Travel Discount Coupon

II0665989

This coupon entitles you
when you book your

GLOBAL TRAVEL NETWORK®
RESERVATION SERVICE

Hotels ♦ Airlines ♦ Car Rentals ♦ Cruises
All Your Travel Needs

Here's what you get: *

♦ A discount of $50 USD on a booking of $1,000** or
  more for two or more people!

♦ A discount of $25 USD on a booking of $500** or more
  for one person!

♦ Free membership for three years, and 1,000 free miles
  on enrollment in the unique Travel Network Miles-to-
  Go® frequent-traveler program. Earn one mile for
  every dollar spent through the program. Redeem
  miles for free hotel stays starting at 5,000 miles. Earn
  free roundtrip airline tickets starting at 25,000 miles.

♦ Personal help in planning your own, customized trip.

♦ Fast, confirmed reservations at any property
  recommended in this guide, subject to availability.***

♦ Special discounts on bookings in the U.S. and around
  the world.

♦ Low-cost visa and passport service.

♦ Reduced-rate cruise packages and special car rental
  programs worldwide.

Visit our website at http://www.travelnetwork.com/Frommer
or call us globally at 201-567-8500, ext. 55. In the U.S., call
toll-free at 1-888-940-5000, or fax 201-567-1838. In Canada,
call at 1-905-707-7222, or fax 905-707-8108. In Asia, call
60-3-7191044, or fax 60-3-7185415.

CAN234

"Amazingly easy to use. Very portable, very complete."

◆

"The only mainstream guide to list specific prices. The Walter Cronkite of guidebooks—with all that implies."

◆

"Complete, concise, and filled with useful information."

◆

"Hotel information is close to encyclopedic."

Frommer's® 98

Cancún, Cozumel & the Yucatán

by Marita Adair

Macmillan • USA

ABOUT THE AUTHOR

Marita Adair's lifelong passion for Mexico's culture, people, and history began at age 11 on her first trip across the border to Nogales. An award-winning travel writer, she logs about 10,000 miles a year traveling in Mexico—by all means of conveyance. Her freelance photographs and articles about Mexico have appeared in numerous newspapers and magazines.

MACMILLAN TRAVEL

A Simon & Schuster Macmillan Company
1633 Broadway
New York, NY 10019

Find us online at **http://www.mgr.com/travel**
or on America Online at Keyword: **Frommer's**

Copyright © 1997 by Simon & Schuster, Inc.
Maps copyright © by Simon & Schuster, Inc.

ISBN 0-02-861583-2
ISSN 1064-1416

Editor: Suzanne Roe Janetta
Production Editor: Lori Cates
Design by Michele Laseau
Digital Cartography by Ortelius Design

SPECIAL SALES

Bulk purchases (10+ copies) of Frommer's and selected Macmillan travel guides are available to corporations, organizations, mail-order catalogs, institutions, and charities at special discounts, and can be customized to suit individual needs. For more information write to: Special Sales, Macmillan General Reference, 1633 Broadway, New York, NY 10019.

Manufactured in the United States of America

Contents

List of Maps

AN INVITATION TO THE READER

In researching this book, I discovered many wonderful places—resorts, inns, restaurants, shops, and more. I'm sure you'll find others. Please tell me about them, so I can share the information with your fellow travelers in upcoming editions. If you were disappointed with a recommendation, I'd love to know that, too. Please write to:

Frommer's Cancún, Cozumel & the Yucatán, '98
Macmillan Travel
1633 Broadway
New York, NY 10019

AN ADDITIONAL NOTE

Please be advised that travel information is subject to change at any time—and this is especially true of prices. We therefore suggest that you write or call ahead for confirmation when making your travel plans. The authors, editors, and publisher cannot be held responsible for the experiences of readers while traveling. Your safety is important to us, however, so we encourage you to stay alert and be aware of your surroundings. Keep a close eye on cameras, purses, and wallets, all favorite targets of thieves and pickpockets.

A FEW WORDS ABOUT PRICES

In December 1994, the Mexican government devalued its currency, the peso. Over the ensuing months, the peso's value against the dollar plummeted from 3.35 pesos against U.S. $1 to nearly 7 pesos against U.S. $1. The peso's value continues to fluctuate—at press time it was around 7.5 pesos to the dollar. Therefore, to allow for inflation, prices in this book (which are always given in U.S. dollars) have been converted to U.S. dollars at a rate of 7 pesos to the dollar, with 15 percent added for inflation. Many moderate-priced and expensive hotels, which often have U.S. toll-free reservation numbers and have many expenses in U.S. dollars, do not lower rates in keeping with the sinking peso.

Mexico has a Value-Added Tax of 15% (Impuesto de Valor Agregado, or IVA, pronounced "ee-bah") on almost everything, including restaurant meals, bus tickets, and souvenirs. (Exceptions are Cancún, Cozumel, and Los Cabos, where the IVA is 10%.) Hotel taxes are 17% everywhere except Cancún, Cozumel, and Los Cabos where they are 12%. The IVA will not necessarily be included in the prices quoted by hotels and restaurants. In addition, prices charged by hotels and restaurants have been deregulated. Mexico's new pricing freedom may cause some price variations from those quoted in this book; always ask to see a printed price sheet and always ask if the tax is included.

WHAT THE SYMBOL MEANS

✪ Frommer's Favorites

Our favorite places and experiences—outstanding for quality, value, or both.

The Best of Cancún, Cozumel & the Yucatán

You've come to the Yucatán to relax on the beach, experience Maya culture, dive and snorkel spectacular coral reefs, bargain for crafts at colorful outdoor markets, and step into the past at world-famous archaeological sites. I've logged thousands of miles crisscrossing the peninsula, and here's my list of personal favorites: the best places to go, the best things to eat, the best places to stay, and must-see, one-of-a-kind experiences.

1 The Best Beach Vacations

- **Cancún and the Costa Turquesa:** There's no question that Mexico's best and most beautiful beaches begin in Cancún and continue south to include both the Punta Allen Peninsula and the Majahual/Xcalak Peninsula. On Cancún Island, the most tranquil waters and beaches face the Bahía de Mujeres. All along the coast, there are extraordinarily inexpensive places to stay right on the powdery, nearly white-sand beaches. See chapter 4.
- **Isla Mujeres:** Pounding waves beat the rocky side of this idyllic island, but the other side, especially Playa Norte close to town, offers perfect, wide beaches. From this island, you can dive in the cave of the sleeping sharks, snorkel just offshore, and take a fascinating boat excursion to the Isla Contoy National Park, which features great birdlife and a fabulous, uninhabited beach. See chapter 5.
- **Playa del Carmen:** The wide and beautiful town beach, which starts by the ferry landing and extends the length of town, is fronted by small hotels and little restaurants. Topless sunbathing, while illegal, seems to be permitted here. See chapter 5.

2 The Best Cultural Experiences

- **Entertainment in the Streets and Parks** (Mérida): No other city in Mexico makes such an effort to entertain its residents and locals the way Mérida does. The city sponsors daily performances of regional song and dance in the streets and parks, including an all-day fair on Sundays featuring antiques vendors, marimba music, and folk ballet dancers reenacting a typical Yucatecan wedding. See chapter 6.

- **Exploring the Inland Yucatán Peninsula:** Travelers who venture only so far as the peninsula's resorts and cities miss the tidy inland villages, where women wear colorful embroidered dresses and life in general goes on as though the modern world, except for highways, doesn't exist. They miss, too, the adventure of seeing ruins deep in jungle settings—ruins that are only now being uncovered. See chapter 6.

- **San Cristóbal de las Casas:** With its 16th-century colonial architecture and pre-Hispanic indigenous influence, visiting the city of San Cristóbal de las Casas is like walking into a living museum. Highland Maya Indians live in remote villages and daily arrive in San Cristóbal wearing colorful and unique handmade clothing. Their outlying villages, too, are like living museums with unusual (to outsiders) dress, religious customs, churches, and ceremonies. See chapter 7.

- **Food:** To enter the region covered in this book is to embark on a culinary tour of some of the country's best foods. Don't miss trying such specialties as *pollo* or *cochinita pibil* (chicken or pork in a savory achiote sauce), *mole chiapaneco* (a Chiapas dish of lightly spicy/sweet mole served over chicken or turkey), Chiapas' dozen or so tamales, Yucatán Maya tamales using the spinach-like chaya leaf and ground, roasted melon seeds, and Caribbean-influenced Tabasco foods such as fried bananas, black beans, and yucca root.

3 The Best Archaeological Sites

- **Uxmal:** No matter how many times you see Uxmal, the splendor of its stone carvings is awesome. A stone rattlesnake undulates across the facade of the Nunnery complex, and 103 masks of Chaac, the rain god, project from the Governor's Palace. See chapter 6.

- **Chichén-Itzá:** Stand beside the giant serpent head at the foot of El Castillo pyramid and marvel at the mastermind who conspired to position the building precisely so that shadow and light would form a serpent's body slithering all the way to the giant head each spring and fall equinox (March 21 and September 21). See chapter 6.

- **Palenque:** The long-ago makers of these powerful Chiapan ruins, located in a dense jungle setting, carved histories in stone that now allow them to speak to us through the centuries. Just imagine the ceremony that must have taken place the day King Pacal was buried below ground in a secret pyramidal tomb, which remained untouched from A.D. 683 until its discovery in 1952. See chapter 7.

4 The Best Active Vacations

- **Scuba Diving:** The coral reefs off the island of Cozumel are Mexico's premier diving destinations, but the diving is also excellent off the shores of Isla Mujeres, Paamul, Akumal, Cancún, and the Majahual/Xcalak Peninsula. On the Yucatán mainland, diving into the deep, dark *cenotes* (sinkholes or natural wells) is an interesting twist on underwater exploration.

- **Sportfishing:** Billfishing for graceful marlin and sailfish is among the popular sports in Cozumel and Playa del Carmen, but you may hook any number of edible fish in these waters. Serious fisherfolk will find bonefish near Punta Allen, south of Tulum, where they can stay at the Cuzan Guest House (☎ 983/4-0358).

- **An Excursion to Bonampak, Yaxchilán, and the Usumacinta River:** Bonampak and Yaxchilán, two remote, jungle-surrounded Maya sites along the Usumacinta

River, can be reached either by air (landing a four-seater plane on a jungle airstrip), or a combination of rafting, hiking, and air. The experience could well be the highlight of any trip.

• **Birding:** All of the Yucatán Peninsula, Tabasco, and Chiapas is bird heaven, with hundreds of species of birds awaiting the birder's gaze and list.

5 The Best Places to Get Away from It All

A few places in Mexico come to mind as total escapes for a moment, a day, a week, or more of sublime tranquillity. Some of these could double as romantic escapes if you're not expecting posh digs.

• **Isla Mujeres, near Cancún:** If there's one island in Mexico that encourages relaxation, this is it. Though the island has plenty of hotels and restaurants, there are no crowds. Guests here bring laziness to new heights, stretching out and dozing beneath shady palms or languidly strolling about, "dressed up" in flip-flops, T-shirts, and shorts. See chapter 5.

• **The Yucatán's Costa Turquesa, south of Cancún:** Away from the busy resort of Cancún, a string of heavenly, quiet getaways, including Capitán Lafitte, Paamul, Xcalacoco, and a portion of Xpuha, offer tranquillity at low prices on beautiful beaches. See chapter 5.

• **The Yucatán's Punta Allen Peninsula:** South of the Tulum ruins, a string of beachside budget inns offers some of the most peaceful getaways in the country. Life here among the birds and coconut palms seems never to have been anything but leisurely. See chapter 5.

• **Cuzan Guest House** (Punta Allen Peninsula; ☎ 983/4-0358): Getting to the isolated lobster-fishing village of Punta Allen is half the adventure, after which you can nest in one of the thatched-roof cottages, swing in a hammock, dine on lobster and stone crabs, and absolutely forget there's an outside world. There are no phones, televisions, or newspapers, and "town" is 35 miles away. Nature trips and fly-fishing are readily arranged. See chapter 5.

• **Rancho Encantado Cottage Resort** (Lago Bacalar; ☎ 800/505-MAYA in the U.S.): Once you see the manicured grounds with hammocks hanging between the trees and the handsomely crafted casitas of the Rancho Encantado Cottage Resort, you'll know you've arrived at *the* place to unwind. The hotel is on the shores of the placid Lake Bacalar, south of Cancún near Chetumal, and there's nothing around for miles. But if you want adventure, you can head a kayak out on the lake; follow a birding trail; take excursions to Belize and to the highly intriguing, but obscure, nearby Maya ruins on the Río Bec ruin route; or sign up for a writing class using jungle-surrounded ruins for inspiration. See chapter 5.

6 The Best Museums

• **Museo de la Isla de Cozumel** (Cozumel): Not just something to do on a rainy day, this well-done museum is worth a visit any time. It unveils the island's past in an informative way not found anywhere else. There's a good bookstore on the first floor and a roof-top restaurant overlooking the Malecón and Caribbean. See chapter 5.

• **Museo de la Cultura Maya** (Chetumal): This new museum showcasing Maya archaeology, architecture, history, and mythology, is one of the best in the country.

It features interactive exhibits and a glass floor that allows visitors to walk above replicas of Maya sites. See chapter 5.

- **Museo Regional de Antropología** (Mérida): Housed in the Palacio Cantón, one of the most beautiful 19th-century mansions in the city, the museum showcases area archaeology and anthropological studies in handsome exhibits. See chapter 6.
- **Museo Regional de Campeche** (Campeche): Rooms in a one-story town house built around an open patio hold Maya artifacts from this ruin-rich state. Of special interest are the jade jewelry and masks found at Calakmul in the southern part of the state. See chapter 6.
- **Museo Olmeca de la Venta** (Villahermosa): The Olmec, considered Mexico's mother culture, are showcased at this park/museum, which features the magnificent stone remains that were removed from the La Venta site in Tabasco state. Stroll through a jungle setting where tropical birds alight, and savor these relics of the mysterious Olmec. See chapter 7.
- **Museo Regional de Antropología Carlos Pellicer** (Villahermosa): Mexican history in the form of objects found at archaeological sites are preserved here, with particular emphasis on the pre-Hispanic peoples of the Gulf Coast region. See chapter 7.

7 The Best Shopping

In resort areas, resort clothing is often a bargain, especially when there's a sale. Be careful about Mexican-made zippers; sometimes they aren't up to the task.

Some tips on bargaining: Bargaining is expected in markets. Start at half the price first quoted to you and agree finally on something in between. You'll get a cheaper per-item price if you buy more than one of the same item. If the vendor senses that you're prepared to walk away, the price will often come down. Even in stores with fixed prices, discounts are often available if you are buying many things, but you'll have to ask for them.

- **Cancún:** Mall after mall on the island contains glitzy boutiques specializing in imported clothing and decorative accessories. See chapter 4.
- **Cozumel:** The downtown area on Avenida Rafael Melgar, which faces the Caribbean, is the best street for strolling in and out of small stores and a few small malls. You'll find stores carrying textiles, copper, pewter, papier-mâché, glass, pottery, and rugs. See chapter 5.
- **Playa del Carmen:** Once a shopping backwater, now the pedestrian-only Avenida 5 is lined with small boutiques selling batik clothing and fabric, Guatemalan textiles, Mexican dance masks, and decorative pottery from Mexico's best pottery villages. See chapter 5.
- **San Cristóbal de las Casas:** Deep in the heart of the Maya highlands, San Cristóbal's shops, open plazas, and markets feature the distinctive waist-loomed wool and cotton textiles of the region, as well as leather shoes, handsomely crude pottery, genre dolls, and Guatemalan textiles. Highland Maya Indians sell direct to tourists from their armloads of textiles, dolls, and handmade miniature likenesses of the Chiapan rebels. See chapter 7.

8 The Hottest Nightlife

In Mexico nightlife runs the gamut from quiet supper clubs with dance floors (although there aren't many of these), to beachside dance floors with live bands, to extended "happy hours" in seaside bars, to some of the flashiest discos in the world. Yes, *discos*. These flamboyant seventies-style clubs may be passé in the rest of the world, but in Mexico, "*dees-cohs*" are more than alive and well—they have a thriving life of their own.

Of the after-dark options in this book, Cancún has the greatest variety and most sophisticated nightlife. From live music in hotel lobby bars to the most cosmopolitan discos around, there's lots to keep you busy from sundown to sunup. Besides Cancún mentioned below, determined night owls in Isla Mujeres and Cozumel can also find a few discos and places to carouse until the wee hours. Most nightspots start up around 9:30 or 10pm and close somewhere between 2am and sunrise.

Here are some favorite hot spots in Cancún (see chapter 4):

- **Mango Tango, Up & Down, Carlos 'n Charlie's, Planet Hollywood, and Dady Rock Bar and Grill:** These Cancún bars all offer tasty food, hot bands, and great dance floors.
- **Azucar Bar Caribeño:** This is the mecca for live Caribbean rhythms in Cancún.
- **The Club Grill:** Located in the luxurious Hotel Ritz-Carlton, this is by far the most elegant evening dining spot on the island. The music is soft and easy.

9 The Most Luxurious Hotels

Cancún, Cozumel, and the Yucatán Peninsula offer a long list of special places where the service is as polished as the quality of the establishment. Below are a few that should be on your short list of posh accommodations, but there are many others.

- **Caesar Park Beach & Golf Resort** (Cancún; ☎ 800/228-3000 in the U.S.): The 18-hole golf course is out the front door, the multifaceted pool claims the side door, and the Caribbean nearly laps the backside foundations. It's so self-contained (three restaurants, tennis, golf, and a fully equipped gym) that some visitors (especially golfers) never feel the need to venture beyond the grounds. See chapter 4.
- **Fiesta Americana Coral Beach** (Cancún; ☎ 800/343-7821 in the U.S.): Lavish use of imported marble and plenty of rich wood accents lead the way to luxurious rooms with views of the Bahía de Mujeres. Sports facilities and one of the best beaches in the city are two superlative draws here. See chapter 4.
- **Ritz-Carlton Cancún** (Cancún; ☎ 800/241-3333 in the U.S.): An ocean of thick carpets, sparkling glass and brass, and rich mahogany surrounds guests who choose this top-notch brand of luxury. The tone is serene and the service impeccable. See chapter 4.
- **Sheraton Resort** (Cancún; ☎ 800/325-3535 in the U.S.): Luxury is the byword in the tower suites located next to this deluxe hotel. Marble floors, cool Caribbean colors and furnishings, along with spacious bathrooms and heavenly views, create rooms you'd just as soon not leave. See chapter 4.
- **Puerto Isla Mujeres Resort & Yacht Club** (Isla Mujeres; ☎ 800/960-ISLA in the U.S.): Spacious, gracious villas face the Laguna Macax where yachts glide up and anchor. Those who immerse themselves in the tranquillity and luxury of this 30-room enclave pass the word on to others who dock for days or weeks on end. See chapter 5.
- **Presidente Inter-Continental Cozumel** (Cozumel; ☎ 800/327-0200 in the U.S.): Not all of the rooms here are luxurious, but the deluxe ground-floor suites with patios offer spacious elegance. This hotel also has the best beach on the island. See chapter 5.

10 The Best Budget Inns

Some inns stand out for their combination of hospitality and simple-but-colorful surroundings. These are places guests return to again and again.

- **Hotel Safari Inn** (Cozumel; ☎ 987/2-0101): The comforts here are simple—a clean, unadorned room, a comfortable king-size bed, good reading lights, powerful air-conditioning, and a great location. The inn is located above the Aqua Safari dive shop (one of the top shops on the island) across from the dive shop's pier (you can book dives and a room at the same time). It's 3 blocks from the plaza and in the heart of the shopping district. What more do you need? See chapter 5.
- **Cabañas Paamul** (Cancún-Tulum Highway; ☎ 99/25-9422): Ten coral-colored bungalows face a beautiful, small cove; a wide, clean, cream-colored beach, and the cerulean Caribbean. Reef diving and snorkeling sites are within a 5-minute walk, but the nearest civilization is at Puerto Aventuras, 2 miles away. See chapter 5.
- **Casa Mexilio Guest House** (Mérida; ☎ 800/538-6802 in the U.S.): Host Roger Lynn has created the atmosphere of a private home in this 19th-century town house, and he offers some of the most unusual guided tours of the area. See chapter 6.
- **Hotel Mucuy** (Mérida; ☎ 99/28-5193): Alfredo and Ofelia Comin, owners of one of the most hospitable budget hotels in the country, strive to make guests feel at home with cheery, clean rooms; comfortable outdoor tables and chairs; a communal refrigerator in the lobby; and laundry facilities. See chapter 6.

11 The Most Authentic Culinary Experiences

- **Los Almendros** (with locations in Cancún ☎ 98/87-1332, Mérida ☎ 99/28-5459, and Ticul ☎ 997/2-0021): This family-owned restaurant chain features Yucatecan specialties. Their famous *poc chuc,* a marinated and grilled pork dish, was created at the original restaurant in Ticul some years ago. See chapters 4 and 6.
- **El Moro** (Cozumel; ☎ 987/2-3029): Take an inexpensive taxi to this popular restaurant where you will enjoy excellently prepared Yucatecan cuisine and the strongest margaritas this side of Acapulco. See chapter 5.
- **El Fogón de Jovel** (San Cristóbal de las Casas; ☎ 967/8-2550): Chiapan food is served at this handsome old town house, with dining under the portals and in rooms built around a central courtyard. The waiters wear indigenous clothing while the food highlights the specialties of Chiapas. Group cooking lessons are available if arranged in advance. See chapter 7.
- **Las Pichanchas** (Tuxtla Gutiérrez; ☎ 961/2-5351): Chiapan variations on sausages, tamales, and beef are featured in this festively decorated restaurant named after the hole-punched pot used to make nixtamal masa dough. See chapter 7.

12 The Best All-Around Restaurants

Besides those listed above, below is another assemblage of good eats.

- **Club Grill** (Cancún; ☎ 98/85-0808): The international cuisine served at this Ritz-Carlton restaurant is as excellent and elegant as the sumptuous setting. Soft, quiet, and utterly refined, dining here is a memorable experience. Plus, there's a dance floor for oh-so-slow and romantic music. See chapter 4.

- **La Dolce Vita** (Cancún; ☎ 98/84-1384): Once you've discovered this Italian restaurant, you'll keep coming back, tempted by blissfully flavorful dishes such as green tagliolini with lobster medallions, linguine with clams or seafood, fresh salmon with cream sauce—well, you get the idea. See chapter 4.

- **Zacil-Ha** (Isla Mujeres; ☎ 987/7-0279): With its sandy floor beneath thatched palapas and palms, it's hard to beat this relaxed and casual place for island atmosphere and well-prepared food—terrific pasta with garlic, shrimp in tequila sauce, fajitas, and delicious mole enchiladas, plus great nachos. See chapter 5.

- **Coco's** (Cozumel; ☎ 987/2-0241): Homesick for breakfast and sandwiches just like home—maybe better? Stop in here for a bagelwich, gigantic blueberry muffin, or, if you're really hungry, the Loco Breakfast. The latter is an inexpensive but more-than-filling he-man or she-woman breakfast feast. See chapter 5.

- **D'Pub** (Cozumel; ☎ 987/2-4132): A high-style Mexican pub by day and a sophisticated English pub and casual restaurant by night, this is the place to imbibe as well as to savor fish and chips and wonderfully fresh, crispy salads that are among the offerings on the extensive international menu. See chapter 5.

- **Prima** (Cozumel; ☎ 987/2-4242): The Italian food here is fresh, fresh, fresh, from the hydroponically grown vegetables to the pasta and garlic bread. And it's all prepared after you walk in, most of it by owner Albert Domínguez, who concocts an unforgettable shrimp fettuccine with pesto, crab ravioli with cream sauce, and crispy house salad in a chilled bowl. See chapter 5.

- **Tarraya Restaurant/Bar** (Playa del Carmen; no phone): Captivating Caribbean waters practically lap the floor of this beachfront restaurant. Locals recommend it as the best place to dine on feasts from the sea. See chapter 5.

- **Madre Tierra** (San Cristóbal de las Casas; ☎ 967/8-4297): Upon arrival in San Cristóbal, I head to this restaurant just for the filling and wonderfully prepared *comida corrida*. It comes with soup; a choice of three entrees, such as pork in adobo sauce, barbecue ribs, perhaps chicken curry, or poblano chile; fruit-flavored purified water; and dessert—all in a cozy setting with classical music playing in the background. See chapter 7.

- **Restaurant Tuluc** (San Cristóbal de las Casas; ☎ 967/8-2090): Another of Mexico's dependable restaurants offering a *comida corrida* that you'll remember and come back for. It includes several choices of everything, served in a warm setting that's ideal for lingering over coffee and dessert. See chapter 7.

2 Getting to Know the Yucatán

Ever since 1841, when American lawyer John Lloyd Stephens published his fascinating travel accounts of exploring the jungles of Yucatán, Chiapas, and Central America in search of pre-Hispanic Maya ruins, the world has been fascinated with travel to the region. Of course, Stephens and Frederick Catherwood, who illustrated the work, and their bevy of porters hacked their way through the jungle and wrote quite a bit about sleepless nights spent fending off their "tormentors," the mosquitos. Although today, even in a short weeklong vacation, travelers can traverse a lot of the territory covered in months by this intrepid pair and their entourage, there's still something of an adventure to be had visiting these regions. Scheduled flights, bus tours via good highways, and cruise ships take visitors nearer to launching points for seeing the ruins. It's simple to choose to take an easy morning tour to a nearby ruin or nature reserve, spend days tramping through jungles, or grind along in a four-wheel-drive vehicle over nearly impassable roads. And in all cases it's easy to mix our explorations with sybaritic days lazing on Mexico's best beaches, with outstretched hands waiting to be filled with an ice-chilled drink—a luxury Stephens and Catherwood might have cherished.

Traveling the two regions covered in this book—the **Yucatán Peninsula** and its neighbor states of **Tabasco** and **Chiapas**—you enter **Mexico's Maya Route,** an area inhabited by the Maya, one of the country's most intriguing indigenous cultures sharing geographic space with Mexico's most famous and most sought-after megaresort, **Cancún;** the island of **Cozumel,** where Mexico's superlative diving is enjoyed offshore; **Isla Mujeres,** Mexico's best laid-back island vacation destination; and the **Costa Turquesa** south of Cancún, with its hidden beachfront inns and splendid beaches. Farther south on the Costa Turquesa are the ruins of **Tulum,** while inland the peninsula's Maya ruins include **Chichén-Itzá, Uxmal, Cobá, Becán, Dzinbanché,** and **Kohunlich.** The premier highlights of Tabasco and Chiapas, located southwest of the Yucatán Peninsula, are the **Museo Olmeca de la Venta,** the majestic Maya ruins of **Palenque,** and the mountain city of **San Cristóbal de las Casas** surrounded by villages of living Maya.

In many ways the mystery, romance, and attraction of the region evoked by Stephens and Catherwood are still evident, even though the area covered in this book is now a metaphor for the country's famed contrasting layers. Along the state of Quintana Roo's Caribbean coastline, glitzy resorts, economical beachside hostelries, and lagoons with world-class snorkeling have sprung up alongside miles of jungle and a few archaeological sites. Inland is more jungle and other ancient sites reached by passing neat, rock-fenced villages. These latter are mostly comprised of white stucco or stick- and mud-walled cottages shaped exactly like Maya homes (called *nah*) occupied in pre-Hispanic times. Completely different are the cities of **Villahermosa,** the capital of Tabasco, a low-elevation, sultry, cosmopolitan city that's the gateway to the ruins of Palenque, and **San Cristóbal de las Casas,** the misty, mountainous 16th-century city located inland that is the hub of the richly colorful highland Maya culture.

1 The Regions in Brief

Three states are included in the Yucatán Peninsula: Quintana Roo, Yucatán, and Campeche.

The Caribbean state of **Quintana Roo** in the east has the best beaches and is also blessed with the resort islands of Cancún, Cozumel, and Isla Mujeres; the ruins of Tulum and Cobá; and the 1.3 million-acre Sian Ka'an Biosphere Reserve south of Cancún. Sultry, rough-edged, and unfriendly, Quintana Roo's capital, **Chetumal,** seems far removed, sitting adjacent to Belize at the southernmost edge of the state, almost an inappropriate capital for an area with such natural and touristic riches. But Chetumal is home to the area's best museum—**Museo de la Cultura Maya**—which is reason enough to spend a half day there. It shares with Campeche state the touristically emerging **Río Bec ruin route,** where "new" Maya sites are being excavated with amazing rapidity.

The wedge-shaped **Yucatán** state in the middle of the region, with delightful **Mérida** as its capital, has among its crowning attractions the ruins of **Uxmal** and **Chichén-Itzá.** The state's **nature reserves** include those for flamingos at Celestún, Río Lagartos, and El Palmar, a 1.2 million-acre reserve established in 1990 on the upper Yucatán coast.

Campeche state, on the peninsula's west coast, faces the Gulf of Mexico and has as its capital the beautiful **walled city** of Campeche. The region is off the beaten path for most tourists, who are drawn to the ruins and beaches of the middle and eastern parts of the peninsula. Among its attractions are the **hat- and basket-weaving towns** of Becal and Halacho, and the ruins of **Edzná.** The Gulf Coast beaches are coarser than those on the Caribbean, and the water tends to be rough and choppy.

The state of **Tabasco** borders the Gulf of Mexico, Campeche on the east, and Chiapas to the south, while **Chiapas,** Mexico's southernmost state, shares borders with Guatemala, Tabasco, Oaxaca, and Veracruz. Chiapas even has a rather insect-infested coastline on the Pacific Ocean.

2 The Yucatán Today

Mexico is undergoing fast-paced and far-reaching change, as are most countries touched by modern technology. Some changes are astounding in their rapidity—the country literally went from the manual typewriter to the computer, almost bypassing entirely the technology of the electric typewriter. On the other hand, many villages and rural communities in this book are without electricity, running water, or a public sewer system. Though lack of reliable telephone service is still one of the country's greatest obstacles to progress, nevertheless, you can reach an AT&T, MCI, or Sprint operator from many Mexican hotels and pay phones. Toll-free telephone

Mexico

UNITED STATES

Tijuana
Mexicali
Ensenada
BAJA
CALIFORNIA
NORTE
Puerto
Penasco
San
Quintin
Nogales
SONORA
15
Hermosillo
16
Isla
Cedros
Guerrero
Negro
Santa
Rosalia
Mulegé
Cuidad
Obregon
Los
Mochis
Culiacán
BAJA
CALIFORNIA
SUR
Loreto
SINALOA
La Paz
Sea of Cortez
Todos Santos
San José
del Cabo
Cabo San Lucas
Mazatlán
40
15

Ciudad
Juárez
45
10
CHIHUAHUA
18
Ojinaga
Chihuahua
Cuauhtémoc
COAHUILA
Delicias
Hidalgo
del Parral
49
Monclova
30
45
Torreo
DURANGO
57
Saltillo
Durango
54
Fresnillo
ZACATECAS
Zacatecas
San
Luis
Potosí

Islas
Marias
San Blas
15
Tuxpan
Tepic
NAYARIT
AGUASCALIENTES
Aguascalientes
Guadalajara
Guanajuato
León
Puerto Vallarta
JALISCO
Lake Chapala
GUANA
JUATO
Morelia
Barra de Navidad
Colima
Uruapan
Pátzcuaro
Manzanillo
COLIMA
MICHOACAN
200
37
Lazaro
Cardenas
Zihuatanejo
& Ixtapa

Pacific

Ocean

0   150 mi
       240 km

N

2-0001

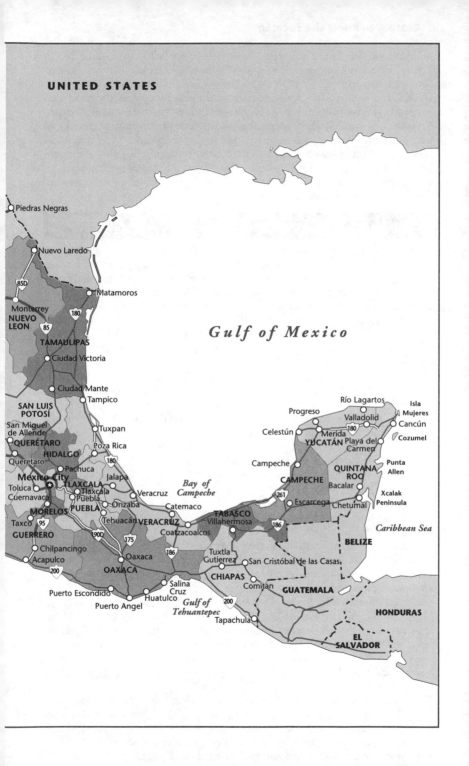

numbers and fax phones that were almost unheard of in Mexico as little as 3 or 4 years ago are not uncommon nowadays in the resorts, cities, and some villages covered in these pages.

These two faces of Mexico, the modern and the past, for now coexist in the areas covered in this book, making it one of the world's most fascinating regions to visit. Traveling cognoscenti, who have watched the modern world supplant the colorful ancient cultures in other countries, covet their forays here because "old" Mexico still exists. They want to absorb as much of the country's rich cultural legacy as they can before it, too, disappears. Other people judge Mexico by its ultra-modern beach resorts, perfectly content not to travel beyond the country's well-known beach meccas. Both kinds of travelers can enjoy this book.

3 The Land & Its People

Many people think that the Yucatán is somewhere in the extreme southeast of Mexico. A look at the map shows that the land of the Maya is actually the far east-central part of the republic. Mérida is north of the major population centers of Mexico City, Guadalajara, Puebla, and Veracruz. Mérida is also surprisingly close to the tip of Florida: From Mexico City to Mérida it's about 600 miles as the crow flies, and from Mérida to Miami it's a mere 675 miles.

Edged by the rough and aquamarine Gulf of Mexico on the west and north, and the clear cerulean blue Caribbean Sea on the east, the peninsula covers almost 84,000 square miles, with nearly 1,000 miles of shoreline. Covered with dense jungle, the porous limestone peninsula is mostly flat, with thin soil supporting a primarily low, scrubby jungle, with almost no surface rivers. Rainwater is filtered by the limestone into underground rivers. *Cenotes,* or collapsed caves, are natural wells dotting the region. The only sense of height comes from the curvaceous terrain rising from the western shores of Campeche inland to the border with Yucatán state. This rise, called the Puuc Hills, is the Maya "Alps," a mere 980 feet high. Locally the hills are known as the Sierra de Ticul or Sierra Alta. The highways undulate a little as you go inland, and south of Ticul there's a rise in the highway that provides a marvelous view of the "valley" and the misty Puuc hills lining the horizon.

Crumbling haciendas surrounded by fields of henequen dot the peninsular landscape. Henequen, a member of the agave family from which hemp is made, was the king crop in the Yucatán in the 19th century, and the industry is still going strong, with rope, packing material, shoes, and purses manufactured from the spiny plant. Besides henequen, other crops in the mostly agricultural peninsula are corn, coconuts, oranges, mangoes, and bananas. In Tabasco and Chiapas, coffee, chocolate, and oil are commercially exploited, but the indigenous people raise some of their own vegetables as well as corn for food and fodder, tend sheep for their wool, and barter for life's other necessities. The highland Maya Indians of Chiapas prefer to live in villages apart from the rest of society, but recently have led a fight for rights regarding land, voting, roads, education, and medical assistance. Electricity and running water are rarities in these Indian villages, though road connections have improved in recent years. The mestizo population residing in formal towns in the highlands has created a modern society with all its conveniences.

Enormous strides in protecting the Yucatán's abundant natural life have been made in the last decade. The nature reserves have not been significantly opened to tourism and may never be, since the idea is to protect them and money is lacking to staff and patrol opened areas. But wildlife, especially birds, is easy to see in or out of a reserve, once you get away from commercialized and developed areas.

Yucatán state's nature reserves include the 118,000-acre **Río Lagartos Wildlife Refuge** north of Mérida, where North America's largest flock of flamingos nests; the **Celestún Wildlife Refuge,** covering more than 14,000 acres, for the protection of flamingos and other tropical birds and plant life; and, adjacent to it, the 123,398-acre **El Palmar Wildlife Refuge,** important for its springs, cenotes, and black mangroves, established in 1990 on the upper Yucatán coast. The state also has incorporated **nature trails** into the archaeological site of Dzibilchaltún, north of Mérida.

In 1989 Campeche state set aside 178,699 acres in the **Calakmul Biosphere Reserve** that it shares with the country of Guatemala. The area includes the state's ruins of Calakmul, as well as significant plants, animals, and birdlife.

Quintana Roo's protected areas are some of the region's most beautiful, wild, and important. In 1986 the state ambitiously set aside the 1.3 million-acre **Sian Ka'an Biosphere Reserve,** protecting a significant part of the coast from development south of Tulum. **Isla Contoy,** also in Quintana Roo, off the coast of both Isla Mujeres and Cancún, is a beautiful island refuge for hundreds of bird species, turtles, and other plants and wildlife. And in 1990 the 150-acre **Jardín Botánica,** south of Puerto Morelos, was opened to the public; along with the Botanical Garden at Cozumel's Chancanaab Lagoon, it gives visitors an excellent idea of the Yucatán's lengthy shoreline, since four of Mexico's eight marine turtle species nest on Quintana Roo's shores—loggerhead, green, hawksbill, and leatherback. More than 600 species of birds, reptiles, and mammals have been counted.

El Triúnfo Biosphere Reserve, near the Lagunas de Montebello in Chiapas, preserves 25,000 acres of the rain forest habitat of the rare and endangered quetzal bird.

Though the Yucatán Peninsula has experienced an invasion of foreign tourism since Cancún opened its first hotel in 1974, the Maya culture has remained amazingly intact, especially in inland villages. Travelers only experiencing Cancún, Cozumel, or Isla Mujeres won't see much of the local culture, but many of the people who serve them also speak Mayan. Many descendants of the peninsula's original inhabitants—who made a living as hunters; henequen, chicle, and coconut plantation workers; fishermen; and crafts people—work in hotels, restaurants, and other resort-oriented businesses. In Chiapas, however, there is a visible separation of cultures and class, with the Spanish descendants owning most of the businesses and land, and indigenous inhabitants primarily living and working separate from them.

On the peninsula, Maya village women wear cool cotton embroidered shifts and go about village life seemingly oblivious to the peninsula's fame as a premier resort destination. Their day-to-day cultural and belief system holds many elements that can be traced to pre-Hispanic times. Though shy, the peninsular Maya are immensely courteous and helpful, and eagerly chat with strangers even when neither can speak the other's language. More than 350,000 Maya living in the Yucatán's three states speak Yukatek Maya and most, especially men, speak Spanish too. Many, especially those serving tourists, slip easily among Maya, Spanish, and English.

Completely different are the estimated 1 million **Tabascan** and **Chiapan Maya,** who speak four different Mayan languages with dozens of dialects and around San Cristóbal weave fabulously designed wool and cotton clothing. The Maya groups around San Cristóbal generally choose not to embrace outside cultures, preferring to live in small mountain hamlets and meeting only for ceremonies and market days. Their forest- and cloud-draped high mountain homeland in Chiapas is cold in

The Yucatán Peninsula

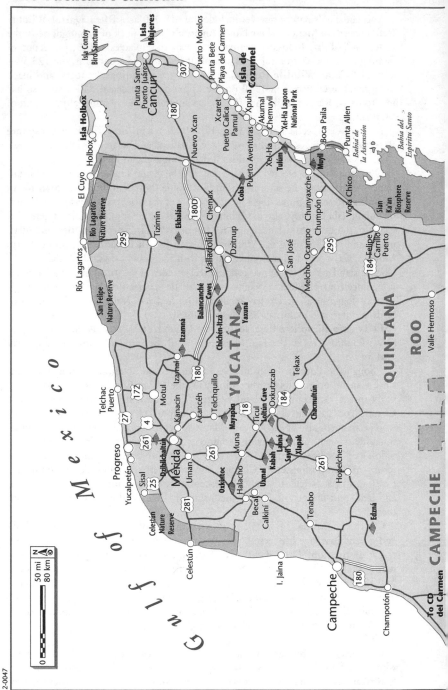

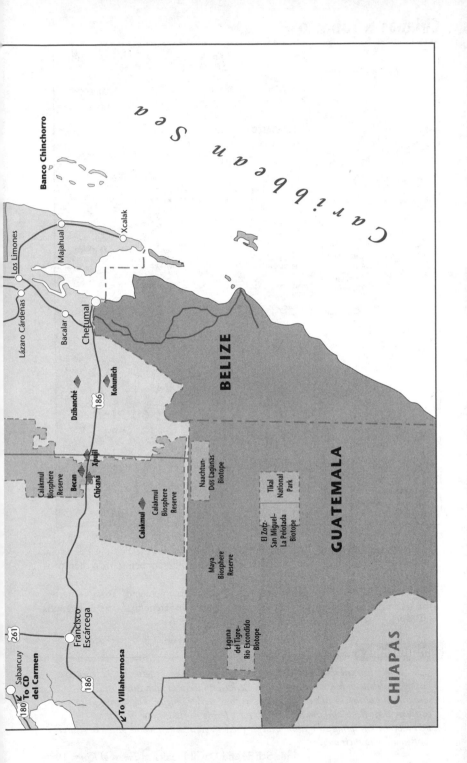

Banco Chinchorro

Caribbean Sea

Los Limones

Majahual

Xcalak

Lázaro Cárdenas

Bacalar

Chetumal

BELIZE

Dzibanché

Kohunlich

186

Calakmul Biosphere Reserve

Becan

Xpujil

Chicaná

Calakmul

Calakmul Biosphere Reserve

Naachtun-Dos Lagunas Biotope

El Zotz-San Miguel-La Pelotada Biotope

Tikal National Park

GUATEMALA

Maya Biosphere Reserve

Laguna del Tigre-Rio Escondido Biotope

CHIAPAS

Francisco Escárcega

261

Sabancuy

180 To CD del Carmen

186

To Villahermosa

15

Chiapas & Tabasco

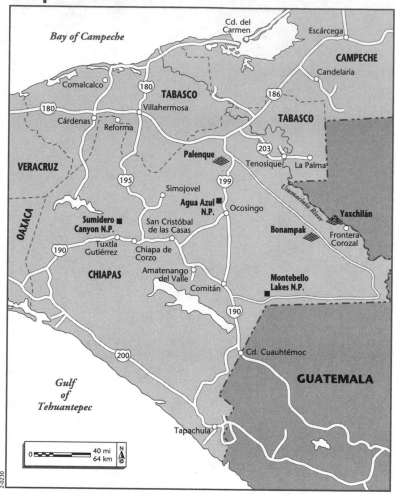

contrast with the heat of the lowland Maya of Tabasco and the Yucatán Peninsula. They, too, live much as their ancestors did but with different beliefs than their peninsular relatives.

However, in modern cities of this area, such as Villahermosa and Tuxtla Gutiérrez, the trappings of modern western culture are more apparent than any indigenous influence.

Impressions

. . . we both learned that the Maya are not just a people of the past. Today, they live in their millions in Mexico, Guatemala, Belize and western Honduras, still speaking one of the 35 Mayan languages as their native tongue. They continue to cultivate their fields and commune with their living world in spite of the fact that they are encapsulated within a larger modern civilization whose vision of reality is often alien to their own.

—Linda Schele and David Freidel, *A Forest of Kings,* 1990

4   A Look at the Past

PRE-HISPANIC CIVILIZATIONS

The earliest "Mexicans" were Stone Age men and women, descendants of the race that had crossed the Bering Strait and reached North America before 10,000 B.C. These were *Homo sapiens* who hunted mastodons and bison, and gathered other food as they could. Later, during the **Archaic period** (5200 to 1500 B.C.), signs of agriculture and domestication appeared: Baskets were woven; corn, beans, squash, and tomatoes were grown; turkeys and dogs were kept for food. By 2400 B.C., the art of pot making had been discovered (the use of pottery was a significant advance). Life in these times was still very primitive, of course, but there were "artists" who made clay figurines for use as votive offerings or household gods and goddesses.

THE PRECLASSIC PERIOD   It was in the Preclassic period (1500 B.C. to A.D. 300) that the area known by archaeologists as Mesoamerica (from the northern Mexico Valley to Costa Rica) began to show signs of a farming culture. They farmed either by the "slash-and-burn" method of cutting grass and trees, then setting fire to the area to clear it for planting, or by constructing terraces and irrigation ducts, a method used principally in the highlands around Mexico City, where the first large towns developed. At some time during this period, religion became an institution as certain men took the role of shaman, or guardian of magical and religious secrets. These were the predecessors of the folk healers and nature priests still found in modern Mexico.

The most highly developed culture of this Preclassic period was that of the Olmec, who flourished from 1500 to 100 B.C. They are considered the first group to create a civilization. Their influence is substantial in the development of the later Maya civilization, but their primary stronghold was in what are today the states of Veracruz and Tabasco. They used river rafts to transport colossal multi-ton blocks of basalt, which were used to carve huge, roundish heads. These sculptures still present problems to archaeologists: What do they signify? The heads seem infantile in their roundness, but all have the peculiar "jaguar mouth" with a high-arched lip that is an identifying mark of the Olmec, and which was borrowed and adapted by many later cultures. They all wear what looks like a helmet. Those with open eyes are slightly cross-eyed. Besides their achievements in sculpture, the Olmec were the first in

Dateline

- **10,000–2,300 B.C.** Pre-Historic Period: Cultivation of chiles, corn, beans, avocado, amaranth, and pumpkin. Mortars and pestles in use. Stone bowls and jars, obsidian knives, and open-weave basketry developed.

- **1500–300** Pre-Classic Period: Olmec culture spreads and develops over Gulf Coast, southern Mexico, Central America, and lower Mexican Pacific Coast and is eventually linked to the development of the Maya culture.

- **1000–900** Olmec San Lorenzo center is destroyed; they begin anew at La Venta.

- **600** La Venta Olmec cultural zenith. Zapotec culture emerges near Monte Albán Oaxaca.

- **500–100 B.C.** The Zapotec flourish and invent the Calendar Round, which is later used near the end of the Olmec period and later by Maya. Olmec culture disintegrates. Teotihuacán settlement is started in central Mexico.

- **A.D. 100** Building begins on Sun and Moon pyramids at Teotihuacán; Palenque dynasty emerges in Yucatán.

- **300–900** Classic period begins: Xochicalco established where pyramids bearing Maya-like figures are eventually built; Maya civilization develops in Yucatán and Chiapas.

- **500–650** Teotihuacán culture from central Mexico exerts strong influence in the Maya world, including intermarrying with the Maya.

- **683** Maya Lord Pacal is buried in an elaborate tomb

continues

below the Palace of the Inscriptions at Palenque.

- **650–800** Teotihuacán burns and is deserted. Cacaxtla, in central Mexico, is at its zenith with brilliantly colored murals of Maya warriors splashed across its walls.
- **750** Zapotecs conquer the Valley of Oaxaca and invent first Mesoamerican writing system.
- **800** Bonampak battle/victory mural painted.
- **900** Postclassic period begins: Toltec culture emerges at Tula and spreads to Chichén-Itzá on the Yucatán Peninsula by 978.
- **909** A small monument at Toniná (near San Cristóbal de las Casas) has this as the last Long Count date discovered so far, symbolizing the end of the Classic Maya era.
- **1156–1230** Tula, the Toltec capital, is abandoned.
- **1290** Zapotec decline and Mixtec emerge at Monte Albán; Mitla becomes refuge of Zapotecs.
- **1325–45** Aztec capital Tenochtitlán founded; Aztecs begin to dominate Mexico but not Chiapas or the Yucatán Peninsula.
- **1443** Calkaní founded after destruction of Mayapán.
- **1511** Santo Domingo–bound Spanish sailors sailing from the Darien Gap near Panama are shipwrecked off the coast of what is today Quintana Roo and two passengers survive. One survivor is a clergyman, Jeronimo de Aguilar, who learns to speak Yukatek Maya and later becomes Cortés's translator. The other, Gonzalo Guerrero, adopts the Maya culture, marries a Maya woman, and has a family. Guerrero eventually leads

continues

Mexico to use a calendar, which was later perfected by the Maya. At Chacan Bacan, a newly uncovered site on the Río Bec ruin route in the southern part of the Yucatán Peninsula, a pyramid was recently unearthed revealing a facade covered with the classic look of the Olmec helmet heads.

Historians speculate that the Maya were influenced by, if not descended from, the mysterious Olmec, but a definitive link between the cultures is missing except for a few archaeological finds. One such find is a stelae, dating from between A.D. 143 and A.D. 156, only recently discovered at La Mojarra ruins on the Gulf Coast, and Izapa, a huge site that rose and flourished between 400 B.C. and A.D. 400 and was found almost intact on the Pacific coast of Chiapas.

Other than conclusions drawn from the stone carvings and historic interpretations of Izapa and La Mojarra, the Maya developmental years remain a mystery. Somewhere along the way they perfected the Olmec and Zapotec calendar and refined and developed their ornate system of hieroglyphic writing and their early architecture. The Maya religion, with its 166 deities, was also being shaped in these early centuries, which were contemporaneous with the Roman Empire. The Maya guided their lives by using a number of interwoven and complex calendars (see the section on Chichén-Itzá in chapter 6).

THE CLASSIC PERIOD   Most artistic and cultural achievement came about during Mexico's Classic period (A.D. 300 to 900), when life began to center in cities. Class distinctions arose as the military and religious aristocracy took control; a class of merchants and artisans grew, with the independent farmer falling under a landlord's control. The cultural centers of the Classic period were Yucatán and Guatemala (also home of the Maya), the Mexican Highlands at Teotihuacán, the Zapotec cities of Monte Albán and Mitla (near Oaxaca), and the cities of El Tajín and Zempoala on the Gulf Coast.

The Maya represented the apex of pre-Columbian cultures. Besides their superior artistic achievements, the Maya made significant discoveries in science, including the use of the zero in mathematics and a complex calendar with which the priests could predict eclipses and the movements of the stars for centuries to come.

The Maya were warlike, raiding their neighbors to gain land and subjects as well as to take captives for their many blood-centered rituals. Recent studies, notably *Blood of Kings* (Braziller, 1986) by Linda

Schele and Mary Ellen Miller, debunked the long-held theory that the Maya were a peaceful people. Scholars continue to decipher the Maya hieroglyphs, murals, and relief carvings to reveal a Maya world tied to a belief that blood sacrifice was necessary for the dynasties of earthly blood kin. Thus, through bloodletting and sacrifice they nourished their gods and ancestors, and honored royal births, deaths, marriages, and accessions during a calendar full of special occasions. Numerous carvings and murals show that members of the ruling class, too, ritualistically mutilated themselves to draw sacrificial blood.

The Classic period ended with a century of degradation and collapse, roughly corresponding to the A.D. 800s. By the early 900s, the great ceremonial centers were abandoned and the jungle took them over, but why classic Maya culture collapsed so quickly is still something of a mystery.

Exactly who inhabited Teotihuacán (100 B.C. to A.D. 700 A.D.—near present-day Mexico City) isn't known, but it is thought to have been a city of 200,000 or more inhabitants covering 9 square miles. At its height, Teotihuacán was the greatest cultural center in Mexico, with tremendous influence as far southeast as Guatemala and including the Yucatán Peninsula. The precise history of the Teotihuacán influence beyond its origins near Mexico City is yet another mystery waiting to be solved.

THE POSTCLASSIC PERIOD—In the Postclassic period (A.D. 900 to 1500), warlike cultures developed impressive societies of their own, although they never surpassed the Classic peoples. Paintings and hieroglyphs of this period show war, migration, and disruption. Somehow the glue of society became unstuck, people wandered from their homes, and the religious hierarchy lost influence.

After the Classic period, the Maya migrated from their historic homelands in Guatemala and Chiapas into the lowlands of the Yucatán (roughly the modern states of Yucatán and Campeche), where they spent 6 centuries, from A.D. 900 to 1500, apparently trying to recover their former greatness.

During this period, the cities near the Yucatán's low western Puuc hills were built. The architecture of the region, called **Puuc style,** is generally characterized by elaborate exterior stonework appearing above door frames and extending to the roofline. Examples of this architecture can be seen in Kabah, Sayil, Labná, and Xlapak. Even though Maya architecture never regained the heights achieved at Palenque or Tikal, the Puuc buildings, such as the

Maya in battle against Spaniards.

- **1516** Gold found on Cozumel in aborted Spanish expedition of Yucatán Peninsula arouses interest of Spanish governor in Cuba, who sends Juan de Grijalva on an expedition, followed by another led by Hernán Cortés.
- **1517** Cortés arrives in Cozumel and rescues Aguilar but Gonzalo Guerrero prefers to remain with his family and adopted culture.
- **1518** Spaniards first visited what is today Campeche.
- **1519** Conquest of Mexico begins: Hernán Cortés and troops arrive near present-day Veracruz.
- **1521** Conquest is complete after Aztec defeat at Tlaltelolco in 1521.
- **1521–1524** Cortés organizes Spanish empire in Mexico and begins building Mexico City on the ruins of Tenochtitlán.
- **1524** First Franciscan friars arrive from Spain.
- **1524–1535** Cortés removed from leadership. Spanish King sends officials, judges, and finally an *audiencia* to govern.
- **1526** Francisco Montejo permitted by King of Spain to colonize the Yucatán.
- **1530** Territory of Tabasco conquered by Francisco Montejo.
- **1535–1821** Viceregal Period: Mexico governed by 61 viceroys appointed by King of Spain. Landed aristocracy, a small elite class owning huge portions of land (haciendas) emerges. Yucatán is led by a governor who reports to the king rather than to viceroys.
- **1540** Campeche, Mérida, and Valladolid are founded.
- **1542** Mérida established as capital of Yucatán Peninsula.

continues

- **1546** Maya rebel and take control of peninsula.
- **1559** French and Spanish pirates attack Campeche.
- **1562** Friar Diego de Landa destroys 5,000 Mayan religious stone figures and burns 27 hieroglyphic painted manuscripts at Maní, Yucatán. Widespread torture and death are meted out to Maya believed to secretly practice pre-Hispanic beliefs.
- **1563–1566** Diego de Landa forced to return to Spain to answer for his actions. In defense of himself he writes his now-famous and invaluable "Yucatán Before and After the Conquest," which was published 298 years later.
- **1579** Diego de Landa dies in the Yucatán.
- **1739** What became known as the "Dresden Codex," a lost Maya calendar text, is purchased in Vienna by the Royal Library of Dresden, where it languishes for more than a century.
- **1767** Jesuits expelled from New Spain.
- **1810–1821** War of Independence: Miguel Hidalgo starts movement for Mexico's independence from Spain, but is executed within a year; leadership and goals change during the war years, but a compromise between monarchy and a republic is outlined by Augustín de Iturbide.
- **1821** Independence from Spain achieved. The Spanish governor of Yucatán resigns and the Yucatán Peninsula becomes an independent country.
- **1822** First Empire: Iturbide ascends throne as Emperor of Mexico.

continues

Codz Poop at Kabah and the palaces at Sayil and Labná, are quite beautiful and impressive.

Finally, in the 1300s, the warlike Aztecs settled west of the Yucatán, in the Mexico Valley on Lake Texcoco (site of Mexico City), with the huge (pop. 300,000) and impressive island city of Tenochtitlán as their capital. The Aztec empire was a more or less loosely united territory of great size, but it did not stretch to Tabasco, Chiapas, and the Yucatán Peninsula. Nevertheless, the Aztec belief in the return of the god/man Quetzalcoatl eventually led to the fall of the Aztecs and all the territory known today as Mexico and Central America.

The Yucatán was also profoundly affected by a strong influence from central Mexico. Evidence of this is the Toltec influence that shows up so strongly at Chichén-Itzá. Some theories claim that a distantly related branch of the Maya people, called the **Putun Maya,** came from the borders of the Yucatán Peninsula between mainland Mexico and the Classic Maya lands in Petén and Chiapas. They spoke the Maya language poorly and used many Nahuatl (Aztec) words.

When the Putun Maya left their ships and moved inland, they became known as the **Itzáes** because, after unsuccessfully trying to conquer Yaxuná, they settled 12 miles north in what eventually became known as Chichén-Itzá (Well of the Itzá), a perfect place because of its access to water and its proximity to centers ripe for conquering. They brought with them years of experience in trading far and wide (thus, so some scholars theorize, came the influence of the Toltec at Chichén-Itzá). Eventually they were successful in conquering other peninsular kingdoms and creating the vast city of Chichén-Itzá.

Another theory to explain the Toltec influence at Chichén-Itzá relates to the legend of **Quetzalcoatl,** a holy man who appeared from central Mexico at the end of the Classic period. This legend is one of the most important tales in Mexican history and folklore. Belief in the return of Quetzalcoatl contributed to the overthrow of the Aztec empire by the Spaniards and to the eventual overthrow of the Maya civilizations living at the time of the Conquest.

Quetzalcoatl means "feathered serpent." Learned beyond his years, he became the high priest and leader of the Toltec at or near Tula and put an end to human sacrifice. Under his influence, the Toltec changed from a group of warriors to peaceful and productive farmers, artisans, and craftsmen. But his success upset the old priests, and they called upon their ancient god of darkness, Texcatlipoca, to degrade Quetzalcoatl in the eyes of the people. One night the priests conspired to dress Quetzalcoatl in ridiculous garb, get him drunk, and tempt him to break his vow of chastity by sleeping with his sister. The next morning the shame of this night of debauchery drove him out of his own land and into the wilderness, where he lived for 20 years. He emerged in Cholula and then in Coatzacoalcos, in the Isthmus of Tehuantepec, bade his few followers farewell, and sailed away, having promised to return in a future age. Legend and Toltec artistic influences noted at Chichén-Itzá in the Yucatán seem to suggest that in fact he landed there and, among the Maya, began his "ministry" again, this time called Kukulkán. He supposedly died there, but the legend of his impending return remained. It was this belief in the return of Quetzalcoatl that led the Aztec Emperor Moctezuma to court the Spanish conqueror Hernán Cortés, whom he believed might be the returning Quetzalcoatl. This toleration of the Spaniards in Mexico brought down the Aztec Empire, and with it came the conquest of Mexico and shortly afterward the conquest of the Yucatán Peninsula.

That Kukulkán led an invasion of Chichén-Itzá was a long-held scholarly theory, but now the scholars are in doubt again. That Kukulkán existed isn't in doubt, but precisely how he fit in is being reexamined. Research revealed in *A Forest of Kings* by Linda Schele and David Freidel (William Morrow and Co., Inc., 1990) shows that the bas-relief history at Chichén-Itzá does not support the theory of a Toltec invasion. Instead, they believe Chichén-Itzá's adoption of Toltec architecture demonstrates that it was a cosmopolitan city that absorbed elements brought by the Itzáes from another region, but that the continuity of buildings and bas-relief figures show it was a continuous Maya site (sans Toltecs). However, not all Mayanists (scholars who study the Maya) raced to embrace this new theory.

According to some authorities, Uxmal was inhabited during this same period (around A.D. 1000), by the tribe known as the **Tutul Xiú,** who came from the region of Oaxaca and Tabasco. Some scholars think that the Xiú took the city from earlier builders because evidence shows that the region around Uxmal was inhabited as early as 800 B.C.

The three great Maya centers of Chichén-Itzá, Mayapán, and Uxmal lived in peace under a confederation: The Itzá ruled in Chichén-Itzá, the Cocom tribe in Mayapán, and the Xiú in Uxmal.

- **1823** The Yucatán Peninsula decides to become part of Mexico.
- **1824** Iturbide is expelled, returns, and is executed by firing squad.
- **1824–1855** Federal Republic Period: Guadalupe Victoria is elected first president of Mexico in 1824; he is followed by 26 presidents and interim presidents, among them José López de Santa Anna.
- **1828** Slavery abolished.
- **1829** Dresden Codex is faithfully reproduced in watercolor and a few copies are published.
- **1836** Santa Anna defeats Texans at Battle of the Alamo, at San Antonio, Texas, but is later defeated and captured at the Battle of San Jacinto outside Houston, Texas.
- **1838** France invades Mexico at Veracruz.
- **1839–1841** Americans John L. Stephens and Frederick Catherwood whack their way to Yucatecan ruins in two journeys that were to become the talk of the literary world.
- **1841–1843** Stephens publishes his three volumes of *Incidents of Travel* illustrated by Catherwood, which stimulate interest in the Yucatán.
- **1845** United States annexes Texas.
- **1846–48** War with the United States: For $15 million Mexico relinquishes half of its national territory to the United States in Treaty of Guadalupe Hidalgo.
- **1847–1866** War of the Castes: Degrading segregationist policies by Yucatán leaders against the Maya cause revolt, upheaval, and decimation of half the

continues

Maya population. Strife lasts well into 20th century. Exportation of *henequén* (agave plant) products, such as hemp for rope, and *chicle* (for gum) bring Yucatán into the world economy.

- **1855–72** Reform Years: Includes a 3-year war in Mexico, pitting cities against villages and rich against poor in search for ideology, stability, and political leadership. Benito Juárez is president in fact and in exile off and on between Reform Wars and during reign of Emperor Maximilian. Juárez nationalizes church property and declares separation of church and state.
- **1858** Campeche and Yucatán become territories.
- **1862** England, Spain, and France send troops to Mexico to demand debt payment and all except France withdraw.
- **1862** Diego de Landa's 1566 account of "Yucatán Before and After the Conquest" is discovered in the Royal Academy of History in Madrid.
- **1863** Campeche gains statehood.
- **1864–67** Second Empire: French Emperor Napoleon Bonaparte III sends Maximilian of Hapsburg to be Emperor of Mexico.
- **1867** Juárez orders execution of Maximilian at Querétaro and resumes presidency in Mexico City until his death in 1872.
- **1872–84** Post-Reform Period: Only four presidents hold office but country is nearly bankrupt.
- **1876–1911** Porfiriato: Porfirio Díaz is president/dictator of Mexico for 35 years, leads country to modernization at the expense

continues

Authorities don't agree on the exact year, but sometime during the 12th century A.D. the people of Mayapán overthrew the confederation, sacked Chichén-Itzá, conquered Uxmal, and captured the leaders of the Itzá and the Xiú. Held in Mayapán, the Itzá and the Xiú princes reigned over but did not rule their former cities. Mayapán remained the seat of the confederation for over 200 years.

The Xiú took their revenge in 1441 when they marched from Uxmal on Mayapán, capturing and destroying the city, and killing the Cocom rulers. They founded a new city at Mani. Battles and skirmishes continued to plague the Maya territory until it was conquered by the Spanish conquistadores.

THE SPANISH CONQUISTADORES

In 1517, the first Spaniards to arrive in what is today known as Mexico skirmished with Maya Indians off the coast of the Yucatán Peninsula. One of these fledgling expeditions ended in shipwreck, leaving several Spaniards stranded as prisoners of the Maya. When word of this new land of riches spread in Cuba, where Hernán Cortés resided, another expedition under his leadership became a reality. When he showed up on the same route as the previous expeditions and landed on the island of Cozumel in February 1519, it changed the course of Mexican history. There he heard of the stranded Spaniards on the mainland and later made contact with them. Soon after, he met the Indian slave Malinche, who spoke both Maya and Nahuatl (the Aztec language), and who, together with Jeronimo de Aguilar, one of the shipwrecked Spaniards, provided the language link between the conquerors and the Aztecs. This liaison facilitated the Spanish conquest of Mexico. When Cortés arrived, the Aztecs didn't rule the Yucatán Maya, but conquering the Aztecs led to total Spanish domination of not only the Yucatán, but of all Mexico. Following the hint of gold, the Spaniards continued on around the Yucatán Peninsula to Campeche and Tabasco, eventually landing on the east coast at what today is Veracruz. From there the conquest was eventually launched. While in Tabasco, Cortés first heard of the Aztecs when he asked the source of the gold the Maya possessed.

When Cortés and his men landed, the Aztec empire was ruled by Moctezuma (often misspelled Montezuma) in great splendor. The emperor was not certain what course to pursue: If the strangers were Quetzalcoatl and his followers returning at last, no resistance must be offered; on the other hand, if the strangers were not Quetzalcoatl, they might be a threat to his empire. Moctezuma tried to bribe them with gold to go away, but this only whetted their appetites. Despite the fact that Moctezuma and his ministers received the conquistadores with full pomp and glory when they reached Mexico City, Cortés eventually took Moctezuma captive.

Though the Spaniards were no match for the hundreds of thousands of Aztecs, they skillfully kept things under their control until two separate consecutive revolts threatened Cortés's entire enterprise. First, Spaniards sent by the governor of Cuba to capture Cortés arrived and sought to discount him and return him to Cuba, or kill him. Cortés left a group of Spaniards in Tenochtitlán while he attacked the Spaniards on the coast and squashed the rebellion. Meanwhile, the Aztecs attacked the Spaniards in Tenochtitlán and drove them out in battle. Cortés then retreated to the countryside, made alliances with non-Aztec tribes, and finally marched on the empire when it was governed by the last Aztec emperor, Cuauhtémoc. Cuauhtémoc defended himself and his people valiantly for almost 3 months, but was finally captured, tortured, and executed.

The Spanish conquest started out as an adventure by Cortés and his men, unauthorized by the Spanish crown or its governor in Cuba. Soon Christianity was being spread through "New Spain." Guatemala and Honduras were explored and conquered, and by 1540 the territory of New Spain included Spanish possessions from Vancouver to Panama. In the 2 centuries that followed, Franciscan and Augustinian friars converted great numbers of Indians to Christianity, and the Spanish lords built up huge feudal estates on which the Indian farmers were little more than serfs. The silver and gold that Cortés had sought made Spain the richest country in Europe.

The conquest of the Yucatán Peninsula, however, occurred separately from what is considered the conquest of Mexico led by Hernán Cortés. In 1526, the King of Spain granted permission to Francisco Montejo to conquer the Yucatán Peninsula. The Maya fought the brutal invaders for 20 years until the peninsula finally came uneasily under the Spanish yoke in 1546. Because the Maya were treated as second-class citizens, unrest festered for 300 years until the Caste War eventually broke out, with the Maya fighting the Spanish for control of the peninsula. The Maya eventually lost, but the

of human rights. Díaz opponents, including Yaqui Indians from Northern Mexico, are exiled to the Yucatán Peninsula to suffer and die as slaves.

- **1902** Quintana Roo becomes Mexican territory.
- **1911–17** Mexican Revolution: Franciso Madero drafts revolutionary plan. Díaz resigns. Leaders jockey for power during period of great violence, national upheaval, and tremendous loss of life.
- **1913** President Madero assassinated.
- **1914, 1916** United States invades Mexico.
- **1915** Payo Obispo becomes capital of territory of Quintana Roo.
- **1917–1940** Reconstruction: Present constitution of Mexico signed; land and education reforms are initiated, and labor unions strengthened; Mexico expels U.S. oil companies and nationalizes all natural resources and railroads. Pancho Villa, Zapata, and Presidents Obregón and Carranza are assassinated.
- **1931** Citizens of Yucatán Peninsula protest division of Quintana Roo territory between the states of Yucatán and Campeche.
- **1935** Quintana Roo is restored to territorial status.
- **1940** Mexico enters period of political stability and makes tremendous economic progress and improvement in the quality of life, although problems of corruption, inflation, national health, and unresolved land and agricultural issues continue.
- **1946** Locals living in the jungle show Giles Healy the magnificent Maya murals at

continues

Bonampak, which he reports to the world.

- **1950** The first train links Campeche with Coatzacoalcos.

- **1952** Dr. Yuri Valentinovich Knorosov, a Russian scholar who had never seen a Maya ruin, publishes the modern-day key to deciphering Maya hieroglyphics; it is not fully accepted for at least 20 years. Mexican archaeologist Alberto Ruz Lhuller uncovers King Pacal's tomb in the Temple of the Inscriptions at Palenque—one of the greatest discoveries of the Maya world.

- **1974** Quintana Roo achieves statehood and Cancún opens to tourism.

- **1982** President Echeverria nationalizes the country's banks.

- **1988** Mexico enters the General Agreement on Trade and Tariffs (GATT).

- **1991** Mexico, Canada, and the United States begin Free Trade Agreement negotiations. Mexico begins massive push to excavate "new" Maya sites and re-excavate and conserve others.

- **1992** Sale of *ejido* land (peasant communal property) to private citizens is allowed. Mexico and the Vatican establish diplomatic relations after an interruption of 100 years.

- **1993** Mexico deregulates hotel and restaurant prices; New Peso currency begins circulation.

- **1994** Mexico, Canada, and the United States sign the North American Free Trade Agreement (NAFTA). An Indian uprising in Chiapas sparks protests countrywide over government policies concerning land distribution,

continues

southern and eastern half of the peninsula remained a virtual no man's land (to outsiders) where the Maya resided almost unfettered by the outside world until coastal development began in the late 1960s. (See also the box "Centuries of Conflict: Spanish & Maya in the Yucatán" in chapter 6).

INDEPENDENCE

Spain ruled Mexico until 1821, when Mexico finally gained its independence after a decade of upheaval. The independence movement had begun in 1810 when a priest, Father Miguel Hidalgo, gave the cry for independence from his pulpit in the town of Dolores, Guanajuato. The revolt soon became a revolution, and Hidalgo, Ignacio Allende, and another priest, José María Morelos, gathered an "army" of citizens and threatened Mexico City. Ultimately Hidalgo was executed, but he is honored as "the Father of Mexican Independence." Morelos kept the revolt alive until 1815, when he, too, was executed.

When independence finally came, Agustín de Iturbide was ready to take over. In 1822 Iturbide founded a short-lived "empire" with himself as emperor. The next year it fell and was followed by the proclamation of a republic, with General Guadalupe Victoria as the first president.

In 1821 the Spanish governor of Yucatán resigned and Yucatán, too, became an independent country. Though it decided to join in a union with Mexico 2 years later, this period of sovereignty is testimony to the Yucatecan spirit of independence. That same spirit arose again in 1846 when Yucatán seceded from Mexico.

At the national level, a succession of presidents and military dictators followed Guadalupe Victoria until the French intervened in Mexico in one of the most bizarre and extraordinary episodes in modern times. In the 1860s, Mexican factions offered Archduke Ferdinand Maximilian Joseph of Hapsburg the crown of Mexico, and with the support of the ambitious French emperor, Napoléon III, the young Austrian actually came to Mexico and "ruled" for 3 years (1864 to 1867), while the country was in a state of civil war. This European interference in New World affairs was not welcomed by the United States, and the French emperor finally withdrew his troops, leaving the misguided Maximilian to be captured and executed by a firing squad in Querétaro. His adversary and successor (as president of Mexico) was Benito Juárez, a Zapotec Indian lawyer and one of the most heroic figures in Mexican history. After victory over Maximilian, Juárez did his best to unify and strengthen his country before dying of a heart attack in 1872. His effect on Mexico's future was profound, however, and his plans and visions bore fruit for decades.

THE PORFIRIATO & THE REVOLUTION

From 1877 to 1911, a period now called the "Porfiriato," the prime role in Mexico was played by Porfirio Díaz, a general under Juárez. Recognized as a modernizer, he was a terror to his enemies and to challengers of his absolute power. During the Díaz years, many who fell into disfavor wound up enslaved in the Yucatán, including the Yaqui Indians of northwestern Mexico. These shockingly brutal years are recorded in *Barbarous Mexico* by John Kenneth Turner (University of Texas Press, 1969). Public opinion forced Díaz to resign in 1911 and he fled to France, where he lived until his death.

After the fall of the Porfiriast dictatorship, several factions split the country. The decade that followed is referred to as the Mexican Revolution. Drastic reforms occurred during this period, and the surge of vitality and progress from this exciting if turbulent time has inspired Mexicans to the present. Succeeding presidents have invoked the spirit of the Revolution, which is still studied and discussed.

BEYOND THE REVOLUTION

The decades from the beginning of the revolution in 1911 to stabilization in the 1940s and 1950s were tumultuous. Great strides were made during these years in distributing land to the peasant populations, irrigation, developing of mineral resources, and establishing education, health, and sanitation programs. However, the tremendous economic pressure Mexico faced from its own internal problems and the world depression of the 1930s did little for political stability. From 1911 to 1940, 16 men were president of Mexico. Some stayed in power a year or less.

From the 1930s through the 1970s, socialism had a strong voice in Mexico; its impact was most marked in the state's attempts to run the country's businesses—not just oil, but railroads, mining, utilities, hotels, motion pictures, the telephone company, supermarkets, and so on.

Miguel Aleman, president from 1946 to 1958, continued progress by building dams, improving highways and railways, and encouraging trade. Yet problems remained, many of which still plague the

bank loans, health, education, and voting and human rights. In an unrelated incident, PRI candidate Luis Donaldo Colossio is assassinated 5 months before the election; replacement candidate Ernesto Zedillo Ponce de Leon is elected and inaugurated as president in December. Within weeks, the peso is devalued, throwing the nation into turmoil.

- **1995** The peso loses half its value within the first 3 months of the year. The government raises prices on oil and utilities. Interest on debt soars to 140 percent; businesses begin to fail; unemployment rises. The Chiapan rebels threaten another rebellion, which is quickly quashed by the government. Former President Carlos Salinas de Gortari, with the devaluation having left his reputation for economic leadership in a shambles, leaves Mexico for the United States. Salinas's brother is accused of plotting the assassination of their brother-in-law, the head of the PRI. The United States extends Mexico $40 billion in loans to stabilize the economy following the peso crisis.

- **1996** Effects of the devaluation continue as in 1995, but many businesses without debt expand and prosper. Mexico begins repaying the loan from the United States extended in 1995; the wife of the president's brother is arrested attempting to remove millions of dollars from a Swiss Bank—drug ties are alleged; former President Salinas's whereabouts unknown, though he speaks out occasionally; the Chiapan

continues

crisis remains unsettled, but some progress has been made.

■ **1997** Mexico continues early repayment of its debt to the United States; Mexico's economy shows signs of improving, but the people struggle under effects of inflation, low pay, and lack of jobs. The Chiapan issue is still not settled, although important agreements have been signed. Drug traffic through Mexico to the United States increases.

country today: The country's booming population created unemployment, wages of the common people were appallingly low, and Aleman's administration was plagued by corruption and graft.

In 1970, Luis Echeverria came to power, followed in 1976 by José López Portillo. During these two presidencies, at the urging of private sector businesses and banks, the country began its enormous development of megaresorts such as Cancún, which, with coastal development continuing into the 1980s, created a completely new tourism sector for the country. This bold idea, to develop undeveloped coastlines and spruce up existing coastal resorts, brought a new kind of leisure traveler to Mexico, billions in income, and created hundreds of thousands of jobs. But also during their presidencies there emerged a studied coolness in relations with the United States and an activist role in international affairs. This period also saw an increase in charges of large-scale corruption in the upper echelons of Mexican society. The corruption, though endemic to the system, was encouraged by the river of money from the rise in oil prices. When oil income skyrocketed, Mexican borrowing and spending did likewise. The reduction of oil prices in the 1980s left Mexico with an enormous foreign bank debt and serious infrastructure deficiencies.

The country inherited by President Miguel de la Madríd Hurtado in 1982 was one without King Oil, and with new challenges to build agriculture, cut expenditures, tame corruption, and keep creditors at bay. He began the process of privatizing government-held businesses (airlines, hotels, banks, and so on) and led the country into membership in GATT (the General Agreement on Tariffs and Trade), an important preparation for entering NAFTA (the North American Free Trade Agreement), which was accomplished during his successor's presidency. De la Madríd also gave the last great thrust to development of the country's coasts before departing from office. Nevertheless, soaring inflation of 200% faced Carlos Salinas de Gortari as he took office in 1989. Salinas's accomplishments included decreasing inflation to 15% annually by adeptly gaining the necessary agreement of industry and labor leaders to hold wages and prices; continuing the privatization of government-held businesses; and leading the country into NAFTA, which over a 15-year period would reduce trade barriers and allow business to flourish more freely among Mexico, the United States, and Canada. During Salinas's 6-year term, Mexico's world position as a country poised for great prosperity strengthened, and Mexican public opinion held

Impressions

The people of Yucatán are above all Yucatecans. They read the poetry of Yucatán, cook according to local recipes, have their own artists and sculptors and universities. Invited to the Rotary Club of Mérida in the large garden of a private house constructed on the model of homes being erected in Paris in 1890, I discovered to my surprise that more of the people in the assemblage had been to Paris or Europe than had been to Mexico City. The Yucatecan, if he need medical treatment of a sort unavailable on the peninsula, will go more readily to Cuba or the United States than to rowdy, politically hostile, and 'savage' Mexico City.

—Michel Peissel, *The Lost World of Quintana Roo,* 1963

his administration in high esteem. But a cloud arose over the country toward the end of the Salinas's era when disgruntled Maya Indians staged an armed uprising after the NAFTA agreement was signed, and assassins' bullets felled both the PRI presidential candidate and the head of the PRI Party. The presidential elections, while automated for the first time and more honest than previous ones, were still marred by allegations of corruption. Still, these incidents failed to dampen Mexico's hope for continued progress when Ernesto Zedillo assumed office in December 1994.

TOWARD THE FUTURE

From the time of the revolution to the present, political parties and their roles have changed tremendously in Mexico. Although one political party, the **Partido Revolucionario Institucional** (PRI, called "el pree") has been in control under that name since 1946, opposition to it has become increasingly vocal and effective in recent years. In the beginning the party had four equal constituent groups—popular, agrarian, labor, and the military. At the risk of greatly oversimplifying a complex history and attendant issues, the widespread perception that the party is out of touch with the common Mexican, and its current problems retaining leadership, are the result of a change in focus away from those groups. The PRI today is heavily backed by, and in turn run by, business and industry leaders.

In 1994 a crisis occurred in Chiapas that has become a focal point for many of the nation's problems. Opposition parties such as the **Partido Acción Nacional** (PAN) had taken up the cause of the seemingly disenfranchised masses, but no one had spoken for or paid much attention to Mexico's millions of poor indigenous and rural poor people for some time. On New Year's Day 1994, militant Maya Indians attacked Chiapan towns, killing many, thus drawing attention to the plight of neglected indigenous groups and others in rural society, which the PRI-led government seemed to relegate to the bottom of the agenda. These groups are still clamoring for land they never received after the Revolution. That population growth has outstripped the availability of distributable land, that Mexico needs large-scale, modern agribusiness to keep up with the country's food needs—these are realities not understood by the millions of rural Mexicans who depend on their small family plot to feed the family. President Carlos Salinas de Gortari's bold, controversial decision in the early 1990s to allow the sale of *ejido* land (peasant communal property) may reflect Mexico's 21st-century needs, but it is at odds with firmly entrenched farm- and land-use traditions born before the 16th-century Conquest of Mexico. These issues of agrarian reform and the lack of other basics of life (roads, electricity, running water, education, health care, and so on) are being raised in areas besides Chiapas, most notably Oaxaca, Chihuahua, Guerrero, Veracruz, and Michoacán. This is a grave and festering problem, made all the more serious now that Mexico is reeling from the devaluation of the peso. Negotiations are ongoing to settle the dispute between the Chiapan Indians and the government, but life in San Cristóbal has returned to normal.

The surprise decision to devalue the currency at the end of 1994 threw domestic and international confidence in Mexico into turmoil. Within 3 months of the devaluation, the peso lost half its value, reducing Mexico's buying power by 50%. After the government issued its harsh economic recovery program, interest rates on credit cards and loans (many of which were variable, not fixed rates in Mexico), soared 80% to 140%. Overnight the cost of gasoline increased 35%, and gas and electricity 20%. As a partial solution, a $40 million loan package offered by the United States to ease the peso crisis used Mexico's sacred petroleum revenue as collateral—a staggering blow to Mexico's national pride. The effect so far has been a loudly expressed

❓ Did You Know?

- Four Maya books (or partial books) survived the 16th-century Maya book burning, but none are in Mexico today.
- The mingling of the blood of Spain with that of Mexico began with the marriage of Gonzalo Guerrero, a Spaniard shipwrecked off the coast of Yucatán in 1511, to a Maya woman with whom he fathered at least three sons. He refused to leave his family and join Cortés. A statue of Guerrero, commemorating the beginning of a new race, stands in Puerto Morelos, south of Cancún.
- The Celustún estuary, on the Yucatán Gulf Coast, is home to the largest flock of flamingos in North America.
- Cacao beans, grown in Tabasco and Chiapas, were Aztec currency.
- Cancún opened to tourism in 1974 with one hotel.
- In 1841 the Texas Navy was hired to protect the Yucatán Peninsula from invasion by Mexico.
- The Maya predicted that the earth's destruction will occur in the year A.D. 2012.
- During the 300 years that Mexico belonged to Spain, no Spanish king ever visited the country.
- Mexico's Indian population was approximately 30 million in 1519. By 1550, it was down to only 3 million, largely because of the spread of diseases brought by the Spaniards.
- Half the population of Mexico is under the age of 16.
- Cortés prevented his troops from returning to Spain by sinking all of his ships.

lack of confidence in the PRI and Zedillo, a dramatically slowed and cautious international investment climate, and a feeling among the citizenry of betrayal by the government. Responsibility for paying for governmental mismanagement of the economy has been shifted to ordinary Mexican citizens who were blindsided by this unexpected financial burden. Ordinary costs of daily living exceeded the ability of average people to pay; businesses closed and jobs were eliminated.

Meanwhile, former president Carlos Salinas de Gortari's brother was jailed and accused of involvement in the assassination of their brother-in-law, the head of the PRI Party. Carlos Salinas de Gortari and his family left Mexico quickly for the United States, after Salinas threatened a hunger strike unless his name was cleared regarding the assassination of his brother-in-law, and after he spoke publicly (an unheard-of breach of conduct by a past president) against the present government's handling of the peso crisis.

It seems incredible that a country so poised for prosperity should career backward so rapidly, and that such an admired and trusted president should so quickly fall from grace—because the people's trust and hopes in government under Salinas were so high, the betrayal is particularly bitter. However, as grim as all this seems, using Mexico's history just this century as a rule, the country bounces back from adversity to become even stronger. A strong popular will to progress undergirds the Mexican spirit, and despite recent sobering events, the country still bustles with commercial activity. Meanwhile, as long as inflation doesn't outpace the effect of the devaluation, the country is quite a bargain; even 2 years after the devaluation many parts of the country are value-priced, if not quite the bargain they were in 1996.

Economically, Mexico, though still a third-world country, is by no means a poor country. Only about a sixth of the economy is in agriculture. Mining is still fairly important. Gold, silver, and many other important minerals are still mined, but the big industry today is oil. Mexico is also well industrialized, manufacturing everything from textiles and food products to cassette tapes and automobiles.

5   Art & Architecture 101

Mexico's artistic and architectural legacy began more than 3,000 years ago. Until the conquest of Mexico in A.D. 1521, art, architecture, politics, and religion in Mexico were inextricably intertwined and remained so in different ways through the colonial period.

World-famous archaeological sites in Mexico—more than 15,000 of them—are individually unique even if built by the same groups of people. Each year scholars decipher more information about the ancient indigenous groups who built these cities, using information they left in bas-relief carvings, sculptures, murals, and hieroglyphics.

Mexico's **pyramids** are truncated platforms, not true pyramids, and come in many different shapes. Many sites have circular buildings, such as El Caracol at Chichén-Itzá, usually called the observatory and dedicated to the god of the wind. El Castillo at Chichén-Itzá has 365 steps—one for every day of the year. The Temple of the Magicians at Uxmal has beautifully rounded and sloping sides. Evidence of building one pyramidal structure on top of another, a widely accepted practice, has been found throughout Mesoamerica.

The Temple of the Inscriptions at Palenque is one of the few pyramids in Mesoamerica with a pyramid built specifically to conceal an underground tomb, although tombs have been found in many other pyramids. Cobá has the longest road (*sacbe*), stretching 62 miles. Numerous sites in Mesoamerica had ballcourts. In Mexico the longest is at Chichén-Itzá—nearly the length of a football field.

Architects of many Toltec, Aztec, and Teotihuacán edifices used a sloping panel (*talud*) alternating with a vertical panel (*tablero*). Elements of this style occasionally show up in the Yucatán. Dzinbanché, a newly excavated site near Lago Bacalar in southern Quintana Roo state, has at least one temple with this characteristic.

The true arch was unknown in Mesoamerica, so the Maya made multiple use of the corbeled arch in which a keystone juts out over the others and is used to build a modified inverted V-shaped arch.

The Olmec, considered the parent culture in Mexico, built pyramids of earth, so little remains to tell us what their buildings looked like. The Olmec, however, left an enormous sculptural legacy from small, intricately carved pieces of jade to 40-ton carved basalt rock heads that were, amazingly, shipped to their homesites by river raft. This legacy of carving was eventually adopted by the Maya.

Throughout Mexico, the pyramids were embellished with carved stone or mural art, not for the purpose of pure adornment, but for religious and historic reasons. **Hieroglyphs,** picture symbols etched on stone or painted on walls or pottery, functioned as the written language of the ancient peoples, particularly the Maya. By deciphering the glyphs, scholars allow the ancients to speak again, giving us specific names to attach to rulers and their families, and demystifying the great dynastic histories of the Maya. For more on this, be sure to read *A Forest of Kings* (1990) by Linda Schele and David Freidel and *Blood of Kings* (1986) by Linda Schele and Mary Ellen Miller. Good hieroglyphic examples can be seen in the site museum at Palenque.

Carving important historic figures on free-standing stone slabs, or *stelae,* was a common Maya commemorative device. Several are in place at Cobá, Calakmul has the most, and good examples are in the Museum of Anthropology in Mexico City and the Carlos Pellicer Museum in Villahermosa.

Pottery played an important role, and different indigenous groups are distinguished by their use of color and style in pottery. The Maya were known for pottery painted with scenes from daily and historic life.

Pre-Hispanic cultures left a number of fantastic painted **murals,** some of which are remarkably preserved, such as those at Bonampak and Cacaxtla. Amazing stone murals or mosaics using thousands of pieces of fitted stone to form figures of warriors, snakes, or geometric designs decorate the pyramid facades at Uxmal and Chichén-Itzá.

With the arrival of the Spaniards a new form of architecture came to Mexico (the next 300 years are known as the Viceregal Period, when Spain's appointed viceroys ruled Mexico). Many sites that were occupied by indigenous groups at the time of the conquest were razed, and in their place appeared Catholic churches, public buildings, and palaces for conquerors and the king's bureaucrats. In the Yucatán existing churches at Izamal, Calkani, Santa Elena, and Muná rest atop former pyramidal structures. Indian artisans, who formerly worked on pyramidal structures, were recruited to give life to the new buildings, often guided by drawings of European buildings. Frequently left on their own, the indigenous artisans sometimes implanted traditional symbolism in the new buildings: a plaster angel swaddled in feathers, reminiscent of the god Quetzalcoatl; or the face of an ancient god surrounded by corn leaves. They used pre-Hispanic calendar counts—the 13 steps to heaven or the nine levels of the underworld—to determine how many florets to carve around the church doorway.

To convert the native populations, New World Spanish priests and architects altered their normal ways of teaching and building. Often before the church was built, an open-air atrium was first constructed so that large numbers of parishioners could be accommodated for service. *Posas* (shelters) at the four corners of churchyards were another architectural technique unique to Mexico, again for the purpose of accommodating crowds during holy sacraments. Because of the language barrier between the Spanish and the natives, church adornment became more graphic. Biblical tales came to life in frescoes splashed across church walls. Christian symbolism in stone supplanted that of pre-Hispanic ideas as the natives tried to make sense of it all. The convenient apparition of the Virgin Mary on former pre-Hispanic religious turf made it "legal" to return there to worship and build a "Christian" shrine. Baroque became even more baroque in Mexico and was dubbed *churrigueresque.*

Almost every village in the Yucatán Peninsula has the hulking remains of enormous fortress-like missions, monasteries, convents, and parish churches. Many were built in the 16th century following the early arrival of Franciscan friars (the Franciscans were the only sect allowed in the Yucatán to Christianize the natives). Highlights include the Mission of San Bernardino de Sisal in Valladolid; the fine altarpiece at Teabo; the folk art retablo at Calkani; the large church and convent at Mani with its unique retablos and limestone crucifix; the facade, altar, and central retablo of the church at Oxkutzcab; the 16-bell espadaña at Ytholin; the baroque facade and altarpiece at Maxcanu; the cathedral at Mérida; the vast atrium and church at Izamal; and the baroque retablo and murals at Tabi.

Concurrent with the building of religious structures, public buildings took shape, modeled after those in European capitals. Colorful locally made tile was used to decorate public walls and church domes. The hacienda architecture sprang up in the countryside, resulting in massive, thick-walled, fortress-like structures built around a central patio. Remains of haciendas, some of them still operating, can be seen in almost all parts of Mexico and espcially in the north-central part of the Yucatán Peninsula where great henequen haciendas were built to process the spiny agave for a world market.

The San Carlos Academy of Art was founded in Mexico City in 1785, taking after the renowned academics of Europe. Though the emphasis was on a European-ized Mexico, by the end of the 19th century the subject matter of easel artists was becoming Mexican: Still lifes with Mexican fruit and pottery and Mexican landscapes with cacti and volcanoes appeared, as did portraits whose subjects wore Mexican regional clothing.

When Porfirio Díaz became president in the late 19th century, the nation's art and architecture experienced another infusion of European sensibility. Díaz idolized Europe, and during this time he lavished on the country a number of striking European-style public buildings, among them opera houses still used today. He provided European scholarships to promising young artists who later returned to Mexico to produce clearly Mexican subject paintings using techniques learned abroad. Partly because of the vast henequen hacienda wealth and partly because the Yucatán Peninsula was so far from the heart of Mexico, it too developed more of an affinity with European and Cuban cultures than it did with Mexico.

While the Mexican Revolution, following the resignation and exile of Díaz, ripped the country apart between 1911 and 1917, the result was the birth of a Mexico claimed and appreciated by Mexicans. In 1923 Minister of Education José Vasconcelos was charged with educating the illiterate masses. As one means of reaching many people, he started the muralist movement when he invited Diego Rivera and several other budding artists to paint Mexican history on the walls of the Ministry of Education building and the National Preparatory School in Mexico City. From then on, the "big three" muralists—David Siquieros, José Clemente Orozco, and Rivera—as well as others depicted Mexico's history on the walls of public buildings throughout the country for all to see and interpret. The years that followed eventually brought about a return to easel art, an exploration of Mexico's culture, and a new generation of artists and architects who were free to invent and draw upon subjects and styles from around the world. The new Museo de Arte Contemporaneo Atenco de Yucatán (MACAY) in Mérida is one place to see regional artists and visiting exhibitions from Mexico and the world.

6 Religion, Myth & Folklore

Mexico is a predominantly Roman Catholic country, a religion introduced by the Spaniards during the Conquest of Mexico. Despite its preponderance, the Catholic faith in many places in Mexico (Chiapas and Oaxaca, for example) has pre-Hispanic overtones. One need only visit the *curandero* section of a Mexican market, or attend a village festivity featuring pre-Hispanic dancers, to understand that supernatural beliefs often run parallel to Christian ones.

Mexico's complicated mythological heritage from pre-Hispanic literature is full of images derived from nature—the wind, jaguars, eagles, snakes, flowers, and more—all intertwined with elaborate mythological stories to explain the universe, climate, seasons, and geography. So strong were the ancient beliefs that Mexico's indigenous peoples built their cities according to the four cardinal points of the compass, with each compass point assigned a particular color (the colors might vary from group to group). The sun, moon, and stars took on godlike meaning and the religious, ceremonial, and secular calendars were arranged to show tribute to these omnipotent gods.

Most groups believed in an underworld (not a hell), usually containing 9 levels, and a heaven of 13 levels, so the numbers 9 and 13 are mythologically significant. The solar calendar count of 365 days and the ceremonial calendar of 260 days are numerically significant. How one died determined where one wound up after death; in the underworld ("Xibalba" to the Maya), in heaven, or at one of the four cardinal points. Everyone had first to make a journey through the underworld.

One of the richest sources of mythological tales is the *Book of Popol Vuh*, a Maya bible of sorts, which was recorded after the Conquest. The *Chilam Balam,* another such book, existed in hieroglyphic form at the Conquest and was recorded using the Spanish alphabet to transliterate Maya words that could be understood by the Spaniards. The *Chilam Balam* differs from the *Popol Vuh* in that it is the collected histories of many Maya communities.

Each of the ancient cultures had its set of gods and goddesses, and while the names might not cross cultures, their characteristics or purposes often did. Chaac, the hook-nosed rain god of the Maya, was Tlaloc, the mighty-figured rain god of the Aztecs; Quetzalcoatl, the plumed-serpent god/man of the Toltecs, became Kukulkán of the Maya. The tales of the powers and creation of these deities make up Mexico's rich mythology. Sorting out the pre-Hispanic pantheon and mythological beliefs in ancient Mexico can become an all-consuming study (the Maya alone had 166 deities), so below is a list of some of the most important gods:

Chaac: Maya rain god.

Ehécatl: Wind god whose temple is usually round; another aspect of Quetzalcoatl.

Itzamná: Maya god above all, who invented corn, cacao, and writing and reading.

Ixchel: Maya goddess of water, weaving, and childbirth.

Kinich Ahau: Maya sun god.

Kukulkán: Quetzalcoatl's name in the Yucatán.

Ometeotl: God/goddess all-powerful creator of the universe, ruler of heaven, earth, and the underworld.

Quetzalcoatl: A mortal who took on legendary characteristics as a god (or vice versa). When he left Tula in shame after a night of succumbing to temptations, he promised to return. He reappeared in the Yucatán. He is also symbolized as Venus, the moving star, and Ehécatl, the wind god. Quetzalcoatl is credited with giving the Maya cacao (chocolate) and teaching them how to grow it, harvest it, roast it, and turn it into a drink with ceremonial and magical properties.

Tlaloc: Aztec rain god.

7 Margaritas, Tamales & Poc Chuc: Food & Drink in Yucatán, Tabasco & Chiapas

True Mexican food usually isn't fiery hot; hot spices are added from sauces and garnishes at the table. While there are certain staples like tortillas and beans that appear almost universally, Mexican food and drink varies considerably from region to region; the regions covered in this book are some of Mexico's best keepers of the country's cuisine.

MEALS & RESTAURANTS
BREAKFAST

Traditionally, businesspeople in Mexico may grab a cup of coffee, or *atole,* and a piece of sweet bread just before heading for work around 8am. Around 10 or 11am it's time for a real breakfast. That's when restaurants fill with men (usually) eating hearty breakfasts that may look more like lunch with steak, eggs, beans, and tortillas.

Foreigners searching for an early breakfast will often find nothing gets going in restaurants until around 9am; that's a hint to bring your own portable coffeepot and coffee, buy bakery goodies the night before, and make breakfast yourself. Markets, however, are bustling by 7am and that's the best place to get an early breakfast. Though Mexico grows flavorful coffee in Chiapas, Veracruz, and Oaxaca, a jar of instant coffee is often all that's offered, especially in budget restaurants.

LUNCH

Between 1 and 5pm patrons again converge for lunch, the main meal of the day, which begins with soup, then rice, then the main course with beans and tortillas and maybe a meager helping of a vegetable, followed by dessert and coffee. Workers return to their jobs until 7 or 8pm.

DINNER

Dinner is late, usually around 9 or 10pm. Although you may see many Mexicans eating in restaurants at night, big evening meals aren't traditional. A typical meal at home would be a light one with leftovers from breakfast or lunch, perhaps soup, or tortillas and jam, or a little meat and rice.

RESTAURANT TIPS & ETIQUETTE

Some of the foreigner's greatest frustrations in Mexico have to do with getting and retaining the waiter and receiving the final bill. If the waiter arrives to take your order before you are ready, you may have trouble getting him again when you *are* ready. Once your meal is before you, and you're close to savoring your last morsel, amazingly an eager waiter often appears to whisk away your plate before you're finished! "¿Puedo retirar?" ("Can I take your plate away?") he asks, nearly clicking his heels with efficiency. At this point guard your plate, for at any moment it could disappear midfork. Finding your waiter to get the check, however, is another matter. It's considered rude for the waiter to bring it before it's requested, so you have to ask for it (sometimes more than once, when at last you've found the waiter).

To summon the waiter, wave or raise your hand, but don't motion with your index finger, which is a demeaning gesture that may even cause the waiter to ignore you. Or if it's the check you want, a smile and a scribbling motion into the palm of your hand can send the message across the room.

FOOD AROUND THE REGIONS

Mexico's regional foods are a mixture of pre-Hispanic, Spanish, and French cuisines, and at their best are among the most delicious in the world. Recipes developed by nuns during colonial times to please priests and visiting dignitaries have become part of the national patrimony, but much of Mexico's cuisine is derived from pre-Hispanic times. For the visitor, finding hearty, filling meals is fairly easy on a budget, but finding truly delicious food is not as easy. However, some of the best food is found in small, inexpensive restaurants where regional specialties are made to please discerning locals.

Tamales are one of Mexico's traditional foods—regional differences make trying them a treat as you travel. Chiapas has many types of tamales, but all are plump and usually come with a sizable hunk of meat and sauce inside. Yucatán tamales often feature a delightful mixture of cornmeal, *chaya* (a spinach-like leaf), and ground, roasted melon seeds.

Tortillas are another Mexican basic, although they are not made or used universally. Tortillas are fried and used as garnish in tortilla and Tarascan soup. Soft tortillas become *tacos* when filled with any number of meats; however, in some places in Mexico what's called a taco on the menu may be more like a flauta elsewhere. An *enchilada* is a tortilla that's stuffed, rolled, covered in a sauce, and garnished. A tortilla filled with cheese and lightly fried is a *quesadilla*. Rolled into a narrow tube, stuffed with chicken, then deep-fried, it's known as a *flauta*. Leftover tortillas cut into wedges and fried until crispy are called *totopos* and are used to scoop up beans and guacamole salad. Yesterday's tortillas mixed with eggs, chicken, peppers, and other spices are called *chilaquiles*. Small fried-corn tortillas are delicious with ceviche; when topped with fresh lettuce, tomatoes, onions, chicken, and sauce they become *tostadas*. Each region has a variation of these tortilla-based dishes.

The Yucatán Peninsula has some of the most varied regional food, including papadzules (stuffed tortillas covered in a tomato sauce), huevos motuleños (fried eggs topped with peas, ham, and grated cheese), poc chuc (a marinated and grilled pork chop), cochinita and pollo pibil (pit-baked pork and chicken in a savory achiote sauce), pavo en relleno negro (stuffed turkey covered in a blackened chile sauce), and lime soup (a chicken broth flavored with lime juice).

Regional drinks are almost as varied as the food in Mexico. Tequila comes from the blue agave grown near Guadalajara. Hot *ponche* (punch) is often found at festivals and is usually made with fresh fruit and spiked with tequila or rum. *Pox* (pronounced posh) is an aguardiente-based drink flavored with fruit and served in Chiapas. Wines from the grape-growing regions of Baja California and the region around Querétaro are sold countrywide. Beer is produced in Monterrey, the Yucatán, and Veracruz. Delicious *aguas frescas* (flavored waters made from flowers, ground rice and melon seeds, watermelon, and other fresh fruits) appear on tables countrywide. *Sangrita* is a spicy tomato/orange-juice and pepper-based chaser for tequila shots.

8 Recommended Books & Recordings

BOOKS
HISTORY

By the time Cortés arrived in Mexico, the indigenous people were already masters of literature, recording their poems and histories by painting in fanfold books (codices) made of deerskin and bark paper or by carving on stone. To record history, gifted students were taught the art of bookmaking, drawing, painting, reading, and writing—abilities the general public didn't have. A contemporary book that tells the story of the Indians' "painted books" is *The Mexican Codices and Their Extraordinary History* (Ediciones Lara, 1985), by María Sten.

The ancient Maya produced two important epic works, the *Book of Popol Vuh* and the *Chilam Balam*. Dennis Tedlock produced the most authoritative translation of the *Popul Vuh* (Simon & Schuster, 1985). Anthropologist Michael D. Coe says, "The *Popul Vuh* is generally considered to be the greatest single work of Native American literature." Unfortunately, other than the *Popul Vuh* and the *Chilam Balam,* there are only four surviving codices (or portions of them) because after the Conquest the Spaniards deliberately destroyed native books. However, several Catholic priests, among them Bernardo de Sahuguin and Diego de Landa (who was one of the book destroyers), encouraged the Indians to record their customs and history. These records are among the best documentation of life before the Conquest.

During the Conquest, Cortés wrote his now-famous five letters to King Charles V, which gave us the first printed Conquest literature, but the most important record is that of Díaz de Castillo. Enraged by an inaccurate account of the Conquest written by a flattering friend of Cortés, 40 years after the conquest Bernal Díaz de Castillo, one of the conquerors, wrote his lively and very readable version of the event, *True History of the Conquest of Mexico;* it's regarded as the most accurate.

In an attempt to defend himself for burning 27 Maya hieroglyphic rolls in 1562, Friar Diego de Landa collected contemporary Maya customs, beliefs, and history and wrote *Relación de las Cosas de Yucatán* (today entitled *Yucatán Before and After the Conquest,* Dover Press, 1978). It was first published in 1566 and remains the most significant record of its kind.

A Short History of Mexico (Doubleday, 1962), by J. Patrick McHenry, is a concise historical account. A remarkably readable and thorough college textbook is *The Course of Mexican History* (Oxford University Press, 1995), by Michael C. Meyer and William L. Sherman. *Sons of the Shaking Earth* (University of Chicago Press, 1959), by Eric Wolf, is an excellent introduction to Mexican history and culture. *Ancient Mexico: An Overview* (University of New Mexico Press, 1985), by Jaime Litvak, is a short, very readable history of pre-Hispanic Mexico.

The Wind That Swept Mexico (University of Texas Press, 1971), by Anita Brenner, is a classic illustrated account of the Mexican Revolution. *Barbarous Mexico,* by John Kenneth Turner (University of Texas Press, 1984), was written in the early 1900s as a shocking exposé of the atrocities of the Porfirio Díaz presidency, which included enslaving Yaqui Indians from Sonora in camps in the Yucatán and Oaxaca. *The Lost World of Quintana Roo,* by Michel Peissel (E.P. Dutton, 1963), is the thrilling account of a young man's journey on foot in search of undiscovered ruins along the Yucatán's almost uninhabited Caribbean coast in the late 1950s.

Passionate Pilgrim, by Antoinette May (Paragon House, 1993), is the fascinating biography of Alma Reed, an American journalist and amateur archaeologist whose life spanned the exciting 1920s to 1960s. Her journalistic assignments included early archaeological digs at Chichén-Itzá, Uxmal, and Palenque; breaking the story to the *New York Times* of archaeologist Edward Thompson's role in removing the contents of the sacred cenote at Chichén-Itzá to the Peabody Museum at Harvard; and serving as a columnist for the *Mexico City News.* She also had a love affair with Felipe Carrillo Puerto, the governor of Yucatán, who commissioned the famous Mexican song, "La Peregrina" in her honor. She later championed the career of Mexican muralist José Clemente Orozco at her art gallery in New York.

CULTURE

Mexican and Central American Mythology (Peter Bedrick Books, 1983), by Irene Nicholson, is a concise illustrated book that simplifies the subject.

Though not focused on life in the Yucatán or Chiapas and Tabasco—where thinking, culture, and customs developed apart from the rest of Mexico—several books, nevertheless, are good background reading on Mexico in general. A good, but controversial, all-around introduction to contemporary Mexico and its people is *Distant Neighbors: A Portrait of the Mexicans* (Random House, 1984), by Alan Riding. In a more personal vein is Patrick Oster's *The Mexicans: A Personal Portrait of the Mexican People* (Harper & Row, 1989), a reporter's insightful account of ordinary Mexican people. A novel with valuable insights into the Mexican character is *The Labyrinth of Solitude* (Grove Press, 1985), by Octavio Paz.

Anyone going to San Cristóbal de las Casas should first read *Living Maya* (Harry N. Abrams, 1987), by Walter F. Morris, with excellent photographs by Jeffrey J. Foxx. The book is all about the Maya living today in the state of Chiapas. Peter Canby's *Heart of the Sky: Travels Among the Maya* (Kodansha International, 1994) takes readers on a rare and rugged journey as he searches to understand the real issues facing the Maya of Mexico and Guatemala today.

The best single source of information on Mexican music, dance, and mythology is Frances Toor's *A Treasury of Mexican Folkways* (Crown, 1967).

ART, ARCHAEOLOGY & ARCHITECTURE

Travelers heading for the Yucatán should consider reading amateur archaeologist John L. Stephens' wonderfully entertaining accounts of travel in that region in the 19th century. His books, *Incidents of Travel in Central America, Chiapas and Yucatán,* and also his account of his second trip, *Incidents of Travel in Yucatán,* have been reprinted by Dover Publications. The series also includes Friar Diego de Landa's *Yucatán Before and After the Conquest.*

The Maya (Thames and Hudson, 1993), by Michael D. Coe, is extremely helpful in relating to the different Maya periods. *A Forest of Kings: The Untold Story of the Ancient Maya* (William Morrow, 1990), by Linda Schele and David Freidel, uses the written history of Maya hieroglyphs to tell the incredible dynastic history of selected Maya sites. You'll never view the sky the same after reading *Maya Cosmos: Three Thousand Years on the Shaman's Path* (William Morrow, 1993) by David Freidel, Linda Schele, and Joy Parker, whose personal insights and scholarly work take us along a very readable path into the amazing sky-centered world of the Maya. *The Blood of Kings: Dynasty and Ritual in Maya Art* (George Braziller, Inc., 1986), by Linda Schele and Mary Ellen Miller, is a pioneer work that unlocks the bloody history of the Maya.

In *Breaking the Maya Code* (Thames & Hudson, 1992) readers follow Michael D. Coe on the fascinating, circuitous hundred-year journey through reading the mysterious written texts left by the Maya in partially remaining books, pottery, murals, and carved in stone. Another must-read, it's a page-turner, modern-day mystery complete with a cast of real-life characters. *Maya History,* by Tatiana Proskouriakoff (University of Texas Press, 1993), is the last work of one of the most revered Maya scholars. Linda Schele, a contemporary Maya scholar, calls Proskouriakoff "the person who was to our field as Darwin was to biology." Her contributions included numerous drawings of now-ruined Maya temples and glyphs, of which there are over 300 in this book.

Try a used bookstore for *Digging in Mexico,* by Ann Axtell Morris (Doubleday, Doran, 1931). The book is as interesting for its photographs of Chichén-Itzá before and during the excavations as it is for the author's lively and revealing anecdotes. Morris was the young writer and artist wife of Earl Morris, director of excavations at Chichén-Itzá during the Carnegie Institution's work there in the 1920s.

In *Maya Missions,* authors Richard and Rosalind Perry (Espadana Press, 1988) reveal the mysteries of the Yucatán Peninsula's many centuries-old colonial-era missions with inviting detail. *An Archaeological Guide to Mexico's Yucatán Peninsula,* by Joyce Kelly (University of Oklahoma, 1993), is a companion to *Maya Missions* that covers the other side of the peninsula's architecture; it is the most comprehensive guide to Maya ruins. Carrying these two books with you will enrich your visit a thousandfold.

Mexico: Splendors of Thirty Centuries (Metropolitan Museum of Art, 1990), the catalog of the 1991 traveling exhibition, is a wonderful resource on Mexico's art from 1500 B.C. through the 1950s. Another superb catalog, *Images of Mexico: The Contribution of Mexico to 20th Century Art* (Dallas Museum of Art, 1987), is a fabulously illustrated and detailed account of Mexican art gathered from collections around the world. *Art and Time in Mexico: From the Conquest to the Revolution* (Harper & Row, 1985), by Elizabeth Wilder Weismann, illustrated with 351 photographs, covers Mexican religious, public, and private architecture with excellent photos and text. *Casa Mexicana* (Stewart, Tabori & Chang, 1989), by Tim Street-Porter, takes readers through the interiors of some of Mexico's finest homes-turned-museums, public buildings, and private homes. *Mexican Interiors* (Architectural Book Publishing Co., 1962), by Verna Cook Shipway and Warren Shipway, uses black-and-white photographs to highlight architectural details from homes all over Mexico.

FOLK ART

Chloë Sayer's *Costumes of Mexico* (University of Texas Press, 1985) is a beautifully illustrated and written work. *Mexican Masks* (University of Texas Press, 1980), by Donald Cordry, based on the author's collection and travels, remains the definitive work on Mexican masks. Cordry's *Mexican Indian Costumes* (University of Texas Press, 1968) is another classic on the subject. Carlos Espejel wrote both *Mexican Folk Ceramics* and *Mexican Folk Crafts* (Editorial Blume, 1975 and 1978), two comprehensive books that explore crafts state by state. *Folk Treasures of Mexico* (Harry N. Abrams, 1990), by Marion Oettinger, curator of folk art and Latin American art at the San Antonio Museum of Art, is the fascinating illustrated story behind the 3,000-piece Mexican folk-art collection amassed by Nelson Rockefeller over a 50-year period, as well as much information about individual folk artists.

NATURE

A Naturalist's Mexico (Texas A&M University Press, 1992), by Roland H. Wauer, is a fabulous guide to birding in Mexico. *A Hiker's Guide to Mexico's Natural History* (Mountaineers, 1995), by Jim Conrad, covers Mexican flora and fauna and tells how to find the easy-to-reach as well as out-of-the-way spots he describes. *Peterson Field Guides: Mexican Birds* (Houghton-Mifflin, 1973), by Roger Tory Peterson and Edward L. Chalif, is an excellent guide to the country's birds. *Birds of the Yucatán* (Amigos de Sian Ka'an) by Barbara MacKinnon has color illustrations and descriptions of 100 birds found primarily in the Yucatán Peninsula. *A Guide to Mexican Mammals and Reptiles* (Minutiae Mexicana), by Normal Pelham Wright and Dr. Bernardo Villa Ramírez, is a small but useful guide to some of the country's wildlife.

RECORDINGS

Mexicans take their music very seriously—notice the tapes for sale almost everywhere, ceaseless music in the streets, and the bus drivers with collections of tapes to entertain passengers. For the collector, choices range from contemporary rock to revolutionary ballads, ranchero, salsa, and romantic trios.

Marimba music is heard often in the Yucatán as well as in Tabasco and Chiapas. Peña Ríos makes excellent marimba recordings. Though marimba musicians seldom ask for requests, some typical renditions would include "Huapango de Moncayo" and "El Bolero de Ravel."

Mariachi music is played and sold all over Mexico. Among the top recording artists is Mariachi Vargas. No mariachi performance is complete without "Guadalajara," "Las Mañanitas," and "Jarabe Tapatió."

Other music from the Yucatán includes the recordings by the Trio Los Soberanos and Dueto Yucalpetén. Typical Yucatecan songs are "Las Golondrinas Yucatecas," "Peregrina," "Ella," "El Pájaro Azul," and "Ojos Tristes." Heartthrob soloists from years past include Pedro Vargas, Pedro Infante, Hector Cabrera, Lucho Gatica, Pepe Jara, and Alberto Vázquez.

For trio music from elsewhere, some of the best are by Los Tres Diamantes and Los Tres Reyes. If you're requesting songs of a trio, good ones to ask for are "Sin Ti," "Usted," "Amor de la Calle," and "Cielito Lindo." Traditional ranchero songs to request, which can be sung by soloists or trios, are "Tú Solo Tú," "No Volveré," and "Adios Mi Chaparita."

One of the best recordings of recent times is the Royal Philharmonic Orchestra's rendition of classic Mexican music titled *Mexicano;* it's one purchase you must make.

3

Planning a Trip to the Yucatán

Before any trip, you need to do a bit of advance planning. When should I go? What's the best way to get there? How much will this trip cost me? And can I catch a festival during my visit? I'll answer these and other questions for you in this chapter.

1 Visitor Information, Entry Requirements & Money

SOURCES OF INFORMATION

The **Mexico Hotline** (☎ 800/44-MEXICO in the U.S.) is a good source for very general informational brochures on the country and for answers to the most commonly asked questions. If you have a fax, Mexico's Ministry of Tourism also offers **FaxMeMexico** (☎ 541/385-9282). Call, provide them with a fax number, and select from a variety of topics—from accommodations (the service lists 400 hotels) to shopping, dining, sports, sightseeing, festivals, and nightlife. They'll fax you the materials you're interested in. Even faster is the **Mexico Ministry of Tourism's web site**: http://www.mexico-travel.com.

The **U.S. Department of State** (☎ 202/647-5225 for travel information, 202/647-9225 for bulletin board information), offers a **Consular Information Sheet** on Mexico, with a compilation of safety, medical, driving, and general travel information gleaned from reports by official U.S. State Department offices in Mexico. You can also request the Consular Information Sheet (☎ 202/647-2000) by fax. The State Department is also on the web at http://www.travel.state.gov/travel_warnings.html and http://www.travel.state.gov/mexico.html. The **Center for Disease Control hotline** (☎ 404/332-4559) is another source for medical information affecting travelers to Mexico and elsewhere. The center's web site, http://www.cdc.gov/, provides lengthy information on health issues for specific countries.

MEXICAN GOVERNMENT TOURIST OFFICES　Mexico has tourist offices throughout the world, including the following:

United States: 70 E. Lake St., Suite 1413, Chicago, IL 60601 (☎ 312/565-2778); 5075 Westheimer, Suite 975, West Houston, TX 77056 (☎ 713/629-1611); 10100 Santa Monica Blvd., Suite 224, Los Angeles, CA 90067 (☎ 310/203-8191); 2333 Ponce de

Leon Blvd., Suite 710, Coral Gables, FL 33134 (☎ **305/443-9160**); 405 Park Ave., Suite 1401, New York, NY 10022 (☎ **212/838-2947**); and the Mexican Embassy Tourism Delegate, 1911 Pennsylvania Ave. NW, Washington, DC 20006 (☎ **202/728-1750**).

Canada: One Place Ville-Marie, Suite 1526, Montréal, PQ H3B 2B5 (☎ **514/871-1052**); 2 Bloor St. W., Suite 1801, Toronto, ON M4W 3E2 (☎ **416/925-1876**). 99 W. Hastings #1610, Vancouver, British Columbia V6C 2W2 (☎ **604/669-3498**).

Europe: Weisenhüttenplatz 26, D 6000 Frankfurt-am-Main 1, Germany (☎ **49/69-25-3413**); 60-61 Trafalgar Sq., London WC2 N5DS, United Kingdom (☎ **171/734-1058**); Calle de Velázquez 126, 28006 Madrid, Spain (☎ **341/261-1827**); 4 rue Notre-Dame-des-Victoires, 75002 Paris, France (☎ **331/4020-0734**); and via Barberini 3, 00187 Rome, Italy (☎ **396/482-7160**).

Asia: 2.15.1 Nagato-Cho, Chiyoda-Ku, Tokyo 100, Japan (☎ **813/580-2962**).

OTHER SOURCES The following newsletters may be of interest to readers: *Mexican Meanderings,* P.O. Box 33057, Austin, TX 78764, offers terrific travel insights aimed at readers who want off-the-beaten-track destinations and experiences. It's published six times annually; a subscription is $18; *Travel Mexico,* Apdo. Postal 6-1007, 06600 Mexico, D.F., from the publishers of the *Traveler's Guide to Mexico,* the book frequently found in hotel rooms in Mexico, covers a variety of topics from archaeology news to hotel packages, new resorts and hotels, and the economy (six times annually, subscription $18).

ENTRY REQUIREMENTS

DOCUMENTS All travelers to Mexico are required to present **proof of citizenship,** such as an original birth certificate with a raised seal, a valid passport, or naturalization papers. Those using a birth certificate should also have a current photo identification such as a driver's license. And those whose last name on the birth certificate is different from their current name (women using a married name, for example) should also bring a photo identification card *and* legal proof of the name change such as the *original* marriage license or certificate (I'm not kidding). This proof of citizenship may also be requested when you want to reenter the United States from Mexico. Photocopies are *not* acceptable.

You must also carry a **Mexican Tourist Permit,** which is issued free of charge by Mexican border officials after proof of citizenship is accepted. The Tourist Permit is more important than a passport in Mexico, so guard it carefully. If you lose it, you may not be permitted to leave the country until you can replace it—a bureaucratic hassle that takes several days to a week at least. (If you do lose your Tourist Permit, get a police report from local authorities indicating that your documents were stolen; having such a report *might* lessen the hassle of exiting the country without all your identification.)

A Tourist Permit can be issued for up to 180 days, and although your stay south of the border may be shorter than that, you should ask for the maximum time, just in case. Sometimes officials don't ask—they just stamp a time limit, so be sure to say "6 months" (or at least twice as long as you intend to stay). If you should decide to extend your stay, you'll eliminate hassle by not needing to renew your papers.

This is especially important for people who take a car into Mexico. Additional documentation is required for driving a personal vehicle in Mexico (see "By Car" under "Getting There," below).

Note that children under age 18 traveling without parents or with only one parent must have a notarized letter from the absent parent or parents authorizing the travel. If one or both parents are deceased, it is probably a good idea to carry along a copy of the death certificate.

Lost Documents   To replace a **lost passport,** contact your embassy or nearest consular agent (see "Fast Facts: Mexico," below). You must establish a record of your citizenship and also fill out a form requesting another Mexican Tourist Permit (assuming it, too, was lost). Without the **Tourist Permit** you can't leave the country, and without an affidavit affirming your passport request and citizenship, you may have hassles at Customs when you get home. So it's important to clear everything up *before* trying to leave. Mexican Customs may, however, accept the police report of the loss of the Tourist Permit and allow you to leave.

CUSTOMS ALLOWANCES   When you enter Mexico, Customs officials will be tolerant as long as you have no illegal drugs or firearms. You're allowed to bring in two cartons of cigarettes, or 50 cigars, plus a kilogram (2.2 lb.) of smoking tobacco; the liquor allowance is 2 liters of anything, wine or hard liquor; you are also allowed 12 rolls of film.

When you're reentering the United States, federal law allows you to bring in duty free up to $400 in purchases every 30 days. The first $1,000 over the $400 allowance is taxed at 10%. You may bring in a carton of cigarettes (200) or 50 cigars or 2kg (4.4 lb.) of smoking tobacco, plus 1 liter of an alcoholic beverage (wine, beer, or spirits).

Canadian citizens are allowed $20 in purchases after a 24-hour absence from the country or $100 after a stay of 48 hours or more.

Going through Customs   Mexican customs inspection has been streamlined. At most points of entry tourists are requested to punch a button in front of what looks like a traffic signal, which alternates on touch between red and green signals. Green light means you can go through without inspection; a red light means your luggage or car may be inspected briefly or thoroughly.

MONEY
CASH/CURRENCY

In 1993, the Mexican government dropped three zeroes from its currency. The new currency is called the *Nuevo Peso,* or New Peso. The purpose was to simplify accounting; all those zeroes were becoming too difficult to manage. Old Peso notes were valid through 1996. Paper currency comes in denominations of 10, 20, 50, and 100 New Pesos. Coins come in denominations of 1, 2, 5, and 10 pesos and 20 and 50 *centavos* (100 centavos make 1 New Peso). The coins are somewhat confusing because different denominations have a similar appearance. You may still see some prices written with *N* or *NP* beside them, which refer to New Pesos. Currently the U.S. dollar equals around NP$8; at that rate an item costing NP$5, for example, would be equivalent to U.S. 63¢.

Before the New Peso was instituted, merchants and others skipped the small change; now they don't. Small change (a peso or less than a peso) is often unavailable, so cashiers often offer gum or candy to make up the difference. Centavos will appear on restaurant bills and credit cards, but are paid differently depending on whether you pay in cash or by credit card. On restaurant bills that you pay in cash, for example, the centavos will be rounded up or down to the nearest 5 centavos. Credit-card bills, however, will show the exact amount (not rounded), and will have *N* written before the amount to denote that the bill is in New Pesos. Be sure to double-check any credit-card vouchers to be sure the *N* or *NP* appears on the total line.

Getting change continues to be a problem in Mexico. Small-denomination bills and coins are hard to come by, so start collecting them early in your trip and continue as you travel. Shopkeepers everywhere seem to always be out of change and small bills; that's doubly true in a market.

Note: The dollar sign ($) is used to indicate pesos in Mexico. To avoid confusion, I will use the dollar sign in this book *only* to denote U.S. currency.

Only dollar prices are listed in this book; they are a more reliable indication than peso prices. Many establishments dealing with tourists quote prices in dollars. To avoid confusion, they use the abbreviations "Dlls." for dollars and "m.n." (*moneda nacional*—national currency) for pesos.

Every effort has been made to provide the most accurate and up-to-date information in this guide, but price changes are inevitable.

EXCHANGING MONEY

The December 1994 devaluation of the peso has had varied meanings for tourists. First, the rate of exchange fluctuates daily, so be careful not to exchange too much of your currency at once. Be sure to allow enough to carry you over a weekend or Mexican holiday, when banks are closed. In general, avoid carrying the U.S. $100 bill, which besides being hard to cash in the past, was the one most commonly counterfeited and people are still wary of it. Since small bills and coins in pesos are hard to come by in Mexico, the U.S. $1 bill is very useful for tipping; I like to carry at least $50 in $1 bills to avoid overtipping in pesos.

Bottom line on exchanging money of all kinds: It pays to ask first and shop around. Banks in Mexico often give a less favorable rate of exchange than the official daily rate, and hotels usually exchange less favorably than do banks. Exchange houses are generally more convenient than banks since they have more locations and longer hours, and the rate of exchange may be the same as the bank or slightly lower or slightly higher. Personal checks may be cashed but not without weeks of delay—a bank will wait for your check to clear before giving you your money. Canadian dollars seem to be most easily exchanged for pesos at branches of Banamex and Bancomer. *Before leaving a bank or exchange house window, always count your change in front of the teller before the next client steps up.*

Banks are open Monday through Friday from 9am to 1:30pm; a few banks in large cities offer extended afternoon hours. Most banks won't exchange money until 10am, when they receive the day's official exchange rate. Large airports have currency-exchange counters that often stay open whenever flights are arriving or departing. Don't go for the first one you see in an airport—there's usually more than one, and you'll often find a better exchange rate farther along the concourse. As a general rule, take a few minutes to scout the exchange houses for the best rate, and then change only enough to tide you over until you can go to a bank, which usually offers better deals.

TRAVELER'S CHECKS

Traveler's checks are readily accepted nearly everywhere, but they can be difficult to cash on a weekend or holiday or in an out-of-the-way place. Their best value is in replacement in case of theft. I usually arrive in Mexico with half of my money in cash (in $1, $20, and $50 bills) and half in traveler's checks ($20 and $50 denominations). Mexican banks sometimes pay more for traveler's checks than for dollars in cash, but in some places *casas de cambio* (exchange houses) pay more for cash than for traveler's checks. Additionally, some but not all banks charge a service fee to exchange either traveler's checks or dollars.

CREDIT CARDS & ATMS

You'll be able to charge some hotel and restaurant bills, almost all airline tickets, and many store purchases on your credit cards. Some establishments charge an additional 3% for use of a credit card, but they usually tell you first. Do not rely on your credit card in out-of-the-way places or in many budget hotels and restaurants. If credit cards are accepted and incur no additional fees, use them whenever possible. The exchange rate may be in your favor when the peso-to-dollar rate is determined later during billing. Such savings can be considerable. You can get cash advances of several hundred dollars on your card, but there may be a wait of 20 minutes to 2 hours. You can't charge gasoline purchases in Mexico.

Visa ("Bancomer" in Mexico), MasterCard ("Carnet" in Mexico), and, less widely, American Express are the most accepted cards. The Bancomer bank, with branches throughout the country, has inaugurated a system of **automatic-teller machines (ATMs)** linked to Visa International's network. If you are a Visa customer, you may be able to get peso cash from one of the Bancomer ATMs.

ATM machines are also associated with other banks and may work with your own bank ATM. There's usually a $200 limit per transaction. A few cautions about using automatic teller machines are in order: First, though ATMs are located next to banks, or in a bank lobby, use the same precautions you would at home—don't use one at night, or on a lonely street, and so on; second, don't depend on them totally for your extra cash—chances are great that you might not have access to one; third, you'll be out of luck if the machine eats your card; fourth, should you be involved in a car or bus hijacking (not that great a threat in the areas covered in this book), thieves have been known to take hostages with ATM cards to the nearest ATM machine to empty their accounts. Thus, as elsewhere in the world, an ATM card can be a blessing and a curse.

BRIBES & SCAMS

At the outset I should mention that the areas covered by this book are not prone to extensive bribes and scams, or even robberies or other malevolent crimes of modern life. The areas and situations in which you are most likely to encounter difficulties are with customs officials at the Mérida airport, with Mérida taxi drivers, with police officers on the outskirts of Mérida, along the lonely highway from Villahermosa through Escarcega to Xpuhil, with traffic police in Chetumal, and an occasional car content thief in Cancún. Generally speaking, there's no need to be overly guarded as you travel this part of the world. In fact, you may discover yourself enveloped in a carefree spirit as you leave thoughts of more crime-prone parts of the world behind. More than likely, anything lost will be returned to you, and it's far more likely that you'll be helped than anything troublesome happening.

If, however, you find yourself hit up for a bribe—called *mordidas* (bites), sometimes masquerading as a tip (*propina*), here's how to deal with it.

Extortion exists everywhere in the world, but in Mexico as in other developing countries, the tolls are smaller and collected more often.

Border officials appear to be slipping back into the petty-extortion habit they largely shed during the administration of President Salinas de Gortari. Just so you're prepared, here are a few hints based on my experiences.

First rule: Even if you speak Spanish, don't say a word of it to Mexican officials. You may appear innocent or even dumb, all the while understanding every word. Border officials are supposed to stamp your passport or birth certificate and perhaps lightly inspect your luggage, and then wave you on through. If the official who inspects your car (if you're driving) or luggage asks for a tip as in "Give me a tip (*propina*)," then he's asking for a bribe. I usually ignore this request, but you'll have to decide for yourself based on your circumstances at the time, especially if the official decides a complete search of your belongings is suddenly in order. If you're charged for the stamping or inspection (for example, the inspector says, "One dollar," followed by an outstretched hand), ask for a receipt (*recibo*; "ray-*see*-bow"). If he says there's no receipt, don't pay the bribe.

Whatever you do, avoid impoliteness, and absolutely *never* insult a Latin American official! When an official's sense of machismo is roused, he can and will throw the book at you, and you may be in trouble. Stand your ground, but do it politely.

How do I know when paying a bribe would be better than fighting it? Here are a couple of scenarios: A driving rain is drenching the world outside, and the scowling border guard or policeman orders everyone out of the vehicle to unpack belongings for inspection—in the rain. Cut your losses and offer a bribe. You're stopped for a traffic infraction that you did or didn't commit, and the policeman keeps inspecting your car documents, your driver's license, or your Tourist Permit, finding things "wrong." If you're in a hurry, offer a bribe. If you're not, offer to follow him to the station. He'll probably not want to do that, and will find some way to save face—your credentials are all right, after all—and move on. You must allow him to save face.

How much should I offer? Usually $3 to $5 or the equivalent in pesos will do the trick. There's supposedly a number to report irregularities with customs officials (☎ toll-free **01-800/0-0148** in Mexico). Your call will go to the office of the Comptroller and Administrative Development Secretariat (SECODAM). It's worth a try. But be sure you have some basic information, such as the name of the person, or badge number, of whomever wanted a bribe or was rude, and the place, time, and day of the event.

2 When to Go

High season in the Yucatán—from just before Christmas through Easter Sunday—is certainly the best time to be in the Yucatán if you're here for calm, warm weather, for snorkeling, diving, and fishing (the calmer weather means clearer and more predictable seas), or to see the ruins that dot the interior of the peninsula. Book well in advance if you're planning to be in Cancún around the holidays.

Low season in Mexico runs from Easter Sunday through approximately December 20, and airlines often offer discounted airfares. Many of these fares are unadvertised, especially during the slowest months mentioned above (mid-summer), and again in January, when the Christmas travelers have dispersed and hotel and airline occupancies are low.

Low season yields even greater discounts in hotel rates than airfares—prices are 20% or more lower than during high season. There's often a lull after New Year's in Cancún and Cozumel—prices can fall to somewhere between high- and low-season norms.

In most of Mexico, July and August are very slow, but there are some exceptions. Mexicans and Europeans take vacations in those months, and some hotels in Isla Mujeres and Playa del Carmen raise their prices in those months.

Generally speaking, Mexico's **dry season** runs from November through April, with the **rainy season** stretching from May through October. It isn't a problem if you're staying close to the beaches, but for those bent on road-tripping to Chichén-Itzá, Uxmal, or other sites, temperatures and humidity in the interior can be downright stifling from May through July. Later in the rainy season the frequency of tropical storms and **hurricanes** increases; such storms, of course, can put a crimp in your vacation. But they can also cool off temperatures, making ruins climbing a sheer joy accompanied by cool air and a slight wind. I especially like November for Yucatán travels.

As for Tabasco and Chiapas, Villahermosa, Tabasco, is sultry and humid all the time. San Cristóbal de las Casas, Chiapas, at an elevation of 7,100, is much cooler than the lowlands, and downright cold in winter.

You may also wish to plan a trip around a **festival,** which in Mérida would be Carnaval during the 3 days before Ash Wednesday, and in San Cristóbal de las Casas, would also be Carnaval (but an entirely different sort of event than in Mérida), Days of the Dead (November 1 and 2), December 12 for the celebration of the Día de Guadalupe, Easter week when there are processions, the Fería de Primavera (the week after Easter), and the Fiesta of San Cristóbal (July 17 to 25).

3 Active Vacations in the Yucatán

Mexico has numerous **golf** courses, especially in the resort areas, and there are excellent ones in Cancún and Playa del Carmen.

Tennis, racquetball, squash, waterskiing, surfing, bicycling, horseback riding, and **scuba diving** are all sports visitors can enjoy. Scuba diving especially is excellent off the Yucatán's Caribbean Coast

Mexico is finally catching up with other countries in ecological adventure and wilderness travel, though most of the national parks and nature reserves are understaffed and/or not staffed by knowledgeable people. The following companies offer a variety of off-the-beaten-path travel experiences:

Apertours, % Dietz Productions, Calle Tonalá 27, San Cristóbal de las Casas, Chiapas (☎ **800/303-4983;** ☎ and fax **967/8-5727;** web site: http://www.mexonline.com/aper1.htm) is led by photographer and San Cristóbal resident Craig Dietz, who offers photography classes for no more than three people at a time. Classes are outdoors, in the villages, and many are scheduled to coincide with special festivals in San Cristóbal.

ATC Tours and Travel, Calle 5 de Febrero no. 15, 29200 San Cristóbal de las Casas, Chiapas (☎ **967/8-2550;** fax 967/8-3145), a Mexico-based tour operator with an excellent reputation, offers specialist-led trips primarily in southern Mexico. In addition to trips to the ruins of Palenque and Yaxchilán (extending into Belize and Guatemala by river, plane, and bus if desired), they also offer horseback tours and day-trips to the ruins of Toniná around San Cristóbal de las Casas, Chiapas; birding in the rain forests of Chiapas and Guatemala (including in the El Triunfo Reserve of Chiapas, where you can see the rare quetzal bird and orchids); hikes out to the shops and homes of native textile artists of the Chiapas highlands; and walks from the Lagos de Montebello in the Montes Azules Biosphere Reserve, with camping and canoeing.

Ecoturismo Yucatán, Calle 3 no. 235, Col. Pensiones, 97219 Mérida, Yuc. (☎ 99/20-2772; fax 99/25-9047), offers a variety of tours including those focused on wildlife (especially birding) and ruins, including the Río Bec ruin route.

Far Flung Adventures, P.O. Box 377, Terlingua, TX 79852 (☎ **800/359-4138** or 915/371-2489), takes clients on specialist-led Mexico river trips, including the Río Usumacinta that runs between Mexico and Guatemala, combining rafting and camping at archaeological sites.

Far Horizons, P.O. Box 91900, Albuquerque, NM 87199-1900 (☎ **800/ 552-4575** or 505/343-9400; e-mail: journey@farhorizon.com; web site: http://

www.farhorizon.com), offers an extensive list of exploration-type tours led by degreed specialists. Among the offerings are a drawing class in the Yucatán and lengthy trips that include the ruins of Río Bec, Dzibanché, Chicanná, Kohunlich, and Palenque.

Mexico Sportsman, 202 Milam Building, San Antonio, TX 78205 (☎ **210/ 212-4567;** fax 210/212-4568) is sport fishing central for anyone interested in advance arrangements for fishing in Cancún and Cozumel. The company offers complete information from the cost (nothing hidden) to the length of a fishing trip, kind of boat, line and tackle used, and whether or not bait, drinks, and lunch are included. Prices are as good as you'll get on-site in Mexico.

Other Americas, 2333 Sunset Blvd., Houston, TX 77005 (☎ **713/526-6175;** fax 713/526-3551), combines photography instruction, culture, language, and adventure travel into colorful, experience-packed trips. Led by well-known photographer Geoff Winningham (head of the Rice University photography program), small groups of between 5 and 18 participants journey off the beaten path to very unusual festivals and events for one-of-a-kind experiences in Mexico.

PanAngling Travel Service, 180 North Michigan Ave., Chicago, IL 60601 (☎ **312/263-5246**) focuses on bonefish and tarpon fishing off the Yucatán Peninsula with stays at some remote and unique lodges.

Trek America, P.O. Box 189, Rockaway, NJ 07866 (☎ **800/221-0596** or 201/ 983-1144; fax 201/983-8551) organizes lengthy, active trips that combine trekking, hiking, van transportation, and camping in the Yucatán Peninsula and Chiapas as well as other places in Mexico.

Victor Emanuel Tours, P.O. Box 33008, Austin, TX 78764 (☎ **800/328-VENT** or 512/328-5221), is an established leader in birding and natural-history tours.

Wildland Adventures, 3516 NE 155th, Seattle, WA 98155 (☎ **800/345-4453**), offers an interesting mix of nature- and history-oriented tours in Mexico. They include the Belize-Yucatán Adventure, using Rancho Encantado on Lake Bacalar as a base for forays into the Río Bec ruin route and Lamanai in nearby Belize.

Wings, Inc., P.O. Box 31930, Tucson, AZ 85751 (☎ **602/749-1967;** e-mail: wings@rtd.com), has a wide assortment of trips, including birding in Chiapas.

4 Health, Safety & Insurance

STAYING HEALTHY

Of course, the very best way to avoid illness or to mitigate its effects is to make sure you're in top health when you travel and that you don't overdo it.

Important note: Antibiotics and other drugs that you'd need a prescription to buy in the States are sold over the counter in Mexican pharmacies. Drugstores, however, won't sell drugs that are controlled in the States—tranquilizers, for instance. High-priced antibiotics cost about the same in Mexico as they do in the United States. Aspirin and over-the-counter sinus medications are difficult, if not impossible, to find in Mexico.

Pack plenty of insect repellent and suntan lotion. When available, these commodities cost at least triple what they do in the States. Lotions with an SPF rating are almost impossible to find.

COMMON AILMENTS

It's a rare person indeed who doesn't experience some degree of gastric upheaval when traveling; see the box on Moctezuma's Revenge for tips on preventing and dealing with **travelers' diarrhea.**

Ay Carumba! Moctezuma's Revenge

Turista, Moctezuma's Revenge, and the Aztec Two-Step, are the names given to the persistent diarrhea, often accompanied by fever, nausea, and vomiting, that attacks so many travelers to Mexico. Doctors, who call it travelers' diarrhea, say it's not caused by just one "bug," or factor, but by a combination of consuming different food and water, upsetting your schedule, being overtired, and experiencing the stresses of travel. Being tired and careless about food and drink is a sure ticket to turista. A good high-potency (or "therapeutic") vitamin supplement, and even extra vitamin C, is a help; yogurt is good for healthy digestion and is becoming much more available in Mexico than in the past.

Preventing Turista: The U.S. Public Health Service recommends the following measures for preventing travelers' diarrhea:

- *Drink only purified water.* This means tea, coffee, and other beverages made with boiled water; canned or bottled carbonated beverages and water; beer and wine; or water you yourself have brought to a rolling boil or otherwise purified. Avoid ice, which may be made with untreated water. However, most restaurants with a large tourist clientele use only purified water and ice.
- *Choose food carefully.* In general, avoid salads, uncooked vegetables, and unpasteurized milk or milk products (including cheese). However, salads in a first-class restaurant, or one serving a lot of tourists, are generally safe to eat. Choose food that is freshly cooked and still hot. Peel fruit yourself. Don't eat undercooked meat, fish, or shellfish.

In addition, something so simple as clean hands can go a long way toward preventing turista. I carry packages of antiseptic towelettes for those times when wash facilities aren't available and to avoid using a communal bar of soap—a real germ carrier.

How to Get Well: If you get sick, there are lots of medicines available in Mexico that can harm more than help. Ask your doctor before you leave home what medicine he or she recommends for travelers' diarrhea.

The Public Health Service guidelines are the following: If there are three or more loose stools in an 8-hour period, especially with other symptoms (such as nausea, vomiting, abdominal cramps, and fever), see a doctor immediately. Dehydration can quickly become life-threatening.

The first thing to do is go to bed and don't move until the condition runs its course. Traveling makes it last longer. Drink lots of liquids: Tea without milk or sugar or the Mexican *té de manzanilla* (chamomile tea) is best. Eat only *pan tostada* (dry toast). Keep to this diet for at least 24 hours, and you'll be well over the worst of it. If you fool yourself into thinking a plate of enchiladas can't hurt or beer or liquor will kill the germs, you'll have a total relapse.

The Public Health Service advises that you be especially careful to replace fluids and electrolytes (potassium, sodium, and the like) during a bout of diarrhea. Do this by drinking Pedialyte, a rehydration solution available at most Mexican pharmacies, or glasses of fruit juice (high in potassium) with honey and a pinch of salt added, or you can also try a glass of boiled pure water with a quarter teaspoon of sodium bicarbonate (baking soda) added. The Center for Disease Control provides excellent suggestions for prevention and medication. (See "Sources of Information," earlier in this chapter, for details.)

Elevation Sickness is another problem travelers experience; San Cristóbal de las Casas is at an elevation of 7,100 feet, as are a number of other central Mexican cities. At high elevations it takes about 10 days to acquire the extra red blood corpuscles you need to adjust to the scarcity of oxygen.

Altitude sickness results from the relative lack of oxygen and the decrease in barometric pressure that characterize high elevations (over 5,000 ft./1,500m). Symptoms include shortness of breath, fatigue, headache, and even nausea.

Take it easy for the first few days after you arrive at a high elevation. Drink extra fluids but avoid alcohol. Remember, food digests more slowly at high altitudes and even a minimal overindulgence can fell the unwary at high elevations. If you have heart or lung problems, talk to your doctor before going above 8,000 feet.

Mosquitoes and gnats are prevalent along the coast and in the Yucatán lowlands. Insect repellent (*rapellante contra insectos*) is a must, and it's not always available in Mexico. If you're sensitive to bites, pick up some antihistamine cream from a drugstore at home. Rubbed on a fresh mosquito bite, the cream keeps the swelling down and reduces the itch.

Scorpions (*alacrán*) may be encountered in lodgings very near jungle settings. Shake out your shoes before donning them. If you're stung, go to a doctor.

MORE SERIOUS DISEASES

You shouldn't be overly concerned about tropical diseases if you stay on the normal tourist routes and don't eat street food. However, both dengue fever and cholera have appeared in Mexico in recent years. Talk to your doctor, or a medical specialist in tropical diseases, about any precautions you should take. You can also get medical bulletins from the U.S. State Department and the Center for Disease Control (see "Sources of Information," above). You can protect yourself by taking some simple precautions. Be careful about what you eat and drink; don't swim in stagnant water (ponds, slow-moving rivers, or wells; avoid mosquito bites by covering up, using powerful repellent, sleeping under mosquito netting, and staying away from places that seem to have a lot of mosquitoes.

EMERGENCY EVACUATION

For extreme medical emergencies there's a service from the United States that will fly people to American hospitals: **Air-Evac,** a 24-hour air ambulance (☎ **800/ 854-2569** in the U.S., or call collect **510/786-1592.** You can also contact the service in Guadalajara (☎ **01-800/90345** or 3/616-9616).

SAFETY

Boisterous drunks aside, I've never had trouble of any kind in Mexico, and seldom feel suspicious of anyone or any situation. You will probably feel physically safer in most Mexican cities and villages than in any comparable place at home.

Crime, however, is more of a problem in Mexico than it used to be. Be smart, be careful, and take all the normal precautions you'd take to deter pickpockets and muggers when traveling to any large American city, for example. As a simple precaution, when you're out for the day, carry only a small amount of cash and leave the rest of your valuables, including credit cards, remaining cash, passport and Tourist Permit in your hotel safe. Conceal your camera rather than strapping it over your shoulder.

Keep a photocopy of your credit cards, driver's license, and passport or birth certificate in a separate place from where you're keeping the originals. (In case you lose, or are relieved of, the originals, these copies will make replacement easier.)

The Traveler's Toolbox

There are a few miscellaneous gadgets and sundries that come in handy time and again in Mexico: a rain poncho for those seasonal and unseasonable rains; arm, waist, or leg money pouches; a washcloth, or better yet, a face sponge (which dries quickly)—you'll rarely find washcloths in a budget-category hotel room, and many first-class hotels don't furnish washcloths either; a basin plug (it's packaged by that name), for all those plugless sinks—a small plastic bag can double as a plug in a pinch; inflatable hangers and a stretch clothesline; a luggage cart saves much effort and tip money—buy a sturdy, steel one with at least 4-inch wheels that can take the beating of cobblestone streets, stairs, and curbs; a heat immersion coil, plastic cup, and spoon for preparing coffee, tea, and instant soup; a small flashlight for those generator-operated places with no lights after 10pm and archaeological sites with dark interiors; and a combination pocketknife for peeling fruit, fixing cameras and eyeglasses, and opening *cervezas* and bottles of wine.

Keep your things with you (rather than putting them in the bus storage compartment) on the less-responsible village buses and some second-class buses on country routes.

And, of course, *never* carry a package back to the States for an acquaintance or a stranger.

See "Sources of Information" at the beginning of this chapter for how to contact the U.S. Department of State for their latest advisories. At press time their crime cautions included warnings about bold highway holdups in the Yucatecan state of Campeche (including robbery of buses on Highway 186 heading east from Escarcega, and between Escarcega and Candalaria), and nighttime bus travel, especially long-distance overnight buses. They urge travelers to contact them for security information before traveling to Chiapas.

Lastly, I urge you not to let these cautionary statements deter you from traveling in Mexico. Were I to write a similar section about travel in the United States, it would take several pages. Mexico is a wonderful country, and your good experiences with its people and culture will far outweigh any negative incidents. I eagerly return there year after year.

INSURANCE

HEALTH/ACCIDENT/LOSS   Even the most careful of us can experience the Murphy's Law of travel—you discover you've lost your wallet, your passport, your airline ticket, or your Tourist Permit. Always keep a photocopy of these documents in your luggage—it makes replacing them easier. To be reimbursed for insured items once you return, you'll need to report the loss to the Mexican police and get a written report. If you don't speak Spanish, take along someone who does. If you lose official documents, you'll need to contact both Mexican and U.S. officials in Mexico before you leave the country.

Health Care Abroad, Wallach and Co. Inc., 107 W. Federal St. (P.O. Box 480), Middleburg, VA 22117 (☎ **800/237-6615** or 540/687-3166) and **World Access,** 6600 W. Broad St., Richmond, VA 23230 (☎ **800/628-4908** or 804/285-3300), offer medical and accident insurance as well as coverage for lost luggage and trip cancellation. Always read the fine print on the policy to be sure that you're getting the coverage you want.

5 Tips for Travelers with Special Needs

FOR SINGLES

Mexico may be an old favorite for romantic honeymoons, but it's also a great place to travel on your own without really being or feeling alone. Although offering an identical room rate regardless of single or double occupancy is slowly becoming a trend in Mexico, most of the inexpensive and moderately priced hotels mentioned in this book still offer singles at lower rates.

Mexicans are very friendly, and it's easy to meet other foreigners. Isla Mujeres, Playa del Carmen, Celestún, Cancún, Palenque, and San Cristóbal are great places to go to on your own.

If you don't like the idea of traveling alone, then try **Travel Companion Exchange,** P.O. Box 833, Amityville, NY 11701 (☎ **516/454-0880;** fax 516/454-0170), which brings prospective travelers together. Members complete a profile, then place an anonymous listing of their travel interests in the newsletter. Prospective traveling companions then make contact through the exchange. Membership costs $99 for 6 months or $159 for a year.

FOR WOMEN

As a frequent female visitor to Mexico, mostly traveling alone, I can tell you firsthand that I feel safer traveling in Mexico than in the United States. Mexicans are very warm and welcoming people, and I'm not afraid to be friendly wherever I go. But I use the same commonsense precautions I use traveling anywhere else in the world—I'm alert to what's going on around me.

Mexicans in general, and men in particular, are nosy about single travelers, especially women. They want to know with whom you're traveling, whether you're married or have a boyfriend, and how many children you have. My advice to anyone asked these details by taxi drivers or other people with whom you don't want to become friendly is to make up a set of answers (regardless of the truth): "I'm married, traveling with friends, and I have three children."

If you're a divorcée, revealing that detail may send out the wrong message about availability. Drunks are a particular nuisance to the lone female traveler. Don't try to be polite—just walk away or duck into a public place.

Generally, lone women will feel comfortable going to a hotel lobby bar, yet are asking for trouble by going into a pulquería or cantina. In restaurants, as a general rule, single women are offered the worst table and service. You'll have to be vocal about your preference and insist on service. Don't tip if service is bad.

FOR MEN

I'm not sure why, but non-Spanish-speaking foreign men seem to be special targets for scams and pickpockets. So if you fit this description, whether traveling alone or in a pair, exercise special vigilance.

FOR FAMILIES

Mexicans travel extensively in their country with their families, so your child will feel very welcome. Hotels will often arrange for a baby-sitter. Several hotels in the middle-to-luxury range have small playgrounds and pools for children and hire caretakers on weekends to oversee them. Few budget hotels offer these amenities.

Before leaving, check with your doctor to get advice on medications to take along. Disposable diapers cost about the same in Mexico but are of poorer quality. Gerber's baby foods are sold in many stores. Dry cereals, powdered formulas, baby bottles, and purified water are all easily available in midsize and large cities.

Cribs, however, may present a problem. Except for the largest and most luxurious hotels, few Mexican hotels provide cribs. However, rollaway beds to accommodate children staying in the room with parents are often available. Likewise, child seats or high chairs at restaurants are rare.

FOR TRAVELERS WITH DISABILITIES

Travelers who are unable to walk or who are in wheelchairs or on crutches discover quickly that Mexico is one giant obstacle course. Beginning at the airport on arrival, you may encounter steep stairs before finding a well-hidden elevator or escalator—if one exists. Airlines will often arrange wheelchair assistance for passengers to the baggage area. Porters are generally available to help with luggage at airports and large bus stations, once you've cleared baggage claim.

In addition, escalators (there aren't many in the country) are often not operating. Few handicapped-equipped rest rooms exist, or when one is available, access to it may be via a narrow passage that won't accommodate a wheelchair or someone on crutches. Many deluxe hotels (the most expensive) now have rooms with baths for the handicapped and handicapped access to the hotel. Those traveling on a budget should stick with one-story hotels or those with elevators. Even so, there will probably still be obstacles somewhere. Stairs without handrails abound in Mexico. Bus drivers generally don't bother with the courtesy step on boarding or disembarking, and the height between the street and the bus step can require considerable force to board. Generally speaking, no matter where you are, someone will lend a hand, although you may have to ask for it.

Few airports offer the luxury of boarding an airplane from the waiting room. You either descend stairs to a bus that ferries you to the waiting plane that's boarded by climbing stairs, or you walk across the airport tarmac to your plane and ascend the stairs. Deplaning offers the same in reverse.

6 Getting There

BY PLANE

The airline situation in Mexico is changing rapidly, with many new regional carriers offering scheduled service to areas previously not served. In addition to regularly scheduled service, charter service direct from U.S. cities to resorts is making Mexico more accessible from the United States.

THE MAJOR INTERNATIONAL AIRLINES   The main airlines operating direct or nonstop flights from the United States to Cancún, Cozumel, and Mérida include **Aero California** (☎ 800/237-6225), **Aeroméxico** (☎ 800/237-6639), **Air France** (☎ 800/237-2747), **American** (☎ 800/433-7300), **Continental** (☎ 800/231-0856), **Lacsa** (☎ 800/225-2272), **Mexicana** (☎ 800/531-7921), **Northwest** (☎ 800/225-2525), **United** (☎ 800/241-6522), and **US Airways** (☎ 800/428-4322).

Excursion and package plans proliferate, especially in the off-season. A good travel agent will be able to give you all the latest schedules, details, and prices, but you may have to investigate the details of the plans to see if they are real deals. You'll also have to sleuth regional airlines for yourself (see "By Plane" under "Getting Around," below), since most travel agents don't have that information.

CHARTERS   Charter flights from cold-weather cities in the United States—most run only in winter—often offer a considerable savings over scheduled airlines because they go direct to the destination (avoiding the necessity of overnighting en route) and they usually include low airfare and hotel. However, these same charters often offer round-trip airfare only, allowing more independent travelers to choose a less expensive hotel, and the option of staying longer and returning on a later charter flight.

Well-known **tour companies** operating charters include **Club America Vacations, Apple Vacations,** and **Friendly Holidays.** You can make arrangements with these companies through your travel agent.

BY CAR

Driving is certainly not the cheapest way to get to Mexico, but it is the best way to see the country. Even so, you may think twice about taking your own car south of the border once you've pondered Mexico's many bureaucratic requirements for doing so.

It's wise to check and double-check all the requirements before setting out for a driving tour of Mexico. Read through the rest of this section, and then address any additional questions you have or confirm the current rules by calling your nearest Mexican consulate, Mexican Government Tourist Office, AAA, or Sanborn's (☎ **800/222-0185** in the U.S.). To check on road conditions, or to get help with any travel emergency while in the country, there's a 24-hour number (toll-free **01-800/9-0329** in Mexico) that you can call. Another 24-hour help number (☎ **5/ 250-0123** or 5/250-0151) is in Mexico City. Both numbers are supposed to be staffed by English-speaking operators.

In addition, check with the U.S. Department of State (see "Sources of Information" at the beginning of this chapter) for their warnings about areas where driving the highways can be dangerous. Their current warnings regarding crime and highway travel are in "Safety," above.

CAR DOCUMENTS

To drive a personal car into Mexico, you'll need a **Temporary Car Importation Permit,** granted upon completion of a long and strictly required list of documents (see below). The permit can be obtained through Banco del Ejército (*Banjercito*) officials, who have a desk, booth, or office at the Mexican Customs (*Aduana*) building after you cross the border into Mexico. Or you can obtain the permit before you travel through Sanborn's Insurance and the American Automobile Association (AAA), each of which maintains border offices in Texas, New Mexico, Arizona, and California. These companies may charge a fee for this service, but it will be worth it to avoid the uncertain prospect of traveling all the way to the border without proper documents for crossing. However, even if you go through Sanborn's or AAA, your credentials *may* be reviewed again by Mexican officials at the border—you must have them all with you since they are still subject to questions of validity.

The following requirements for border crossing were accurate at press time:

- *A valid driver's license,* issued outside of Mexico.
- *Current, original car registration and a copy of the original car title.* If the registration or title is in more than one name and not all the named people are traveling with you, then a notarized letter from the absent person(s) authorizing use of the vehicle for the trip is required; have it ready just in case. The car registration and your credit card (see below) must be in the same name.
- *An original notarized letter from the lien or lease holder,* if your registration shows a lien or lease, giving you permission to take the vehicle into Mexico.
- *A valid international major credit card.* Using only your credit card, you are required to pay a $12 car-importation fee. The credit card must be in the same name as the car registration.

Note: Those without credit cards will forego the $12 importation fee and instead will be required to post a cash bond based on the value of the car. The rules and procedures are complicated (and expensive), so contact AAA or Sanborn's for details.

• *A signed declaration promising to return to your country of origin with the vehicle.* This form is provided by AAA or Sanborn's before you go or by Banjercito officials at the border. There's no charge. The form does not stipulate that you return through the same border entry you came through on your way south.

You must carry your Temporary Car Importation Permit, Tourist Permit, and, if you purchased it, your proof of Mexican car insurance in the car at all times.

Important reminder: Someone else may drive the car, but the person (or relative of the person) whose name appears on the Car Importation Permit must *always* be in the car at the same time. (If stopped by police, a nonregistered family member driver, driving without the registered driver, must be prepared to prove familial relationship to the registered driver—no joke.) Violation of this rule makes the car subject to impoundment and the driver to imprisonment and/or a fine.

Only under certain circumstances will the driver of the car be allowed to leave the country without the car. If it's undrivable, you can leave it at a mechanic's shop if you get a letter to that effect from the mechanic and present it to the nearest Secretaria de Hacienda y Credito Público (a treasury department official) for further documentation, which you then present to a Banjercito official upon leaving the country. Then you must return personally to retrieve the car. If the driver of the car has to leave the country without the car due to an emergency, the car must be put under Customs seal at the airport, and the driver's Tourist Permit must be stamped to that effect. There may be storage fees. If the car is wrecked or stolen, your Mexican insurance adjuster will provide the necessary paperwork for presentation to Hacienda officials.

If you receive your documentation at the border (rather than through Sanborn's or AAA), Mexican border officials will make two copies of everything and charge you for the copies.

The Temporary Car Importation Permit papers may be issued for as long as 6 months, and the Tourist Permit may be issued for up to 180 days; but they might stamp it for half that, or even 30 days, so state your preference *before* the official stamps your papers. It's a good idea also to overestimate the time you'll spend in Mexico, so that if something unforeseen happens and you have to—or want to—stay longer, you'll avoid the long hassle of getting your papers renewed.

Important note: Whatever you do, don't overstay either permit. Doing so invites heavy fines and/or confiscation of your vehicle, which will not be returned. Remember also that 6 months does not necessarily work out to be 180 days—be sure that you return before whichever expiration date comes first.

Other documentation is required for an individual's permit to enter Mexico—see "Entry Requirements," above.

MEXICAN AUTO INSURANCE

Although auto insurance is not legally required in Mexico, driving without it is foolish. U.S. insurance is invalid in Mexico; to be insured there, you must purchase Mexican insurance. Any party involved in an accident who has no insurance is automatically sent to jail and his or her car is impounded until all claims are settled. This is true even if you just drive across the border to spend the day, and it may be true even if you're injured.

I always buy my car insurance through **Sanborn's Mexico Insurance,** P.O. Box 310, Dept. FR, 2009 S. 10th, McAllen, TX 78505-0310 (☎ **800/222-0158** in the U.S. or 210/686-0711 in Texas; fax 210/686-0732). The company has offices at all of the border crossings in the United States. Their policies cost the same as the competition's do, but you get legal coverage (attorney and bail bonds if needed) and a detailed mile-by-mile guide to your proposed route—to me, this last part is the kicker. With the ongoing changes in Mexico's highway system, it's inevitable that your log will occasionally be a bit outdated. But for the most part having this guide is like having a knowledgeable friend in the car telling you how to get in and out of town, where to buy gas (and which stations to avoid), what the highway conditions are, and what scams you need to watch out for. It's especially helpful in remote places. Most of Sanborn's border offices are open Monday through Friday, and a few are staffed on Saturday and Sunday. You can purchase your auto liability and collision coverage by phone in advance and have it waiting at a 24-hour location if you are crossing when the office is closed. The annual insurance includes a type of evacuation assistance in case of emergency, and emergency evacuation insurance for shorter policies is available for a small daily fee. They also offer a medical policy.

AAA also sells insurance.

All agencies selling Mexican insurance will show you a full table of current rates and recommend the coverage they think is adequate. The policies are written along lines similar to those north of the border, with the following exception: The contents of your vehicle aren't covered. If you need to, it's now possible to get your policy term lengthened by fax from the insurer. However, if you are staying longer than 48 days, it's more economical to buy a nonrefundable annual policy. There are policies for short trips and annual policies. The latter may be better for those who make frequent trips to Mexico. Be sure the policy you buy will pay for repairs in either the United States or Mexico and will pay out in dollars, not pesos.

PREPARING YOUR CAR

Check the condition of your car thoroughly before you cross the border. Parts made in Mexico may be inferior, but service generally is quite good and relatively inexpensive. Carry a spare radiator hose and belts for the engine fan and air conditioner. Be sure your car is in tune to handle Mexican gasoline. Also, can your tires last a few thousand miles on Mexican roads?

Don't forget a flashlight and a tire gauge—Mexican filling stations generally have air to fill tires but no gauge to check the pressure. When I drive into Mexico, I always bring along a combination gauge/air compressor—sold at U.S. automotive stores—that plugs into the car cigarette lighter, making it a simple matter to check the tires daily.

Not that many Mexican cars comply, but Mexican law requires that every car have **seat belts** and a **fire extinguisher.** Be prepared!

CROSSING THE BORDER WITH YOUR CAR

After you cross the border into Mexico from the United States and you've stopped to get your **Tourist Card** and **Car Permit,** somewhere between 12 and 16 miles down the road you'll come to a Mexican customs post. In the past, all motorists had to stop and present travel documents and possibly have their cars inspected. Now there is a new system under which some motorists are stopped at random for inpection. All car papers are examined, however, so you must stop. If the light is green, go on through after your papers are examined; if it's red, stop for inspection. On the Baja Peninsula the procedures may differ slightly—first you get your Tourist Permit, then farther down the road you may or may not be stopped for the car inspection.

RETURNING TO THE UNITED STATES WITH YOUR CAR

The car papers you obtained when you entered Mexico *must* be returned when you cross back with your car or at some point within the time limit of 180 days. (You can cross as many times as you wish within the 180 days.) If the documents aren't returned, heavy fines are imposed ($250 for each 15 days late), and your car may be impounded and confiscated or you may be jailed if you return to Mexico. You can only return the car documents to a Banjercito official on duty at the Mexican Customs (*Aduana*) building *before* you cross back into the United States. Some border cities have Banjercito officials on duty 24 hours a day, but others do not; some also do not have Sunday hours. On the U.S. side, Customs agents may or may not inspect your car from stem to stern.

BY SHIP

Numerous cruise lines serve the Mexican Caribbean. Possible trips might run from Miami to the Caribbean (which often includes stops in Cancún, Playa del Carmen, and Cozumel).

If you don't mind making last-minute arrangements, several cruise-tour specialists arrange substantial discounts on unsold cabins. One such company is **The Cruise Line, Inc.,** 4770 Biscayne Blvd., Penthouse 1–3, Miami FL 33137 (☎ **800/ 327-3021** or 305/576-0036).

7 Getting Around

An important note: If your travel schedule depends on an important connection, say a plane trip between points, or a ferry or bus connection, use the telephone numbers in this book or other information resources mentioned here and find out if the connection you are depending on is still available. Although I've done my best to provide accurate information, transportation schedules can and do change.

BY PLANE

To fly from point to point within Mexico, you'll rely on Mexican airlines. Mexico has two privately owned large national carriers: **Mexicana** (☎ **800/531-7921** in the U.S.) and **Aeroméxico** (☎ **800/237-6639** in the U.S.), in addition to several up-and-coming regional carriers. Mexicana and Aeroméxico both offer extensive connections to the United States as well as within Mexico.

Several of the new regional carriers are operated by or can be booked through Mexicana or Aeroméxico. Regional carriers are **Aerocancún** (see Mexicana) and **Aerocaribe** (see Mexicana). The regional carriers are expensive, but they go to places that are difficult to reach. In each applicable section of this book, I've mentioned regional carriers with all pertinent telephone numbers.

Regional airlines affiliated with Mexicana and Aeroméxico cost much more to book from the United States than if booked in Mexico and paid in pesos. Of course, if a connection is critical, you'll want to book from the United States, but if you can wait, or want to take a chance that seats will be available, you can save at least one-third or sometimes even one-half of the fare by waiting until you're in Mexico to book a flight.

Because major airlines can book some regional carriers, read your ticket carefully to see if your connecting flight is on one of these smaller carriers—they may leave from a different airport or check in at a different counter.

AIRPORT TAXES

Mexico charges an airport tax on all departures. Passengers leaving the country on an international departure pay $12 in cash—dollars or the peso equivalent. (That tax is usually included in your ticket.) Each domestic departure you make within Mexico costs around $8, unless you're on a connecting flight and have already paid at the start of the flight. You shouldn't be charged again if you have to change planes for a connecting flight.

RECONFIRMING FLIGHTS

Although airlines in Mexico say it's not necessary to reconfirm a flight, I always do. Aeroméxico seems particularly prone to canceling confirmed and ticketed reservations. Also, be aware that airlines routinely overbook. To avoid getting bumped, check in for an international flight the required hour and a half in advance of travel.

BY BUS

Bus service in the Yucatán Peninsula is beginning to catch up to the high standard seen elsewhere in Mexico. Buses are frequent, readily accessible, and can get you to almost anywhere you want to go. Buses are an excellent way to get around, and they're often the only way to get from large cities to other nearby cities and small villages. Ticket agents can be quite brusque or indifferent, especially if there's a line; in general, however, people are willing to help, so never hesitate to ask questions if you're confused about anything. *Important Notes:* There's little English spoken at bus stations, so come prepared with your destination written down, then double-check the departure several times just to make sure you get to the right departing lane on time.

Dozens of Mexican companies operate large, air-conditioned, Greyhound-type buses between most cities. Travel classes are generally labeled first, second, and deluxe; the latter is referred to by a variety of names—*plus, de lujo, ejecutivo, primera plus,* and so on. The deluxe buses often have fewer seats than regular buses, show video movies en route, are air-conditioned, and have few stops; some have complimentary refreshments. Many run express (without stops) from origin to the final destination. They are well worth the few dollars more you'll pay than you would for first-class buses. First-class buses may get there as fast as a deluxe bus, but without the comfort; they may also have many stops—you'll have to ask. Second-class buses have many stops and often cost only slightly less than first-class or deluxe buses. In rural areas, buses are often of the schoolbus variety, with lots of local color.

Whenever possible, it's best to buy your reserved-seat ticket, often via a computerized system, a day in advance on many long-distance routes and especially before holidays. Schedules are fairly dependable, so be on time.

Many Mexican cities have new central bus stations, much like sophisticated airport terminals. Routes and times change, and the only place to receive current information is directly at the bus station.

For long trips, *always* carry food, water, toilet paper, and a sweater (in case the air-conditioning is too strong).

A Safety Precaution: The U.S. State Department notes that bandits target long-distance buses traveling at night, but there have also been daylight robberies as well. I've always avoided overnight buses, primarily because they usually must negotiate mountain roads in the dark, which I prefer not to risk. The State Department particularly warns about hijackings on Highway 186 between Escarcega and Xpujil in the southern Yucatán Peninsula. (See "Sources of Information," above, for contact information, and "Safety," above, for specific areas of caution.)

See the appendix for a list of helpful bus terms in Spanish.

BY CAR

Most Mexican roads are not up to U.S. standards of smoothness, hardness, width of curve, grade of hill, or safety marking. Avoid driving at night—the trucks, carts, pedestrians, and bicycles usually have no lights, and you can hit potholes, animals, rocks, dead ends, or bridges out with no warning. Enough said!

You will also have to get used to the "spirited" style of Mexican driving. Be prepared for new procedures, as when a truck driver flips on his left-turn signal when there's not a crossroad for miles. He's probably telling you the road's clear ahead for you to pass—after all, he's in a better position to see than you are. It's difficult to know, however, whether he really means that he intends to pull over on the left-hand shoulder. Another strange custom (to foreigners) decides who crosses a one-lane bridge first when two cars approach from opposite directions—the first car to flash its headlights has the right of way. Still another custom that's very important to respect, especially on the narrow roads of the Yucatán Peninsula, is how to make a left turn. Never turn left by stopping in the middle of a highway with your left signal on. Instead, pull off the highway onto the right shoulder, wait for traffic to clear, then proceed across the road. Other driving exasperations include following trucks without mufflers and pollution-control devices for miles. Under these conditions, drop back and be patient, take a side road, or stop for a break when you feel tense or tired.

GASOLINE

There's one government-owned brand of gas and one gasoline station name throughout the country—**Pemex** (Petroleras Mexicanas). There are two types of gas in Mexico: **nova,** an 82-octane leaded gas, and **magna sin,** an 87-octane unleaded gas. Magna sin is sold from brilliantly colored pumps and costs around $1.20 a gallon; nova costs slightly less. In Mexico, fuel and oil are sold by the liter, which is slightly more than a quart (40 liters equals about 10½ gallons). Nova is readily available. Magna sin is now available in most areas of Mexico, along major highways, and in the larger cities. Plan ahead; fill up every chance you get, and keep your tank topped off. *Important Note:* No credit cards are accepted for gas purchases.

Here's what to do when you have to fuel up. First rule is to keep your eyes on the pump meters as your tank is being filled. Check that the pump is turned back to zero, go to your fuel filler cap and unlock it yourself, and watch the pump and the attendant as the gas goes in. Though many service-station attendants are honest, many are not. It's better to ask for a specific peso amount rather than saying "full." This is because the attendants tend to overfill, splashing gas on the car and anything within range.

As there are always lines at the gas pumps, attendants often finish fueling one vehicle, turn the pump back quickly (or don't turn it back at all), and start on another vehicle. You've got to be looking at the pump when the fueling is finished because it may show the amount you owe for only a few seconds. This "quick draw" from car to car is another good reason to ask for a certain peso amount of gas. If you've asked for a certain amount, the attendant can't charge you more for it.

Once the fueling is complete, let the attendant check the oil or radiator or put air in the tires. Do only one thing at a time, be with him as he does it, and don't let him rush you. Get into these habits, or it'll cost you.

If you get oil, make sure the can that is tipped into your engine is a full one. Check your change and, again, don't let them rush you. Check that your locking gas cap is back in place.

DRIVING RULES

If you park illegally or commit some other infraction and are not around to discuss it, police are authorized to remove your license plates (*placas*). You must then go to the police station and pay a fine to get them back. Mexican car-rental agencies have begun to weld the license tag to the tag frame; you may want to devise a method of your own to make the tags more difficult to remove. Theoretically, this may encourage a policeman to move on to another set of tags, one easier to confiscate. On the other hand, he could get his hackles up and decide to have your car towed. To weld or not to weld is up to you.

Be attentive to road signs. A drawing of a row of little bumps means there are speed bumps (*topes*) across the road to force you to reduce speed while driving through towns or villages—and there seem to be thousands of topes on the Yucatán Peninsula. Slow down when coming to a village whether you see the sign or not—sometimes they install the bumps but not the sign!

Mexican roads are never as well marked as you'd like—when you see a highway route sign, take note and make sure you're on the right road. Don't count on plenty of notice of where to turn, even on major interchanges; more often than not, the directional sign appears without prior notice exactly at the spot where you need to make a decision. Common road signs include these:

Camino en Reparación	Road repairs
Conserva Su Derecha	Keep right
Cuidado con el Ganado, el Tren	Watch out for cattle, trains
Curva Peligrosa	Dangerous curve
Derrumbes	Falling rocks
Deslave	Caved-in roadbed
Despacio	Slow
Desviación	Detour
Disminuya Su Velocidad	Slow down
Entronque	Highway junction
Escuela	School (zone)
Grava Suelta	Loose gravel
Hombres Trabajando	Men working
No Hay Paso	Road closed
Peligro	Danger
Puente Angosto	Narrow bridge
Raya Continua	Continuous (solid) white line
Tramo en Reparación	Road under construction
Un Solo Carril	One-lane road
Zone Escolar	School zone

TOLL ROADS

Mexico charges among the highest tolls in the world to use its network of new toll roads. As a result, they are comparatively little used. Generally speaking, using the toll road between Cancún and Mérida will cut your travel time from 5 hours to 4. The old road, on which no tolls are charged, is generally in good condition and offers the most scenic route through villages; traffic is generally light.

MAPS

Guia Roji, AAA, and International Travel Map Productions have good maps to Mexico. In Mexico, maps are sold at large drugstores, at bookstores, and in hotel gift shops.

BREAKDOWNS

Your best guide to repair shops is the Yellow Pages. For specific makes and shops that repair them, look under "Automoviles y Camiones: Talleres de Reparación y Servicio"; auto-parts stores are listed under "Refacciones y Accesorios para Automoviles." On the road, often the sign of a mechanic simply says TALLER MECÁNICO.

I've found that the Ford and Volkswagen dealerships in Mexico give prompt, courteous attention to my car problems, and prices for repairs are, in general, much lower than those in the United States or Canada. I suspect other big-name dealerships give similar satisfactory service. Often they will begin work on your car right away and make repairs in just a few hours, sometimes minutes. Hondas are now manufactured in Mexico, so those parts will become more available.

If your car breaks down on the road, help might already be on the way. Radio-equipped green repair trucks manned by uniformed English-speaking officers patrol the major highways during daylight hours to aid motorists in trouble. These **"Green Angels"** will perform minor repairs and adjustments for free, but you pay for parts and materials.

MINOR ACCIDENTS

When possible, many Mexicans drive away from minor accidents to avoid hassles with police. If the police arrive while the involved persons are still at the scene, everyone may be locked in jail until blame is assessed. In any case you have to settle up immediately, which may take days of red tape. Foreigners who don't speak fluent Spanish are at a distinct disadvantage when trying to explain their side of the event. Three steps may help the foreigner who doesn't wish to do as the Mexicans do: If you're in your own car, notify your Mexican insurance company, whose job it is to intervene on your behalf. If you're in a rental car, notify the rental company immediately and ask how to contact the nearest adjuster. (You did buy insurance with the rental—right?) Finally, if all else fails, ask to contact the nearest Green Angel, who may be able to explain to officials that you are covered by insurance.

See also "Mexican Auto Insurance" in "By Car" under "Getting There," above.

PARKING

When you park your car on the street, lock it up and leave nothing within view inside (day or night). I use guarded parking lots, especially at night, to avoid vandalism and break-ins. This way you also avoid parking violations. When pay lots are not available, small boys, and sometimes older men, usually offer to watch your car for you—tip them well on your return.

CAR RENTALS

Car-rental rules change often in Mexico. The best prices are obtained by reserving your car in the United States a week or more in advance of travel. Cancún, Mérida, Villahermosa, and now Playa del Carmen have international companies such as Avis, Hertz, and National plus many local companies. You'll find rental desks at airports, all major hotels, and many travel agencies. Renting a car during a major holiday may prove difficult. To avoid being stranded without a vehicle, if possible plan your arrival a day or two before the anticipated rush of travelers.

Cars are easy to rent if you have a credit card (American Express, Visa, and MasterCard), are 25 or over, and have a valid driver's license and passport with you. Without a credit card you must leave a cash deposit, usually a big one. Rent-here/leave-there arrangements are usually simple to make but costly.

COSTS   Don't underestimate the cost of renting a car. And unfortunately, the devaluation of the peso has not resulted in lower car-rental costs in Mexico. When I checked recently, the basic cost of a 1-day rental of a Volkswagen Beetle, with unlimited mileage (but before 15% tax and $15 daily insurance) was $45 in Cancún and $38 in Mérida. Renting by the week gets you a lower daily rate.

It makes a difference where you rent, for how long, and when. If you have a choice of renting in Mérida and driving to Cancún, you might save more money than if you rent in Cancún. Mileage-added rates can run up the bill considerably, so avoid those. Car-rental companies will write up a credit-card charge in U.S. dollars or in pesos at the end of the trip, but you must leave a signed credit-card voucher when you rent the car. *Important Tip:* Take advantage of Avis's prepay offer. You *prepay* the daily rental by credit card before you go and receive a considerable discount. Under this plan, you pay tax and insurance in Mexico, but your low daily rate is confirmed in the states.

RENTAL CONFIRMATION   Make your reservation directly with the car-rental company. Write down your confirmation number and request that a copy of the confirmation be mailed to you (rent at least a week in advance so the confirmation has time to reach you). Present this confirmation slip when you appear to collect your car. If you're dealing with a U.S. company, the confirmation must be honored, even if the company has to upgrade you to another class of car—don't allow them to send you to another agency. The rental confirmation will also display the agreed-on price, which protects you from being charged more in case there is a price change before you arrive. Insist on the rate printed on the confirmation slip.

CAR RENTAL INSURANCE   Many credit-card companies offer their cardholders free rental-car insurance. *Don't use it in Mexico,* for several reasons. Even though car insurance is supposedly optional in Mexico, there may be major consequences if you don't have insurance. First, if you buy insurance, in case of damage you pay only the deductible, which limits your liability. Second, if you have an accident or your car is vandalized or stolen and you don't have insurance, you'll have to pay for everything before you can leave the rental-car office. This includes the full value of the car if it is unrepairable—a determination made only by the rental-car company. While your credit card may eventually pay your costs, you will have to lay out the money in the meantime. Third, if an accident occurs, everyone may wind up in jail until guilt is determined, and if you are the guilty party, you may not be released from jail until restitution is paid in full to the rental-car owners and to injured persons—made doubly difficult if you have no car insurance. Fourth, if you elect to use your credit-card insurance anyway, the rental company may ask you to leave them a cash bond, or a credit-card voucher with a high amount filled in.

Insurance is offered in two parts. **Collision and damage** insurance covers your car and others if the accident is your fault, and **personal accident** insurance covers you and anyone in your car. I always take both.

DEDUCTIBLES   Be careful—deductibles vary greatly; some are as high as $2,500, which comes out of your pocket immediately if the car is damaged. Hertz's deductible is $1,000 on a VW Beetle; Avis's deductible is $500 for the same car. You will be asked to sign two separate credit-card vouchers, one for the insurance, which is torn up on your return if there's no damage to the car, and one for the rental. Don't fail to get information about deductibles.

DAMAGE   Always inspect your car carefully and mark all problem areas. Make sure you check hubcaps, windshield (for nicks and cracks), tire tread, muffler (is it smashed?), trim (is it loose or damaged?), head and taillights, spare tire and tools (in the trunk), seat belts (required by law), gas cap, outside mirror, floor mats, and note any dents or nicks in body or fenders. Check to see if car is equipped with a fire extinguisher (it should be under the driver's seat, as required by law).

Note every damaged or missing area, no matter how minute, on your rental agreement or you will be charged for all missing or damaged parts, including missing car tags, should the police confiscate your tags for a parking infraction (which is very costly). I can't stress enough how important it is to check your car carefully. A tiny nick in a windshield can grow the length of the glass while in your care, and you'll be charged for a replacement windshield if you didn't note the nick at the time of rental.

FINE PRINT   Read the fine print on the back of your rental agreement and note that insurance is invalid if you have an accident while driving on an unpaved road.

TROUBLE NUMBER   One last detail to see to before starting out with a rental car: Be sure you know the rental company's trouble number. Get the direct number to the agency where you rented the car and write down its office hours. The large firms have toll-free numbers, but they may not be well staffed on weekends.

PROBLEMS, PERILS, DEALS   At present, I find the best prices are through Avis, and that's the company I use; generally I am a satisfied customer, though I sometimes have to dig in my heels and insist on proper service. I have had even more difficult problems with other agencies. I have encountered certain kinds of situations that could occur with any company. These problems have included an attempt to push me off to a no-name company rather than upgrade me to a more expensive car when a VW Beetle wasn't available; and poorly staffed offices with no extra cars, parts, or mechanics in case of a breakdown. Since potential problems are varied, I'd rather deal with a company based in the States so at least I have recourse if I am not satisfied.

BY TAXI

Most airports and bus stations in large cities have *colectivo* (minibuses or minivans) or fixed-rate taxis to town. The colectivo is always the least expensive way to go. Buy a special colectivo ticket from a booth that's usually located near the exit door or main airport concourse. The taxi ticket booth is also in close proximity to the colectivo, but the price may be more than double that of a colectivo.

Taxis in the area covered by this book aren't metered, so you must agree on a price before you get in. Taxi prices to the most common destinations are usually posted inside the front door of most hotels. Use these prices as guides to taxi costs, since taxi drivers are notorious for bargaining high. Mérida taxi drivers are the most difficult to deal with since some like to confuse visitors by quoting in dollars when the passenger thinks the price is in pesos.

8 Tips on Accommodations

Here are some tips on getting the most for your money when it comes to accommodations.

Note: Some hotels, especially in more touristed areas, accept credit cards; Visa, MasterCard, and, less widely, American Express are the most accepted cards.

Note: All hotels listed in this book have private baths, unless otherwise noted. Fewer and fewer hotels in Mexico have rooms without private baths. The few bathless rooms listed in this book will be somewhat cheaper, but not necessarily by very much, than those with baths.

- Rooms with air-conditioning are almost always more expensive than those with only fans. Rooms with a view of the street may be more expensive (not to mention noisier) than those with windows opening onto an airshaft. Water views cost more than garden or street views at the same resort. A room with a balcony or patio, however, may cost the same as one without.

- Hotels a block or two from the beach may cost 50% less than those right on the sand. Similarly, hotels on the main square are often slightly higher priced than hotels a block or two away.

- Some hotels, especially inexpensive and moderately priced hotels, offer single room rates that are cheaper than the double room rates. Ask about single rooms if you are traveling alone. Many hotels, however, charge the same rate for singles and doubles. For more on single rooms, see "For Singles," under "Tips for Travelers with Special Needs," above.

- If you ask a desk clerk to price a room, the quote he gives you may not be for the cheapest room available. If that's what you want, then ask to see a cheaper room by saying *"quiero ver un cuarto más barato, por favor"*—it can't hurt.

- By law, hotel rates should be posted within view of the reception desk, but they rarely are. If a hotel's quoted rate seems too high, ask to see their official rate sheet and ask about discounts (*discuento*) and promotional rates (*tarifas promocionales*). Walk away if the price seems too high.

    Additionally, budget quality hotels may charge you 10% to 15% more if you want a receipt. Since it isn't wise to pay a desk clerk for a room without getting a receipt for your payment—for example, readers have reported paying an evening clerk on check-in, only to discover upon checkout that the day clerk has no record of the transaction—I carry a pad of receipts, so they won't have to use their official ones. As an alternative, I've asked them to write, sign, and date an informal receipt in my notebook.

- If you're traveling in the off-season (and not during a Mexican holiday), it is not necessary to make reservations at an inexpensive or moderately priced hotel. Arrive at your destination early in the day and target your choice of hotel. This will save you the price of a long-distance call to reserve a room and the uncertainty of not knowing whether your reservation deposit has been received. Mexican hotels often do not respond to reservation requests made by mail, even though they may honor such requests on arrival—you just never know. (However, deluxe and first-class hotels penalize walk-in guests without a reduced-rate hotel package by charging high daily rates.)

- If you arrive in a city without a hotel reservation, call a hotel from the public telephone/fax office in most bus stations and airports. For only the cost of a local call, you'll be assured of a room when you arrive. In addition, you will not incur hefty taxi fares while you shop for a hotel. If you don't speak Spanish and if the person at the telephone office isn't busy, ask him or her to make the call for you.

- Most hotels allow children under age 12 to stay for free in their parents' room. Many hotels will accommodate kids with a roll-away bed. When making your reservation, always verify that the hotel has this service and note the name of the person with whom you spoke.

- Although Mexican campsites are not of the same quality as those in the United States, a few beach destinations south of Cancún have designated camping areas; you'll find rustic campgrounds at Playa del Carmen, Punta Bete, Xcacel, Xpuha, and the Punta Allen Peninsula; there's a fine trailer park on the beach at Paamul and hookups available on the Xcalak/Majahual Peninsula.

- Finally, some destinations *do* have cheaper places to stay than those I've written up for this book. But I purposely have not listed rock-bottom hotels in this guide because of frequent reports of thefts at such places—especially of cameras and money from backpackers. While nothing can guarantee complete security, I have chosen hotels that feel safe.

9 Tips on Package Deals

Package deals, which usually include round-trip airfare and accommodations, offer some of the best values to the coastal resorts, especially during high season—from December until after Easter. Off-season packages can be real bargains. However, to know for sure if the package will save you money, you must price the package yourself by calling the airline for round-trip flight costs and the hotel for rates. Take into consideration that round-trip transportation from the airport to your hotel is often included in package rates and can save you $20 to $30 in such places as Cancún, Mérida, or Villahermosa.

Packages are usually per person, and single travelers pay a supplement. In the high season a package may be the only way of getting to certain places in Mexico because wholesalers have all the airline seats. In this book, better hotels in Cancún or Mérida are more likely to offer packages. The cheapest package rates will be those in hotels in the lower range, always without as many amenities as higher-priced hotels. You can still use the public areas and beaches of more costly hotels without being a guest.

Travel agents have information on specific packages.

DIVING PACKAGES   In Cozumel, you may be able to save money by purchasing diving packages, which include the price of the hotel and a given number of dives. Many divers, however, save more money by staying in a cheaper hotel than a package calls for and booking dives directly with a diving concession. This method may be particularly practical in the fall, when stormy seas often preclude diving, and you therefore won't have to pay for unused dives.

FAST FACTS: Mexico

Abbreviations   Dept. = apartments; Apdo. = post office box; Av. = Avenida; Calz. = Calzada (boulevard). "C" on faucets stands for *caliente* (hot), and "F" stands for *fría* (cold). PB (*planta baja*) means ground floor.

Business Hours   In general, Mexican businesses in larger cities are open between 9am and 7pm; in smaller towns many close between 2 and 4pm. Most are closed on Sunday. Bank hours are Monday through Friday from 9 or 9:30am to 1pm. A few banks in large cities have extended hours.

Camera/Film   Buying a camera can be inconvenient in Mexico, but there are cheap, imported models available. Film costs about the same as that in the United States. Bring along extra camera batteries: AA batteries are generally available, but AAA and small disc batteries for cameras and watches are rare.

Important note about camera use: Tourists wishing to use a video camera at any archaeological site in Mexico and a still or video camera at many museums operated by the Instituto de Historia y Antropología (INAH) may be required to pay $4 per camera. (In most museums camera use is not permitted.) When you pay the fee, your camera will be tagged and you are permitted to use the equipment. Watchmen are often posted to see that untagged cameras are not used. Such fees are noted in the listings for specific sites and museums.

It's courteous to ask permission before photographing anyone. In some areas, such as around San Cristóbal de las Casas, Chiapas, there are other restrictions on photographing people and villages. Such restrictions are noted in specific cities, towns, and sites.

Doctors/Dentists   Every embassy and consulate is prepared to recommend local doctors and dentists with good training and modern equipment; some of the doctors and dentists even speak English. See the list of embassies and consulates under "Embassies/Consulates," below, and remember that at the larger ones, a duty officer is on call at all times. Hotels with a large foreign clientele are often prepared to recommend English-speaking doctors. Almost all first-class hotels in Mexico have a doctor on call.

Drug Laws   Don't use or possess illegal drugs in Mexico. Mexicans have no tolerance for drug users, and jail is their solution, with very little hope of getting out until the sentence (usually a long one) is completed or heavy fines or bribes are paid. (*Important Note:* It isn't uncommon to be befriended by a fellow user, only to be turned in by that "friend"—he's collected a bounty for turning you in. It's a no-win situation!) Bring prescription drugs in their original containers. If possible, pack a copy of the original prescription with the generic name of the drug.

I don't need to go into detail about the penalties for illegal drug possession upon return to the United States. Customs officials are also on the lookout for diet drugs sold in Mexico, possession of which could also land you in a U.S. jail because they are illegal here. If you buy antibiotics over the counter (which you can do in Mexico)—say, for a sinus infection—and still have some left, you probably won't be hassled by U.S. Customs.

Drugstores   Drugstores (*farmacías*) will sell you just about anything you want, with a prescription or without one. Mexico does have a controlled medicine list, which is different from that of the U.S. However, over-the-counter medicines such as aspirin, decongestants, or antihistamines are rarely sold. Most drugstores are open Monday through Saturday from 8am to 8pm. If you need to buy medicines after normal hours, ask for the *farmacía de turno*—pharmacies take turns staying open during off-hours. Find any drugstore, and in its window may be a card showing the schedule of which drugstore will be open at what time.

Electricity   The electrical system in Mexico is 110 volts, 60 cycles; the same as in the United States and Canada. However, in reality it may cycle more slowly and overheat your appliances. To compensate, select a medium or low speed for hair dryers and curling irons, though they may still overheat. Older hotels still have electrical outlets for flat two-prong plugs; you'll need an adapter for using any modern electrical apparatus that has an enlarged end on one prong or that has three prongs to insert. Many first-class and deluxe hotels have the three-holed outlets (*trifacicos* in Spanish). Those that don't may loan adapters, but to be sure, it's always better to carry your own.

Embassies/Consulates   They provide valuable lists of doctors and lawyers, as well as regulations concerning marriages in Mexico. Contrary to popular belief, your embassy cannot get you out of a Mexican jail, provide postal or banking services, or fly you home when you run out of money. Consular officers can provide you with advice on most matters and problems, however. Most countries have a representative embassy in Mexico City, and many have consular offices or representatives in the provinces.

The Embassy of **Australia** in Mexico City is at Jaime Balmes 11, Plaza Polanco, Torre B (☎ 5/395-9988 or 5/566-3053); it's open Monday through Friday from 8am to 1pm.

The Embassy of **Canada** in Mexico City is at Schiller 529, in Polanco (☎ 5/724-7900); it's open Monday through Friday from 9am to 1pm and 2 to 5pm (at other times the name of a duty officer is posted on the embassy door). In Acapulco, the Canadian consulate is in the Hotel Club del Sol, Costera Miguel Alemán, at the corner of Reyes Católicos (☎ 74/85-6621); it's open Monday through Friday from 8am to 3pm.

The Embassy of **New Zealand** in Mexico City is at Homero 229, 8th floor (☎ 5/250-5999 or 5/250-5777); it's open Monday through Thursday from 9am to 2pm and 3 to 5pm and Friday from 9am to 2pm.

The Embassy of the **United Kingdom** in Mexico City is at Lerma 71, at Río Sena (☎ 5/207-2569 or 5/207-2593); it's open Monday through Friday from 9am to 2pm. There are honorary consuls in the following cities: Acapulco, Hotel Las Brisas, Carretera Escénica (☎ 74/84-6605 or 74/84-1580); Ciudad Juárez, Calle Fresno 185 (☎ 16/7-5791); Guadalajara, Paulino Navarro 1165 (☎ 3/611-1678); Oaxaca, Ev. Hidalgo 817 (☎ 951/6-5600); Tampico, 2 de Enero 102-ASur (☎ 12/12-9784 or 12/12-9817); Tijuana, Blv. Salinas 1500 (☎ 66/81-7323); and Veracruz, Emparan 200 PB (☎ 29/31-0955).

The Embassy of the **United States** in Mexico City is next to the Hotel María Isabel Sheraton at Paseo de la Reforma 305, at the corner of Río Danubio (☎ 5/211-0042). There are U.S. Consulates General in Ciudad Juárez, López Mateos 924-N (☎16/13-4048); Guadalajara, Progreso 175 (☎ 3/625-2998); Monterrey, Av. Constitución 411 Poniente (☎ 83/45-2120); and Tijuana, Tapachula 96 (☎66/81-7400). There are U.S. Consulates in Hermosillo, Av. Monterrey 141 (☎ 62/17-2375); Matamoros, Av. Primera 2002 (☎ 88/12-4402); Mérida, Paseo Montejo 453 (☎ 99/25-5011); Nuevo Laredo, Calle Allende 3330 (☎ 871/4-0512). In addition, Consular Agencies are in Acapulco (☎ 74/85-6600 or 5-7207); Cabo San Lucas (☎ 114/3-3566); Cancún (☎ 98/83-0272); Mazatlán (☎ 69/13-4444, ext. 285); Oaxaca (☎ 951/4-3054); Puerto Vallarta (☎ 322/2-0069); San Luis Potosí (☎ 481/2-1528); San Miguel de Allende (☎ 465/2-2357 or 465/2-0068); Tampico (☎ 12/13-2217); and Veracruz (☎ 29/31-5821).

Emergencies　The 24-hour Tourist Help Line in Mexico City is ☎ 5/250-0151.

Guns　I probably don't need to mention this, but just in case, it is unlawful to enter Mexico with a weapon unless you have a special hunting permit issued by the Mexican government. There are several military roadblocks in the peninsula and in Tabasco and Chiapas established specifically to look for guns first and drugs second. Don't tempt them.

Legal Aid　International Legal Defense Counsel, 111 S. 15th St., 24th Floor, Packard Building, Philadelphia, PA 19102 (☎ 215/977-9982), is a law firm specializing in legal difficulties of Americans abroad. See also "Embassies/Consulates" and "Emergencies," above.

Mail　Mail service south of the border tends to be slow and undependable—though it is improving. If you're on a 2-week vacation, it's not a bad idea to buy and mail your postcards in the arrivals lounge at the airport to give them maximum time to get home before you do.

For the most reliable and convenient mail service, have your letters sent to you ℅ the American Express offices in major cities, which will receive and forward mail for you if you are one of its clients (a travel-club card or an American Express traveler's check is proof). They charge a fee if you wish to have your mail forwarded.

It's also possible to have mail sent care of *Lista de Correos* (General Delivery), followed by the Mexican city, state, and country. In Mexican post offices there may actually be a "lista" posted near the Lista de Correos window bearing the names of all those for whom mail has been received. If there's no list, ask and show them your passport so they can riffle through and look for your letters. The central post office—not a branch—will receive Lista de Correos mail. In many post offices mail is returned to the sender after 10 days. Make sure people don't send you letters too early.

In major Mexican cities there are also branches of such U.S. express mail companies as UPS, Federal Express, and DHL, as well as private mail boxes such as Mail Boxes Etc.

Newspapers/Magazines Two English-language newspapers, the *News* and the *Times,* are published in Mexico City and distributed all over the country. They carry world news and commentaries. Newspaper kiosks in Mérida and Cancún will carry a selection of English-language magazines and perhaps the *New York Times* or *Chicago Tribune.*

Police Police in general in Mexico are to be suspected rather than trusted; however, you'll find many who are quite honest and helpful with directions, even going so far as to lead you where you want to go.

Rest Rooms The best bet in Mexico is to use rest rooms in restaurants and hotel public areas. Always carry your own toilet paper and hand soap, neither of which is in great supply in Mexican rest rooms. Public facilities, usually near the central market, vary in cleanliness and usually have an attendant who charges a few pesos for toilet use and a few squares of toilet paper. Pemex gas stations have improved the maintenance of their rest rooms along major highways. No matter where you are, even if there's enough water pressure to carry away paper in the toilet, there will be a wastebasket for paper disposal—which can be a disgusting sight. Because so many toilets won't flush paper, people will throw used paper on the floor rather than put it in the toilet; thus, you'll see the basket no matter what quality of place you are in. There's often a sign telling you whether or not to flush paper.

Taxes There's a 12% to 17% IVA tax on goods and services in the areas covered in this book, and it may or may not be included in the posted price. This tax is 12% in Cancun, Cozumel, and Isla Mujeres and 17% elsewhere.

Telephone/Fax Telephone area codes are gradually being changed all over the country. Some cities are even adding exchanges and changing whole numbers, often without notification to the subscriber. Telephone courtesy messages announcing a phone number change are nonexistent in Mexico. You can try operator assistance for difficult-to-reach numbers, but often the phone company doesn't inform its operators of recent changes. People who have fax machines often turn them off when their offices are closed. Many fax numbers are also regular telephone numbers; you have to ask whoever answers your call for the fax tone (*Por favor darme el tono por fax*). Telephone etiquette in Mexico does not prompt the answerer to offer to take a message or to have someone return your call; you'll have to make these suggestions yourself. In addition, etiquette doesn't necessarily require that a business answer its phone by saying its name; often you'll have to ask if you have the right place.

Save money on long-distance calls by calling collect. If that's not possible, then the least expensive option is to use a *larga distancia* office, found in most towns. Generally there's a service charge of about $2.50 to $3.50 in addition to the cost of the call. Using the phone in your hotel room can be the most expensive way to call; a hefty service charge is often added to the price of the call—even if you are calling a toll-free number. Many budget hotels, however, charge the same rates as those at a larga distancia office; ask before you call. Camino Real hotels charge for call attempts even when no one answers.

The **country code** for dialing Mexico from abroad is **52.** For more on placing long-distance calls within Mexico or to Mexico from abroad, consult "Telephones & Mail" in the appendix.

Time Central standard time prevails throughout most of Mexico. The west-coast states of Sonora, Sinaloa, and parts of Nayarit are on Mountain standard time. The state of Baja California Norte is on Pacific time, but Baja California Sur is on Mountain time. **Daylight saving time** arrived in Mexico in 1996.

Water Most hotels have decanters or bottles of purified water in the rooms, and the better hotels have either purified water from regular taps or special taps marked AGUA PURIFICADA. In the resort areas, especially in the Yucatán, hoteliers are beginning to charge for in-room bottled water. If the water in your room is an expensive imported variety such as Evian, for sure there's an extra charge for using it. Virtually any hotel, restaurant, or bar will bring you purified water if you specifically request it, but you'll usually be charged for it. Bottled purified water is sold widely at drugstores and grocery stores.

Cancún 4

Say the word "Cancún" to most people, and they'll think of fine sandy beaches, limpid, incredibly blue Caribbean waters, and expensive luxury resorts—these images are all true. Isla Cancún is lined with shopping centers and upscale resort hotels, many of which are luxurious by any world standard. Ciudad Cancún (Cancún City), on the mainland, grew up with hotels more for the budget-minded traveler and boasts a downtown area chockablock with restaurants, each trying to outdo the others to attract clientele.

Twenty years ago, the name Cancún meant little to anyone, but these days Cancún is the magic word in Mexican vacations. A hook-shaped island on the Caribbean side of the Yucatecan coast, Cancún opened for business in 1974 with one hotel and a lot of promotion, after being judged the best spot in the country for a new jet-age resort. Meanwhile, Ciudad Cancún popped up to house the working populace that flocked to support the resort.

Cancún is a perfect resort site, with powdery limestone sand beaches, and air and water temperatures that are just right. Furthermore, Cancún can be a starting point for exploration of other Yucatecan lures. The older, less expensive island resorts of Isla Mujeres and Cozumel are close at hand. The Maya ruins at Tulum, Chichén-Itzá, and Cobá are within driving distance, as are the snorkeling reserves of Xcaret and Xel-Ha. And along the coast south of Cancún, in places such as Playa del Carmen, new resorts in all price ranges are popping up.

Cancún today is a city of 450,000 people and boasts more than 18,000 hotel rooms between the mainland city and the resort-filled island. The 14-mile-long island's resorts together make for quite a variegated display of modern architectural style; they seem to get grander and more lavish each year.

Fans of Cancún see its similarity to U.S. resorts as a plus—a foreign vacation without foreign inconveniences. Cancún is a good place to ease into Mexican culture, though it's not at all like the rest of the country, or even like the rest of the Yucatán Peninsula. But if you like beaches, Cancún and the coast to its south have the best beaches in Mexico. Food and drinks are just one sybaritic step from your lounge chair.

1 Orientation

ARRIVING & DEPARTING
BY PLANE

Several airlines connect Cancún with other Mexican and Central American cities. **Aeroméxico** (☎ 98/84-3571 or 98/84-1186 in Cancún) offers service from Mexico City, Mérida, and Tijuana. **Mexicana** (☎ 800/5-0220 for 24-hour reservations, or 98/87-4444 or 98/87-2769 in Cancún) flies in from Guadalajara, Mexico City, and Flores, Guatemala. Regional carriers **Aerocozumel** and **Aerocaribe** (☎ 98/84-2000, both affiliated with Mexicana) fly from Cozumel, Havana, Mexico City, Tuxtla Gutiérrez, Villahermosa, Mérida, Oaxaca, Veracruz, and Cuidad del Carmen. The regional airline **Aviateca** (☎ 98/84-3938 or 98/87-1386) flies from Cancún to Mérida, Villahermosa, Tuxtla Gutiérrez, Guatemala City, and Flores (near Tikal). **Avio Quintana** (☎ 98/86-0422) flies a 19-passenger plane to and from Chetumal Monday through Saturday. **Taesa** (☎ 98/87-4314) has flights from Tijuana, Chetumal, Mérida, and other cities within Mexico.

You'll want to confirm departure times for flights back to the States; here are the Cancún airport numbers of the major international carriers: **American** (☎ 98/86-0151), **Continental** (☎ 98/86-0005 or 98/86-0006), **Northwest** (☎ 98/86-0044 or 98/86-0046), and **United** (☎ 98/86-0158).

Special minibuses (colectivos) run from Cancún's international airport into town. Tickets are purchased as you exit the building. Rates for a cab are double or triple the colectivo fare depending on your destination. The least expensive way to get to the ferry to Isla Mujeres is to take the colectivo to the bus station in downtown Cancún and from there bargain for a taxi. Most major rental-car firms have outlets at the airport, so if you're renting a car, consider picking it up and dropping it off at the airport to save on airport-transportation costs.

There is no colectivo service returning to the airport from Ciudad Cancún or the Zona Hotelera, so you'll have to hire a taxi. Ask at your hotel what the fare should be.

BY BUS

Cancún's bus terminal is in downtown Ciudad Cancún at the intersection of avenidas Tulum and Uxmal. All out-of-town buses arrive here. The terminal has been renovated and is divided into two parts: The air-conditioned ADO and Greenline ticket windows and waiting rooms occupy the right half of the building; the left half holds the unair-conditioned second-class ticket windows.

The difference between first- and second-class buses here is that first-class buses are usually air-conditioned, often have video movies, sometimes have a snack area aboard, and have fewer, if any, stops en route to the destination. Second-class buses may also be air-conditioned and often also offer limited-stop service to the destination. Often, the price difference between the two is not great.

Bus travel note: Bus travel in this region changes more than any in the country. So services and buslines could be dramatically changed (usually improved) when you travel.

Autotransportes Playa Express runs buses from Cancún to Playa del Carmen and Tulum almost every 20 minutes between 6am and 9pm from their ticket counter opposite the bus station near the corner of avenidas Tulum and Pino. They also have frequent service to Xcaret, Tulum, the Capitan Lafitte resort, Puerto Aventuras, Xpuha, Akumal, and Felipe Carrillo Puerto. Check on their Tulum service that includes entry and transportation to the entrance of the ruins (as opposed to letting you off on the highway).

In the second-class bus terminal section are **ATS (Autotransportes del Sureste)** and **Autotransportes de Oriente (ADO)** buses. ATS has service every 20 minutes to Playa del Carmen. Other ATS buses travel to Palenque, San Cristóbal, Mérida, Valladolid, and Chetumal. ADO buses go frequently to Mérida, on both the short route (via the toll road) and long route (via the free road), as well as to Chichén-Itzá, Izamal, and Tizimin. **Transportes de Lujo Linea Dorado,** despite its name, is a second-class line. Its buses go hourly to Playa del Carmen, Xcaret, Tulum, Lago Bacalar, Oxkutzcab, and Ticul.

In the first-class part of the station are **Greenline Paquete** and **ADO** buses with their separate air-conditioned waiting room on the far right. ADO buses go to Mérida and Valladolid almost twice hourly until 11:30pm; the company also has daily service to Mexico City, Veracruz, and Villahermosa. Greenline Paquetes offer packages (*paquetes*) to popular nearby destinations. The package to Chichén-Itzá departs at 9am and includes the round-trip air-conditioned bus ride, with video for the 3-hour trip, entry to the ruins, 2 hours at the ruins, lunch, a brief stop for shopping, and a visit to a cenote. The tour returns to Cancún by 5pm. The trip to Xcaret (which is much cheaper than the same trip offered at the Xcaret terminal office) includes round-trip transportation and entry to the park; the tours depart daily at 9 and 10am and return at 5pm. Package trips to Cozumel depart at 8, 9, and 10am (returning at 5pm) and include round-trip, air-conditioned bus transportation to and from Playa del Carmen and the ferry ticket to and from Cozumel. Buying a Greenline Paquete takes the mystery out of getting to Cozumel, but you can do this simple trip on your own, by bus from this terminal, for half the price of the paquete.

VISITOR INFORMATION

The State Tourism Office (☎ 98/84-8073) is centrally located downtown on the east side of Avenida Tulum immediately left of the Ayuntamiento Benito Juárez building between avenidas Cobá and Uxmal. It's open daily from 9am to 9pm. A second tourist information office (☎ **98/84-3238** or 98/84-3438) is located on Avenida Cobá at Avenida Tulum, next to Pizza Rolandi, and is open Monday through Friday from 9am to 9pm. Hotels and their rates are listed at each office, as are ferry schedules.

Of particular help to anyone planning a trip to the area is **Mexico Self-Serve (ELECTUR),** a World Wide Web site that will make hotel and car reservations and gladly answer myriad travel-related questions via the Internet. Contact them at their World Wide Web site (http://www.mexicoweb.com/cancun) or by e-mail (mexico@cancun.rce.com.mx).

A warning: The friendliest people in town are often representatives of time-share real estate businesses who snag your attention by offering "information." Their real mission, however, is to get you to attend a spiel about the wonders of a Cancún time-sharing or condo purchase. They'll go so far as to shout and beckon at you across a busy street. Perhaps just as bad, or maybe worse, in some hotels they're in cahoots with reception desk clerks who give them your name and room number, so they can pester you either just after you've checked in or with an early morning call inviting you to a "free" breakfast or some other enticement. Don't get suckered in by these sales professionals.

Pick up free copies of the monthly *Cancún Tips* booklet and a seasonal tabloid of the same name. Both are useful and have fine maps. The publications are owned by the same people who own the Captain's Cove restaurants, a couple of sightseeing boats, and time-share hotels, so the information (though good) is not completely unbiased. Don't be surprised if, during your stay, one of their army of employees touts the joys of time-sharing, though more subtly than the others.

CITY LAYOUT

There are two Cancúns: **Isla Cancún** (Cancún Island) and **Ciudad Cancún** (Cancún City). The latter, on the mainland, has restaurants, shops, and less expensive hotels, as well as all the other establishments that make life function—pharmacies, dentists, automotive shops, banks, travel and airline agencies, car-rental firms—all within an area about 9 blocks square. The city's main thoroughfare is **Avenida Tulum.** Heading south, Avenida Tulum becomes the highway to the airport and to Tulum and Chetumal on farther south; heading north, it intersects the highway to Mérida and the road to Puerto Juárez and the Isla Mujeres ferries.

The famed **Zona Hotelera** (alternately called the **Zona Turística**) stretches out along Isla Cancún, a sandy strip 14 miles long shaped like a "7." It's now joined by bridges to the mainland at the north and south ends. Avenida Cobá from Cancún City becomes Paseo Kukulkán, the island's main traffic artery. Cancún's international airport is just inland from the south end of the island.

FINDING AN ADDRESS   The street-numbering system is leftover from Cancún's early days. Addresses are still given by the number of the building lot and by the manzana (block) or super-manzana (group of city blocks). The city is still relatively small, and the downtown section can easily be covered on foot.

On the island, addresses are given by kilometer number on Paseo Kukulkán or by reference to some well-known location.

2 Getting Around

BY BUS

In town, almost everything is within walking distance. **Ruta 1** and **Ruta 2** ("Hoteles") city buses travel frequently from the mainland to the beaches along Avenida Tulum (the main street) and all the way to Punta Nizuc at the far end of the Zona Hotelera on Isla Cancún. **Ruta 8** buses go to Puerto Juárez/Punta Sam for ferries to Isla Mujeres. They stop on the east side of Avenida Tulum. Both these city buses operate between 6am and midnight daily. Beware of private buses plying the same route; they charge far more than the public ones. The public buses have the fare amount painted on the front; when last I checked it was 2.5 pesos.

BY TAXI

Settle on a price in advance. Ask at your hotel about the going price for a taxi from there to your destination on the island or in town or to the airport. There's a wide variation in prices if you're starting on the island; however, taxis around the downtown area are relatively inexpensive.

BY MOPED

Mopeds are a dangerous way to cruise around through the very congested traffic. Rentals start at $25 for a day. A credit-card voucher is required as security for the moped. You should receive a crash helmet (it's the law) and instructions on how to lock the wheels when you park. Read the fine print on the back of the rental agreement regarding liability for repairs or replacement in case of accident, theft, or vandalism. You rent at considerable risk.

BY RENTAL CAR

There's really no need to have a car in Cancún, since bus service is good, taxis on the mainland are relatively inexpensive, and most things in Ciudad Cancún are within walking distance. But if you do rent, the cheapest way is to arrange for the rental before you leave your home country. If you rent on the spot after arrival, the daily cost of a rental car will be around $65 to $75 for a VW Beetle. Hertz has opened an office in Playa del Carmen, so it's now possible to rent a Hertz car in Cancún and drop it off in Playa del Carmen. For more details, see "Getting Around" in chapter 3.

Important note: Observe all speed zones on the island and the mainland. Police give tickets to speeders.

FAST FACTS: Cancún

American Express The local office is at Av. Tulum 208 and Agua (☎ 98/84-1999, 98/84-4243, or 98/87-0831), open Monday through Friday from 9am to 2pm and 4 to 6pm and Saturday from 9am to 1pm. It's 1 block past the Plaza México.

Area Code The telephone area code is **98.** See also "Telephones," below.

Climate It's hot but not overwhelmingly humid. The rainy season is May through October. August through October is the hurricane season, which brings erratic weather. November through February can be cloudy, windy, somewhat rainy, and even cool, so a sweater is handy, as is rain protection.

Consulates The **U.S. Consular Agent** is in the Plaza Caracol Two, third level, no. 320-323, Blv. Kukulkán km 8.5 (☎ **98/83-0272**). The office is open Monday through Friday from 9am to 2pm and 3 to 6pm. The **Canadian Consulate** is in the Plaza Mexico 312 (☎ **98/84-3716**). The office is open Monday through Friday from 10am to 2pm.

Crime Car break-ins are just about the only crime, and they happen frequently, especially around the shopping centers in the Zona Hotelera. VW Beetles and Golfs are frequent targets. Don't leave valuables in plain sight. Though pickpockets haven't been a problem in the past, thieves appear worldwide, so it pays to keep an eye on your purse and wallet. Men shouldn't keep their wallet in a back pocket.

Currency Exchange Most banks are downtown along Avenida Tulum and are usually open Monday through Friday from 9:30am to 1:30pm. In the hotel zone you'll find banks in the Plaza Kukulkán and next to the Convention center. There are also many *casas de cambio* (exchange houses). Downtown merchants are eager to change cash dollars, but island stores don't offer good exchange rates. Avoid changing money at the airport as you arrive, especially at the first exchange booth you see—its rates are less favorable than any in town or others farther inside the airport concourse.

Drugstores Next to the Hotel Caribe Internacional, **Farmacia Canto,** at Avenida Yaxchilán 36, at Sunyaxchen (☎ **98/84-4083** or 98/84-9330), is open 24 hours.

Emergencies To report an emergency dial ☎ **06,** which is supposed to be similar to 911 in the United States. For first aid, the Cruz Roja (**Red Cross;** ☎ **98/84-1616**) is open 24 hours on Avenida Yaxchilán between avenidas Xcaret and Labná, next to the Telemex building. **Total Assist,** a small nine-room emergency hospital with English-speaking doctors at Claveles 5, SM22, at Avenida Tulum (☎ **98/84-1058** or 98/84-1092), is open 24 hours. Desk staff may have limited

English. **Clínica Quirurgica del Caribe,** at SM63, Mz Q, Calle 3 inte. no. 36 (☎ 98/84-2516), is open 24 hours. "Urgencias" means "Emergencies."

Luggage Storage/Lockers Hotels will generally tag and store excess luggage while you travel elsewhere.

Newspapers/Magazines For English-language newspapers and books, go to **Fama** on Avenida Tulum between Tulipanes and Claveles (☎ 98/84-6586), open daily from 8am to 10pm. (Avoid filling out a contest flier here that will result in a call from a time-share promoter.)

Police To reach the police (Seguridad Pública), dial ☎ 98/84-1913 or 98/84-2342. The *Procuraduria del Consumidor* (consumer protection agency) is opposite the Social Security Hospital at Av. Cobá 10 (☎ 98/84-2634 or 98/84-2701).

Post Office The main post office is at the intersection of Avenidas Sunyaxchen and Xel-Ha (☎ 98/84-1418). It's open Monday through Friday from 8am to 7pm and Saturday from 9am to 1pm.

Safety There is very little crime in Cancún. People in general are safe late at night in touristed areas; just use ordinary common sense. As at any other beach resort, don't take money or valuables to the beach. See "Crime," above.

Swimming on the Caribbean side presents real dangers from undertow. See "The Beaches" in "Beaches, Water Sports & Other Things to Do," below, for flag warnings.

Seasons Technically, high season is December 15 through Easter; low season is May through November, when prices are reduced 10% to 30%. Some hotels are starting to charge high-season rates between July and September when travel is high for European and school-holiday visitors. There's a mini-low season in January just after the Christmas–New Year's holiday.

Telephones The phone system for Cancún changed in 1992. The area code, which once was 988, is now 98. All local numbers now have six digits instead of five; all numbers begin with 8. If a number is written ☎ 988/4-1234, when in Cancún you must dial ☎ 84-1234.

3 Accommodations

Island hotels run almost the gamut, but extravagance is the byword in the more recently built hotels, many of which are awash in a sea of marble and glass, with white-gloved bellmen in waistcoats. Some hotels, however, while exclusive, effect a more relaxed attitude.

The water is placid on the upper end of the island facing Bahía de Mujeres, while beaches lining the long side of the island facing the Caribbean are subject to choppier water and crashing waves on windy days (for more information on swimming safety, see "Beaches, Water Sports & Other Things to Do," later in this chapter). Be aware that the farther you go south on the island, the longer it takes (20 to 30 minutes in traffic) to get back to the "action spots," which are primarily between the Plaza Flamingo and Punta Cancún on the island and along Avenida Tulum on the mainland.

During the off-season (from April to November), prices go down. Hotels also often have discounted prices from February up to Easter week. *Important note on prices:* Cancún's higher-priced hotels have not reduced rates in proportion to the devaluation of the peso. In fact, their prices are as high as or higher than before the devaluation. Although rack rates (the hotel's rate to the public) are high and are the ones I

Isla Cancún (Zona Hotelera)

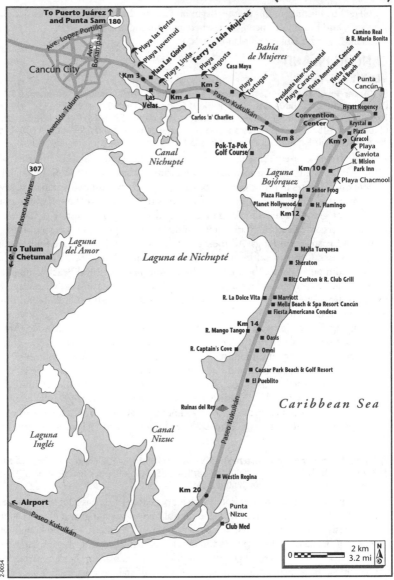

list here, a package that includes hotel and airline ticket will save you money. To avoid paying the rack rates, ask about special promotional rates (*tarifa promocional*) and meal credits. Note that the price quoted to you when you call a hotel's reservation number from the U.S. doesn't include Cancún's 12% tax. Prices can vary wildly from hotel to hotel at different times of the year, so it pays to shop around.

Cancún hoteliers, even in budget and moderately priced hotels, are beginning to quote rates in dollars instead of pesos, to buffer themselves against the falling value of the peso. At inexpensive and moderately priced hotels, you're usually better off insisting on a quote in pesos; the top hotels quote rates only in dollars.

The hotel listings in this chapter begin on Cancún Island, the most expensive place to stay, and finish in Cancún City, where bargain lodgings abound.

Parking is available at all island hotels.

CANCÚN ISLAND
VERY EXPENSIVE

✪ **Caesar Park Beach & Golf Resort.** Paseo Kukulcán km 17, Retorno Lacandones, 77500 Cancún, Q. Roo. ☎ **800/228-3000** in the U.S., or 98/81-8000. Fax 98/85-2437. 411 rms, 16 suites. A/C MINIBAR TV TEL. High season standard rooms $275–$350 double; Royal Beach Club $300–$485 double; suites $375–$500. Low season standard rooms $200–$300; Royal Beach Club $250–$290; suites $300–$350.

A true resort in every sense of the word, the Caesar Park, which is affiliated with the Westin chain and is a member of the Leading Hotels of the World, opened in 1994 on 250 acres of prime Cancún beachfront property with two restaurants, seven pools, and an 18-hole, par-72 golf course across the street. Like the sprawling resort, rooms are grandly spacious and immaculately decorated in an austere Japanese way (the owners are Japanese). Marble floors and baths throughout are softened with area rugs and pastel furnishings. All rooms have sea views and some have both sea and lagoon views. Other amenities in each luxurious room include robes, house shoes, hair dryers, and safety deposit boxes. Suites have coffeemakers. Royal Beach Club guests enjoy nightly cocktails and a manager's cocktail party on the patio each Tuesday. The elegant Royal Beach Club rooms are set off from the main hotel in two- and three-story buildings (no elevators) and have their own check-in and concierge service.

Dining/Entertainment: Spices Restaurant serves the cuisines of Mexico, Argentina, and Italy while Sirenita offers selections from Japanese cuisine.

Services: Laundry and room service, ice machine on each floor, concierge, tour desk, beauty salon, gift shop and boutiques, golf clinic, car rental.

Facilities: 18-hole, par-72 golf course; seven swimming pools with a swim-up bar; two whirlpools; two lighted tennis courts; water-sport center; large, fully equipped gym with daily aerobics; massage; beauty salon; and sauna. A Kids Club is part of the gym program. Greens fee is $75 for 18 holes for guests and $95 for nonguests; carts cost $22.

✪ **Fiesta Americana Coral Beach.** Km 9.5 Paseo Kukulkán, 77500 Cancún, Q. Roo. ☎ **800/343-7821** in the U.S., or 98/83-2900. Fax 98/83-3225. 602 suites. A/C MINIBAR TV TEL. High season $370 double. Low season $260 double.

This sophisticated, spectacular hotel, which opened in 1991, has a lot to recommend it: perfect location; gracious service; grand public areas; the full gamut of water sports, beach activities, and indoor tennis. It's enormous in a Mexican way and grandly European in its lavish public halls and lobby. It's embellished with elegant dark green granite from France, deep red granite from South Africa, black and green marble from Guatemala, beige marble from Mexico, a canopy of stained glass from Guadalajara, and hardwood floors from Texas. The elegant choices are, of course, carried into the guest rooms, which are decorated with more marble, area rugs, and tasteful use of Mexican decorative arts. All rooms have balconies facing the ocean. Master suites have double vanities, dressing room, bathrobes, whirlpool baths, and large terraces; all rooms have hair dryers. Two concierge floors feature daily continental breakfast and evening cocktails, and a 24-hour reception-cashier. Two junior suites are equipped for guests with disabilities.

The hotel's great Punta Cancún location (opposite the convention center, and within walking distance of shopping centers and restaurants) has the advantage of facing the beach to the north, meaning the surf is calm and just perfect for swimming.

Dining/Entertainment: Three elegant restaurants serve seafood, international, and Mexican fare. There are five bars.

Services: Laundry and room service, travel agency, car rental, and massage.

Facilities: A 660-foot-long, free-form swimming pool; swim-up bars; 1,000 feet of beach; three indoor tennis courts with stadium seating; gymnasium with weights, sauna, and massage; water-sport rentals on the beach; business center; tennis pro shop; fashion and spa boutiques; and beauty and barber shops.

✪ Hotel Melia Cancún Beach & Spa Resort. Km 16.5 Paseo Kukulkán, 77500 Cancún, Q. Roo. ☎ **800/336-3542** in the U.S., or 98/85-1114. Fax 98/85-1263. 450 rms and suites. A/C MINIBAR TV TEL. High season $290–$325 double; $420 suite. Low season $220–$275 double; $410 suite.

You can't miss this palatial hotel. The eight-storied circular interior is a jungle of plants set against a fountain. The marble-and-teakwood backdrop is decorated with majolica pottery from Guanajuato and lacquer chests from Olinalá, Guerrero. This is another of Cancún's hotels that could easily become an island—everything is here, even a pampering spa and a golf course. The spacious rooms, all with sitting areas and balconies, are appropriately stylish and feature in-room security boxes and purified tap water. There are four rooms on the first floor especially equipped with extra-wide bathrooms for guests with disabilities.

Dining/Entertainment: Four restaurants feature foods from France, Mexico, and the United States and include a daily breakfast buffet and poolside dining. Three bars serve guests all day. The lobby bar features Latin rhythms starting at 8pm.

Services: Laundry and room service, travel agency, shops, car rental, and baby cribs and baby-sitters.

Facilities: Three pools; beach; 18-hole, par-54 golf course on the property; three lighted tennis courts; Ping-Pong; volleyball; complete spa with gymnasium, massage, sauna, whirlpool, facials, seaweed and mud therapy, body scrubs, aerobic and aquatic classes, weights, hydromassage showers, and dressing room; and beauty and barber shop. During high season or times of high hotel occupancy there's a full daily list of activities for children, posted in the lobby.

✪ Ritz-Carlton Hotel. Retorno del Rey, off Paseo Kukulkán km 13.5, 77500 Cancún, Q. Roo. ☎ **800/241-3333** or 98/85-0808. Fax 98/85-1015. 272 rms. 100 suites. A/C MINIBAR TV TEL. High season $395–$525 double; $595–$985 suite. Low season $295–$395 double; $400–$670 suite. Free guarded parking.

On 7¹/₂ acres, the nine-story Ritz-Carlton is easily the island's most elegant hotel and a member of Leading Hotels of the World. People who stay here are accustomed to the finest of everything—impeccable service, crystal chandeliers, stained glass, elegant marble, luxurious furniture, fresh flowers, silver and crystal in the dining rooms, and lush carpets throughout.

The spacious guest rooms are as sumptuous as the public areas. Each room has safety deposit boxes, electronic locks, and twice-daily maid service. Suites are large, and some have a large dressing area, two TVs, balconies, and 1¹/₂ baths. Marble baths have telephones, separate tubs and showers, lighted makeup mirror, weight scales, and hair dryers. Floors 8 and 9 are for Ritz-Carlton Club members and offer guests special amenities, including five mini-meals a day. The hotel fronts a 1,200-foot white-sand beach, and prices depend on whether your room is oceanfront, or ocean or garden view. Special packages may offer some cost-saving incentives and are worth exploring.

Dining/Entertainment: Of the three exceedingly stylish restaurants, The Grill, a fashionable English pub, is one of the best restaurants in the city (See "Where to Dine," below), offering grilled specialties, nightly entertainment, and a dance floor.

The Caribe Bar and Grill is open for snacks during pool hours. The lobby bar opens at 5pm daily, offering tea and later live music between 7:30 and 11pm.

Services: Laundry and dry cleaning, room service, travel agency, concierge.

Facilities: A swimming pool, three lighted tennis courts, fully equipped gym with exercise equipment and massages, pharmacy/gift shop, boutiques, beauty and barber shops.

EXPENSIVE

✪ **Camino Real Cancún.** Paseo Kukulkán, 77500 Punta Cancún (Apdo. Postal 14), Cancún, Q. Roo. ☎ **800/722-6466** in the U.S., or 98/83-0100. Fax 98/83-1730. 381 rms and suites. A/C MINIBAR TV TEL. High season $290 double; $355 suite; $310 Camino Real Club. Low season $205 double; $240 suite; $230 Camino Real Club. Daily fee for guarded parking adjacent to hotel.

On 4 acres right at the tip of Punta Cancún, the Camino Real is among the island's most appealing places to stay. The rooms are elegantly outfitted with pink breccia-marble floors, tropical high-backed raffia easy chairs, and drapes and spreads in soft pastel colors. Some rooms in the new 18-story Camino Real Club have elegant Mexican decor, while standard rooms in this section are much like rooms in the rest of the resort. Master suites have expansive views, large dining tables with four chairs, and hot tubs on the balconies. Camino Real Club guests receive a complimentary full breakfast daily in the Beach Club lobby, as well as complimentary cocktails and snacks there each evening. Lower-priced rooms have lagoon views.

Dining/Entertainment: Three restaurants include a beach and poolside snack bar with seafood specialties; indoor casual dining with flame-broiled meat; and an elegant evening-only restaurant featuring Chinese cuisine. There's a children's menu at the more casual restaurants. A Mexican fiesta takes place on Saturday nights. The lobby bar features Mexican music nightly from 5:30 to 7:30pm, and the seaview disco swings into action Monday through Saturday at 9:30pm.

Services: Laundry and room service, travel agency, car rental, in-room safety boxes, baby-sitting (with advance notice).

Facilities: Freshwater pool; private saltwater lagoon with sea turtles and tropical fish; private beach; sailing pier; water-sports center. There are also three lighted tennis courts, beach volleyball, boutiques, and barber and beauty shops.

✪ **Fiesta Americana Cancún.** Km 7.5 Paseo Kukulkán, 77500 Cancún, Q. Roo. ☎ **800/343-7821** in the U.S., or 98/83-1400. Fax 98/83-2502. 281 rms. A/C MINIBAR TV TEL. High season $160 double. Low season $140 double. Low-season rates include breakfast; also ask about summer "Fiesta" packages. Free parking.

With colorful stucco walls and randomly placed balconies and windows, the Fiesta Americana has old-world charm. Originally built with honeymooners in mind, it's smaller than most island accommodations and is Cancún's most intimate hotel. On the best beach facing the calm Bahía de Mujeres, the large, quiet rooms are beautifully furnished with balconies facing the ocean. The location is ideal—it's right across the street from shopping malls and restaurants near the convention center.

Dining/Entertainment: The hotel's three restaurants cover your dining needs, from formal dining to light meals poolside (where there's a swim-up bar). The lobby bar, open most of the day, features piano entertainment in the evening between 8 and 11pm. Caliente Sports/TV Betting Bar has big-screen TVs for viewing sporting events.

Services: Laundry and room service, travel agency, and wedding arrangements.

Facilities: One swimming pool, water-sports rental on the beach, boutiques, wheelchairs.

Hyatt Cancún Caribe. Km 10.5 Paseo Kukulkán, 77500 Cancún, Q. Roo. ☎ **800/233-1234** in the U.S., 98/83-1234, or 98/83-0044. Fax 98/83-1349. 300 rms. A/C MINIBAR TV TEL. High season $255 double; Regency room $320. Low season $195 double; Regency room $250. Free parking.

This sedate Hyatt Caribe is south of Punta Cancún, where there's another Hyatt—the Regency. Because of its dramatic crescent shape, all units face the sparkling Caribbean and have terraces on which to enjoy the view. Regency rooms, set off by themselves, have their own pool and such in-room amenities as lighted makeup mirrors, weight scales, hair dryers, robes, and security boxes. Regency guests also receive a complimentary continental breakfast, evening drinks, and crudités.

Dining/Entertainment: Four restaurants serve all guests' dining needs. The Casis Bar has live music nightly.

Services: Room and laundry service, travel agency, and car rental.

Facilities: Swimming pool, beach, beauty shop, pharmacy, and boutiques.

Krystal Cancún. Km 7.5 Paseo Kukulkán, 77500 Cancún, Q. Roo. ☎ **800/231-9860** in the U.S., or 98/83-1133. Fax 98/83-1790. 364 rms. A/C MINIBAR TV TEL. High season $210–$450 double. Low season $140–$170 double. Free parking.

The Krystal Cancún lies on Punta Cancún along with the Camino Real and the Hyatt Regency, near the convention center, shops, restaurants, and clubs. The Krystal uses lots of cool marble in its decor. The guest rooms, in two buildings, have bamboo furniture, drapes and spreads in earthy tones, two double beds, and water views. The hotel's tap water is purified, and there are ice machines on every floor. The presidential suites have private pools. Club Krystal rooms come with in-room safety boxes, complimentary continental breakfast, and evening canapés and drinks; guests in those rooms also have access to the Club Lounge, a rooftop sun lounge with a whirlpool and concierge service.

Dining/Entertainment: Among the hotel's four restaurants are two that have gained countrywide recognition for fine cuisine—Bogart's, a chic dining room with a Moroccan "Casablanca" theme, and the luxurious Hacienda El Mortero, a replica of a colonial hacienda featuring Mexican cuisine. The hotel also hosts theme nights throughout the week. In the evening there's live entertainment in the lobby bar. Christine's, one of the most popular discos in town, is open nightly.

Services: Laundry, room service, travel agency, and car and moped rental.

Facilities: Swimming pool complex overlooking the Caribbean and a beach with fairly safe swimming; pharmacy; barber and beauty shop; boutiques and a silver shop; two tennis courts with an on-duty tennis pro; a racquetball court; a dive shop; and a fitness club with whirlpool, sauna, and massage facilities.

Marriott Casamagna. Km 20 Paseo Kukulkán, 77500 Cancún, Q. Roo. ☎ **800/228-9290** in the U.S., or 98/85-2000. Fax 98/85-1385. 450 rms and suites. A/C MINIBAR TV TEL. High season $210–$275 double; $325–$450 suite. Low season $140–$170 double; $235–$325 suite. Ask about seasonal "super-saver" packages.

Luxury is this hotel's hallmark. Entering through a half-circle of Roman columns, you pass through a long, domed foyer to a wide, lavishly marbled 44-foot–high lobby. The lobby expands in three directions with wide, Mexican cantera-stone arches branching off outdoors, where columns vanish into shallow pools like Roman baths. Guest rooms have contemporary furnishings, tiled floors, and ceiling fans; most have balconies. All suites occupy corners and have enormous terraces, ocean views, and TVs in both the living room and bedroom.

Dining/Entertainment: The hotel's four restaurants feature the cuisines of Japan, Mexico, and the United States. The lobby bar features nightly mariachi music, while Sixties nightclub features hits from the '50s through the '70s, with space for dancing.

Services: Laundry and room service, travel agency, and car rental.

Facilities: Beach; swimming pool; two lighted tennis courts; health club with saunas, whirlpool, aerobics, and juice bar; and beauty and barber shop.

Presidente Inter-Continental Cancún. Km 7 Paseo Kukulkán, 77500 Cancún, Q. Roo. ☎ **800/327-0200** in the U.S., or 98/83-0200. Fax 98/83-0200. 292 rms. A/C MINIBAR TV TEL. High season $230–$290 double. Low season $180–$255 double. Free parking.

On the island's best beach facing the placid Bahía de Mujeres, the Presidente's location is tops. Elegant and spacious, the Presidente sports a modern design with lavish marble and wicker accents. Rooms have king-size beds, private balconies, tastefully simple unfinished pine furniture, and in-room safes. Sixteen rooms on the first floor have patios with outdoor whirlpool tubs. The club floors offer robes, magnified makeup mirrors, complimentary continental breakfast, evening drinks and canapés, and use of a private key-activated elevator. Two rooms are available for guests with disabilities and two floors are reserved for nonsmokers. Coming from Cancún City, you'll reach the Presidente on the left side of the street before you get to Punta Cancún—it's behind the golf course and next to million-dollar homes.

Dining/Entertainment: The fine-dining restaurant features foods from France, Greece, Italy, Spain, and Morocco. El Caribeño, a three-level palapa restaurant by the beach and pool, serves all meals (see "Dining," below).

Services: Laundry and room service, travel agency, car rental.

Facilities: Two landscaped swimming pools with a waterfall; whirlpools; fitness center; a great beach fronting the calm Bahía de Mujeres; lighted tennis courts; water-sports equipment rental; and marina.

۞ Sheraton Resort. Km 13.5 Paseo Kukulkán, 77500 Cancún, Q. Roo. ☎ **800/325-3535** in the U.S., or 98/83-1988. Fax 98/85-0974. 748 rms and suites. A/C MINIBAR TV TEL. High season $225–$300 double. Low season $195–$250 double. Ask about summer "Temptation" packages. Free parking.

These three lavish, pyramid-style buildings are set on their own vast stretch of beach. The impressive lobby has large expanses of green tiles and a dramatic stainless-steel sculpture of birds in flight. Emerald lawns extend in every direction from the main buildings, and a small reconstructed Maya ruin crowns a craggy limestone hillock. Rooms and suites are luxurious, with views of the Caribbean (to the east) or of the lagoon (to the west). In the V-shaped tower section, all units have in-room security boxes, and guests enjoy the services of a personal butler who attends to a variety of tasks from shoe shining to snack service. There's a nonsmoking floor, and rooms are available for guests with disabilities.

Dining/Entertainment: Four restaurants cover every aspect of dining, from grilled food by the beach to lavish breakfast buffets to Italian feasts to Mexican food. There are five bars, including the lobby bar where there's live music from noon to midnight.

Services: Laundry and room service, travel agency, car rental, massage, and baby-sitting.

Facilities: Three swimming pools; six lighted tennis courts with tennis pro on duty; beach; fitness center with sauna, steam bath, and whirlpool; mini-golf; aerobics; swimnastics; arts and crafts; Spanish classes; children's playground; basketball court; table games; pharmacy; beauty and barber shop; business center; flower shop; and boutiques.

Westin Regina Cancún. Km 20 Paseo Kukulkán, 77500 Cancún, Q. Roo. ☎ **800/228-3000** in the U.S., or 98/85-0086. Fax 98/85-0074. 385 rms. A/C MINIBAR TV TEL. High season $200–$250 single or double. Low season $165–$200. Free parking.

The strikingly austere but grand and beautiful architecture, immediately impressive with its elegant use of stone and marble, is the stamp of leading Latin American architect Ricardo Legorreta. The hotel is divided into two sections, the main hotel and the more exclusive six-story hot-pink tower section. Standard rooms are unusually large and beautifully furnished in cool, contemporary furniture. Those on the sixth floor have balconies and first-floor rooms have terraces. Rooms in the tower all have ocean or lagoon views, oodles of marble, furniture with Olinalá lacquer accents, Berber carpet area rugs, oak tables and chairs, and marble terraces with lounge chairs. Bear in mind that this hotel is a 15- to 20-minute ride from the "action" strip that lies between the Plaza Flamingo and Punta Cancún. Buses stop in front and taxis are readily available.

Dining/Entertainment: Three restaurants and two bars keep guests fueled.

Services: Laundry and room service, baby-sitting, concierge, travel agency, car rental, purified tap water, and ice machine on each floor.

Facilities: Five swimming pools; four whirlpools; beach; two lighted tennis courts; gymnasium with Stairmaster, bicycle, weights, aerobics, sauna, steam, and massage; pharmacy/gifts; boutiques; beauty and barber shop.

MODERATE

Calinda Viva Cancún. Km 8.5 Paseo Kukulkán, 77500 Cancún, Q. Roo. ☎ **800/228-5151** in the U.S., or 98/83-0800. Fax 98/83-2087. 210 rms. A/C TV TEL. High season $145–$185 double. Low season $130 double. Free parking.

From the street, this hotel looks like a blockhouse, but on the ocean side you'll find a small but pretty patio garden and Cancún's best beach that is also safest for swimming. Its location is ideal, close to all the shops and restaurants clustered near Punta Cancún and the convention center. You have a choice of rooms with either lagoon or ocean view. The rooms are large and indistinguished in decor, but comfortable with marble floors and either two double beds or a king-size bed. At least 162 rooms have refrigerators and 64 have kitchenettes.

Dining/Entertainment: The main restaurant, La Fuente, serves all three meals. La Palapa and La Parilla, both beside the pool, serve drinks and light meals; Bar La Terraza is in the lobby.

Services: Laundry and room service, travel agency.

Facilities: Swimming pool for adults and one for children, one lighted tennis court, water-sports equipment rental, marina, pharmacy, and gift shop.

✪ **Club Med.** Punta Nizuc, km 22 Paseo Kukulkán, 77500 Cancún, Q. Roo. ☎ **800/258-2633** in the U.S. and Canada, or 98/85-2900. Fax 98/85-2290. 406 rms. A/C. $125 per night per person; $875–$1000 per week per person. Single occupancy available at an extra charge. Land and air packages available from selected cities and zones. Children 12 and over are welcome. Rates vary with the season and include all meals, domestic drinks, and most activities. Excursions are extra.

Club Meds are the standard-setters among all-inclusive resorts, and this one is no exception. Guests get a lot for the money. Set on a secluded, exquisitely manicured peninsula, Club Med is more like a country club than a hotel resort. Activities are spread out all over the grounds, so there's no feeling of bumping into crowds. There are more room varieties here than at some Club Meds. Rooms are in two- and three-story buildings (no elevators); all have two full beds that can be moved (unlike some other Club Meds, where beds are fixed). Some units have views of the gardens and lagoon, and others have views of the ocean. The clientele includes a mixture of people from the United States and Canada, and from France and other countries where there is a big interest in the Yucatán. In keeping with that cultural mix, staff members speak many languages. Club Med is the farthest accommodation away from Cancún, lying nearer the airport than town—a factor to consider if you're planning much shopping or dining away from the club. However, most people who choose a Club Med vacation plan to spend most of their time there. There's an extra charge for scuba diving, which ranges from beginner to advanced, excursions, horseback riding, and deep-sea fishing.

Dining/Entertainment: Three restaurants serve an international mix of food. Every evening the staff performs—anything from comedy or magic routines in the bar to a full-scale song-and-dance show in the auditorium, followed by dancing in the nightclub.

Services: Travel agency, tours to Isla Mujeres, Cobá, Tulum, Chichén-Itzá, Mérida, and Uxmal.

Facilities: Sports include waterskiing from a special beach, windsurfing, sailing, snorkeling in a protected reserve at the village, beaches, pool, eight composition tennis courts with four lit for night play, fitness center, aerobics/calisthenics, volleyball and basketball, Ping-Pong and bocce ball, horseback riding, scuba diving equipment and pier. A pharmacy, boutique, and massage and hair salon complete the facilities.

Flamingo Cancún. Km 11.5 Paseo Kukulkán, 77500 Cancún, Q. Roo. ☎ **98/83-1544.** Fax 98/83-1029. 162 rms. A/C MINIBAR TV TEL. High season $175 double. Low season $145 double. Free unguarded parking across the street in the Plaza Flamingo.

The Flamingo seems to have been inspired by the dramatic, slope-sided architecture of the Camino Real, but the Flamingo is considerably smaller. The clean, comfortable, and modern guest rooms form a courtyard facing the swimming pool. A colorful open-air restaurant faces the pool, where guests lounge with a view of the Caribbean. The Flamingo is in the heart of the island hotel district, opposite the Flamingo Shopping Center and close to other hotels, shopping centers, and restaurants.

Dining/Entertainment: La Joy Restaurant and Don Francisco Restaurant are both open daily. El Coral is the lobby bar.

Services: Laundry and room service, travel agency, and car rental.

Facilities: Swimming pool and beach.

Misión Miramar Park Inn. Km 9.5 Paseo Kukulkán, 77500 Cancún, Q. Roo. ☎ **800/ 448-8355** in the U.S., or 98/83-1755. Fax 98/83-1136. 189 rms. A/C MINIBAR TV TEL. $175 double.

Each of the ingeniously designed rooms has views of both the lagoon and ocean. Public spaces throughout the hotel have lots of dark wood, cream-beige stucco, red tile, and pastel accents. The big swimming pool is next to the beach. Rooms are on the small side but comfortable, with bamboo furniture offset by pastel-colored cushions and bedspreads; bathrooms have polished limestone vanities.

Dining/Entertainment: Two restaurants serve cuisine of Mexico and the United States. There's live music nightly in the lobby bar, and the bar by the pool serves guests during pool hours. Batacha nightclub also has live music for dancing from 9pm to 4am Tuesday through Sunday.

Services: Laundry and room service, travel agency, and car rental.

Facilities: Pool, beach, pharmacy, and gift shop.

INEXPENSIVE

Hotel Aristos. Km 12 Paseo Kukulkán (Apdo. Postal 450), 77500 Cancún, Q. Roo. ☎ **800/ 527-4786** in the U.S., or 98/83-0011. 244 rms (all with bath). A/C TV TEL. High season $100–$130 double. Low season $85 double. Free parking; unguarded.

This was one of the island's first hotels. Rooms are neat and cool, with red-tile floors, small balconies, and yellow Formica furniture. All rooms face either the Caribbean or the paseo and lagoon; rooms with the best views (and no noise from the paseo) are on the Caribbean side. The hotel has one restaurant and several bars and offers room and laundry service, a travel agency, and baby-sitting service. The central pool overlooks the ocean with a wide stretch of beach one level below the pool and lobby. You'll also find a marina with water-sports equipment and two lighted tennis courts. Beware of spring break here, when the hotel caters to the crowd with loud music poolside all day.

El Pueblito. Km 17.5 Paseo Kukulkán, 77500 Cancún, Q. Roo. ☎ **98/85-0422** or 98/85-0797. Fax 98/85-0422. 239 rms. A/C TV TEL. High season $155. Low Season $95–$130. Ask about discounts.

Dwarfed by its ostentatious neighbors, El Pueblito nevertheless has several three-story buildings (no elevators) terraced in a V shape down a gentle hillside toward the sea. A meandering swimming pool with waterfalls runs between the two series of buildings. Rooms have modern furnishings with rattan furniture, bedspreads too short for the beds, travertine marble floors, and large bathrooms. Many have balconies facing the pool or sea. The hotel does not post swimmer warning flags, even during extremely dangerous swimming conditions, so use caution in ocean swimming here. Two restaurants and a bar are on the grounds. Try to get a ground-floor room, since a two- or three-story flight of stairs with each trip to your room could get old. The hotel is located toward the southern end of the island past the Caesar Park Resort.

CANCÚN CITY

MODERATE

Mexhotel Centro. Yaxchilán 31, SM 22. Cancún, Q. Roo. ☎ **800/221-6509** in the U.S., or 98/84-3078. Fax 84/34-7881. 81 rms. A/C TV TEL. High season $65–$85 double. Low season $60–$70 double.

The former Hotel Plaza del Sol has been incorporated into a small shopping mall and has new owners. The three stories of rooms (with elevator) front a lovely palm-shaded pool area with comfortable tables and chairs and restaurant. Standard rooms have two double beds framed with wrought iron headboards and overhead reading lights, desks, tile floors, and large tile baths with separate sinks. It's a nice hotel, but the prices are high for the location. Ask about a discount. The hotel is between Jazmines and Gladiolas, catercorner from **Périco's.**

INEXPENSIVE

✪ **Hotel Antillano.** Claveles 37, 77500 Cancún, Q. Roo. ☎ **98/84-1532.** Fax 98/84-1878. 47 rms, 2 suites. A/C TV TEL. High season $45 double. Low season $35 double.

This is an excellent choice and one of the nicer downtown establishments. For the quality, you'd expect to pay a good deal more. Rooms overlook either Avenida Tulum, the side streets, or the interior lawn and large pool, with the latter being the most desirable since they are quieter. Each room has nicely coordinated furnishings, one or two double beds, a sink area separate from the bath, red-tile floors, and a small TV. There's a small bar to one side of the reception area and a travel agency in the lobby. The hotel offers guests use of its beach club on the island. Baby-sitting can be arranged. To find it from Tulum, walk west on Claveles a half block; it's opposite the **Restaurant Rosa Mexicana**. Parking is on the street.

✪ **Hotel Hacienda Cancún.** Sunyaxchen 39–40, 77500 Cancún, Q. Roo. ☎ **98/84-3672.** Fax 98/84-1208. 40 rms. A/C TV. High season $26 double. Low season $21 double.

This extremely pleasing little hotel is another great value. The guest rooms are clean and plainly furnished but very comfortable, and all have two double beds and windows (but no views). There's a nice small pool and cafe under a shaded palapa in the back. The hotel is also a member of the Imperial Las Perlas beach club in the Zona Hotelera. To find it from Avenida Yaxchilán, turn west on Sunyaxchen; it's on your right next to the Hotel Caribe International, opposite 100% Natural. Parking is on the street.

Hotel Parador. Tulum 26, 77500 Cancún, Q. Roo. ☎ **98/84-1922.** Fax 98/84-9712. 66 rms. A/C TV TEL. High season $41 double. Low season $32 double. Ask about promotional rates.

One of the most popular downtown hotels, the three-story Parador is conveniently located. Guest rooms are arranged around two long, narrow garden courtyards leading back to a pool (with separate children's pool) and grassy sunning area. The rooms are modern, each with two double beds, a shower, and cable TV. Help yourself to bottled drinking water in the hall. There's a restaurant/bar, plus it's next to **Pop's** restaurant almost at the corner of Uxmal. Rates are almost always discounted from those quoted here. Street parking is limited.

Hotel Rivemar. Tulum 49–51, 77500 Cancún, Q. Roo. ☎ **98/84-1199.** 36 rms. A/C or FAN TV TEL. $23–$30 double.

Right in the heart of downtown Cancún, this hotel is perfectly located and offers good value. Rooms are clean, each with tile floors, two double beds, and small baths. Most rooms have air-conditioning, with only seven having fan only. All rooms have windows, some with street views and some with hall view. The hotel is at the corner of Crisantemas, $1^1/_2$ blocks north of the corner of Avenidas Cobá and Uxmal.

4 Dining

Restaurants change names with amazing rapidity in Cancún, so the restaurants I've chosen are a mix of those with dependable quality and staying power and those that were newly thriving when I checked them for this edition.

One of the first things you'll notice on arrival in Cancún is the invasion of U.S. franchise restaurants. You'll see them almost everywhere you look, including Wendy's, Subway, McDonalds, Pizza Hut, Tony Roma's, Ruth's Chris Steak House, KFC, TGI Friday's, and Burger King. Among the most economical chains are Vips and Denny's, which are also in several locations.

CANCÚN ISLAND
VERY EXPENSIVE

Captain's Cove. Km 15 Paseo Kukulkán. ☎ **98/85-0016.** Main courses $18–$40; breakfast buffet $8–$10. Daily 7:30am–11pm. INTERNATIONAL.

Though it sits almost at the end of Paseo Kukulkán far from everything, the Captain's Cove continues to pack customers in on its several dining levels. Diners face big open windows overlooking the lagoon and Royal Yacht Club Marina. During breakfast there's an all-you-can-eat buffet. Lunch and dinner main courses of steak and seafood are the norm, and there's a menu catering especially to children. For

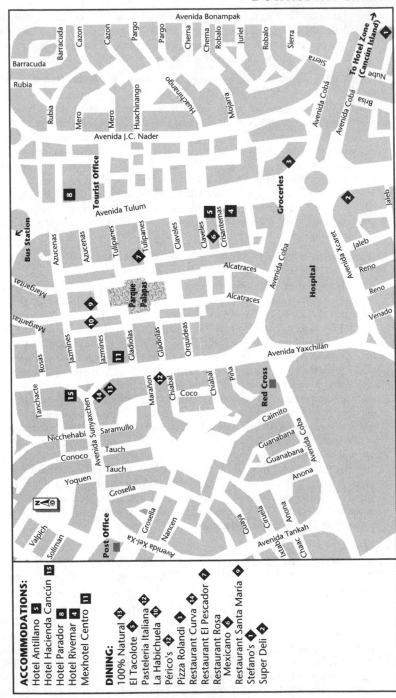

Avenida Bonampak

To Hotel Zone (Cancún Island)

Barracuda
Barracuda
Cazon
Cazon
Pargo
Pargo
Cherna
Cherna
Robalo
Juriel
Robalo
Sierra

Rubia

Nube

Brisa

Avenida Cobá
Avenida Cobá

Rubia
Mero
Mero
Huachinango

Huachinango

Mojarra

Sierra

Jaleb

Avenida J.C. Nader

Tourist Office

3

Avenida Xcaret

Jaleb

Reno

Reno

Venado

8

2

Avenida Tulum

Bus Station

Groceries

Azucenas
Azucenas
Tulipanes
Tulipanes
Claveles
Claveles
Crisantemas

5
4
6
1

Alcatraces

Alcatraces

Avenida Coba

Hospital

Margaritas

Parque Palapas

9

10

Margaritas

Jazmines
Jazmines
Gladiolas
Gladiolas
Orquideas

Rosas

11

Avenida Yaxchilán

Marañon
Chiabal
Coco
Chiabal
Piña

12

Tanchacte

15
14
13

Avenida Sunyaxchen

Red Cross

Niccehabi

Saramullo

Caimito

Conoco

Tauch

Guanabana

Avenida Coba

Yoquen

Tauch

Guanabana

Grosella

Anona

Valpich
Soliman

Post Office

Grosella
Nancen

Avenida Xel-Xa

Guaya
Ciruela
Anona
Ixtaba
Chaac

Avenida Tankah

dessert there are flaming coffees, crêpes, and Key lime pie. Clever and sophisticated time-share hawkers approach arriving patrons, so be aware that the friendly greeters may have ulterior motives as they express interest in how you're enjoying your vacation. The restaurant is on the lagoon side opposite the Omni Hotel.

✪ **Club Grill.** Ritz-Carlton Hotel, km 13.5 Paseo Kukulkán. ☎ **98/85-0808.** Reservations required. Main courses $40–$50. Daily 7pm–11pm. INTERNATIONAL.

Cancún's most elegant and stylish restaurant is also its best. Even rival restaurateurs give it an envious thumbs up. The gracious service starts as you enter the anteroom with its comfortable couches and chairs and selection of cognacs and Cuban cigars. It continues into the candlelit dining room with padded side chairs and tables shimmering with silver and crystal. Under the trained eye of chef de cuisine John Patrick Gray, elegant plates of peppered scallops, truffles, and potatoes in tequila sauce, or grilled lamb, or mixed grill arrive without feeling rushed after the appetizer. The restaurant has both smoking and nonsmoking sections (a rarity in Mexico). A band plays romantic music for dancing from 8pm on. This is the place for that truly special night out.

✪ **María Bonita.** Hotel Camino Real, Punta Cancún. ☎ **98/83-1730.** Main courses $15–$30. Daily 6pm–11pm. REGIONAL/MEXICAN/NOUVELLE MEXICAN.

Enjoy Mexico at its very best—it's music, food, and atmosphere—in an authentic setting that captures the essence of Mexico with every bite and glance. Overlooking the water, the interior is divided by cuisine—La Cantina Jalisco includes an open, colorful Mexican kitchen (with pots and pans on the wall) and Tequila bar (with more than 50 different tequilas); the Salon Michoacán in the center features food from that state's cuisine; and the Patio Oaxaca is on the lower level. The menu includes foods from these three states, as well as the best of Mexico's other cuisines, as excellently prepared as you'll find them anywhere, with a few international dishes thrown in for variety. While you dine, you'll be serenaded by duets, marimba music, jarocho, and the ever-enchanting mariachis. The different peppers used in sauces and preparation are explained on the front of the menu, and each dish is marked for its heat quotient (from zero chiles to two chiles); dishes without a chile mean they're not picante at all. A nice starter is the Mitlan salad, which has Oaxaca cheese slices (the state is known for its excellent cheese) dribbled with a little olive oil and a coriander dressing. The stuffed chile "La Doña"—a poblano pepper (mildly hot) filled with lobster and huitlacoche, in a cream sauce—comes as either an appetizer or main course and is wonderful. The restaurant is separate from the hotel (to the left of the entrance) and is entered from the street.

EXPENSIVE

El Caribeño. In the Presidente Inter-Continental Hotel, km 7.5 Paseo Kukulkán. ☎ **98/83-0200.** Main courses $8–$20; breakfast buffet $10. Daily 7am–11pm. MEDITERRANEAN.

Especially nice for breakfast, lunch, or dinner, El Caribeño sits on the beach with a stunning view of the Bahía de Mujeres and Isla Mujeres in the distance. The breakfast buffet is a sumptuous affair including made-to-order omelets and a gorgeous array of tropical fruits and fresh sweet rolls. Lunch is a good choice since you'll be able to see the sea and will pay a bit less for your main courses. But dinner is quiet, romantic, and charming; you can order from the lunch menu at dinner, even though there's a less extensive and more expensive dinner menu. Try the fresh fish prepared Yucatecan style in achiote sauce. The restaurant is on the grounds of the Presidente Inter-Continental, on your left as you face toward the convention center on Paseo Kukulkán.

✪ **La Dolce Vita.** Km 14.6 Paseo Kukulkán. ☎ **98/84-1384.** Reservations required for dinner. Main courses $10–$21. Mon–Fri 1pm–midnight; Sat–Sun 5pm–midnight. ITALIAN.

Prepare to dine on some of the best Italian food in Mexico. Now at its new location on the lagoon and opposite the Marriott Casamagna, the casually elegant La Dolce Vita is even more pleasant and popular than at its old garden location downtown. Appetizers include pâté of quail liver and carpaccio in vinaigrette, or watercress salad. You can order such pastas as green tagliolini with lobster medallions, linguine with clams or seafood, or rigatoni Mexican style (with chorizo, mushrooms, and chives), as an appetizer for half price or as a main course for full price. Other main courses include veal with morels, fresh salmon with cream sauce, scampi, and various fish.

La Fisheria. Plaza Caracol, Second Floor. ☎ **98/83-1395.** Main courses $6–$18. Daily 11am–11:30pm. SEAFOOD.

Patrons find a lot to choose from at this restaurant overlooking Boulevard Kukulkán and the lagoon. The expansive menu offers shark fingers with a jalapeño dip, grouper fillet stuffed with seafood in a lobster sauce, Acapulco-style ceviche (in a tomato sauce), New England chowder, steamed mussels, grilled red snapper with pasta—well I think you can get the idea. The menu changes daily, but there's always tik-n-xic—that great Yucatecan grilled fish marinated in achiote sauce. And for those not inclined toward seafood, pizza might do, or one of the grilled chicken or beef dishes.

Mango Tango. Km 14 Paseo Kukulkán, opposite Jack Tar Village. ☎ **98/85-0303.** Main courses $6–$16; dinner show $25–$35. Daily 2pm–2am. INTERNATIONAL.

Mango Tango's made a name for itself with its floor shows (see "Cancún After Dark," below), but its kitchen is no slouch. Try the peel-your-own shrimp, Argentine-style grilled meat with chimichuri sauce, and other grilled specialties. The Mango Tango Salad has shrimp, chicken, avocado, red onion, tomato and mushrooms on mango slices. Pasta includes Mango Tango rice with seafood and fried bananas. The creole gumbo comes with lobster, shrimp, and squid.

✪ **Savios.** Plaza Caracol. ☎ **98/83-2085.** Main courses $8.25–$20. Daily 10am–11:30pm. ITALIAN.

Savios, in stylish black and white with tile floors and green marble-topped tables, is on two levels and faces Paseo Kukulkán through two stories of awning-shaded windows. Its bar is always crowded with patrons sipping everything from cappuccino to imported beer. Repeat diners look forward to large fresh salads and richly flavored, subtly herbed Italian dishes. I recommend the ravioli stuffed with ricotta and spinach in a delicious tomato sauce.

CANCÚN CITY
EXPENSIVE
✪ **La Habichuela.** Margaritas 25. ☎ **98/84-3158.** Reservations recommended in high season. Main courses $8–$30. Daily 1pm–midnight. GOURMET SEAFOOD/BEEF/MEXICAN.

In a garden setting with tables covered in pink-and-white linens and soft music in the background, this restaurant is an ideal setting for romantic, gourmet dining. For an all-out culinary adventure, try Habichuela (string bean) soup; shrimp in any number of sauces including Jamaican tamarindo, tequila, and a ginger and mushroom combination; and the Maya coffee with Xtabentun. The grilled seafood and steaks are excellent as well, but this is a good place to try a Mexican specialty such as enchiladas suizas or tampiqueña-style beef. For something totally new, try the "Cocobichuela," which is lobster and shrimp in a curry sauce served in a coconut shell and topped with fruit.

MODERATE

100% Natural. Av. Sunyaxchen 6. ☎ **98/84-3617.** Breakfast $2.25–$3.25; spaghetti $5; fruit or vegetable shakes $2.50; sandwiches and Mexican plates $3–$6. Daily 7am–11pm. SEMI-VEGETARIAN.

Of all the 100% Naturals around Mexico, this has one of the most appealing settings, with white rattan tables on a white tile floor and large dining areas on the street or interior patio. For great mixed-fruit shakes and salads, this is the place. Coffee is expensive ($1.50) but comes with several refills. Full meals include large portions of chicken or fish, spaghetti, or soup and sandwiches. Dine on the pretty patio in back to avoid the roar of Sunyaxchen. The restaurant is near the corner of avenidas Yaxchilán and Sunyaxchen opposite the Hotel Caribe Internacional. Two other locations with higher prices are in the Zona Hotelera at Plaza Terramar (☎ 98/83-1180; open 24 hours) and Plaza Kukulkán (☎ 98/85-2904; open 7am to 11pm).

Périco's. Yaxchilán 61. ☎ **98/84-3152.** Main courses $6–$18. Daily 1pm–1am. MEXICAN/SEAFOOD/STEAKS.

Périco's—with colorful murals that almost dance off the walls, a bar area overhung with baskets and with saddles for bar stools, colorfully bedecked leather tables and chairs, and witty waiters—is always booming and festive. The extensive menu offers well-prepared steak, seafood, and traditional Mexican dishes for moderate rates (except lobster). This is a place not only to eat and drink but to let loose and join in the fun, so don't be surprised if everybody drops their forks and dons huge Mexican sombreros to bob and snake in a conga dance around the dining room. It's fun whether or not you join in. There's marimba music from 7:30 to 10:30pm, and mariachis from 10:30pm to midnight. This is a popular spot, so expect a crowd if you get there after 8pm; go around 7pm if you want to secure a seat.

✪ **Restaurant El Pescador.** Tulipanes 28, off Av. Tulum. ☎ **98/84-2673.** Main courses $8–$25; Mexican plates $5–$9. Daily 11am–10:30pm. SEAFOOD.

There's often a line at this restaurant, which opened in 1980 serving well-prepared fresh seafood on its streetside patio and in an upstairs venue overlooking Tulipanes. Feast on shrimp cocktail, conch, octopus, Créole-style shrimp (camarones à la criolla), charcoal-broiled lobster, and stone crabs. Zarzuela is a combination seafood plate cooked in white wine and garlic. There's a Mexican-specialty menu as well. Another branch, **La Mesa del Pescador,** is in the Plaza Kukulkán on Cancún Island and is open the same hours but is more expensive.

✪ **Restaurant Los Almendros.** Av. Bonampak and Sayil. ☎ **98/87-1332.** Main courses $4–$6. Daily 10:30am–11pm. YUCATECAN.

To steep yourself in Yucatecan cuisine head directly to this large, colorful, air-conditioned restaurant. Many readers have written to say they ate nearly every meal here, since the food and service are good and the illustrated menu, with color pictures of dishes, makes ordering easy. Some of the regional specialties include lime soup, poc chuc, chicken or pork pibil, and such appetizers as panuchos Yucatecos. The combinado Yucateco is a sampler of four typically Yucatecan main courses—pollo, poc chuc, sausage, and escabeche. A second location opened in 1994 on Cancún Island on Paseo Kukulkán across from the convention center. To find the downtown location, go to the corner of Tulum and Cobá, walk toward Cancún Island (east) 2 long blocks, and turn right on Avenida Bonampak; it's opposite the bullring 7 short blocks ahead.

Restaurant Rosa Mexicano. Claveles 4. ☎ **98/84-6313.** Reservations recommended for parties of six or more. Main courses $6–$12; lobster $20. Daily 5–11pm. MEXICAN HAUTE.

This beautiful little place has candlelit tables and a plant-filled patio in back, and it's almost always packed. Colorful paper banners and piñatas hang from the ceiling, efficient waiters wear bow ties and cummerbunds color-themed to the Mexican flag, and a trio plays romantic Mexican music nightly. The menu features "refined" Mexican specialties. Try the pollo almendro, which is chicken covered in a cream sauce sprinkled with ground almonds, or the pork baked in a banana leaf with a sauce of oranges, lime, chile ancho, and garlic. The steak tampiqueño is a huge platter that comes with guacamole salad, quesadillas, beans, salad, and rice.

INEXPENSIVE

Pizza Rolandi. Cobá 12. ☎ **98/84-4047.** Pasta $5–$8; pizza and main courses $4–$9. Mon–Sat 1pm–midnight; Sun 1pm–11pm. ITALIAN.

At this shaded outdoor patio restaurant you can choose from almost two dozen different wood-oven pizzas and a full selection of spaghetti, calzones, and Italian-style chicken and beef and desserts. There's a full bar list as well.

✪ **Restaurant Curva.** Av. Yaxchilán at Sunyaxchen. No phone. Breakfast $1.75–$2.50; comida corrida $2.50–$3. Mon–Sat 9am–5pm. MEXICAN.

It's worth the wait for a seat at one of the six tables in this tiny, and spotless, storefront cafe. You'll join young office workers and students for an inexpensive home-style lunch. The daily comida includes soup, rice, beans, and meat. There's usually a choice of main courses, such as beef tips, pozole, pollo adobado, and pollo frito. Lingering is not appreciated during lunchtime.

Restaurante Santa María. Azucenas at Parque Palapas. ☎ **98/84-3158.** Main courses $3.50–$9; tacos 75¢–$5;. Daily 5pm–10pm. MEXICAN.

The open-air Santa María restaurant is a clean, gaily decked-out place to sample authentic Mexican food. It's cool and breezy with patio dining that's open on two sides and furnished with leather tables and chairs covered in multicolored cloths. A bowl of frijoles de olla and an order of beefsteak tacos will fill you up for a low price. You may want to try the tortilla soup or enchiladas, or go for one of the grilled U.S.-cut steaks, order of fajitas, ribs, or grilled seafood, all of which arrive with a baked potato.

Stefano's. Bonampak 177. ☎ **98/84-1715.** Main courses $4–$6; pizza $4.75–$6.75. Wed–Mon 2pm–midnight. ITALIAN/PIZZA/PASTA.

Tourists are beginning to find Stefano's, which serves Italian food with a few Mexican accents. For example, on the menu you'll find a huitlacoche and shrimp pizza, rigatoni in tequila sauce, and seafood with chile peppers, nestled proudly alongside the Stefano special pizza, made with fresh tomato, cheese, and pesto, and calzones stuffed with spinach, mozzarella, and tomato sauce. For dessert the ricotta strudel is something out of the ordinary, or else try the tiramisú. There are lots of different coffees and mixed drinks, as well.

COFFEE AND PASTRIES

Pasteleria Italiana. Av. Yaxchilán 67, SM 25, near Sunyaxchen. ☎ **98/84-0796.** Pastries $1.75–$2.25; ice cream $2; coffee $1–$2. Mon–Sat 9am–10pm, Sun 2–9pm. COFFEE/PASTRIES/ICE CREAM.

More like a casual neighborhood coffeehouse than a place aimed at tourists, this shady little respite has been doing business here since 1977. You'll spot it by the white awning that covers the small outdoor, plant-filled table area. Inside are refrigerated cases of tarts and scrumptious-looking cakes, ready to be carried away in their entirety or by the piece. The coffeehouse is in the same block as Périco's, between Maraño and Chiabal.

A DELICATESSEN

Super Deli. Tulum at Xcaret/Cobá. ☎ **98/84-1412.** Breakfast $2–$7.50; sandwiches $5–$7.50; pizzas $5.75–$8. Daily 24 hours. DELICATESSEN.

You can't miss the trendy green awning of the outdoor restaurant here. It's very popular for light or substantial meals any time, and inside is a well-stocked, medium-size grocery store with an excellent delicatessen. Dining choices include pizza, pasta, steaks, burgers, baguette sandwiches, a variety of coffees, wine, and beer. There's another branch on the island in the Plaza Nautilus.

5 Beaches, Water Sports & Other Things to Do

Although most people come to Cancún to kick back and relax on the beach, options for exploring beyond your selected beach chair are numerous. If you need a travel agent, I highly recommend **Mayaland Tours,** Av. Tulum at Cobá in the Hotel América (☎ 98/87-2450; fax 98/87-2438). The company pioneered tourism in the Yucatán and has a better handle on it than most others. Their double-decker buses run the route south to Tulum and Xel-Ha and elsewhere, and now they're a full-service travel agency handling not only tours all over the Yucatán Peninsula, but plane reservations. They own hotels in Mérida, Uxmal, and Chichén-Itzá and can arrange a free rental car with reservations at their hotels. Besides the suggestions listed below, see also "Road Trips from Cancún" at the end of the chapter for suggestions on getting to the ruins of **Chichén-Itzá, Cobá,** and **Tulum;** the water parks of **Xcaret** and **Xel-Ha; El Eden,** a 500,000-acre private biological reserve northwest of Cancún; and the 2 million–acre **Sian Ka'an Biosphere Reserve** south of Cancún and Tulum.

However, before venturing out of Cancún, the first thing to do is explore the Zona Hotelera on Isla Cancún, just to see the fabulous resort itself (with the amazing variety of architecture) and to get your bearings. Frequent Ruta 1 or Ruta 2 buses marked "Hoteles" and those marked "Turismo" run from the mainland city along the full 12 miles to the end of the island. These buses are inexpensive, and you can get on and off anywhere to visit hotels, shopping centers, and beaches (but you pay to ride again).

THE BEACHES   The best stretches of beach are dominated by the big hotels. All of Mexico's beaches are public property, so you can use the beach of any hotel by walking through the lobby. Be especially careful on beaches fronting the open Caribbean, where the undertow can be deadly. Swim where there's a lifeguard. By contrast, the waters of Mujeres Bay (Bahía de Mujeres) at the north end of the island are usually calm. Get to know Cancún's water-safety pennant system, and make sure to check the flag at any beach or hotel before entering the water. Here's how it goes:

- White   Excellent
- Green   Normal conditions (safe)
- Yellow   Changeable, uncertain (use caution)
- Black or Red   Unsafe—use the swimming pool instead!

Here in the Caribbean, storms can arrive and conditions can change from safe to unsafe in a matter of minutes, so be alert: If you see dark clouds heading your way, make your way to shore and wait until the storm passes and the green flag is displayed again.

Playa Tortuga (Turtle Beach) is the public beach. Besides swimming, you can rent a sailboard and take lessons there. There's a small but beautiful portion of public beach on Playa Caracol, by the Xcaret Terminal. Both of these face the calm waters of Bahía de Mujeres, and for that reason are much better than those facing the Caribbean.

WATER SPORTS Many beachside hotels offer water-sports concessions that include rental of rubber rafts, kayaks, and snorkeling equipment. On the calm Nichupte Lagoon are outlets for renting **sailboats, water jets,** and **water skis.** Prices vary and are often negotiable, so check around.

Besides **snorkeling** at Garrafón National Park (see "Boating Excursions," below), travel agencies offer an all-day excursion to the natural wildlife habitat of Isla Contoy, which usually includes time for snorkeling. It costs more than doing it on your own from Isla Mujeres (see chapter 5 for details).

You can arrange a day of **deep-sea fishing** at one of the numerous piers or travel agencies for around $150 to $250 for 4 hours for up to four people.

Scuba trips run around $60 and include two tanks. **Scuba Cancún,** Paseo Kukulkán km 5, on the lagoon side (☎ **98/83-1011,** fax 98/84-2336; open 8:30am to 6pm, phone reservations available in the evenings from 7:30 to 10:30pm using the fax line), offers a 4-hour resort course for $70. Full certification takes 4 to 5 days and costs around $350. Scuba Cancún also offers diving trips to 12 nearby reefs, including Cuevones at 30 feet and the open ocean at 50 to 60 feet (offered in good weather only). The average dive is around 35 feet. The farthest reef is about 40 minutes away. Drift diving is the norm here, and the big attractions are the coral reefs, where there are hundreds of fish. One-tank dives cost $45, and two-tank dives cost $55. Dives usually start around 10am and return by 2:15pm. Snorkeling trips cost $25 and leave every afternoon after 2pm going to shallow reefs about a 20-minute boat ride away.

For windsurfing, go to the Playa Tortuga public beach, where there's a **Windsurfing School** (☎ 98/84-2023) with equipment for rent.

BOATING EXCURSIONS The island of Isla Mujeres, just 10 miles offshore, is one of the most pleasant day-trips from Cancún. At one end is El Garrafón National Underwater Park, which is excellent for snorkeling. And at the other end is a delightful village with small shops, restaurants, and hotels, and Playa Norte, the island's best beach. (See chapter 5 for more on Isla Mujeres.) If you're looking for relaxation and can spare the time, Isla Mujeres is worth several days.

There are four ways to get there: by frequent public ferry from Puerto Juárez, which takes between 20 and 45 minutes; by shuttle boat from Playa Linda or Playa Tortuga (a 1-hour ride) but with irregular service; by the Watertaxi (also with limited service), next to the Xcaret Terminal; and by one of the day-long pleasure boats, most of which leave from the Playa Linda pier. The cost of the public ferry from Puerto Juárez is three times cheaper than any of those from Cancún Island.

It's easy to go on your own. The inexpensive Puerto Juárez **public ferries** are just a few miles from downtown Cancún. From Cancún City, take the Ruta 8 bus on Avenida Tulum to Puerto Juárez; the ferry docks in downtown Isla Mujeres by all the shops, restaurants, hotels, and Playa Norte. You'll need a taxi to go to Garrafón Park at the other end of the island. You can stay as long as you like on the island (even overnight) and return by ferry, but be sure to ask about the time of the last returning ferry—don't depend on the posted hours. (For more details and a shuttle schedule, see chapter 5.)

Pleasure boat cruises to Isla Mujeres are a favorite pastime here. Modern motor yachts, catamarans, trimarans, and even old-time sloops take swimmers, sunners, snorkelers, and shoppers out onto the limpid waters. Some tours include a snorkeling stop at Garrafón, lunch on the beach, and a short time for shopping in downtown Isla Mujeres. Most leave at 9:30 or 10am; last about 5 or 6 hours; and include continental breakfast, lunch, and rental of snorkel gear. Others, particularly the sunset and night cruises, go to beaches away from town for pseudo-pirate shows and include a lobster dinner or Mexican buffet. If you want to actually see Isla Mujeres, go on a morning cruise, or go on your own using the public ferry at Puerto Juárez mentioned above.

Tour companies are also beginning to offer cruises that emphasize Cancún's natural attributes. The **lagoons** along the Zona Hotelera are ideal for spotting herons, egrets, and crabs in the mangroves. Often billed as **jungle cruises,** they don't go to a jungle, but they usually include time for lagoon snorkeling, which is not the best place to snorkel. Other excursions go to the **reefs** in glass-bottom boats, so you can have a near-scuba–diving experience and see many colorful fish. However, the reefs are a distance from shore and impossible to reach on windy days with choppy seas. They've also suffered from overuse, and their condition is far from pristine. The **Nautibus** (☎ 98/83-3552 or 98/83-2119), one of those offering glass-bottom boat trips to the reefs, has been around for years. The morning and afternoon trips in a glass-bottom boat from the Playa Linda Pier to the Chitale coral reef to see colorful fish takes about 1 hour and 20 minutes. Around 50 minutes is consumed going to and from the reef. Still other boat excursions visit Isla Contoy, a **national bird sanctuary** that's well worth the time. If you are planning to spend time in Isla Mujeres, the Contoy trip is easier and more pleasurable to take from there.

The operators and names of boats offering excursions change often. To find out what's available when you're there, check with a local travel agent or hotel tour desk, because they should have a wide range of options. You can also go to the Playa Linda Pier either a day ahead or the day of your intended outing and buy your own ticket for trips on the Nautibus or to Isla Mujeres. If you go on the day of your trip, arrive at the pier around 8:45am since most boats leave around 9 or 9:30am.

RUINAS EL REY Cancún has its own **Maya ruins.** It's a small site and not impressive compared to ruins at Tulum, Cobá, or Chichén-Itzá. The Maya fishermen built this small ceremonial center and settlement very early in the history of Maya culture. It was then abandoned, to be resettled later near the end of the Postclassic period, not long before the arrival of the conquistadores. The platforms of numerous small temples are visible amid the banana plants, papayas, and wildflowers. A new golf course has been built around the ruins, but there is a separate entrance for sightseers. You'll find the ruins about 13 miles from town, at the southern reaches of the Zona Hotelera, almost to Punta Nizuc. Look for the Caesar's Palace hotel on the left (east), then the ruins on the right (west). Admission is $4.50 (free on Sundays and holidays); the hours are daily from 8am to 5pm.

A MUSEUM To the right side of the entrance to the Cancún Convention center is the Museo Arqueológico de Cancún, a small but interesting museum with relics from archaeological sites around the state. Admission is $1.75 (free on Sundays and holidays); the hours are Tuesday to Saturday from 9am to 7pm, Sunday from 10am to 5pm.

BULLFIGHTS Cancún has a small bullring (☎ 98/84-8372) near the northern (town) end of Paseo Kukulkán opposite the Restaurant Los Almendros. Bullfights are held every Wednesday at 3:30pm during the winter tourist season. There are usually four bulls. Travel agencies in Cancún sell tickets: $45 for adults and $25 for children.

6 Shopping

Although shops in Cancún are more expensive than their equivalents in any other Mexican city, most visitors spend a portion of their time browsing.

There are several **open-air crafts markets** easily visible on Avenida Tulum in Cancún City and near the convention center in the hotel zone.

Malls on Cancún Island are air-conditioned, sleek, and sophisticated. Most of these are located one after another on Paseo Kukulkán between km 7 and km 12— Plaza Lagunas, Costa Brava, La Mansión, Mayfair, Plaza Terramar, Plaza Caracol, Plaza Flamingo, and Plaza Kukulcán. These malls offer shops selling everything from fine crystal and silver to designer clothing and decorative objects. Numerous restaurants are interspersed among the shops, many with prices higher than their branches on the mainland. Stores are generally open daily from 10am to 8 or 10pm. Stores in malls near the convention center generally stay open all day, but some, and especially in malls farther out, close between 2 and 5pm. Here's a brief rundown on the malls and some of the shops they contain. Inside the **Plaza Kukulkán** you'll find a branch of Banco Serfin, OK Maguey Cantina Grill, a movie theater with U.S. movies, Tikal, a shop with Guatemalan textile clothing, several crafts stores, a liquor store, a bathing suit specialty store, a record and tape outlet, all leather goods including shoes and sandals, and another specializing in silver from Taxco. In the food court are a number of U.S. franchise restaurants including Ruth's Chris Steakhouse, plus one featuring specialty coffee.

Planet Hollywood anchors the **Plaza Flamingo,** but inside you'll also pass branches of Bancrecer, Denny's, Subway Sandwiches, and La Casa del Habana for Cuban Cigars.

The long, meandering **Plaza Caracol** holds outlets for Cartier jewelry, Aca Joe, Guess, Señor Frog clothing, Waterford crystal, Samsonite luggage, Thomas Moore Travel, Gucci, Fuji film, Mr. Papa's, and La Fisheria restaurant.

Mayfair Plaza/Centro Comercio Mayfair is the oldest, with an open bricked center that's lively with people sitting in open-air restaurants and bars such as Tequila Sunrise, Fat Tuesday, El Mexicano (a dinner show restaurant), Hard Rock Café, Pizza Hut, and several stores selling silver, leather, and crafts.

7 Cancún After Dark

One of Cancún's draws is its active nightlife. Sometimes there's entertainment enough just strolling along thriving Avenida Tulum, where restaurant employees show off enticing sample plates to lure in passersby. But the **Centro Comercio Mayfair** on the island is just about the liveliest place for spending an evening hanging out, going from restaurant to drinking establishment to restaurant. It's one of the first shopping centers on the island, and the only one with a large open-air center that's ideal for sitting outside to eat and drink and meet other vacationers having a good time. Snazzy discos and a variety of lobby entertainment are all part of the island nighttime scene at many of the better hotels.

CONVENTION CENTER   The long-awaited convention center is open with slick (and I mean slick) marble floors, arcades of fashionable shops and restaurants, entertainment, meeting rooms, and an auditorium.

THE PERFORMING ARTS   Nightly performances of the **Ballet Folklórico de Cancún** (☎ 98/83-0199, ext. 193 and 194) are held at the Cancún Convention

Center. Tickets are sold between 8am and 9pm at a booth just as you enter the convention center. You can go for dinner and the show, or just the show. Dinner/show guests pay around $35 and arrive at 6:30pm for drinks, which is followed by dinner at 7pm and the show at 8pm. The price includes an open bar, dinner, show, tax, and tip. Guests preferring only the show arrive at 7:30pm and pay $25. Several hotels host **Mexican fiesta nights,** including a buffet dinner and a folkloric dance show; admission, including dinner, ranges from $35 to $50. A Ballet Folklórico appears Monday through Saturday nights in a 1 hour and 15 minute show at the Continental Villas Plaza (☎ **98/85-1444,** ext. 5690). The Hyatt Regency Cancún (☎ **98/83-1234**) has a dinner, folkloric show, and mariachi fiesta Tuesday through Sunday nights during the high season, as does the Camino Real (☎ **98/83-1200**). **El Mexicano restaurant** (☎ **98/84-4207**) in the Costa Blanca shopping center hosts a tropical dinner show every night as well as live music for dancing. The entertainment alternates each night with mariachis entertaining intermittently from 7:30 to 11pm and a folkloric show from 8 to 9:30pm.

You can also get in the party mood at **Mango Tango,** Paseo Kukulkán km 14 (☎ **98/85-0303**), a lagoon-side restaurant/dinner show establishment. Diners can choose from two levels, one nearer the music and the other overlooking it all. Music is loud and varied. The 1 hour and 20 minute dinner show begins at 8pm nightly and costs $25 to $35. At 9:30pm live reggae music begins, and there's no cover. If you want to enjoy the show without a meal, just order a drink and be seated at an upper level table and order a drink. It's opposite the Jack Tar Village.

For something that mingles tourists with the locals, on Fridays at 7:30pm head for the downtown **Parque de las Palapas** (the main park) for Noches Caribeños, where live tropical music is provided at no charge for anyone who wants to listen and dance.

THE CLUB & MUSIC SCENE   Clubbing in Cancún, still called discoing here, is a raucous affair. Several of the big hotels have nightclubs, usually a disco, or entertain in their lobby bars with live music. The discos are expensive, however. Expect to pay a cover charge of $10 to $20 per person in the discos or show bars and $5 to $8 for a drink. Numerous restaurants, such as **Carlos 'n Charlie's, Planet Hollywood, Hard Rock Café, Fat Tuesday, Señor Frog, TGI Friday's,** and **Périco's** (for the last see "Where to Eat," above), double as nighttime party spots; the first four attract hordes of spring breakers and offer wildish fun at a fraction of the prices of more costly evening entertainment at discos. Certainly the most sophisticated and upscale of all Cancún's nightly gathering spots is the Club Grill restaurant of the **Ritz-Carlton Hotel,** where diners with reservations enjoy soft, low-key music to dance by.

Azucar Bar Caribeño, adjacent to the Hotel Camino Real (☎ **98/83-0441**), offers spicy tropical dancing of the salsa, meringue, and bolero kind, with bands from Cuba, Jamaica, and the Dominican Republic; it's open Monday to Saturday from 9:30pm to 4am.

La Boom, Bulevar Kukulkán km 3.5 (☎ **98/83-1152**), has two sections: On one side is a video bar and on the other is a bilevel disco with the required cranium-cracking music. There's blessed air-conditioning in both places. Each night there may be a special client-getting attraction like no cover, free bar, ladies' night, or bikini night. It's open nightly from 8pm to 6am. A sound-and-light show begins at 11:30pm in the disco.

Carlos 'n Charlie's, Paseo Kukulkán km 4.5 (☎ **98/83-0846**), is a reliable place to find both good food and packed frat house–level entertainment in the evenings. There's a dance floor to go along with the live music that starts nightly around 9pm. A cover charge is implemented if you're not planning to eat. It's open daily from noon to 2am.

With taped music, **Carlos O'Brien's,** Tulum 29, SM 22 (☎ **98/84-1659**), is one of the tamer of the Carlos Anderson restaurants/night spots in town (Señor Frog and Carlos 'n Charlie's are two others), but it has its lively moments, depending on the crowd. It's open daily from 11am to 12:30am.

Christine's, at the Hotel Krystal on the island (☎ **98/83-1793**), is one of the most popular discos. The dress code is no shorts or jeans. It opens at 9:30pm nightly.

Dady'O, Paseo Kukulkán km 9.5. (☎ **98/83-3333**), is the current heavyweight champion, with lines long enough to make you think you're in New York or L.A. It opens at 9:30pm nightly.

Dady Rock Bar and Grill, Paseo Kukulkán km 9.5 (☎ **98/83-1626**), the offspring of Dady'O, opens early (7pm) and goes as long as any other night spot (the wee hours) offering a new twist on entertainment with a combination of live bands and DJ-orchestrated music, along with an open bar, full meals, a buffet, and dancing.

Hard Rock Café, in the Mayfair Shopping Center (☎ **98/83-2024**), entertains with a live band at 10:30pm every night except Wednesday. Other hours you'll get your share of lively recorded music to munch by—the menu combines the most popular foods from American and Mexican cultures. It's open daily from 10am to 2am.

Planet Hollywood, Flamingo Shopping Center, Paseo Kukulkán km 11 (☎ **98/ 85-3022**), is the trendy brainchild of Sylvester Stallone, Bruce Willis, and Arnold Schwarzenegger. It's both a restaurant and nighttime music/dance spot with megadecible live music. It's open daily from 11am to 2am.

Tequila Sunrise Grill Bar & Fiesta, in the Mayfair Shopping Center above the Pizza Hut, is a restaurant, but it's also a lively dancing spot with tempting music drifting down to the plaza below; there's no cover, and it's open daily from 7pm to 4am.

Up & Down, Paseo Kukulkán km 15.5 (☎ **98/85-2909**), a glitzy high-tech disco (downstairs) and splashy restaurant with quieter music (upstairs), offers night owls a wide choice in evening entertainment. It's in front of the Hotel Oasis.

SPORTS WAGERING   This form of entertainment seems to be sweeping Mexico's resorts. TV screens mounted around the room at **LF Caliente** (☎ **98/83-3704**), at the Fiesta Americana Hotel, show all the action in race track, football, soccer, and so on in a bar/lounge setting.

8 Road Trips from Cancún

Outside of Cancún are all the many wonders of the Yucatán Peninsula; you'll find the details in chapters 5 and 6. Cancún can be a perfect base for day- or overnight trips or the starting point for a longer exploration. Any travel agency or hotel tour desk in Cancún can book these tours, or you can elect to do them on your own via local bus or rental car. The Maya ruins to the south at **Tulum** or **Cobá** should be your first goal, then perhaps the *caleta* (cove) of **Xel-Ha** or the new lagoon day-trip to **Xcaret.** And if you're going south, consider staying a night or two on the island of **Cozumel** or at one of the budget resorts on the **Tulum coast** or **Punta Allen,** south of the Tulum ruins. **Isla Mujeres** is an easy day trip off mainland Cancún (see chapter 5).

About 80 miles south of Cancún begins the **Sian Ka'an Biosphere Reserve,** a 1.3 million–acre area set aside in 1986 to preserve a region of tropical forests, savannas, mangroves, canals, lagoons, bays, cenotes, and coral reefs, all of which are home to hundreds of birds and land and marine animals (see chapter 5 for details). The Friends of Sian Ka'an, a nonprofit group based in Cancún, offers biologist-escorted day-trips (weather permitting) from the **Cabañas Ana y José** just south of the Tulum ruins on Monday, Tuesday, Friday, and Saturday for $50 per person using their vehicle or $40 per person if you drive yourself. The price includes chips and soft drinks, round-trip van transportation to the reserve from the Cabañas, a guided boat/birding trip through one of the reserve's lagoons, and use of binoculars. Tours can accommodate up to 19 people. Trips start from the Cabañas at 9:30am and return there around 2:30pm. For reservations, contact Amigos de Sian Ka'an, Cobá 5, Plaza America (☎ **98/84-9583;** fax 98/87-3080) in Cancún. Office hours are 9am to 3pm and 6 to 8pm.

Although I don't recommend it, by driving fast or catching the right buses, you can go inland to **Chichén-Itzá,** explore the ruins, and return in a day, but it's much better to spend at least 2 days seeing Chichén-Itzá, Mérida, and Uxmal. See chapter 6 for transportation details and further information on these destinations.

Reserva Ecologíca El Eden, established in 1990, is a privately owned 500,000-acre reserve dedicated to research for biological conservation in Mexico. Only 30 miles northwest of Cancún, it takes around 2 hours to reach the center of the reserve deep in the jungle. It's intended as an overnight (or more) excursion for people hungering to know more about the biological diversity of the peninsula. Within the reserve, or near to it, are found marine grasslands, mangrove swamps, rain forests, savannas, wetlands, and sand dunes, plus evidence of archaeological sites and at least 205 different species of birds, plus orchids, bromeliads, and cacti. Among the animals are spider monkeys, jaguars, cougars, deer, and ocelots. The "eco-scientific" tours offered include naturalist-led bird watching, animal tracking, star gazing, spotlight surveys for nocturnal wildlife, and exploration of cenotes and Maya ruins. Comfortable, basic accommodations are provided. Tours include transportation from Cancún, 1 or 2 nights accommodation at La Savanna Research Station, meals, nightly cocktail, guided nature walks, and tours. Contact Reserva Ecologíca El Eden, Apdo. Postal 770, 77500 Cancún, Q. Roo (☎ and fax **98/80-5032**). E-mail: mlazcano@cancun.rce.com.mx. Web addresses: http://www.ucr.edu/pril/peten/ images/el eden/home.html and http://www.iminet.com/mexico/eden.html.

Isla Mujeres, Cozumel & the Caribbean Coast

Once obscured by Cancún's glitter, Mexico's other Caribbean vacation spots have shouldered their way into the tourist spotlight. **Isla Mujeres,** just a short ferry ride from Cancún, offers low-priced and low-key Caribbean relaxation. The island of **Cozumel,** somewhere on the spectrum between Isla Mujeres's slow pace and Cancún's fast-lane bustle, has scuba and snorkeling opportunities that compare with any in the world. And the Quintana Roo coast, dubbed the **Costa Turquesa** (Turquoise Coast) or the **Tulum Corridor** as far as Tulum, stretches south from Cancún all the way to Chetumal—230 miles of powdery white-sand beaches, short, scrubby jungle, crystal-clear lagoons full of coral and colorful fish, a few flashy resorts, and inexpensive hideaways. It also includes some hideaway nuggets on both the **Punta Allen Peninsula** and the **Majahual Peninsula.**

Chapter 6 supplies full information on points west of Cancún, such as Chichén-Itzá and Mérida. Let's look now at the islands off the peninsula and the mainland coast south of Cancún.

EXPLORING MEXICO'S CARIBBEAN COAST
ISLA MUJERES

Many people enjoy a brief day-trip to Isla Mujeres on a party boat from Cancún, which is fine if you don't have much time. However, most of these trips provide little time in the village, and you get no sense of what island life is like. Besides loafing, fishing, and snorkeling, diving is one of the island's main attractions. I recommend at least two nights on Isla Mujeres, and you could even spend a whole week relaxing here. Some people over-winter here for months.

Passenger ferries go to Isla Mujeres from Puerto Juárez near Cancún, and car ferries to Isla Mujeres leave from Punta Sam, also near Cancún. More expensive passenger ferries, with less frequent departures than from Puerto Juárez, also go to Isla Mujeres from the Playa Linda pier on Cancún Island.

COZUMEL

This truly laid-back island getaway is a perfect place to relax for a week or more, with opportunities for the best diving in Mexico, good fishing, and excursions to villages and ruins only a ferry ride away on the mainland. If you're considering a package (usually offered for 3 or 4 nights), remember that you'll spend a day coming and going. Buy a longer package if you can. But remember

On the Road in the Yucatán

Here are a few things to keep in mind if you're planning to hit the road and explore the Yucatán.

Except in Cancún, Isla Mujeres, Playa del Carmen, and Cozumel, exchanging money is difficult along this coast. And though Isla Mujeres and Cozumel are breezy enough to keep them at bay, everywhere else on this coast mosquitoes are numerous and fierce, so bring plenty of mosquito repellent that has DEET as the main ingredient. (Avon's Skin So Soft, a bath oil that's acquired quite a reputation in the States for its unexpected effectiveness as an almost pleasant-smelling mosquito repellent, is practically useless here.)

The most economical way, although not the best way, to see the Yucatán is by bus. Although service is still best between the major cities, since 1992 it has improved considerably to other parts of the peninsula as well. There are more deluxe buses and you can sometimes purchase tickets in advance—often selecting your seat on a computer screen. Using buses as the primary means of transportation will add more days to your trip. On highways, you can still flag down buses that are going your way and hop aboard, though you'll spend a lot of time waiting at intersections, particularly near Uxmal and Kabah and along the Caribbean coast. If you're waiting on a busy route—say between Cancún and Tulum—many full buses will pass you by. Distances are deceiving. For example, a bus trip using the new highway from Mérida to Cancún takes 4 hours; bus travel between Mérida and Palenque takes 9 hours. To find the fastest bus, get in the habit of asking if a bus goes *sin escalas* or *directo* (nonstop or direct); either may mean no stops or only a couple of stops as opposed to many stops on a regular bus.

The best way to see the Yucatán is by car. It's one of the most pleasant parts of the country for a driving vacation. The jungle- and beach-lined roads, while narrow and without shoulders, are generally in good condition and have little traffic (except the stretch from Cancún to Tulum). And they are straight, except in the southern part of Yucatán state and west to Campeche, where they undulate through the Yucatán "Alps."

that there are many inexpensive places to stay that won't be part of a package deal, and you can still do all the diving and sightseeing you want.

A car/passenger ferry runs between Puerto Morelos (south of Cancún) and Cozumel. Passenger ferries also run between Playa del Carmen and Cozumel—the preferred way to go, if you aren't flying directly there from your home base.

THE COSTA TURQUESA

Signs pointing to brand-new, expensive resort developments are sprouting up all along Highway 307 from Cancún south to **Tulum,** a stretch known both as the "Tulum Corridor," referring to the distance from Cancún to Tulum, and the "Costa Turquesa," south from Cancún to Chetumal on the Belize border. Some new resorts are actually under construction, whereas others may never progress further than a big sign and a pipe dream. This frenzy of construction is changing the character of the corridor, but there are still plenty of small, inexpensive beachfront hideaways, as well as luxury places, just a short distance from the highway. And south of Tulum, almost 100 miles of this coast have been saved from developers and set aside as the Sian Ka'an Biosphere Reserve.

The four-lane toll road between Cancún and Mérida is complete but actually ends short of either city. Costing around $20 one-way, it cuts the trip from 5 to around 4 hours. The old two-lane free road is still in fine shape and passes through numerous villages with many speed-control bumps (*topes*)—this route is much more interesting. New directional signs seem to lead motorists to the toll road (*cuota*) and don't mention the free road (*libre*), so if you want to use it, ask locals for directions.

A new four-lane stretch of road going out of Cancún south to Playa del Carmen is finished. Originally it was to extend to Chetumal, but the local rumor is that a new toll road instead will parallel the existing two-lane Highway 307 and connect Cancún and Chetumal. Meanwhile, traffic is quite heavy from Cancún to Tulum, and drivers go too fast. A stalled or stopped car is hard to see, and there are no shoulders for pulling off the roadway. Follow these precautions for a safe journey: Never turn left while on the highway (it's against Mexican law anyway). Always go to the next road on the right and turn around and come back to the turnoff you want. Occasionally, a specially constructed right-hand turnoff, such as at Xcaret and Playa del Carmen, allows motorists to pull off to the right in order to cross the road when traffic has passed. Don't speed and don't follow the car in front of you too closely. There have been many accidents and fatalities on this road lately, and these precautions could save your life. After Tulum, traffic is much lighter, but follow these precautions anyway.

Be aware of the long distances in the Yucatán. Mérida, for instance, is 400 miles from Villahermosa, 125 miles from Campeche, and 200 miles from Cancún. Leaded gas (*nova*) is readily available in the Yucatán; unleaded gas (*magna sin*) is available at most stations.

Note: Gas stations are found in all major towns, but they're open only from around 8am to around 7pm. If you're planning to rent a car to travel the area, see "Car Rentals" in chapter 3, "Planning a Trip to the Yucatán."

A trip down the coast is a great way to spend a day of a vacation centered in Cancún. The most popular agency-led tour out of Cancún is to the ruins of Tulum, followed by a stop at Xel-Ha for a swim and/or snorkeling in the beautiful clear lagoon. Once a placid and little-known spot, Xcaret Lagoon opened in 1991 as a full-blown tourist attraction for people who plan to spend the day.

The Costa Turquesa is best experienced in a car. (See chapter 4, "Cancún," for information on rentals.) It's not impossible to get around by bus, but doing so requires careful planning, more time, and lots of patience. Besides Cancún, Playa del Carmen has the best selection of bus services. There are frequent buses between Cancún and Chetumal that stop at the more populous towns—Playa del Carmen, Tulum, and Felipe Carrillo Puerto. These buses will also let you off if you want to go to Xel-Ha, Xcaret, Paamul, or other spots, but you'll have to walk the mile or so from the highway to your destination. However, a few bus lines now take passengers directly into these popular day-trip destinations. (See "By Bus" in chapter 3, "Planning a Trip to the Yucatán," for details.) To return on buses not offering door-to-door service, you'll have to walk back and wait on a sweltering highway along with hordes of ravenous mosquitoes to flag a passing bus—and be prepared to watch buses pass you by if they're full. Hitching a ride with other travelers is another possibility, though I don't recommend hitchhiking on the highway. You can always hire a taxi for the return to Cancún.

Highway 307 south of Cancún is flanked by jungle on both sides, except where there are beaches and beach settlements. Traffic, which was once scarce, can be dangerously dense. (See "On the Road in the Yucatán," above.)

Here are some drive times from Cancún: Puerto Morelos (port for the car ferry to Cozumel and a sleepy beachside town), 45 minutes; Playa del Carmen (a laid-back beachside village), 1 hour; Xcaret Lagoon and Paamul, 1 1/4 hours; Akumal, 1 3/4 hours; Xel-Ha and Tulum, around 2 hours; and Chetumal, about 5 hours.

THE PUNTA ALLEN & MAJAHUAL PENINSULAS

These two areas will appeal to people looking for totally off-the-beaten-track travel, and/or for world-class adventure sports. Punta Allen's saltwater fly-fishing is extraordinary, and the Chinchorro Banks, 22 miles off Majahual's little village of Xcalak, is perhaps the last example of a pristine Caribbean reef—the diving is spectacular. Both places are hard to get to, have beautiful beaches, are overrun by exotic birdlife and jungle flora, and have a few laid-back, rustic inns to stay at.

THE RÍO BEC RUIN ROUTE

Between Lago Bacalar and Escarcega, in Campeche state, is the Río Bec ruin route, where several "new" sites are open to the public and others are available with special permission.

CHETUMAL

Though Chetumal is the capital of Quintana Roo state, it is an ugly and unfriendly city with little to recommend it. It's best to think of it as a gateway to Guatemala, Belize, the several ruins near the city, and the excellent diving and fishing to be had off the Xcalak Peninsula. In 1995 a fantastic museum opened in Chetumal, and the reexcavation of many of the ruins near Chetumal may be a reason for a detour there, but Lago Bacalar is the preferred place to stay near Chetumal.

1   Isla Mujeres

10 miles N of Cancún

For total, laid-back, inexpensive Caribbean relaxation, it's hard to beat Isla Mujeres. Often called the "poor man's Cancún," Isla Mujeres is a bargain compared to Cancún—and I much prefer it. The sand streets have been bricked, and some of the original Caribbean-style clapboard houses remain to add a colorful and authentic reminder of the island's past. Suntanned visitors hang out in open-air cafes and stroll streets lined with souvenir vendors who beckon them like carnival barkers.

As packed as days can be—with trips to the Isla Contoy bird sanctuary and excellent diving, fishing, and snorkeling—in the evenings most people find the slow, relaxing pace one of the island's biggest draws. It is then that the island is bathed in a cool breeze, perfect for casual open-air dining and drinking in small streetside restaurants. Most people pack it in as early as 9 or 10pm, when most of the businesses close. Restless night owls, however, will find kindred souls at a few bars on Playa Norte that stay open until the wee hours.

There are at least two versions of how Isla Mujeres ("Island of Women") got its name. The more popular story claims that pirates parked their women here for safekeeping while they were marauding the Spanish Main. The other account attributes the name to conquistador Francisco Hernández de Córdoba, who was reportedly impressed by the large number of female terra-cotta figurines he found in temples on the island.

ESSENTIALS
GETTING THERE & DEPARTING

Puerto Juárez, just north of Cancún, is the dock for the passenger ferries to Isla Mujeres. The *Caribbean Queen* makes the 45-minute trip many times daily. The newer *Caribbean Express* makes thè trip in 20 minutes; both are inexpensive. Ferries run frequently between 6am and 8pm. Pay at the ticket office, or if the ferry is about to leave, you can pay aboard.

Taxi fares are now posted by the street where the taxis park; be sure to check the rate before agreeing to a taxi, since these drivers will gleefully charge the uninformed double the posted rate.

Isla Mujeres is so small that a vehicle isn't necessary, but if you're taking a vehicle to Isla Mujeres, you'll use the **Punta Sam** port a little farther past Puerto Juárez. The ferry runs the 40-minute trip five or six times daily all year except in bad weather (check with the tourist office in Cancún for a current schedule). Cars should arrive an hour in advance of the ferry departure to register for a place in line and pay the posted fee.

There are also boats to Isla Mujeres from the Playa Linda pier in Cancún, but they're less frequent and much more expensive than those from Puerto Juárez. The Playa Linda ferries simply don't run if there isn't a crowd. A new **Watertaxi** (☎ 98/86-4270 or 98/86-4847) to Isla Mujeres operates from Playa Caracol, between the Fiesta Americana Coral Beach Hotel and the Xcaret terminal on the island, with prices about the same as those from Playa Linda, both of which are about four times the cost of the public ferries from Puerto Juárez. Their scheduled departures are 9 and 11am and 1 and 3pm with returns from Isla Mujeres at 10am, noon, 2pm, and 5pm.

To get to either Puerto Juárez or Punta Sam from Cancún, take any Ruta 8 city bus from Avenida Tulum. If you're coming from Mérida, you can either fly to Cancún and then proceed by bus to Puerto Juárez, or you can take a first- or second-class bus directly from the Mérida bus station to Puerto Juárez; they leave several times a day. From Cozumel, you can either fly to Cancún (there are daily flights) or take a ferry to Playa del Carmen (see the Cozumel section below for details), where you can catch a bus to Puerto Juárez.

ORIENTATION

Ferries arrive at the dock in the center of town. Unless you're loaded with luggage, you don't need transportation, since most hotels are close by. However, tricycle taxis are the least expensive and a merry way to get to your hotel; you and your luggage pile in the open carriage compartment while the "driver" effortlessly peddles through the streets. Regular taxis are always lined up in a parking lot to the right of the pier. Their rates are posted where they line up. The price gets lower if you wait until all passengers have left the area. Negotiate directly with the driver, not a representative who recruits passengers on the pier by quoting half the price the driver actually charges.

VISITOR INFORMATION

The **City Tourist Office** (☎ and fax **987/7-0316**) is on the second floor of the Plaza Isla Mujeres. You'll find it at the northern end of Juárez, between López Mateos and Matamoros, It's open Monday through Friday 9am to 2:30pm and 7 to 9pm. Also look for *Islander,* a free publication with history, local information, advertisements, and a list of events (if any).

ISLAND LAYOUT

Isla Mujeres is about 5 miles long and 2¹/₂ miles wide. The **ferry docks** are right at the center of town, within walking distance of most hotels, restaurants, and shops. The street running along the waterfront is **Rueda Medina,** commonly called the **Malecón.** The **market** (Mercado Municipal) is by the post office on **Calle Guerrero,** an inland street at the north edge of town, which, like most streets in the town, is unmarked.

GETTING AROUND

A popular form of transportation on Isla Mujeres is the electric golf cart, available for rent at many hotels for $10 per hour or $50 per day. They don't go more than 20 miles per hour, so don't expect to speed around the island, but they're fun. Anyway, on Isla Mujeres you aren't there to hurry. Many people enjoy touring the island by moto, the local sobriquet for motorized bikes and scooters. If you don't want to fool with shifting gears, rent a fully automatic one for around $25 to $30 per day or $6 per hour. They come with seats for one person, but some are large enough for two. Whatever you rent, take time to get familiar with how the vehicles work, and be careful on the road as you approach blind corners and hills where visibility is poor. There's only one main road with a couple of offshoots, so you won't get lost. Be aware that the rental price does not include insurance, and any injury to yourself or the vehicle will come out of your pocket. Bicycles are also available for rent at some hotels for $5 per day.

FAST FACTS: ISLA MUJERES

Area Code   The area code of Isla Mujeres is 987. The first digit for all telephone numbers on the island has been changed from 2 to 7.

Hospital   The Hospital de la Armada, on Medina at Ojon P. Blanco (☎ 987/ 7-0001). It's half a mile south of the town center.

Post Office/Telegraph Office   The correo is on Calle Guerrero, by the market.

Telephone   There's a long-distance telephone office in the lobby of the Hotel María José, Avenida Madero at Medina, open Monday through Saturday from 9am to 1pm and 4 to 8pm. There are Ladatel phones accepting coins and prepaid phone cards at the plaza.

Tourist Seasons   Isla Mujeres's tourist season (when hotel rates are higher) is a bit different from that of other places in Mexico. High season runs December through May, a month longer than in Cancún; some hotels raise their rates in August and some hotels raise their rates beginning in mid-November. Low season is June through mid-November.

BEACHES, WATER SPORTS & OTHER ATTRACTIONS
THE BEACHES

The most popular beach in town used to be called Playa Cocoteros (Coco for short). Then, in 1988, Hurricane Gilbert destroyed the coconut palms on the beach. Gradually, the name has been changed to **Playa Norte,** referring to the long stretch of beach that extends around the northern tip of the island, to your left as you get off the boat. This is a truly splendid beach—a wide swath of fine white sand and calm, lucidly clear, turquoise-blue water. Topless sunbathing is tolerated here. The beach is easily reached on foot from the ferry and from all downtown hotels. Water-sports

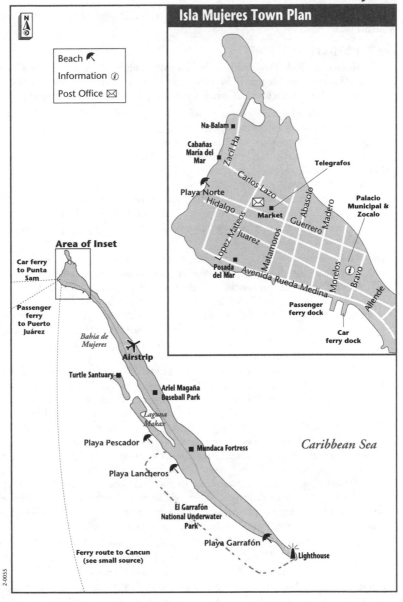

Isla Mujeres Town Plan

equipment, beach umbrellas, and lounge chairs are available for rent. Those in front of restaurants usually cost nothing if you use the restaurant as your headquarters for drinks and food. New palms are beginning to sprout all over Playa Norte, and it won't be long until it will be deserving of its previous name.

Garrafón National Park is known best as a snorkeling area, but there is a nice stretch of beach on either side of the park. **Playa Lancheros** is on the Caribbean side of Laguna Makax. Local buses go to Lancheros, then turn inland and return downtown. The beach at Playa Lancheros is nice, but the few restaurants there are high-priced.

WATER SPORTS

SWIMMING   Wide Playa Norte is the best swimming beach, with Playa Lancheros second. There are no lifeguards on duty on Isla Mujeres, and the system of water-safety flags used in Cancún and Cozumel isn't used here either. Be very careful!

SNORKELING   By far the most popular place to snorkel is **Garrafón National Park,** at the southern end of the island, where you'll see numerous schools of color-ful fish. The well-equipped park has beach chairs, changing rooms, rental lockers, showers, and a snack bar. Admission is $2. Also good for snorkeling is the **Manchones Reef,** which is just off shore and reached by boat, where a bronze cross was installed in 1994.

Another excellent location is in the **Bahía de Mujeres** near the lighthouse at the southern tip of the island, where the water is about 6 feet deep. Boatmen will take you for around $10 per person if you have your own snorkeling equipment, or $15 more if you use theirs.

DIVING   Several dive shops have opened on the island, most offering the same trips. The traditional dive center is **Buzos de México,** on Rueda Medina at Morelos (☎ **987/7-0500**), next to the boat cooperative. Dive instructor Carlos Gutiérrez speaks English, French, and Italian and offers certification (5 to 6 days for $300) and resort courses ($80 with three dives), and makes sure all dives are led by certified dive masters. **Bahia Dive Shop,** on Rueda Medina 166 across from the car-ferry dock (☎ and fax **987/7-0340**), is a full-service shop with dive equipment for sale and rent and resort and certification classes.

All 30- to 40-foot dives cost $40 to $70 for a two-tank trip; equipment rental costs $15. Cuevas de los Tiburones (Caves of the Sleeping Sharks) is Isla's most famous dive site and costs $60 to $80 for a two-tank dive at a depth of 70 feet. There are actually two places to see the sleeping sharks—the Cuevas de Tiberones and La Punta. During a storm, the arch that was featured in a Jacques Cousteau film collapsed, but the caves are still there. However, your chance of actually seeing sleeping sharks, by the way, is about one in four; fewer sharks are present than in the past. The best time to see them is January through March. Other dive sites include a wreck 9 kilome-ters off shore; Banderas Reef, between Isla Mujeres and Cancún, where there's always a strong current; Tabos Reef on the eastern shore; and Manchones Reef, 1 kilome-ter off the southeastern tip of the island, where the water is 15 to 35 feet deep. The best season for diving is from June through August, when the water is calm.

FISHING   To arrange a day of fishing, ask at the **Sociedad Cooperativa Turística** (boatmen's cooperative; ☎ **987/7-0274**) or the travel agency mentioned below, un-der Isla Contoy. The cost can be shared with four to six others and includes lunch and drinks. All year you'll find bonito, mackerel, kingfish, and amberjack. Sailfish and sharks (hammerhead, bull, nurse, lemon, and tiger) are in good supply in April and May. In winter, larger grouper and jewfish are prevalent. Four hours of fishing close to shore costs around $100; 8 hours farther out goes for $240. The coopera-tive is open Monday through Saturday from 8am to 1pm and 5 to 8pm, and Sun-day from 7:30 to 10am and 6 to 8pm.

A TURTLE SANCTUARY

Easily the most interesting outing on the island is to this reserve dedicated to preserving Caribbean sea turtles and educating the public about them.

As few as 20 years ago fishermen converged on the island nightly from May through September waiting for these monster-size turtles to lumber ashore to deposit their flimsy Ping-Pong-ball–sized eggs. Totally vulnerable once the turtles begin laying their eggs, and exhausted when they finished, the turtles were easily captured and slaughtered for their highly prized meat, shell, and eggs. Then a concerned fisherman, Gonzalez Cahle Maldonado, began convincing fishermen to spare at least the eggs, which he protected. It was a start. Following his lead, the Fishing Secretariat founded this **Centro de Investigaciones** 10 years ago; it's funded by both the government and private donations. Since then at least 28,000 turtles have been released and every year local schoolchildren participate in the event, thus planting the notion of protecting the turtles within a new generation of islanders.

Six different species of sea turtles nest on Isla Mujeres. An adult green turtle, the most abundant species, measures 4 to 5 feet in length and can weigh as much as 450 pounds when grown. At the center, visitors walk through the indoor and outdoor turtle pool areas, watching the creatures paddling around. The turtles are separated by age, from newly hatched up to one year. Besides protecting the turtles that nest on Isla Mujeres of their own accord, the program also calls for capturing the turtles at sea and bringing them to enclosed compounds to mate and later to be freed to nest on Isla Mujeres. They are tagged and then released. While in the care of the center, these guests receive a high-protein diet and reportedly grow faster than in the wild. People who come here usually end up staying at least an hour, especially if they opt for the guided tour, which enhances a visit. The permanent shelter has large wall paintings of all the sea turtles of the area. The sanctuary is on a spit of land separated from the island by Bahía de Mujeres and Laguna Makax; you'll need a taxi to get there. Admission is $1; the shelter is open daily from 9am to 5pm.

A MAYA RUIN

Just beyond the lighthouse, at the southern end of the island, is a pile of stones that formed a small Maya pyramid before Hurricane Gilbert struck. Believed to have been an observatory built to the moon goddess Ixchel, now it's reduced to a rocky heap. The location, on a lofty bluff overlooking the sea, is still worth seeing. If you're at Garrafón National Park and want to walk, it's not too far. Turn right from Garrafón. When you see the lighthouse, turn toward it down the rocky path.

A PIRATE'S FORTRESS

The Fortress of Mundaca is about 2¹/₂ miles in the same direction as Garrafón, about half a mile to the left. The fortress was built by the pirate Mundaca Marecheaga, who in the early 19th century arrived at Isla Mujeres and proceeded to set up a blissful paradise in a pretty, shady spot while making money from selling slaves to Cuba and Belize.

A VISIT TO ISLA CONTOY

If at all possible, plan to visit this pristine, uninhabited island, 19 miles by boat from Isla Mujeres, which was set aside as a national wildlife reserve in 1981. The oddly shaped 3.8-mile-long island is covered in lush vegetation and harbors 70 species of birds and a host of marine and animal life. Bird species that nest on the island include pelicans, brown boobies, frigates, egrets, terns, and cormorants. Flocks of flamingos arrive in April. June, July, and August are good months to spot turtles that bury their eggs in the sand at night. Most excursions troll for fish (which will be your lunch), anchor en route for a snorkeling expedition, and skirt the island at a leisurely pace for close viewing of the birds without disturbing the habitat, then pull ashore. While the captain prepares lunch, visitors can swim, sun, follow the nature trails, and visit the fine nature museum. For a while the island was closed to visitors, but it's reopened now after rules for its use and safety were agreed to by fishermen and those bringing visitors. The trip from Isla Mujeres takes a minimum of 1 ¹/₂ hours one-way, more if the waves are choppy. Because of the tight-knit boatmen's cooperative, prices for this excursion are the same everywhere—$30. You can buy a ticket at the **Sociedad Cooperativa Turística** (☎ 987/7-0274) on Avenida Rueda Medina, next to Mexico Divers and Las Brisas restaurant, or at one of several travel agencies, such as **La Isleña,** on Morelos between Medina and Juárez (☎ 987/7-0578). La Isleña is open daily from 7am to 9pm and is a good source for tourist information. Contoy trips leave at 8:30am and return around 4pm.

Three types of boats go to Contoy. Small boats have one motor and seat eight or nine people. Medium-size boats have two motors and hold 10. Large boats have a toilet and hold 16 passengers. Most boats have a sun cover. The first two types are being phased out in favor of larger, better boats. Boat captains should respect the cooperative's regulations regarding capacity and should have enough life jackets to go around. Snorkeling equipment is usually included in the price, but double-check that before heading out. I highly recommend the services of English-speaking boat owner **Ricardo Gaitan** (☎ 987/7-0434), who has two boats: the *Afroditi,* a 30-foot speedboat holding up to 15 people, and the 37-foot trimaran *Pelicano,* good for day-trips and overnight excursions. It sleeps up to six people or carries 15 passengers for day-trips. Call him, or write to him directly: P.O. Box 42, 77400 Isla Mujeres, Q. Roo.

SHOPPING

Shopping is a casual activity here. There are only a few glittery, sleek shops. But you may be bombarded by shop owners, especially on Hidalgo, selling Saltillo rugs, onyx, silver, Guatemalan clothing, blown glassware, masks, folk art, beach paraphernalia, and T-shirts in abundance. Prices are also lower than in Cancún or Cozumel, but with the overeager sellers, bargaining is necessary to achieve a satisfactory price.

One store stands out from the rest: **La Loma,** Guerrero 6 (☎ 987/7-0223), stocks a great variety of good folk art, including Huichol yarn "paintings," masks, silver chains and coins, a good selection of textiles, Oaxacan wood carvings, Olinalá lacquer objects, and colorful clay candelabras from Izúcar de Matamoros. You'll see it opposite the left side of the church beside La Peña restaurant, and almost next to the Hotel Perla del Caribe II. It's open Monday through Saturday from 10am to 3pm and 5 to 8pm.

WHERE TO STAY

There are plenty of hotels in all price ranges on Isla Mujeres. Rates are at their peak during high season, which is the most expensive and most crowded time to go. Elizabeth Wenger of **Four Seasons Travel** in Montello, WI (☎ 800/552-4550) specializes in Mexico travel and especially books a lot of hotels in Isla Mujeres. Her service is invaluable in high season when hotel occupancy is high.

VERY EXPENSIVE

✪ **Puerto Isla Mujeres Resort & Yacht Club.** Puerto de Abrigo Laguna Macax, Isla Mujeres, Q. Roo. ☎ **800/960-ISLA** in the U.S., 987/7-0330 or 987/83-3208 in Cancún. Fax 987/ 83-0485 or 98/83-1228 in Cancún. 30 rms. A/C MINIBAR TV TEL. High season $270 suite. Low season $225 suite. Villas $250–$530. Rates include transportation from Cancún and daily continental breakfast and dinner.

The concept here—an exclusive glide-up yachting/sailing resort—is new not only to Isla Mujeres, but to all of Mexico. Opened in 1995 and facing an undeveloped portion of the glass-smooth, mangrove-edged Macax Lagoon, Puerto Isla Mujeres's modern suites and villas, with sloping white stucco walls and red tile roofs, are spread across spacious palm-filled grounds. Beautifully designed with Scandinavian and Mediterranean elements, guest quarters feature tile, wood-beamed ceilings, natural wood and marble accents, televisions with VCRs, stereos with CD changers, and living areas. Villas have two bedrooms upstairs with a full bath and a small bathroom downstairs with a shower. Each villa also features a small, stylish kitchen area with dishwasher, microwave, refrigerator, and coffeemaker. A whirlpool is on the upper patio off the master bedroom. Since weather is of consideration to the boating crowd, nightly turndown service leaves the next day's weather forecast on the pillow beside the requisite chocolate. The beach club, with refreshments, is a water-taxi ride across the lagoon on a beautiful stretch of beach. A staff biologist can answer questions about birds and water life on Isla Mujeres. Besides two meals, an afternoon snack is delivered to each room. More suites and villas are on the drawing board.

Dining/Entertainment: Two excellent restaurants, one indoors and one outdoors by the pool, gourmet deli, small grocery store.

Services: Transportation from the Cancún airport by Chevy Suburban and private yacht to Isla Mujeres; full-service marina with 60 slips for 30- to 60-foot vessels, short- and long-term dockage, fueling station, charter yachts and sailboats, and sailing school; mopeds, golf carts, bicycles, and water-sports equipment for rent; video and CD library.

Facilities: Laundry and room service, nearby beach club, free-form swimming pool with swim-up bar.

EXPENSIVE

Hotel Cabañas María del Mar. Av. Carlos Lazo 1, 77400 Isla Mujeres, Q. Roo. ☎ 800/ 826-6842 in the U.S., or 987/7-0179. Fax 987/7-0173. 56 rms. A/C. High season $70–$75 double. Low season $45–$50 double. Rates include continental breakfast.

A good choice, the Cabañas María del Mar is located on Playa Norte, a half block from the Hotel Nabalam. There are three completely different sections to this hotel. The older two-story section, behind the reception area and beyond the garden, offers nicely outfitted rooms facing the beach, all with two single or double beds, refrigerators, and balconies with ocean views. Eleven single-story cabañas closer to the reception and pool are rather dark and are the lowest priced. The newest addition, El Castillo, is across the street and built over and beside Buho's restaurant. It contains all "deluxe" rooms, but some are larger than others; the five rooms on the ground floor all have large patios and are the most appealing. Upstairs rooms have small balconies. Most have one double bed. All have ocean views, blue-and-white tile floors, and tile lavatories and are outfitted in natural-toned neocolonial furniture. There's a small, unkempt pool in the garden. The owners also have a bus for tours and a boat for rental, as well as golf cart and moto rental.

To get here from the pier, walk left 1 block, then turn right on Matamoros. After 4 blocks, turn left on Lazo, the last street. The hotel is at the end of the block.

✪**Hotel Na Balam Beach Hotel.** Zacil Ha 118, 77400 Isla Mujeres, Q. Roo. ☎ **987/7-0279.** Fax 987/7-0446. E-mail: nabalam@cancun.rce.com.mx. 31 suites. A/C and FAN. High season $95 suite. Low·season $80 suite. Free unguarded parking.

This two-story hotel near the end of Playa Norte is my favorite of the island's lodgings, with its comfortable rooms on a quiet, ideally located portion of the beach. It seems to get better each year. Rooms are in three sections, with some facing the beach and others across the street in a garden setting where there's a swimming pool. All rooms have either a patio or balcony. Each fashionably furnished, spacious suite contains two double beds, a seating area, and folk-art decorations. Though other rooms are newer, my preference is the older section with a bottom-floor patio facing the peaceful palm-filled sandy inner yard and Playa Norte. Tuesday through Thursday, yoga lessons are offered; ask about the time and price. The restaurant, Zacil-Ha, is one of the island's most popular (see "Where to Dine," below). To find it from the pier, walk 5 blocks to López Mateos; turn right and walk 4 blocks to Lazo (the last street). Turn left and walk to the sandy road parallel to the beach and turn right. The hotel is half a block farther.

MODERATE

Hotel Perla del Caribe I. Av. Madero 2 (at Guerrero), 77400 Isla Mujeres, Q. Roo. ☎ **800/ 258-6454** in the U.S., or 987/7-044. Fax 987/7-0011. 86 rms. A/C (44 rms) and FAN (42 rms). High season $55–$65 double. Low season $40–$45 double.

The Perla del Caribe I and its sister Perla del Caribe II at Av. Norte and Guerrero always seem a bit overpriced no matter what the peso is doing; it's worth it to ask about discounts and packages. Located on the eastern shore, where a heavy surf crashes rhythmically against a newly built seawall, you can't swim or enjoy a beach here, but it's one of the few island hotels with a pool—and it's a nice one, though not shaded and not as idyllic as the one at the Hotel Posada del Mar. In short, you're paying for a pool, the water-side location, motel-like rooms, and a restaurant on the grounds. Rooms are comfortable but ordinary with tile floors and balconies. A hotel representative often meets the ferries to transport guests and their luggage to the hotel. The hotel also rents golf carts to buzz around town. It's 5 blocks inland from the ferry pier, at the corner of Madero and Guerrero.

✪ **Hotel Posada del Mar.** Av. Rueda Medina 15, 77400 Isla Mujeres, Q. Roo. ☎ **800/ 221-6509** in the U.S., or 987/7-0044. Fax 987/7-0266. E-mail: hposada@cancun.rce.com.mx. Web site: iminet.com/mexico/posada.htm. 40 rms. A/C TEL. High season $54–$60 double. Low season $42–$48 double. Ask about special: 7 nights for the price of 5.

Attractively furnished, quiet, and comfortable, this long-established hotel faces the water and a wide beach 3 blocks north of the ferry pier, and it has one of the few swimming pools on the island. The very spacious rooms, all with a fresh coat of white paint, are in a large garden palm grove in either a three-story building or in one-story bungalow units. For the spacious quality of the rooms and the location, this hotel is among the best buys on the island. A wide, seldom used but appealing stretch of Playa Norte is across the street. An extremely appealing casual palapa-style bar and a lovely pool are set on the back lawn, and the popular restaurant Pinguino (see "Where to Dine," below) is by the sidewalk at the front of the property. Ask about specials— 4 nights for the price of 3 and 7 nights for the price of 5. From the pier, go left for 4 blocks; the hotel is on the right.

INEXPENSIVE

Hotel Belmar. Av. Hidalgo 110, 74000 Isla Mujeres, Q. Roo. ☎ **987/7-0430.** Fax 987/ 7-0429. 11 rms. A/C and FAN TV TEL. High season $45 double. Low season $30 double.

Situated above Pizza Rolandi (consider the restaurant noise), this hotel is run by the same people who serve up those wood-oven pizzas. Each of the simple but stylish rooms comes with two twin or double beds and handsome tile accents. Prices are high for no views, but the rooms are very pleasant. On the other hand, this is one of the few island hotels with televisions (bringing in U.S. channels) in the room. The hotel is between Madero and Abasolo, 3½ blocks from the passenger ferry pier.

✪ **Hotel D'Gomar.** Rueda Medina 50, 77400 Isla Mujeres, Q. Roo. ☎ **987/7-0540.** 16 rms. FAN and A/C. High season $30–$35 double. Low season $20–$25 double.

You can hardly beat this hotel for comfort at reasonable prices. Rooms, with rattan furniture, all have two double beds, pink walls and drapes, and a wall of windows providing great breezes and picture views. The higher prices are for air-conditioning, which is hardly needed with the fantastic breezes and ceiling fans. Manager Manuel Serano says, "We make friends of all our clients," and indeed I think he does. The only drawback is that there are five stories of rooms and no elevator. But it's conveniently located catercorner (look right) from the ferry pier, and the rooftop views can't be beat anywhere on the island. The name of the hotel is the most visible sign on the "skyline."

✪ **Hotel Francis Arlene.** Guerrero 7, 77400 Isla Mujeres, Q. Roo. ☎ and fax **987/7-0310,** 988/84-3302 in Cancún. 17 rms. A/C or FAN. High season $25–$35 double. Low season $20–$24 double.

The Magaña family operates this neat little two-story inn behind the family home, which is built around a small, shady courtyard. You'll notice the tidy cream-and-white facade of the building from the street. Rooms are clean and comfortable, with tile floors and all-tile baths, and soap and towels laid out on your bed. Each downstairs room has a refrigerator and stove; each upstairs room comes with a refrigerator and toaster. All have either a balcony or a patio. Rates were substantially better if quoted in pesos and are reflected above. In dollars they are 15% to 20% higher. It's 5$^{1}/_{2}$ blocks inland from the ferry pier, between Abasolo and Matamoros.

Hotel Vistamar. Av. Rueda Medina, 77400 Isla Mujeres, Q. Roo. ☎ **987/7-0209.** 36 rooms (all with bath). A/C or FAN. High season $15–$18 double. Low season $11–$15.50 double.

The name means "sea view," which is indeed what you get if you select a room facing the Malecón. Other rooms have interior windows without views. All units have green-tile floors and ruffled bedspreads and are extremely simple but well kept. Of course, rooms with air-conditioning command the highest prices. The hotel is across from a nice stretch of beach and shoreline, and Playa Norte is almost around the corner. The hotel is on the Malecón, between Abasolo and Matamoros, 1$^{1}/_{2}$ blocks to the left of the ferry pier.

WHERE TO DINE

The **Municipal Market,** next door to the telegraph office and post office on Avenida Guerrero, has several little cookshops operated by obliging and hard-working señoras and enjoyed by numbers of tourists. On Sunday, Nacho Beh, El Rey del Taco (The King of the Taco), prepares sublime cochinita pibil tacos. Get there early.

At the **Panadería La Reyna,** at Madero and Juárez, you can pick up inexpensive sweet bread, muffins, cookies, and yogurt. It's open Monday through Saturday from 7am to 9:30pm.

As in the rest of Mexico, a **cocina economica** restaurant literally means "economic kitchen." Usually aimed at the local population, these are almost universally great places to find good food at rock-bottom prices. That's especially so on Isla Mujeres, where you'll find several.

MODERATE

✪ **Las Palapas Chimbo's.** Playa Norte. No phone. Breakfast $2–$3; sandwiches and fruit $2–$3.50; seafood $5–$8. Daily 8am–6pm. SEAFOOD.

If you're looking for a beachside palapa-covered restaurant where you can wiggle your toes in the sand while scarfing down fresh seafood, this is the best of them. Locals recommend it as their favorite on Playa Norte. Try the delicious fried fish (a whole one), which comes with rice, beans, and tortillas. You'll notice the bandstand and dance floor that have been added to the middle of the restaurant, and especially the sex-hunk posters all over the ceiling—that is, when you aren't gazing at the beach and the Caribbean. Chimbo's becomes a disco at night, and draws a motley crew of drinkers and dancers. (See "Isla Mujeres After Dark," below, for details.) To find it from the pier, walk left to the end of the Malecón, then right onto the Playa Norte; it's about half a block on the right.

✪ **Pinguino.** In the Hotel Posada del Mar, Av. Rueda Medina 15. ☎ **987/7-0300.** Breakfast $2–$3; main courses $3.75–$6.75; daily special $6. Daily 7am–9pm; bar open to midnight. MEXICAN/SEAFOOD.

The best seats on the waterfront are on the deck of this restaurant/bar, especially in late evening when islanders and tourists arrive to dance and party. This is the place to splurge on lobster—you'll get a beautifully presented, large, sublimely fresh lobster tail with a choice of butter, garlic, and secret sauces. Breakfasts include fresh fruit, yogurt, and granola or sizable platters of eggs, served with homemade wheat bread. At night it's one of "the" places to be. Pinguino is in front of the hotel, 3 blocks west of the ferry pier.

Pizza Rolandi. Av. Hidalgo. ☎ **987/7-0429.** Main courses $3.75–$27; pizza $6–$18. Daily 1–11pm. ITALIAN.

Pizza Rolandi, a chain that saves the day with dependably good, reasonably priced food amid other expensive resorts, comes through in Isla Mujeres as well. In the casual dining room, in an open courtyard of the Hotel Belmar, you can munch on plate-size pizzas, pastas, and calzones cooked in a wood oven. There's also a more expensive menu with fish, beef, and chicken dishes. Guitarists often perform in the evenings. It's 3¹/₂ blocks inland from the pier, between Madero and Abasolo.

✪ **Zacil-Ha.** At the Hotel Na Balam, Playa Norte. ☎ **987/7-0279.** Breakfast $3.50–$4.50; main courses $6–$9. Daily 7:30am–10pm; breakfast 7:30–10:30am, lunch 12:30–3:30pm, dinner 7–10pm. INTERNATIONAL.

At this restaurant you can enjoy some of the island's best food while sitting among the palms and gardens at tables on the sand. The serene environment is enhanced by the food—terrific pasta with garlic, shrimp in tequila sauce, fajitas, seafood pasta, and delicious mole enchiladas. Main courses come with a vegetable and rice. Between the set hours for meals you can have all sorts of enticing food, such as blender vegetable and fruit drinks, tacos and sandwiches, ceviche, and terrific nachos. It's likely you'll stake this place out for several meals before you leave. It's at the end of Playa Norte and almost at the end of Calle Zacil-Ha.

INEXPENSIVE

✪ **Cafecito.** Calle Juárez. ☎ **987/7-0438.** Coffee drinks $1–$3; crepes $1.75–$3.75; breakfast $2–$4; main courses $4.75–$7. Mon–Wed and Fri–Sat 8am–noon and 6–10pm; Thurs and Sun 8am–noon. CREPES/ICE CREAM/COFFEES/FRUIT DRINKS.

Sabina and Luis Rivera own this cute, Caribbean-blue corner restaurant where you can begin the day with flavorful coffee and a croissant and cream cheese, or end it with a hot-fudge sundae. Terrific crepes are served with yogurt, ice cream, fresh fruit, or chocolate sauces, as well as ham and cheese. The two-page ice-cream menu satisfies most any craving—even one for waffles with ice cream and fruit. The three-course, fixed-price dinner starts with soup, then a main course such as fish or curried shrimp with rice and salad, followed by dessert. It's 4 blocks from the pier at the corner of Juárez and Matamoros.

✪ **Chen Huaye.** Bravo 6. No phone. Breakfast $1.75–$2.50; main course $1.75–$5. Thurs–
Tues 9am–11pm. MEXICAN/HOME COOKING.

The Juanito Tago Trego family owns this large lunchroom where tourists and locals
find a variety of pleasing dishes at equally pleasing prices. Light meals include
empañadas, Yucatecan salubites, panucos, and quesadillas. The *tamal costado,* a tamal
stuffed with hunks of chicken and baked in a banana leaf, is a daily special. Main
courses might include breaded pork chops, chicken in adobado, or fried chicken. The
name, by the way, is Maya for "only here." It's between Guerrero and Juárez; you'll
spot it by the wagon wheel in front.

✪ **Cocina Economica Carmelita.** Calle Juárez 14. ☎ **987/7-0136.** Meal of the day $3. Daily
12:30–5pm. MEXICAN/HOME COOKING.

Few tourists find their way to this tiny restaurant, open only for lunch. But locals
know they can get a filling, inexpensive, home-cooked meal prepared by Carmelita
in the back kitchen and served by her husband at the three cloth-covered tables in
the front room of their home. Two or three comida corridas are available each day
and are served until they run out. They begin with black bean soup and include a
fruit water drink. If offered, try the *Brazo de la Reina,* which is a large, sliced, very
flavorful and filling Maya tamal stuffed with hard-boiled eggs and spices. If it's not
on the menu, make a request and see if it can be prepared during your stay. Other
selections include paella or *cochinita pibil,* and Sunday is *pozole* day. It's two blocks
from the passenger ferry pier, between Bravo and Allende.

ISLA MUJERES AFTER DARK

Those in a party mood by day's end might want to start out at the beach bar of the
Hotel Na Balam on Playa Norte, which hosts a crowd until around midnight. On
Saturday and Sunday there's live music here between 4 and 7pm. **Las Palapas
Chimbo's** restaurant on the beach becomes a jivin' dance joint with a live band from
9pm on. Farther along the same stretch of beach, **Buho's,** the restaurant/beach bar
of the Posada María del Mar, has its moments as a popular, low-key hangout.
Pinguino's in the Hotel Posada del Mar offers a most convivial late-night hangout.
There are two places to be: the restaurant/bar, where the manager, Miguel, whips up
some potent concoctions at the bar and the band plays nightly during high season
from 9pm to midnight, and the more tranquil but totally delightful poolside bar, with
swings under a giant palapa.

2 Cozumel

44 miles SE of Cancún

Cozumel, 12 miles from Playa del Carmen, comes from the Maya word *Cuzamil,* meaning "land of the swallows." It's Mexico's largest Caribbean island, 28 miles long and
11 miles wide, but it's only 3% developed, leaving vast stretches of jungle and uninhabited shoreline. The only town is San Miguel de Cozumel, usually called just San Miguel.

Today Cozumel is one of the Yucatán's top resort destinations as well as the
country's scuba-diving capital. It's also home to two species of birds that are found
nowhere else—the Cozumel vireo and the Cozumel thrasher. If Cancún is the jet-
set's port of call and Isla Mujeres is the poor man's Cancún, Cozumel is a little bit
of both. More remote than the other two, this island (pop. 60,000) is a place where
people come to get away from the day-tripping atmosphere of Isla Mujeres or the
megadevelopment of Cancún.

All the necessities for a good vacation are here: excellent snorkeling and scuba places, sailing and water sports, expensive resorts and modest hotels, elegant restaurants and taco shops, and even a Maya ruin or two. If, after a while, you do get restless, the ancient Maya city of Tulum, the lagoons of Xel-Ha and Xcaret, or the nearby village of Playa del Carmen provide convenient and interesting excursions.

During pre-Hispanic times the island was one of three important ceremonial centers (Izamal and Chichén-Itzá were the other two). Salt and honey, trade products produced on the island, further linked Cozumel with the mainland; they were brought ashore at the ruins we know today as Tulum. The site was occupied when Hernán Cortés landed here in 1519. Before his own boat docked, Cortés's men sacked the town and took the chief's wife and children captive. According to Bernal Díaz del Castillo's account, everything was returned. Diego de Landa's account says Cortés converted the Indians and replaced their sacred Maya figures with a cross and a statue of Mary in the main temple at Cozumel. After the Spanish Conquest, the island was an important port; however, diseases brought by the foreigners decimated the population, and by 1570 it was almost uninhabited.

The inhabitants returned later, but the War of the Castes in the 1800s severely curtailed Cozumel's trade. Cozumel continued on its economic roller coaster, and after the Caste War it again took its place as a commercial seaport. Merchants exported henequen, coconuts, sugarcane, bananas, chicle, pineapples, honey, and wood products, though in 1955 Hurricane Janet all but demolished the coconut palm plantations. In the mid-1950s Cozumel's fame as a diving destination began to grow, and real development of the island as the site for a vacation resort evolved along with Cancún beginning in the mid-1970s.

ESSENTIALS
GETTING THERE & DEPARTING

BY PLANE   **Aero Cozumel,** a Mexicana affiliate, has numerous flights to and from Cancún and Mérida. **Mexicana** flies from Mexico City. **Taesa** flies from Cancún, Chetumal, and Mérida.

Here are some telephone numbers for confirming departures to and from Cozumel: Aero Cozumel (☎ **987/2-3456** or 988/4-2002 in Cancún; fax 987/2-0877 in Cozumel); Continental (☎ **987/2-0847** in Cozumel); Mexicana (☎ **987/2-0157** or 987/2-2945 at the airport; fax 987/2-2945); and Taesa (☎ **987/2-4420**).

You can't get a colectivo van from town to the airport, but taxis go to the airport for $6 to $8.

BY FERRY   Passenger ferries to Cozumel depart from Playa del Carmen on the mainland; there is also a car ferry from Puerto Morelos. You can catch a bus to Playa del Carmen from Cancún.

The Car Ferry from Puerto Morelos: The first thing to know is that you're better off without a car in Cozumel; parking is difficult. A solution is to drive to Playa del Carmen, find a reliable place to leave your car, and take the passenger ferry. If you do want to take your car over, the terminus in Puerto Morelos (☎ **987/1-0008**), the largest establishment in town, is very easy to find. The car-ferry schedule is complicated and may change, so double-check it before arriving in Puerto Morelos. On Monday, the ferry leaves at 7pm; on Tuesday at 11am; on Wednesday through Sunday at 6am. The crossing takes approximately 3 hours.

Cargo takes precedence over cars. Officials suggest that camper drivers stay overnight in the parking lot to be first in line for tickets. In any case, *always arrive at least 3 hours in advance of the ferry's departure to purchase a ticket and to get in line.*

Since passenger-boat service between Playa del Carmen and Cozumel is quite frequent now, I don't recommend that foot passengers bother with this boat.

When returning to Puerto Morelos from Cozumel, the ferry departs from the international cruise-ship pier daily. Get in line about 3 hours before departure, and double-check the schedule by calling ☎ **987/2-0950.** The fare is $35 for a car and $6 per passenger.

The Passenger Ferry from Playa del Carmen: There are several passenger ferries running between Cozumel and Playa del Carmen. The WJ *México III*, a modern water jet, makes the trip in 45 minutes compared to 60 on the *Cozumeleño*. The WJ *México III* costs $8.25 round-trip and is enclosed, and usually air-conditioned, with cushioned seats and video entertainment. The *Cozumeleño,* an open-top, enclosed-bottom vessel, runs the route for $5 round-trip. In Playa del Carmen, the ferry dock is 1¹/₂ blocks from the main square and from where buses let off passengers. Both companies have ticket booths at the main pier in Cozumel. Since schedules change frequently, be sure to double-check them at the docks—especially the time of the last ferry back, if that's the one you intend to use. Be prepared for seasickness on windy days.

From Playa del Carmen to Cozumel, The WJ *Mexico III* runs every hour or every 2 hours between 5:30am and 8:45pm. The *Cozumeleño* runs five times between 9:30am and 6:30pm.

From Cozumel to Playa del Carmen, the WJ *Mexico III* runs approximately every hour or hour and a half between 4am and 8pm. The *Cozumeleño* runs four times, between 8am and 5:30pm.

ORIENTATION

ARRIVING   Cozumel's **airport** is immediately north of downtown. Aero Transportes' colectivo vans at the airport provide transportation into town and to the north or south hotel zone. Buy your ticket as you exit the terminal. Cozumel now has two **cruise ferry docks.** The newest one, Puerto Mayo, about a mile south of the older one, dubbed the Intenational Pier, is controversial because it was built over North Paraiso Reef—the reef with the best shore diving and snorkeling possibilities. Dive operators, the town, and ecological preservation activists from around the world protested the building of this pier—without success.

VISITOR INFORMATION   The **State Tourism Office** (☎ and fax **987/2-0972**) is on the second floor of the Plaza del Sol commercial building facing the central plaza and is open from Monday through Friday from 8:30am to 3pm.

CITY LAYOUT   San Miguel's main waterfront street is called **Avenida Rafael Melgar,** running along the western shore of the island. Passenger ferries dock right in the center, opposite the main plaza and Melgar. Car ferries dock south of town at the International Pier near the hotels Sol Caribe, La Ceiba, and Fiesta Inn. Cruise ships dock at the International Pier and at the new Puerto Mayo Pier.

The town is laid out on a grid, with avenidas running north and south, calles running east and west. The exception is **Avenida Juárez,** which runs right from the passenger-ferry dock through the main square and inland. Juárez divides the town into northern and southern halves.

Heading inland from the dock along Juárez, you'll find that the avenidas you cross are numbered by fives: 5a av., 10a av., 15a av. If you turn left and head north, calles are numbered evenly: 2a Norte, 4a Norte, 6a Norte. Turning right from Juárez heads you south, where the streets are numbered: 1a Sur (also called Adolfo Salas), 3a Sur, 5a Sur.

ISLAND LAYOUT   The island is cut in half by one road, which runs past the airport and the ruins of San Gervasio to the almost uninhabited southern coast of the island. The northern part of the island has no paved roads. It's scattered with small, badly ruined Maya sites, from the age when "Cuzamil" was a land sacred to the moon goddess Ixchel. San Gervasio is accessible by motor scooter and car.

Most inexpensive hotels are in the town of San Miguel. Moderate to expensive accommodations are north and south of town. Many cater to divers. Beyond the hotels to the south is **Chankanaab National Park,** centered on the beautiful lagoon of the same name. Beyond Chankanaab are **Playa Palancar** and, offshore, the **Palancar Reef** (*arrecife*). At the southern tip of the island are **Punta Celarain** and the lighthouse.

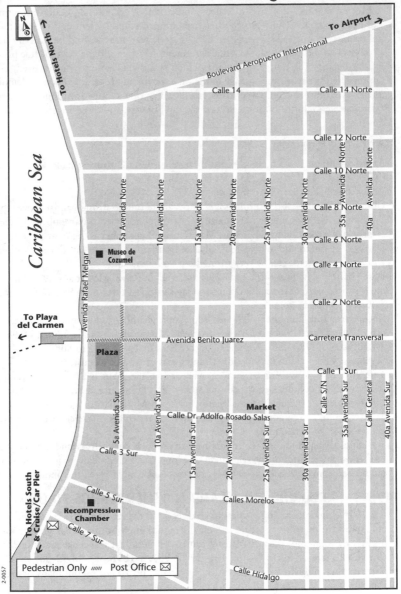

To Airport →

To Hotels North →

Boulevard Aeropuerto Internacional

Calle 14   Calle 14 Norte

Caribbean Sea

Calle 12 Norte

Calle 10 Norte

5a Avenida Norte   10a Avenida Norte   15a Avenida Norte   20a Avenida Norte   25a Avenida Norte   30a Avenida Norte   35a Avenida Norte   40a Avenida Norte

Calle 8 Norte

Calle 6 Norte

■ Museo de Cozumel

Calle 4 Norte

Avenida Rafael Melgar

Calle 2 Norte

To Playa del Carmen ←

Avenida Benito Juarez   Carretera Transversal

Plaza

Calle 1 Sur

Market

Calle S/N   35a Avenida Sur   Calle General   40a Avenida Sur

5a Avenida Sur   10a Avenida Sur   Calle Dr. Adolfo Rosado Salas

15a Avenida Sur   20a Avenida Sur   25a Avenida Sur   30a Avenida Sur

Calle 3 Sur

To Hotels South & Cruise/Car Pier

Calle 5 Sur

■ Recompression Chamber

✉ Calle 7 Sur

Calles Morelos

Calle Hidalgo

| Pedestrian Only ////// Post Office ✉ |

2-0057

The eastern, seaward shore of the island is mostly surf beach, beautiful for walking but dangerous for swimming.

GETTING AROUND You can walk to most destinations in town. However, getting to outlying hotels and beaches, including the Chankanaab Lagoon, requires a taxi.

Car rentals are as expensive here as in other parts of Mexico. Open-top jeeps are popular for rental, but be aware: They roll over easily and many tourists have been injured or killed using them. See "By Car" under "Getting Around" in chapter 3 for specifics.

Moped rentals are all over the village and cost about $25 for 24 hours, but terms and prices vary. Carefully inspect the actual moped you'll be renting to see that all the gizmos are in good shape: horn, light, starter, seat, mirror. And be sure to note all damage to the moped on the rental agreement. Most important, read the fine print on the back of the rental agreement, which states that you are not insured, are responsible for paying any damage to the bike (or for all of it if it's stolen or demolished), and must stay on paved roads. It's illegal to ride a moped without a helmet. *Important note:* North/south streets have the right of way, and these drivers don't slow down.

FAST FACTS: COZUMEL

American Express   The local representative is Fiesta Cozumel, Calle 11 no. 598 (☎ **987/2-0725** or 987/2-0433; fax 987/2-1044).

Area Code   The telephone area code is 987.

Climate   From October through December there can be strong winds all over the Yucatán, as well as some rain. In Cozumel, wind conditions in November and December can make diving dangerous. May through September is the rainy season.

Diving   If you intend to dive, remember to bring proof of your diver's certification. Underwater currents can be very strong here, so be cautious.

Post Office   The post office (*correo*) is on Avenida Rafael Melgar at Calle 7 Sur, at the southern edge of town; it's open Monday through Friday from 9am to 6pm and Saturday from 9am to noon.

Recompression Chamber   The recompression chamber (*cámara de recompreción*) is on Calle 5 Sur 1 block off Melgar between Melgar and Avenida 5 Sur (☎ **987/ 2-2387**; fax 987/2-1430). Normal hours are 8am to 1pm and 4 to 8pm.

Seasons   High season is Christmas through Easter, and in August.

Telephone   The **Calling Station** on Melgar at Calle 3 Sur is a full-service phone center with air-conditioned booths, no surcharges, fax service, and a bulletin board where you can leave messages for friends. It's open Monday through Saturday from 8am to 11pm, and Sunday from 9am to 10pm. You can also make collect calls from the Sports Page restaurant.

Besides these, long-distance telephones are on Salas between Avenidas 5 Sur and 10 Sur on the exterior of the telephone building. Use a credit card to get an American operator; make it collect; or have a pile of coins ready to feed the phone.

DIVING, EXPLORING THE ISLAND & OTHER THINGS TO DO

For **diving** and **snorkeling** it's best to go directly to the recommended shops below. For **island tours, ruins tours** on and off the island, **glass-bottom boat tours, fiesta nights, fishing,** and other activities, I can recommend the travel agency **InterMar Cozumel Viajes,** Calle 4 Norte. 101-B (☎ **987/2-1098**; fax 987/2-0895). The office is close to the main plaza between Avenida 5 and 10 Norte. But many of these you can do on your own without purchasing a tour.

A FESTIVAL

Carnaval/Mardi Gras is Cozumel's most colorful fiesta. It begins the Thursday before Ash Wednesday with daytime street dancing and nighttime parades on Thursday, Saturday, and Monday (the best).

FUN ON & UNDER THE WATER

SNORKELING   Anyone who can swim can go snorkeling. Rental of the snorkel (breathing pipe), goggles, and flippers should cost only about $4 for half a day; a 2-hour snorkeling trip costs $15. The brilliantly colored tropical fish provide a dazzling show. Chankanaab Park is one of the best places to go on your own for an abundant fish show.

Agency-arranged **snorkeling excursions** cost around $40 for a 10am–3pm trip that includes snorkeling at three different reefs, lunch, beer, and soft drinks. Two-hour snorkeling trips through the dive shops recommended below cost $15 and usually leave around 2:30pm.

SCUBA DIVING   Cozumel is Mexico's dive capital. Various establishments on the island rent scuba gear—tanks, regulator with pressure gauge, buoyancy compensator, weight belts, mask, snorkel, and fins. Many will also arrange a half-day expedition in a boat, complete with lunch, for a set price—usually around $40. Sign up the day before if you're interested. A two-tank morning dive costs around $50; some shops are now offering an additional afternoon one-tank dive for $9 for those who took the morning dives, or $25 for a one-tank dive. However, if you're a dedicated diver, you may save many dollars by buying a diving package that includes air transportation, hotel, and usually two dives a day. There's a recompression chamber on the island (see "Fast Facts: Cozumel," above).

The underwater wonders of the famous **Palancar Reef** are offshore from the beach of the same name. From the car-ferry pier south to Punta Celarain is more than 20 miles of offshore reefs. In the famous blue depths, divers find caves and canyons, small and large colorful fish, and an enormous variety of sea coral. The **Santa Rosa Reef** is famous for its depth, sea life, coral, and sponges. **San Francisco Reef,** off the beach by the same name south of town, has a drop-off wall, but it's still fairly shallow and the sea life is fascinating. The **Chankanaab Reef,** where divers are joined by schools of tropical fish, is close to the shore by the national park of the same name. It's shallow and good for novice divers. Next after Chankanaab going south on the eastern road, **Yucab Reef** has beautiful coral.

Numerous vessels on the island operate daily diving and snorkeling tours, so if you aren't traveling on a prearranged dive package, the best plan is to shop around and sign up for one of those. Of Cozumel's many dive shops, two are among the top: Bill Horn's **Aqua Safari,** in front of the Aqua Safari Inn and next to the Vista del Mar Hotel on Melgar at Calle 5 (☎ 987/2-0101; fax 987/2-0661) and in the Hotel Plaza Las Glorias (☎ 987/2-3362 or 987/2-2422), a PADI five-star instruction center, has full equipment and parts, a good selection of books, and its own pier just across the street. Its Web site is aquasafari.com. **Dive House,** on the main plaza (☎ 987/ 2-1953 and fax 987/2-0368), offers PADI and NAUI SSI instruction. Both shops offer morning and night dives, and afternoon snorkeling trips.

You can save money by renting your gear at a beach shop, such as the two mentioned above, and diving from shore. The shops at the Plaza Las Glorias and La Ceiba hotels are good for shore diving—you'll find plenty to see as soon as you enter the water. It costs about $6 to rent one tank and weights.

A new twist in underwater Yucatán is **cenote diving and snorkeling.** The peninsula's underground cenotes (say-*noh*-tehs), or sinkholes—which were sacred to the Maya—lead to a vast system of underground caverns, where the gently flowing water is so clear divers appear to be floating on air through caves that look just like those on dry land, complete with stalactites and stalagmites, plus tropical fish, eels, and turtles. These caverns were formed millions of years ago during the last two glacial eras, but only in recent years has this other world been opened to certified divers. The experienced cave divers and owners of **Yucatec Expeditions** (☎ and fax 987/ 2-4618 or 987/4-7835) offer this unique experience five times weekly from Playa del Carmen (you take the ferry with your gear and they meet you with vans there). Cenotes are 30 to 45 minutes from Playa del Carmen and a dive in each cenote lasts around 45 minutes. Snorkelers paddle around the cenotes, while divers explore the depths. Dives are within the daylight zone, about 130 feet into the caverns and no more than 60 feet deep. There's plenty of natural light. Company owners Sheila Gracey, German Yañez Mendoza, and Jorge Gonzalez inspect diving credentials carefully and have a list of requirements divers must meet before cave diving is permitted. They also offer the equivalent of a resort course in cave diving and a full cave diving course. A snorkeling trip to two cenotes runs around $70, while a two-cenote dive costs around $130, and a two-cavern dive runs $160.

WINDSURFING   Raul de Lille, one of Mexico's top windsurfing champions, offers windsurfing classes and equipment rentals at the beach in front of Sol Cabañas del Caribe, on the north side. For information call ☎ **987/2-0017;** fax 987/2-1942.

BOAT TRIPS   Boat trips are another popular pastime at Cozumel. Some excursions include snorkeling and scuba diving or a stop at a beach for lunch. Various types of tours are offered, including rides in **glass-bottom boats** for around $30. These usually start at 9am and end at 1pm and include beer and soft drinks.

FISHING   The best months for fishing are April through September, when the catch will be blue and white marlin, sailfish, tarpon, swordfish, dorado, wahoo, tuna, and red snapper. Fishing costs $450 for six people all day or $80 to $85 per person for a half day for four people. (See chapter 3, "Active Vacations in the Yucatán," for arranging fishing in advance.)

A TOUR OF THE ISLAND

Travel agencies can book you on a group tour of the island for around $35, depending on whether the tour includes lunch and a stop for snorkeling. A taxi driver charges $60 for a 4-hour tour. A 4-hour horseback riding tour of the island's interior to the ruins and jungle costs around $40; call **Rancho Buenavista** (☎ **987/2-1537**) for information, or the InterMar Viajes travel agency mentioned above.

You can easily rent a motorbike or car for half a day to take you around, but observe the warning above under "Getting Around"—an open-air jeep or jeep-like vehicle is a popular rental vehicle, but every year tourists are injured or killed using these vehicles. I would add that motorbikes and motorcycles can be equally as risky to use.

North of town, along Avenida Rafael Melgar (which becomes Carretera Pilar), you'll pass a marina and a string of Cozumel's first hotels as well as some new condominiums. A few of the hotels have nice beaches. This road ends just past the hotels. You can backtrack to the transversal road that cuts across the island from west (the town side) to east and links up with the eastern highway that brings you back to town.

The more interesting route begins by going south of town on Melgar (which becomes Costera Sur or Carretera a Chankanaab) past the **Hotel Barracuda** and **Sol Caribe.** After about 3 miles you'll see a sign pointing left down an unpaved road a short distance to the **Rancho San Manuel,** where you can rent horses. There are only seven horses here, but a guide and soft drink are included in the price. Rides cost $20 per hour. It's open daily from 8am to 4pm.

About 5 miles south of town you'll come to the big **Sol Caribe** (which is closed) and **La Ceiba** hotels and also the car-ferry dock for ferries to Puerto Morelos. Go snorkeling out in the water by the Hotel La Ceiba and you might spot a sunken airplane, put there for an underwater movie. Offshore, from here to the tip of the island at Punta Celarain, 20 miles away, is the **Underwater National Park,** so designated to protect the reef from damage by visitors. Dive masters warn not to touch or destroy the underwater growth.

CHANKANAAB NATIONAL PARK   This lagoon and botanical garden is a mile past the big hotels and 5$^1/_2$ miles south of town. It has long been famous for the color and variety of its sea life. The intrusion of sightseers began to ruin the marine habitat, so now visitors must swim and snorkel in the open sea, not in the lagoon. The beach is wide and beautiful, with plenty of shady thatched umbrellas to sit under, and the snorkeling is good—lots of colorful fish. Arrive early to stake out a chair and palapa before the cruise-ship visitors arrive. There are rest rooms, lockers, a gift shop, several snack huts, a restaurant, and a snorkeling-gear–rental palapa.

Surrounding the lagoon, the botanical garden, with shady paths, has 352 species of tropical and subtropical plants from 22 countries and 451 species from Cozumel. Several Maya structures have been re-created within the gardens to give visitors an idea of Maya life in a jungle setting. There's a small natural history museum as well. Admission to the park costs $3; it's open daily from 8am to 5pm.

THE BEACHES   Ten miles past the Chankanaab National Park, you'll come to **Playa San Francisco** and, south of it, **Playa Palancar.** Besides the beach at Chankanaab Lagoon, they're the best on Cozumel. Food (usually overpriced) and equipment rentals are available. On the east side of the island, the **Playa Bonita Beach Club,** near Playa Chiqueros, has water-sports and windsurfing-equipment rentals. The restaurant is open daily from 10am to 5pm.

PUNTA CELARAIN   After Playa San Francisco, you plow through the jungle on a straight road for miles until you're 17$^1/_2$ miles from town. Finally, though, you emerge near the southern reaches of the island on the east coast. The **lighthouse** you see in the distance is at Punta Celarain, the island's southernmost tip. The sand track is unsuitable for motorbikes, but in a car you can drive to the lighthouse in about 25 minutes.

THE EASTERN SHORE   The road along the east coast of the island is wonderful. There are views of the sea, the rocky shore, and the pounding surf. On the land side are little farms and forests. Exotic birds take flight as you approach, and monstrous (but harmless) iguanas skitter off into the undergrowth.

Most of the east coast is unsafe for swimming because the surf can create a deadly undertow that will pull you far out to sea in a matter of minutes. There are always cars pulled off along the road here, with the occupants spending the day on the beach but not in the churning waters. Three restaurants catering to tourists are along this part of the coast, complete with sombrero-clad iguanas for a picture companion.

Halfway up the east coast, the paved eastern road meets the paved transversal road (which passes the ruins of San Gervasio) back to town, 9$^1/_2$ miles away. The east-coast road ends when it turns into the transversal, petering out to a narrow track of sandy road by a nice restaurant in front of the Chen Río Beach; vehicles, even motorbikes, will get stuck on the sand road. If you're a bird watcher, leave your vehicle on the highway here and walk straight down the sandy road. Go slowly and quietly and at least you'll spot many herons and egrets in the lagoon on the left that parallels the path. Much farther on are Maya ruins.

MAYA RUINS

One of the most popular island excursions is to **San Gervasio** (100 B.C. to A.D. 1600). A road leads there from the airport, or you can continue on the eastern part of the island following the paved transversal road. The worn sign to the ruins is easy to miss, but the turnoff (left) is about halfway between town and the eastern coast. Stop at the entry gate and pay the $1 road-use fee. Go straight ahead over the potholed road to the ruins about 2 miles farther and pay the $3.50 to enter; camera permits cost $4 for each still or video camera you want to bring in. A small tourist center at the entrance has cold drinks and snacks for sale.

When it comes to Cozumel's Maya remains, getting there is most of the fun, and you should do it for the trip, not for the ruins. The buildings, though preserved, are crudely made and would not be much of a tourist attraction if they were not the island's only cleared and accessible ruins. More significant than beautiful, the site was once an important ceremonial center where the Maya gathered, coming even from the mainland. The important deity here was Ixchel, known as the goddess of weaving, women, childbirth, pilgrims, the moon, and medicine. Although you won't see any representations of her at San Gervasio today, Bruce Hunter, in his *Guide to Ancient Maya Ruins*, writes that priests hid behind a large pottery statue of her and became the voice of the goddess speaking to pilgrims and answering their petitions. She was the wife of Itzamná, preeminent among Maya gods.

Tour guides charge $10 for a tour for one to six people, but it's not worth it. Find a copy of the green booklet *San Gervasio*, sold at local checkout counters or bookstores, and tour the site on your own. Seeing it takes 30 minutes. Taxi drivers offer a tour to the ruins for about $25; the driver will wait for you outside the ruins.

PARQUE ARQUEOLÓGICA

This park contains reproductions of many of Mexico's important archaeological treasures, including the 4-foot-high Olmec head and the Chaac-Mool seen in Chichén-Itzá. A Maya couple demonstrate the lifestyle of the Maya in a *nah*, or thatch-roofed oval home. The park is a nice addition to the island's cultural attractions and is well worth visiting—but slather on the bug repellent before you begin exploring. The park is open daily from 8am to 6pm; admission is $1.50. To get there, turn left on the unmarked road across from the International Pier, off Costera Sur just south of the La Ceiba hotel, then left on Avenida 65 Sur and follow the signs.

A HISTORY MUSEUM

The **Museo de la Isla de Cozumel,** on Avenida Melgar between Calles 4 and 6 Norte, is more than just a nice place to spend a rainy hour. On the first floor an excellent exhibit showcases endangered species, the origin of the island, and its present-day topography and plant and animal life, including an explanation of coral formation. Upstairs, showrooms feature the history of the town; artifacts from the island's pre-Hispanic sites; and colonial-era cannons, swords, and ship paraphernalia. It's open daily from 10am to 6pm. Admission is $1.75; guided tours in English are free. There's a rooftop restaurant open long hours.

TRIPS TO THE MAINLAND
PLAYA DEL CARMEN & XCARET

Going on your own to the nearby seaside village of **Playa del Carmen** and the **Xcaret** nature park is as easy as a quick ferry ride from Cozumel. (For ferry information, see "Getting There & Departing," above.) Both are covered in detail later in this chapter. Cozumel travel agencies offer an Xcaret tour that includes the ferry fee, transportation to the park, and the admission fee for $45.

CHICHÉN-ITZÁ, TULUM & COBÁ

Travel agencies can arrange day-trips to the fascinating ruins of **Chichén-Itzá** either by air or by bus. Departure times vary depending on which transportation you choose. It costs less for an excursion to the ruins of **Tulum,** overlooking the Caribbean, and **Cobá,** in a dense jungle setting, since these ruins are closer, but they are a complete architectural contrast to Chichén-Itzá. Such a trip begins at 9am and returns around 6pm.

In case you want to see the world.

At American Express, we're here to make your journey a smooth one. So we have over 1,700 travel service locations in over 120 countries ready to help. What else would you expect from the world's largest travel agency?

do more®

Travel

In case you want to be welcomed there.

We're here to see that you're always welcomed at establishments everywhere. That's why millions of people carry the American Express® Card—for peace of mind, confidence, and security, around the world or just around the corner.

do more

Cards

And just in case.

We're here with American Express® Travelers Cheques and Cheques *for Two*.® They're the safest way to carry money on your vacation and the surest way to get a refund, practically anywhere, anytime.

Another way we help you...

do more

Travelers Cheques

SHOPPING

Shopping has improved beyond the ubiquitous T-shirt shops into expensive resortwear, silver, and better decorative and folk art. Most of the stores are on Avenida Melgar; the best shops for high-quality Mexican folk art are **Los Cinco Soles, Talavera,** and **Playa del Angel.** Prices for serapes, T-shirts, and the like are normally less expensive on the side streets off Melgar.

If you want to pick up some Mexican tapes and CDs, head to **Discoteca Holly-wood,** at Juárez 421 (☎ 987/2-4090); it's open Monday through Saturday from 9am to 10pm. Self-billed as the "Paradise of the Cassette," this store stocks a large selection.

WHERE TO STAY

Cozumel's hotels are in three separate locations: The oldest resorts, most of which are expensive, line beaches and coral and limestone outcroppings north and south of town; the more budget-oriented inns are in the central village; and other relatively inexpensive hotels lie both immediately north and south of town. *Note:* There's one **central reservations number** for many (not all) of the island's hotels (☎ 800/327-2254 in the U.S. and Canada). As an alternative to a hotel, **Casa Cozumel Vacation Villas** and Condos, Av. 10 Sur no. 124, 77600 Cozumel, Q. Roo (☎ 800/558-5145 in the U.S., or 987/2-2259; fax 987/2-2348), offers a wide range of accommodations and prices.

HOTELS NORTH OF TOWN

I'll start with the northernmost hotels going through town and move onward to the end of the southern hotel zone. Like beaches south of town, those along the northern shore appear sporadically and some hotels have enclosed them with retaining walls. **Carretera Santa Pilar** is the name of Melgar's northern extension, so just take Melgar north and all the hotels are lined up in close proximity to each other on the Santa Pilar Beach a short distance from town and the airport.

Moderate

Cabañas del Caribe. Km 4.5 Carretera Santa Pilar (Apdo. Postal 9), 77600 Cozumel, Q. Roo. ☎ **800/336-3542** in the U.S., 987/2-0017, or 987/2-0072. Fax 987/2-1599. 48 rms. A/C. High season $135 double. Low season $105 double. Free parking.

Built in two sections, the hotel gives you two choices of room styles. Standard rooms in the two-story section adjacent to the lobby are smallish (but very nice) and decorated in southwest shades of apricot and blue. All have small sitting areas and either a porch or balcony facing the beach and pool. The one-story bungalow/cabaña section has a similar decor, but rooms are larger and have patios on the beach.

Dining/Entertainment: The main restaurant is in a glassed-in terrace on the beach, and there's a poolside spot for snacks.

Services: Travel agency.

Facilities: Swimming pool; water-sports equipment for rent including sailboats, jet skis, as well as diving, snorkeling, and windsurfing equipment; pharmacy; gift shop.

Condumel. Carretera Pilar, 77600 Cozumel, Q. Roo. ☎ **987/2-0892.** Fax 987/2-0661. E-mail: condumel@aquasafari.com. 8 condos. A/C and FAN. High season $125 double. Low season $100 double.

These spacious condos are an appealing option, especially if you plan to stay on the island a while. Maya carvings decorate the limestone edifice; king-size beds and hammock hooks provide a choice of sleeping accommodations. The full kitchens have toaster ovens and coffeemakers; the baths include tubs and bidets. The owner, Bill

Horn, also owns the Aqua Safari dive shop and provides dive packages. The condos are on the left just before the marina, about two miles north of town.

Hotel El Cozumeleño Beach Resort. Km 2 Carretera Santa Pilar (Apdo. Postal 53), 77600 Cozumel, Q. Roo. ☎ **800/221-6509** in the U.S., or 987/2-0050. Fax 987/2-0381. 100 rms. A/C TEL. High season $95–$140 double. Low season $55–$120 double.

The Cozumeleño has been fluctuating between being an all-inclusive resort and not being one. The rates above reflect an all-inclusive status and several variations in price depending on the months booked. The five-story hotel (with elevator) has one of the nicest stretches of coral-free beach on the island. The expansive marble-floored lobby, scattered with groupings of pastel chairs and couches, is a popular gathering place. The glassed-in dining room looks out onto the Caribbean, as do all the spacious and nicely furnished guest rooms.

Dining/Entertainment: Two restaurants, one by the beach and pool and the other indoors, serve all three meals. A karaoke bar provides music to drink by.

Services: Laundry and room service, travel agency, auto and moped rental.

Facilities: Palm-shaded pool, tennis court, water-sports equipment, 19-hole miniature golf course, game room, gym, and diving center.

Hotel Fontan. Km 2.5 Carretera Santa Pilar, 77600 Cozumel, Q. Roo. ☎ **800/221-6509** in the U.S., or 987/2-0300. Fax 987/2-0105. 48 rms. A/C TV TEL. High season $95–$125 double. Low season $80–100 double. Free unguarded parking.

Rooms on all four floors of this tan-colored hotel are well maintained and have private balconies; most have ocean views. Baths all have showers. There's a nice pool by the beach (held up by a retaining wall) that's surrounded by lounge chairs. There's a restaurant/bar, plus a dock for water sports. The hotel is an excellent value for your money.

HOTELS IN TOWN

Expensive

✪ **Hotel Plaza Las Glorias.** Km 1.5 Av. Rafael Melgar, 77600 Cozumel, Q. Roo. ☎ **800/ 342-AMIGO** or 987/2-2000. Fax 987/2-1937. 170 rms. A/C MINIBAR TV TEL. High season $224 double. Low season $145 double.

An all-suite hotel, this one offers the top-notch amenities of the expensive hotels farther out, but it's within 5 blocks of town. Beyond the expansive, comfortable lobby is the pool, with a swim-up bar, a multilevel deck, a shored-up beach, and the ocean. Most of the large, nicely furnished rooms all have cool tile floors, separate sunken living rooms, and balconies with views. Standard in-room amenities include hair dryers, purified tap water, and in-room safety deposit boxes.

Dining/Entertainment: During high season there's usually a buffet at breakfast and lunch. The main restaurant features different specialties nightly. There's palapa dining outside for all meals (weather permitting). The popular lobby bar features a large-screen TV that brings in major sports events. In high season there's often live entertainment (soft music) there as well and a happy hour with two-for-one drinks between 5 and 7pm.

Services: Laundry and room service, fully equipped dive shop with PADI and NAUI certification available

Facilities: Swimming pool with swim-up bar by the beach, diving pier, organized pool games, recreational director, travel agency, concierge.

Moderate

Hotel Barracuda. Av. Rafael Melgar 628 (Apdo. Postal 163), 77600 Cozumel, Q. Roo. ☎ **987/2-0002** or 987/2-1243. Fax 987/2-0884 or 987/2-3633. 50 rms. A/C and FAN. High season $70 double. Low season $65 double.

You won't think much of this plain tan-colored building a short walk south of town, but the view from within is outstanding. Rustic carved-wood furnishings decorate the cozy rooms, all with balconies looking out to sea. There's a refrigerator in each room as well. An inner hallway leading to the rooms blocks out the noise from the road. There's no pool, but lounge chairs are lined up on an elevated strip of sand, and stairs lead down to a good snorkeling area. There is a small oceanfront cafe serving breakfast and snacks, plus a good dive shop. The hotel is on Costera Sur, a 10-minute walk from town; from the pier walk right; the hotel is on your right. Street parking is readily available.

✪ **Hotel Suites Bazar Colonial.** Av. 5 Sur no. 9 (Apdo. Postal 286), 77600 Cozumel, Q. Roo. ☎ **987/2-0506.** Fax 987/2-1387. 28 rms. A/C TV TEL. High season $70 double. Low season $50 double.

Across the street from the El Marqués hotel is a collection of shops and this nice four-story hotel—with an elevator. It's a good deal for the money, especially if you like to spread out. The lobby is far back past the shops. You get a quiet, spacious, furnished studio or a one-bedroom apartment with red tile floors on the first floor; second- and third-floor rooms have kitchenettes. The street is closed to traffic. From the plaza, walk half a block south on Avenida 5 Sur; the hotel is on the left.

Inexpensive

B & B Caribo. 799 Av. Juárez, 77600 Cozumel, Q. Roo. ☎ and fax **800/830-5558** in the U.S., or 987/2-3195. 10 rms (8 with bath). A/C or FAN. $60–$70 double. Rates include continental breakfast.

This blue-and-white residence behind a short, white iron fence looks like one of the finer residences in this neighborhood. The 10 rooms continue the crisp blue-and-white decor and come with cool tile floors, white furniture, blue bedspreads, and big bottles of purified drinking water. Besides having fans, all rooms are air-conditioned. Eight rooms have private baths. Two rooms have a shared bath in the middle, and these have fans but no air-conditioning. Rooms either have one or two double beds or a double and a single. The two most expensive rooms have kitchens. A bakery is located in the front of the house. To find the Caribo from the plaza, walk 6½ blocks inland on Juárez, and it's on the left.

Hotel Aguilar. Calle 3 Sur no. 95, 77600 Cozumel, Q. Roo. ☎ **987/2-0307.** Fax 987/2-0769. 32 rms. A/C and FAN. High season $45 double. Low season $35 double.

Behind its white stucco walls you'll find a clean, quiet little respite focused on a large pool and a plant-filled courtyard within walking distance of the downtown action. The spotless rooms come with fresh paint, lights over the beds, tile floors, two double beds (firm) covered with ruffled spreads, and glass windows with good screens. You can rent a car (expensive), boat, or motor scooter in the lobby. To find the hotel, turn right at the ferry pier on Melgar, then turn left on Calle 3 Sur.

Hotel El Marqués. Av. 5 Sur no. 180, 77600 Cozumel, Q. Roo. ☎ **987/2-0677.** Fax 987/2-0537. 40 rms. A/C. High season $40 double. Low season $30 double. Discounts for two or more nights.

Each of the sunny rooms here has gold trim and Formica-marble countertops, French provincial overtones, gray-and-white tile floors, and two double beds. The junior suites have refrigerators; full suites have refrigerators, stoves, and sitting areas. Third-floor rooms have good views. The staff is friendly and attentive. To find it from the plaza, turn right (south) on Avenida 5 Sur; the hotel is near the corner of Salas, on the right up the stairs next to Coco's restaurant.

✪ **Hotel Flamingo.** Calle 6 Norte no. 81, 77600 Cozumel, Q. Roo. ☎ **987/2-1264.** 22 rms. FAN. High season $34 double. Low season $26 double.

Built in 1986, the Flamingo offers three floors of quiet rooms, a grassy inner court-yard, and very helpful management. Second- and third-story rooms are spacious. All have white tile floors. Rooms in the front of the building have balconies overlook-ing the street. Some doubles have one bed; others have two. Soft drinks and bottled water are available from the refrigerator in the lobby. Trade paperbacks are by the reception desk and a TV in the lobby is for guests. You get a lot for your money here. To find it, walk 5 blocks north on Melgar from the plaza and turn right on Calle 6; the hotel is on the left between Melgar and Avenida 5. Street parking is available.

✪ **Hotel Mary-Carmen.** Av. 5 Sur no. 4 (Apdo. Postal 14), 77600 Cozumel, Q. Roo. ☎ **987/ 2-0581.** 30 rms. A/C or FAN. High season $45 double. Low season $35 double.

Watched over by eagle-eyed señoras, the two stories of rooms at the Mary-Carmen surround an interior courtyard shaded by a large mamey tree. Rooms are clean and carpeted, with well-screened windows facing the courtyard. Most have two double beds. Upstairs rooms have fan only, while first-floor rooms have both fan and air-conditioning. It's half a block south of the main plaza, or *zócalo*, on the right.

Hotel Maya Cozumel. Calle 5 Sur (Apdo. Postal 23), 77600 Cozumel, Q. Roo. ☎ **987/ 2-0011.** Fax 987/2-0781. 38 rms. A/C TEL. $48 double.

Maya touches decorate the lobby and rooms in this pretty, apricot-and-white hotel. A long, green lawn and small, clean pool are framed by two three-story buildings and flowering shrubs. Paintings of Maya deities decorate the walls in the large rooms; some have leather lounge chairs. TVs with cable connection are available in 15 rooms. The rates stay the same year-round. Street parking is limited. From the ferry pier turn right (south) and walk 3 blocks on Melgar, then turn left on Calle 5. The hotel is on the left between Melgar and 5 Avenida Sur.

✪ **Hotel Safari Inn.** Av. Melgar at Calle 5 Sur (Apdo. Postal 41), 77600 Cozumel, Q. Roo. ☎ **987/2-0101.** Fax 987/2-0661. E-mail: dive@aquasafari.com. 12 rms. A/C. $40 double.

The nicest budget hotel in town is above and behind the Aqua Dive Shop. Natural colors and stucco pervade the interior of this three-story (no elevator) establishment. The huge rooms come with firm beds, built-in sofas, and tiled floors. The hotel caters to divers and offers some good dive packages through its dive shop, Aqua Safari—one of the most reputable on the island. To find it from the pier, turn right (south) and walk $3^1/2$ blocks on Melgar; the hotel is on your left facing the Carib-bean at the corner of Calle 5 Sur.

HOTELS SOUTH OF TOWN

The best beaches are south of town, but not all the best ones have hotels on them. Each hotel has either a swimming pool, a tiny cove, a dock, or all three. You'll be able to swim, sun, and relax at any of these hotels and most are diver-oriented. **Costera Sur,** also called **Carretera a Chankanaab,** is the southern extension of Melgar, so just follow Melgar south through town to reach these hotels, which are, generally speaking, farther apart than those north of town.

Very Expensive

✪ **Presidente Inter-Continental Cozumel.** Km 6 Costera Sur, 77600 Cozumel, Q. Roo. ☎ **800/327-0200** in the U.S., or 987/2-0322. Fax 987/2-1360. 253 rms. A/C MINIBAR TV TEL. High season $235–$360 double. Low season $180–$295 double. Discounts and pack-ages available. Free parking.

The first thing you'll notice here is the palatial scale of the place and the masterful, grand combination of marble with hot-pink stucco and stone as you enter. Near the Chankanaab Lagoon, the hotel, surrounded by shady palms, spreads out on a beautiful beach with no close neighbors. Rates vary widely, depending on your view and the time of year you travel, even within seasons. There are four categories of rooms—some have balconies and garden views, while very spacious rooms come with balconies and ocean views. Deluxe beachfront rooms have comfortable patios and direct access to the beach on the ground floor. On the second floor there are balconies with ocean views. These deluxe rooms exude luxury, while other rooms in the hotel may be disappointing by comparison, with musty smelling air-conditioning and bedspreads too short for the bed. The no-smoking rooms are all on the fourth level, and two rooms are set aside for guests with disabilities. Naturally, each category of room has a different price. Absolutely ask about discounts and packages and stay in a deluxe room if at all possible.

Dining/Entertainment: The Arrecife restaurant serves international specialties and is open daily from 6pm to midnight. Caribeño, by the pool and beach, is open from 7am to 7pm.

Services: Laundry and room service, travel agency, car and motorbike rental.

Facilities: Swimming pool, two tennis courts, water-sports equipment rental, dive shop and dive-boat pier, pharmacy, boutiques.

Expensive

La Ceiba Beach Hotel. Km 4.5 Costera Sur (Apdo. Postal 284), 77600 Cozumel, Q. Roo. ☎ **800/221-6509** in the U.S., 987/2-0065, or 987/2-0844. 113 rms. A/C MINIBAR TV TEL. High season $140 double. Low season $115 double. Diving packages available. Free parking.

Across from the Sol Caribe, on the beach side of the road, La Ceiba is named for the lofty and majestic tree, sacred to the Maya, which grows in the tropics. It's a popular hotel, and the large lobby seems to always be abustle with guests. The guest rooms, while not necessarily outfitted in the latest style, are nicely furnished, large, and comfortable; all have ocean views and balconies. The swimming pool is only steps from the beach.

The emphasis here is on water sports, particularly scuba diving, and if this is your passion, be sure to ask about the special dive packages when you call for reservations.

Dining/Entertainment: The Galleon Bar/Restaurant, off the lobby, has walls shaped like an old ship and is open for all meals. Chopaloca, by the beach, is open daily from early morning until almost midnight.

Services: Laundry and room service, travel agency.

Facilities: Large, free-form swimming pool by the beach; tennis court; water sports; dive shop and dive-boat pier; roped-off area for snorkeling.

Moderate

Galápagos Inn. Km 1.5 Costera Sur (Apdo. Postal 289), 77600 Cozumel, Q. Roo. ☎ **987/2-0663** or 987/2-1133; or call Aqua-Sub Tours at 800/847-5708 in the U.S., or 713/783-3305 in Texas. 54 rms. A/C. High season $480–$580 single; $360–$435 per person double. Low season 3-night package $515 single; $390 per person double. Package rates include all meals and two days diving. Longer diving packages and lower rates for nondivers available.

Homey, shady, and done in colonial style with white stucco and redbrick accents, this older inn is usually peopled by divers who have signed up for one of the several money-saving 3-, 5-, and 7-night package deals. The inn, located a mile south of the main square, has its own small swimming pool and a bit of walled-in beach. A row of hammocks swing under a long thatched roof by the ocean, where there's nothing but the sound of surf and breezes. Some rooms have balconies or terraces on the beach. All have ocean views. The rooms themselves are rather nondescript—comfortable and functional but not much else. One restaurant serves all meals with specific meal times. The bar, with drinks only, is open daily from 7 to 11pm. There's a fully equipped dive shop; dives take off from the hotel's pier.

WHERE TO DINE

Zermatt, a terrific little bakery, is on Avenida 5 at Calle 4 Norte. On Calle 2 Norte, half a block in from the waterfront, is the **Panificadora Cozumel,** excellent for a do-it-yourself breakfast or for picnic supplies. It's open from 6am to 9pm daily.

VERY EXPENSIVE

✪ **Café del Puerto.** Av. Melgar 3. ☎ **987/2-0316.** Reservations recommended. Main courses $15–$35. Daily 5pm–11pm. INTERNATIONAL.

For a romantic dinner with a sunset view, try this restaurant. After being greeted at the door, climb the spiral staircase to the main dining room or continue to a higher loft, overlooking the rest of the dining room. Soft piano music entertains in the background. The service is polished and polite, and the menu is sophisticated, with dishes like mustard steak flambé, shrimp brochette with bacon and pineapple, and prime rib. From the pier, cross the street and turn left on Melgar; it's almost immediately on your right.

Pepe's Grill. Av. Rafael Melgar at Salas. ☎ **987/2-0213.** Reservations recommended. Main courses $15–$30; children's menu $6.50. Daily 5–11:30pm. GRILLED SPECIALTIES.

Pepe's started the grilled-food tradition in Cozumel and continues to be a popular trendsetter with low lights, soft music, solicitous waiters, and excellent food—the perpetual crowd is here for a reason. The menu is extensive, with flame-broiled specialties such as beef fillet Singapore and shrimp Bahamas. The children's menu offers breaded shrimp and fried chicken. For dessert try the cajeta crepes.

MODERATE

✪ **D'Pub.** Calle 4 Norte. ☎ **987/2-4132.** Reservations recommended in high season. Main courses $6–$16. Mon–Sat 11pm–midnight, Sun 5pm–midnight; Pub/Botanera Mon–Sat 11am–5pm. SEAFOOD/INTERNATIONAL.

Nothing here is quite what you expect. It's in a new building that's architecturally like the old island frame houses with cutout wood trim. Then it's a handsome English-style pub with a mahogany bar glimmering with shiny glass and brass while coupling the best of a Mexican cantina (the equivalent of a Mexican pub), offering delicious snacks free with inexpensive drinks—but that's only between 11am and 5pm. After 5pm it's transformed from casual to elegant, becoming a stylish restaurant with cloth-covered tables where good service brings terrific crispy fresh salads, curried chicken, large seafood platters, fish and chips, barbecue chicken, roast beef sandwiches, fajitas, stir-fried vegetables, steaks, and an enormous Mexican combo including roasted chicken, rice, beans, guacamole, an enchilada, and a quesadilla. You can dine inside or on the veranda or patio in back overlooking the shaded garden. In the main room as you enter, casual couches and conversational areas are conducive to leisurely drinking, chatting, card playing, or backgammon, or watching ESPN, CNN, WGN Chicago, or sporting events (the television is played at low volume). The gracious owners, Anibal and Mercedes de Iturbide, are almost always on hand. To get there from the plaza, turn left (north) on Avenida 5 Norte, walk two blocks and turn right on Calle 4 Norte; it's behind Zermatt bakery, on your right midway up the block.

✪ **El Moro.** 75 bis Norte 124. ☎ **987/2-3029.** Main courses $4–$12; margaritas $3; beers $1.25. Fri–Wed 1–11pm. Closed Thursday. REGIONAL.

Crowds flock to El Moro for its wonderfully prepared food and service but not for the decor, which is orange, orange, orange, and Formica. And it's away from everything—a taxi is a must—costing around $1.50 one-way. But you won't care as soon as you taste anything, and especially if you sip even a little of their giant, wallop-packing margaritas. The pollo Ticuleño (a specialty from the town of Ticul) is a ribsticking, delicious, layered plate of smooth tomato sauce, mashed potatoes, crispy baked corn tortilla, and batter-fried chicken breast, all topped with shredded cheese and green peas. Besides the regional food, other specialties of Mexico arrive from the kitchen piping hot, such as enchiladas and seafood prepared many ways, plus grilled steaks, sandwiches, and, of course, nachos to go with that humdinger of a margarita. El Moro is 12¹/₂ blocks inland from Melgar between Calles 2 and 4 Norte.

La Choza. Salas 198 at Av. 10 Sur. ☎ **987/2-0958.** Breakfast $2.80; main courses $8–$16. Daily 7:30am–11pm. YUCATECAN.

Tables full of diners look out the big open-air windows on the corner of Salas and Avenida 10 Sur. The restaurant looks like a big Maya house with white stucco walls and a thatched roof. Platters of chiles stuffed with shrimp, pollo en relleno negro (chicken in a blackened pepper sauce), puerco entometado (pork stew), and beefsteak in a poblano pepper sauce, are among the truly authentic specialties.

Pizza Rolandi. Av. Melgar, between calles 6 and 8 Norte. ☎ **987/2-0946.** Main courses $8–$13; pizza $9–$14; daily specials $5–$13. Mon–Sat 11am–11pm; Sun 5–11pm. ITALIAN.

Deck chairs and glossy wood tables make the inviting interior garden a restful place in daytime, and it becomes romantic with candlelight at night. The specialty here (as in their branches in Isla Mujeres and Cancún) is wood-oven–baked pizzas. But for a change, check out the pasta prepared five ways and the weekly specials. The latter may be a special appetizer of sea bass carpaccio, pizza, pasta, or fish with an Italian twist. To get there from the pier, turn left (north) on Melgar and walk 4 blocks; it's on your right.

✪ Prima. Calle Salas 109. ☎ **987/2-4242.** Pizzas $5–$14; pastas $5–$15; calzones $3.75–$5.25. Daily 3–11pm. ITALIAN.

One of the few good Italian restaurants in Mexico, Prima gets better every year. Everything is fresh—the pastas, calzones, vegetables, and sourdough pizza. Owner Albert Domínguez grows most of the vegetables in his hydroponic garden on the island. The menu changes daily and might include shrimp scampi, fettucine with pesto, and lobster and crab ravioli with cream sauce. The fettucine Alfredo is wonderful, as are the puff-pastry garlic "bread" and fresh house salad. Dining is upstairs on the breezy terrace. Next door is **Prima Deli,** serving great sandwiches on fresh-baked bread and aromatic coffee from 9am to 7pm. To get to either place from the pier, turn right (south) on Melgar and walk two blocks to Calle 5 Sur and turn left. Prima is visible on your left between avenidas 5 and 10 Sur. Hotel delivery is available.

INEXPENSIVE

Café Caribe. Av. 10 Sur 215. ☎ **987/2-3621.** Coffee and pastries $1.50–$4. Mon–Sat 8am–1pm and 6–9:30pm. PASTRIES & COFFEE.

This cute little cafe behind a facade of fuchsia and dark green may become your favorite place to start or finish the day or for something in between. You'll find ice cream, milk shakes, freshly made cheesecake and carrot cake, waffles, bagels, croissants, and biscuits filled with cheese and cream, ham and cheese, or butter and marmalade. Nine different coffees are served, including Cuban, cappuccino, espresso, and Irish. To get there from the plaza, turn right (south) on Avenida 5 Sur, walk 1 block and turn left on Calle Salas, then right on Avenida 10; it's on your left.

Casa de Denis. Calle 1 Sur. ☎ **987/2-0067.** Breakfast $1.75–$3.75; main courses $4.75–$12. Mon–Sat 7am–11pm. REGIONAL/INTERNATIONAL.

This yellow, wooden house holds a great home-style Mexican restaurant. Small tables are scattered outside on the pedestrian-only street and in two rooms separated by a foyer filled with family photos. More tables are set in the back on the shady patio. You can make a light meal from empanadas filled with potatoes, cheese, or fish; or go for the full comida of fried grouper, rice, and beans; or better yet, try one of the regional specialties such as pollo pibil or pork brochette seasoned with the subtle flavor of achiote. Groups of four or more can request a special meal in advance. To get there from the plaza, walk a half block inland up Calle 1 Sur; it's on your right.

✪ **Coco's.** Av. 5 Sur no. 180, at the corner of Calle Salas. ☎ **987/2-0241.** Breakfast $3–$5.75. Tues–Sun 7am–noon. Closed the last 2 weeks of September and the first week of October. MEXICAN/AMERICAN.

Once discovered, Coco's becomes a favorite. Tended by owners Terri and Daniel Ocejo, it's clean and welcoming to the tourist, right down to the free coffee refills and the ready purified ice water. Plan to indulge in Stateside favorites like hash browns, cornflakes and bananas, gigantic blueberry muffins, cinnamon rolls, and cream-stuffed rolls, plus something unique like a bagelwich or a sandwich on an English muffin. Mexican specialties include huevos rancheros, huevos mexicanas, and eggs scrambled with chiles and covered with melted cheese. And you can order them with Egg Beaters™ eggs, if you wish. The really famished should inquire about the inexpensive but outrageously filling "Loco" breakfast. A gift section at the front includes gourmet coffee, local honey, bottles of hot pepper, chocolate, *rompope,* and vanilla. Plus there's a paperback book exchange. To get there from the plaza, turn right (south) on Avenida 5 Sur. Coco's is on your right beside the entry to the Hotel El Marqués.

Comida Casera Toñita. Calle Salas 265, between calles 10 and 15 Norte. ☎ **987/2-0401.** Breakfast $1.75–$3; main courses $3.75–$5; daily specials $3; fruit drinks $1.75. Mon–Sat 8am–6pm. HOME-STYLE YUCATECAN.

The owners have taken the living room of their home and made it into a comfortable dining room, complete with filled bookshelves and classical music playing in the background. Whole fried fish, fish fillet, fried chicken, and beefsteak prepared as you wish are on the regular menu. Daily specials give you a chance to taste authentic regional food, including a pollo a la naranja, chicken mole, pollo en escabeche, and pork chops with achiote seasoning. To reach Toñita's, walk south from the plaza on Avenida 5 Sur for 1 block, then turn left on Calle Salas and walk east 1 1/2 blocks; the restaurant is on your left.

✪ **Frutas Selectas.** Calle Rosado Salas 352. ☎ **987/2-5560.** Breakfast $1.75–$3.25; salads $1.75–$3; sandwiches $1.55–$3; fruit and vegetable juices 95¢–$1.55; coffee 75¢. Mon–Sat 7am–2pm and 5–9pm. FRUIT/PASTRIES.

The sweet smell of fruit will greet you as you enter Frutas Selectas. Downstairs is a grocery store specializing in fresh fruit, and upstairs is the sleek, cheery restaurant with windows on two sides. Juices, licuados, "the best coffee in town," yogurt, veggie sandwiches, a salad bar, fruit shakes, baked potatoes with a variety of toppings, and pastries are served. From the plaza, turn right and walk 1 block south on Avenida 5 Sur, then turn left on Calle Salas and walk 3 blocks east. It's on your right between 15th and 20th Norte.

✪ **The Waffle House.** Av. Melgar. ☎ **987/2-0545** or 987/2-3065. Waffles $3.15–$5; breakfast $3.25–$4; main courses $5–$9. Daily 6am–1pm and 6–10pm. BREAKFAST/DESSERTS/MEXICAN.

Tables are often full since The Waffle House has far more business than it has space to handle. The name is a bit misleading since you can order way more than waffles, and you can also have breakfast any time. Jeanie De Lille, the island's premier pastry chef, bakes crisp, light waffles and serves them in many ways, including the waffle ranchero with eggs and salsa, the waffle Benedict with eggs and hollandaise sauce, and waffles with whipped cream and chocolate. Hash browns, homemade breads, and great coffee are other reasons to drop in for breakfast mornings and evenings. The menu has been expanded to include fried fish, tamales, *carne asada tampiqueña,* and several pasta dishes, and there is a full bar. To get there from the pier, turn right (south) on Melgar and walk 4 blocks; it's on your left between the Aqua Safari and the Hotel Vista del Mar.

COZUMEL AFTER DARK

Cozumel is a town frequented by sports-minded visitors who play hard all day and wind down early at night. People sit in outdoor cafes around the *zócalo* (plaza) enjoying the cool night breezes until the restaurants close. **Carlos 'n Charlie's** and the **Hard Rock Café,** both on Melgar left of the pier, are two of the liveliest places in town. **Karen's Grill and Pizza,** on Avenida 5 between Juárez and Calle 2 Norte, features live entertainment in the evenings.

Scaramouche, a popular disco, on Melgar at Salas, is open nightly from 10pm to 3am. The cover charge varies.

3 Puerto Morelos

21 miles S of Cancún

Most people come here to take the car ferry to Cozumel, several hours away. Puerto Morelos has begun to resume the building boom that was beginning when Hurricane Gilbert came through.

ESSENTIALS
GETTING THERE

BY BUS   Buses from Cancún's bus station going to Tulum and Playa del Carmen usually stop here, but be sure to ask in Cancún if your bus makes the Puerto Morelos stop.

BY CAR   Drive south from Cancún along Highway 307 to the km 31 marker. There are a couple of worthwhile stops along Highway 307 on the way to Puerto Morelos. **Croco Cun,** a zoological park where crocodiles are raised, is one of the most interesting attractions in the area—don't be put off by the comical name. Though far from grand, the park has exhibits of crocodiles in all stages of development, as well as many native animals that once roamed the Yucatán Peninsula. The snake exhibit is fascinating, though it may make you think twice about roaming in the jungle. The rattlesnakes and boa constrictors are particularly intimidating, and the tarantulas are downright enormous. Children enjoy the guides' enthusiastic tours and are entranced by the spider monkeys and wild pigs. Wear plenty of bug repellent and allow an hour or two for the tour, followed by a cool drink in the restaurant. Croco Cun is open daily from 8:30am to 5:30pm. Admission is $5, and free for children under 6. The park is at km 31 on Highway 307.

About half a mile before Puerto Morelos is the 150-acre **Jardín Botánico,** opened in 1990. A natural, protected showcase for native plants and animals, it's open Tuesday through Sunday from 9am to 4pm. Admission is $3.75; it's worth the money—

and every minute of the hour or more it will take to see it. Slather on the mosquito repellent, though.

The park is divided into six parts: an epiphyte area (plants that grow on others); Maya ruins; an ethnographic area, with a furnished hut and typical garden; a chiclero camp about the once-thriving chicle (chewing gum) industry; a nature park, where wild vegetation is preserved; and mangroves. Wandering along the marked paths, you'll see that the dense jungle of plants and trees is named and labeled in English and Spanish. Each sign has the plant's scientific and common names, the use of the plant, and the geographic areas where it is found in the wild. It's rich in bird and animal life, too, but to catch a glimpse of something you'll have to move quietly and listen carefully.

BY THE PUERTO MORELOS–COZUMEL CAR FERRY　　The dock (☎ 987/ 1-0008), the largest establishment in town, is very easy to find. Look to the Cozumel section above for details on the car-ferry schedule, but several points bear repeating here: The car-ferry schedule is complicated and may change, so double-check it before arriving. And always arrive at least 3 hours in advance of the ferry's departure to purchase a ticket and to get in line.

ORIENTATION

There's one public telephone in Puerto Morelos (☎ 987/2-0070; fax 987/1-0081), at the Caseta de Larga Distancia, next to the Zenaida Restaurant a block south of the main entry street leading to the highway. You can make calls there, and supposedly they'll take messages and pass along hotel-reservation requests. It's open Monday through Saturday from 8am to 1pm and 4 to 7pm. On the highway, near the Puerto Morelos junction, you'll see a gas station with public phones (including Ladatel phones that accept prepaid phone cards) and a supermarket on the right.

EXPLORING AROUND PUERTO MORELOS

Visitors to Puerto Morelos enjoy seaside relaxation without the crowds and high prices of Cancún, Cozumel, or Playa del Carmen. The beaches here are as beautiful as any along the coast, but they don't look like it because the deposits of seaweed and other wave-brought debris mar the visual appeal. Plus, except for **Los Pelicanos,** there are no seaside restaurants selling drinks and food and no thatched beach umbrellas under which to seek shelter from the midday sun. Though the village is attracting more resort development now, and other businesses are popping up too, you make your own fun here—which is precisely its appeal to some people. As for **diving and fishing,** try **Sub Aqua Explorers** (☎ 987/1-0012; fax 987/1-0162), on the main square. More than 15 dive sites are nearby and many are close to shore. A two-tank dive costs around $60 and night dives $55. Two hours of fishing costs around $80 and snorkeling excursions run around $5.

WHERE TO STAY

Cabañas Puerto Morelos. Apdo. Postal 1524, 77501 Cancún, Q. Roo. ☎ **987/1-0004.** E-mail: 102312.3506@compuserve.com. Reservations: Niki Seach, 7912 NE Ochoa, Elk River, MN 55330. ☎ and fax 612/441-7630. E-mail: 102301.2317@compuserve.com. 4 cabañas. High season $450–$750 per week; $70 per night. Low season $275–$450 per week; $50 per night.

If you're looking for something comfortable and reasonable, away from the crowds and near the beach, this is a good place to consider, especially for a long stay. Connie and Bill Butcher created this shady hideaway with lots of extra touches. It consists of three one-bedroom cabañas and a two-bedroom house. The cabañas, all with tile floors, have kitchens equipped with coffeemakers and juicers, plus bottled water, several beers, and soft drinks to get guests started. You'll also find paperback books and colorful furniture with folk art accents. There's a shady place outside for dining or lounging. The Butchers are known for their willingness to help guests enjoy the area. Most rooms are booked in advance from the United States, but you can take a chance on a vacancy if you're in the area. This spot is 12 miles from the Cancún airport. To find it from the Puerto Morelos zócalo, turn left at the edge of the zócalo as you come from the highway. Go 3 blocks and it's on the left behind a white wall and gate. Ring the bell.

Caribbean Reef Club. Villa Marina, 77501 Puerto Morelos, Q. Roo. ☎ **800/322-6286** or 987/1-0191. Fax 987/1-0190. 21 suites. A/C and FAN TV. High season $145. Low season $115.

Opened in 1991, this is the nicest place to stay in Puerto Morelos, and it's right on the beach. The units (called suites, but they're really like upscale apartments) come with marble floors, neutral-toned furniture, and windows on the garden all facing the sea. All come with one bedroom (most with two double beds), combination kitchenette with living room (and sleeper sofa), remote-control TV, and two bathrooms with showers (some have a combo tub/shower). Besides air-conditioning, each also has a fan. There's a nice-size pool next to the beach. The hotel offers complimentary use of snorkeling gear, small sailboats, and windsurf boards. A comfortable and breezy beachfront restaurant on the property serves all three meals daily between 8am and 9pm—it's the best restaurant in Puerto Morelos. To find it, follow directions through Puerto Morelos to the ferry pier and the complex is just beyond it.

Ojo de Agua. Calle Ejer Mexicano, 77501 Puerto Morelos, Q. Roo. ☎ **987/1-0027.** 16 rms. FAN. High season $50–$60 double. Low season $45–$55 double.

This family-style, two-story hotel on the beach is ideal for a long weekend or extended stay, especially in the 12 rooms with kitchens. Each room contains a white tile floor, natural-tone furniture, and a table and chairs. Most rooms have one double and one twin bed, but two come with king-size beds. There's a free-form pool by the ocean. Restaurants are within easy walking distance and dive gear and trips are available through the hotel. To find it from the plaza, turn left on the last street that parallels the ocean. The hotel is at the far end on the left.

Posada Amor. Apdo. Postal 806, 77580 Cancún, Q. Roo. ☎ **987/1-0033.** 20 rms (8 with bath). $24 double without bath; $30 double with bath; $35 for a room with 4 beds and bath.

The simple, cheery little rooms at the Posada Amor, with screens and mosquito netting, are plain but adequate (and overpriced). They're clustered around a patio in back of the restaurant. The posada's restaurant is rustic and quaint like an English cottage—with whitewashed walls, small shuttered windows, and open rafters—and is decorated with primitive paintings and flowers on each table. The food is tasty, with many regional specialties, sandwiches, a comida corrida for $4, and a Sunday buffet for $5.75. It's open daily from 7:30am to 11pm. To get here, when you enter town, turn right; with the town square on the left, follow the main street leading to the ferry; the hotel is about a block down on the right.

WHERE TO DINE

Besides the above-mentioned Posada Amor, and the best restaurant in town on the covered patio of the Caribbean Reef Club, Los Pelicanos is worth trying.

Los Pelicanos. On the oceanside behind and right of the zócalo. ☎ **987/1-0014.** Main courses $5.50–$16; lobster $25. Daily 10am–10pm. SEAFOOD.

Since this village has few restaurants, Los Pelicanos holds almost a captive audience for central village beachside dining. You'll notice the inviting restaurant down a block to the right of the plaza on the street paralleling the ocean. Select a table inside under the palapa or outside on the terrace (wear mosquito repellent in the evenings). From the terrace you have an easy view of pelicans swooping around the dock. The seafood menu has all the usual offerings, from ceviche to conch made three ways to shrimp, lobster, and fish. There are grilled chicken and steak for those who don't want seafood.

EN ROUTE TO PLAYA DEL CARMEN

Heading south on Highway 307 from Puerto Morelos, it's only 20 miles to Playa del Carmen, so you'll be there in half an hour or less. However, you'll pass several small beach resorts en route. The two more upscale places below are run by the reputable Turquoise Reef Group. And less than 3 miles before Playa del Carmen, you'll pass several roads that head out to the relaxed, isolated small hotels at **Punta Bete,** which is the name of a fine beach—not a town. If you turn left and follow a small unpaved trail at the km 52 marker and PUNTA BETE sign, you'll find two small, inexpensive groups of bungalows at the end of the trail and on a fine stretch of beach, which you'll have almost to yourself.

If you come here between July and October, you can walk the beach at night to watch for **turtles** lumbering ashore to lay their eggs, or watch the eggs hatch and the tiny, vulnerable turtles scurry to the ocean in November and December. However, turtles will not lay eggs where there is too much light, so as development continues (and more lights are installed) we'll see fewer turtles nesting.

WHERE TO STAY & DINE IN PUNTA BETE

If you're seeking low-cost, comfortable isolation, turn left at the Punta Bete sign on the highway. The narrow, overgrown road you follow isn't much, and you may even wonder if it is the right one. Have faith and keep bearing right. Soon you'll see a sign pointing right to the Cabañas Bahía Xcalacoco or straight ahead to the Cabañas Xcalacoco. (There's another group of cabañas to the left of the Cabañas Xcalacoco, with nearly the same name, but the upkeep and service are totally undependable, and I don't recommend it.) Even if you don't stay here, you can use the restaurants as a base and come for the day from Playa del Carmen. The beach is beautiful and almost uninhabited. In fact, though you're only 4 miles from Playa del Carmen the solitude and lack of crowds makes it seem more like civilization is 1,000 miles away. It is a perfect getaway if you aren't looking for luxury.

✪ **Cabañas Bahía Xcalacoco.** Apdo. Postal 176, 77710 Playa del Carmen, Q. Roo. No phone. 2 rms (both with bath). $35 double.

Ricardo and Rosa Novelo opened their own small inn in 1996, with two small white-washed rooms in a shady thicket by the beach. Rosa, the powerhouse cook and general manager, keeps things running smoothly, while Ricardo takes guests fishing and snorkeling. The rooms are small and plain, but comfortable—however, there's no electricity, so you learn to work the kerosene lamp. Rosa serves guests in the small restaurant—expect sizable portions at very reasonable prices. The fish dinner is large and excellent. Ask about jungle trails to Maya ruins near the cabañas.

Cabañas Xcalacoco. Km 52 Carretera Cancún–Tulum (Apdo. Postal 176), 77710 Playa del Carmen, Q. Roo. No phone. 7 cabañas (all with bath). $25 with one bed; $35 with two beds; RVs and campers $4 per person. Discounts available in low season.

Next door to the Cabañas Bahía is this long-established set of cabañas, which are tidy, whitewashed buildings with small porches, all right on the beach. All have baths; five have king-size beds, and the others have two double beds each. Since there's no electricity, kerosene lamps light rooms in the evenings. Camping facilities are available for those in recreational vehicles and others wishing to hang a hammock under

The Yucatán´s Upper Caribbean Coast

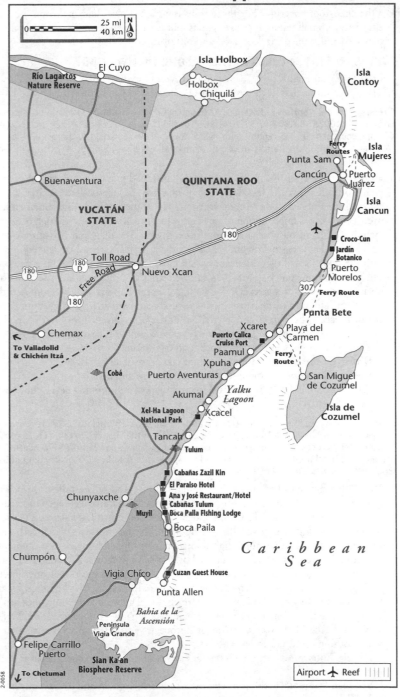

25 mi
40 km
0

N

El Cuyo

Río Lagartos
Nature Reserve

Isla Holbox

Holbox
Chiquilá

Isla
Contoy

Ferry
Routes

Isla
Mujeres

Punta Sam

Cancún

Puerto
Juárez

QUINTANA ROO
STATE

Isla
Cancun

Buenaventura

180

Croco-Cun

Jardín
Botanico

YUCATÁN
STATE

Toll Road

180
D

180
D

Free Road

180

Nuevo Xcan

Puerto
Morelos

307

Ferry Route

Punta Bete

Chemax

To Valladolid
& Chichén Itzá

Cobá

Xcaret

Puerto Calica
Cruise Port

Paamul

Xpuha

Playa del
Carmen

Ferry
Route

Puerto Aventuras

Akumal

Yalku
Lagoon

San Miguel
de Cozumel

Xel-Ha Lagoon
National Park

Xcacel

Isla de
Cozumel

Tancah

Tulum

Chunyaxche

Muyil

Cabañas Zazil Kin

El Paraíso Hotel

Ana y José Restaurant/Hotel

Cabañas Tulum

Boca Palla Fishing Lodge

Boca Paila

Caribbean
Sea

Chumpón

Vigia Chíco

Cuzan Guest House

Punta Allen

Bahía de la
Ascensión

Felipe Carrillo
Puerto

Peninsula
Vigia Grande

Sian Ka´an
Biosphere Reserve

To Chetumal

2-0058

Airport ✈ Reef ||||||

a thatched-roof covering. For those folks there's a shower and bathroom but no electricity. A small restaurant serves guests, but it's always a good idea to bring along packaged and canned snacks, water, and soft drinks.

WHERE TO STAY & DINE FARTHER ALONG HIGHWAY 307

Continuing on Highway 307, a few miles beyond the Punta Bete turnoff, you'll see a large sign on the left to the entrance to La Posada del Capitán Lafitte.

✪ **La Posada del Capitán Lafitte.** Km 62 Carretera Cancún–Tulum, 77710 Playa del Carmen, Q. Roo. ☎ **800/538-6802** or 303/674-9615 in the U.S., or 987/3-0214. Fax 987/3-0213. 40 bungalows. A/C or FAN. High season $165 double. Low season $120 double. Christmas, New Year's, Thanksgiving, and part of Feb are higher. Minimum 3-night stay. Rates include breakfast and dinner. Free parking.

From the highway, drive a mile down a rough dirt road that heads toward the ocean. Here you can enjoy the feeling of being on a private, nearly deserted island but enjoy all the amenities of a relaxing vacation. The numerous units of Capitán Lafitte stretch out along a huge portion of powdery white beach with space enough between them to feel luxuriously separate from other guests. The one- and two-story white stucco bungalows are smallish but very comfortable, stylishly furnished, and equipped with tile floors, small tiled bathrooms, and either two double or one king-size bed and an oceanfront porch. There's 24-hour electricity (a plus you learn to value on isolated stretches of this coast). If you wish, coffee can be served in the room as early as 6:30am. There's a turtle patrol in which guests can participate during summer on nearby beaches where green and loggerhead turtles nest. Divers from North America make up a sizable portion of the clientele here, as well as repeat visitors who come annually just for the peace, quiet, beach, and relaxation.

Dining/Entertainment: One restaurant takes care of all meals.

Services: Laundry and room service, travel agency, and dive shop.

Facilities: You'll find a large, raised swimming pool and sunning deck, clubhouse, and excellent dive shop.

Shangri-La Caribe. Km 69.5 Carretera Cancún–Tulum (Apdo. Postal 253), 77710 Playa del Carmen, Q. Roo. ☎ **800/538-6802** or 303/674-9615 in the U.S, or 987/3-0611. Fax 987/3-0500. FAN. 50 oceanview bungalows, 5 beachfront cabañas. High season $170 oceanview double; $220 beachfront double. Low season $127 oceanview double; $177 beachfront double. (Book well in advance during high season.) Free parking.

After Punta Bete and La Posada del Capitán Lafitte—and only a mile or so before you reach Playa del Carmen on Highway 307—you'll see the Volkswagen plant and a huge sign for the Shangri-La Caribe and another resort called Las Palapas. Turn left at the VW building, and you'll find the Shangri-La a mile straight ahead on a semipaved road. The two-story, high-domed, palapa-topped bungalows meander to the ocean, linked by sidewalks and edged by tropical vegetation. All come with two double beds, nice tile baths, and a hammock strung on the patio or balcony. Prices get higher the closer you get to the beach and are higher for two-bedroom casas. Though you're very close to Playa del Carmen, hotel guests are the only ones using the beach, and the feeling is one of being many relaxing miles from civilization. You'll share this beachside retreat with lots of European vacationers to whom wearing a whole bathing suit is not important.

Dining/Entertainment: One restaurant serves all three meals, and the bar is open long hours.

Services: Car rental and bus or taxi tours to nearby lagoons and to Tulum, Cobá, and Chichén-Itzá.

Sea Turtles of the Yucatán

At least four species of marine turtles nest on the beaches of Quintana Roo—the loggerhead, green, hawksbill, and leatherback varieties. Of these, the leatherback is almost nonexistent, and the loggerhead is the most abundant—but all are endangered.

Most turtles lay eggs on the same beach year after year, and as often as three times in a season. Strolling along the beach late at night in search of giant turtles (prime egg-laying hours are between 10pm and 3am) is a special experience that will make you feel closer to the Yucatán's environment. It may take you a while to get used to the darkness, but don't use your flashlight—lights of any kind repel the turtles. Laying the eggs is tough work—a female will dig nonstop with back flippers for more than an hour; the exercise leaves its head and legs flushed. Depositing the 100 or more eggs takes only minutes; then she makes the nest invisible by laboriously covering it with sand and disappears into the sea. Each soft-shelled egg looks like a Ping-Pong ball.

Hatchlings scurry to the sea 45 days later, but successful incubation depends on the temperature and depth of the nest. When conditions are right, the hatch rates of fertile eggs are high; however, only 5% of those that do make it to the sea escape predators long enough to return.

Despite recent efforts to protect Mexico's turtles, the eggs are still considered an aphrodisiac, and there's a market for them; turtles are killed for their shells and meat as well. Since turtle life expectancy is more than 50 years, killing one turtle kills thousands more. Costly protection programs include tagging the female and catching the eggs as they are deposited, then removing them to a protected area and nest of identical size and temperature.

Facilities: The large, inviting pool is surrounded by a sundeck, and there are horses for rent at $25 an hour. The Cyan-Ha Diving Center on the premises offers diving, snorkeling, and fishing trips, and equipment rental for these sports. May and June are best for fishing with abundant marlin, sailfish, and dorado.

4 Playa del Carmen

20 miles SW of Puerto Morelos, 44 miles SW of Cancún, 6.5 miles N of Xcaret, and 8 miles N of Puerto Calica

This rapidly expanding Caribbean village grew up around the mainland terminus of the passenger-boat service to Cozumel. Travelers soon discovered that Playa del Carmen's long stretches of white beach were far better than those on Cozumel, and it has developed quite a tourist trade of its own. The tide of progress is rolling on with the appearance of the all-inclusive Diamond Resort and the Hotel Continental Plaza Playacar, both new resorts south of the center of town, as well as new sewage and water lines, telephone service, and more brick-paved streets. The town doubled in size in 1993 and is preparing for 50,000 inhabitants by the year 2000.

Time-share hawkers ply their same fake, friendly ways in Playa, but not in the numbers present in Cancún. Topless sunbathing, though against the law in Mexico, seems condoned here—including leisurely topless strolling anywhere there's a beach. It's so casually topless, in fact, that there was a sign in the post office to the effect of NO TOPLESS IN HERE.

Avenida Juárez (also known as Avenida Principal) leads into town and has always been considered "main street," but the four-lane Avenida 30, 5 blocks from the beach, has been paved and is positioned as another "main street."

Playa del Carmen is something of a fork in the road for southbound travelers—you can go by ferry east to Cozumel or continue south to Xcaret, Puerto Calica, Akumal, Tulum, Cobá, Punta Allen, Majahual, Lago Bacalar, and Chetumal on Highway 307.

Though Playa has lost its innocence, it's still a peaceful place where you can hang out on the beach for hours without feeling the need to explore. However, get there quickly—it's changing fast.

ESSENTIALS
GETTING THERE & DEPARTING

BY BUS   There are three bus stations in Playa del Carmen, all on Avenida Principal (the main street): **Transportes de Oriente, Playa Express,** and **ATS** are a half block north of the plaza and Avenida 5 on Avenida Principal; **Expreso Oriente** is on the corner of Avenida 5 and Avenida Principal; and the **ADO** station is 4 blocks west of the plaza.

ATS offers service to and from Cancún every 15 minutes. ATS buses also go to Xcaret (five times) and to Tulum (11 times), as well as to Cobá, Chetumal, and Palenque. Second-class Oriente buses travel the route to and from Tulum, Cobá, and Bacalar. Several de paso ADO buses pass through Playa del Carmen on the way to Cancún. And several ADO buses go to Valladolid, Chichén-Itzá, and Mérida.

Expreso Oriente goes to Villahermosa, Mérida, Tulum, Cancún, Felipe Carrillo Puerto, and Chetumal.

BY CAR   The turnoff to Playa del Carmen from Highway 307 is plainly marked, and you'll arrive on the town's widest street, Avenida Principal, also known as Avenida Benito Juárez (not that there's a street sign to that effect).

BY THE PLAYA DEL CARMEN–COZUMEL PASSENGER FERRY   See the Cozumel section above for the details on the passenger ferry service between Playa del Carmen and Cozumel.

BY TAXI   Taxi fares to the Cancún airport are high, but there is a service offering shared taxi rides for $14 per person. Check at your hotel or at the Caribe Maya restaurant on Avenida 5 at Calle 8 for information and reservations.

ORIENTATION

ARRIVING   The ferry dock in Playa del Carmen is 1 1/2 blocks from the main square and within walking distance of hotels. Buses are along Avenida Principal, a short distance from hotels, restaurants, and the ferry pier. Tricycle taxis are the only vehicular traffic allowed between the bus stations and Avenida 5 and the ferry. A number of these efficient taxis meet each bus and ferry and can transport you and your luggage to any hotel in town. The new Puerto Calica Cruise Pier is almost 8 miles south of Playa del Carmen; taxis meet each ship.

CITY LAYOUT   Villagers know and use street names, but few street signs exist. The main street, **Avenida Principal,** also known as **Avenida Benito Juárez,** leads into town from Highway 307, crossing Avenida 5 one block before it ends at the beach next to the main plaza, or zócalo. Traffic is diverted from Avenida Principal at Avenida 10. **Avenida 5,** the other main artery (closed to traffic from Avenida Principal to Calle 6) leads to the ferry dock, two blocks from the zócalo; most restaurants

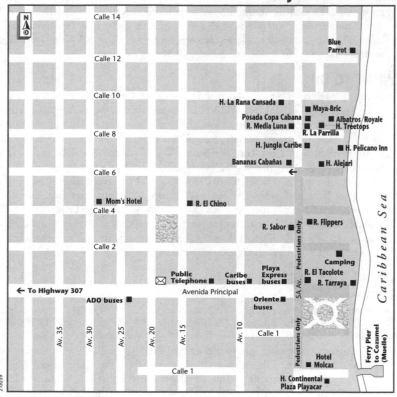

and hotels are either on Avenida 5, or a block or two off of it. The village's beautiful beach parallels Avenida 5 and is only a block from it.

FAST FACTS: PLAYA DEL CARMEN

Area Code   The telephone area code is 987.

Messages   Mom's Hotel acts as an unofficial message center, with a bulletin board posting messages for traveling friends, people needing rides, house or room rentals, or items for sale.

Money Exchange   There are two branches of the Cicsa Money Exchange, one at the foot of the pier and the other at the Rincón del Sol plaza on Avenida 5 at Calle 8. Both are open Monday through Friday from 7:30am to 7:30pm and Saturday from 7:30am to 1pm and 3:30 to 6:30pm.

Parking   Because of the pedestrian-only blocks and increasing population and popularity of Playa, parking close to hotels has become more difficult. The most accessible parking lot is the Estacionamiento Mexico at the corner of Avenida Principal and Avenida 10, open daily 24 hours; the fee is $1.25 per hour and $8 per day.

Post Office   The post office is on Avenida Principal 3 blocks north of the plaza, on the right past the Hotel Playa del Carmen and the launderette.

Seasons   High season is December through Easter and August. Low season is all other months, but November is becoming very popular.

Telephones   Most hotels have phones and faxes now; often both are on the same phone line. So, to send a fax call and ask for the fax tone: "Por favor, dar me el tono por el fax." The **Calling Station** on the street leading up from the ferry pier is a full-service phone center with air-conditioned booths, no surcharges, fax service, and a bulletin board where you can leave messages for friends. It's open Monday through Saturday from 8am to 11pm, and Sunday from 9am to 10pm.

WHAT TO DO

Playa is for relaxing. But beyond that, the island of **Cozumel** is a quick ferry ride away; **Tulum, Xel-Ha, Xcaret,** and **Xcalacoco** are easy excursions. Avenida 5 is lined with two dozen nice-looking, small shops selling imported batik clothing, Guatemalan fabric clothing, masks, pottery, hammocks, and a few T-shirts. Reef diving can be arranged through **Tank-Ha Dive Shop** (☎ and fax **987/3-0302**), at the Hotel Maya Bric. Snorkeling trips cost $25 and include soft drinks and equipment. Two-tank dive trips are $65; resort courses are available. For **cavern diving,** see "Scuba Diving" in "Cozumel," above, where small groups are met in Playa del Carmen for this new one-of-a-kind experience. An 18-hole championship **golf course** (☎ **987/ 3-0624**), designed by Robert Von Hagge, is open adjacent to the Continental Plaza Playacar. Greens fee is $75 and the price includes a cart and tax. Two **tennis** courts are also available at the club there.

WHERE TO STAY
EXPENSIVE
Continental Plaza Playacar. Km 62.5 Frac. Playacar, 77710 Playa del Carmen, Q. Roo. ☎ **800/88-CONTI** in the U.S., or 987/3-0100. Fax 987/3-0105. 185 rms. A/C TV TEL. High season $195–$450 double. Low season $145–$340 double. Ask about special packages.

The village's most upscale resort hotel opened in 1991 on 308 acres spreading out along the beach beyond the ferry pier, a short walk from the village center. Almost 200 Maya ruins were found during development of the resort. The entry leads through a sunny, wide marble lobby beyond which you see the pool and beach. The large, nicely furnished rooms all have in-room safety deposit boxes, purified tap water, tile floors, large baths, wet bars with refrigerators, and balconies with sea views. Rates vary depending on your view—garden, ocean, parking lot, or brick wall—and on whether you have one or two bedrooms. To find it from the ferry pier, turn left when you get off the ferry and follow the road a short distance until you see the Playacar sign. If you're driving in, turn right at the last street before the main street dead-ends and you'll see signs to the hotel about two blocks ahead.

Dining/Entertainment: La Pergola, with pool, beach, and ocean view, serves international food daily for breakfast and dinner. La Sirena is the poolside restaurant. The stylish and welcoming lobby bar is open between 7am and 1am daily with live music in the evenings.

Services: Laundry and room service, baby-sitting, gift shop and boutiques, travel agency, and tours to nearby archaeological zones and lagoons.

Facilities: Oceanside pool with swim-up bar, water-sports equipment, one lighted tennis court.

MODERATE
✪ **Albatros Royale.** Calle 8 (Apdo. Postal 31), 77710 Playa del Carmen, Q. Roo. ☎ **800/ 538-6802** in the U.S. and Canada, or 987/3-0001. 31 rms. FAN. High season $80 double. Low season $60 double. Rates include breakfast.

This "deluxe" sister hotel to the neighboring Pelicano Inn (see below) rises up on a narrow bit of land facing the beach. The two stories of rooms all have tile floors, tile baths with marble vanities and showers, balconies or porches, and most have ocean views. Most have two double beds, but seven have queen-size beds. Breakfast is taken almost next door at the Pelicano Inn. To get here from the corner of Avenida 5 and Calle 8 (where you'll see the Rincón del Sol center), turn toward the water on Calle 8; it's midway down the block on your left. Street parking is scarce.

Hotel Alejari. Calle 6 (Apdo. Postal 166), 77710 Playa del Carmen, Q. Roo. ☎ **987/3-0374.** Fax 987/3-0005. 23 rms. A/C or FAN. High season $55 double; $65 double with kitchenette; $60 double two-story unit with kitchen. Low season $50 double; $60 double two-story unit with kitchen. Rates include breakfast. Free guarded parking.

Built around a fastidiously kept flower-filled inner yard, this small hotel is just off Avenida 5 and half a block from the beach. Though overpriced compared to newer similarly priced hotels in Playa, rooms are clean, each with white walls, ruffled nylon bedspreads, and a small vanity with mirror in the bedroom. Ground-level rooms have two double beds. Rooms with kitchens have a kitchen and living room downstairs, and the bedroom, with a king-size bed, is up a narrow stairway. The restaurant is open daily from 8am to 4pm and breakfast is served between 8 and 11am.

La Jungla Caribe. Av. 5 Norte at Calle 8 (Apdo. Postal 180), 77710 Playa del Carmen, Q. Roo. ☎ **987/3-0650.** 25 rms. A/C TV. High season $65–$75 double; $95–$120 suite. Low season $57–$65 double; $75–$100 suite.

La Jungla Caribe offers a lot of quality for the bucks. Rolf Albrecht, the mastermind behind the hotel, envisioned a lot of space and comfort for guests, so even the standard rooms have plenty of room, with grey-and-black marble floors and large bathrooms. There's a catwalk to the "tower" section of suites. A pool is on the first level and a restaurant overlooks Calle 8.

✪ **Pelicano Inn.** On the beach between calles 6 and 8 (Apdo. Postal 31), 77710 Playa del Carmen, Q. Roo. ☎ **800/538-6802** in the U.S., or 987/3-0997. Fax 987/3-0998. 38 rms. FAN and A/C. High season $65–$90 double. Low season $50–$77 double. Rates include breakfast.

Larry Beard demolished his old seaside hotel Albatros and in its place created a handsome white-stucco pueblo-style hotel bearing no resemblance to its funky predecessor. The spacious rooms, in one-, two-, and three-level tiers, have tile floors and baths, overbed reading lights, and balconies or patios outfitted with hammocks. Most rooms have two double beds, and several have only one—but none have bedspreads. Once you see it, you'd expect to pay a good deal more. Rates vary according to the view—garden, sea, or beachfront—and the time of year. There are two low-season rates, with the higher one in place from July through mid-December. The restaurant, open 7:30am–6pm, is one of the best (see "Where to Dine," below), and guests partake of the all-you-can-eat breakfast buffet. From Avenida Principal, walk 4 blocks north on Avenida 5, then turn right half a block on Calle 8, where a path on the right between two lots leads into the hotel. (You don't have to trudge across the beach as in the past.)

INEXPENSIVE

✪ **Hotel Maya-Bric.** Av. 5 Norte, 77710 Playa del Carmen, Q. Roo. ☎ and fax **987/3-0011.** 29 rms. A/C and FAN. High season $40 double. Low season $35 double. Free guarded parking.

The colorful exterior and flowers will draw your eye to this two-story beachfront inn. Each of the well-kept rooms has two double beds with fairly firm mattresses; some have ocean views. The buildings frame a small pool where guests gather for card games and conversation. The Maya-Bric is one of the quietest hotels in town; it's well-supervised by the Briseño family owners and is frequented by loyal guests who return annually. The gates are locked at night, and only guests are allowed to enter. A small restaurant by the office sometimes serves breakfast and snacks during the high season. Air-conditioning is being added to all rooms. The on-site dive shop, Tank-Ha (See "What to Do," above), rents diving and snorkeling gear and arranges trips to the reefs.

Mom's Hotel. Av. 30 at Calle 4, 77710 Playa del Carmen, Q. Roo. ☎ and fax **987/3-0315.** 12 rms. AC or FAN. High season $35 double. Low season (May, June, Sept–Nov) $25 double. Discounts for lengthy stays.

Though away from the beach, this is a good choice if all the beachside inns are full or if your stay is long. Rooms, all facing the interior courtyard, are fairly large and sunny; each comes with tile floors, one or two double beds, and bedside reading lights. Three rooms have air-conditioning. There's a small pool in the sunny court- yard and a bulletin board for messages to other travelers. A bar and restaurant were in the planning stage when I checked. To find it from the corner of Avenida 5 and Calle 4, walk 5 blocks inland; it's at the corner of Calle 4 and Avenida 30.

Posada Copa Cabana. Av. 5 (Apdo. Postal 103), 77710 Playa del Carmen, Q. Roo. ☎ **987/ 3-0218.** 8 rms, 2 cabañas. FAN. High season $40 double. Low season $35 double.

Hammocks are stretched in front of each room and on the porch of each cabaña at this pleasant, palm-shaded inn, and the patio Restaurant Soluna fills up the court- yard to the right. Each of the clean, simply furnished rooms has one or two double beds on concrete platforms and pink-and-gray tile floors. Vanities and sinks are conveniently placed outside the baths. There's good cross-ventilation through well-screened windows. To get here from the plaza, turn right on Avenida 5 and walk 3 blocks; it's on your right between calles 8 and 10. There is no parking on Avenida 5, but there's limited parking nearby.

La Rana Cansada. Calle 10, 77710 Playa del Carmen, Q. Roo. ☎ and fax **987/3-0389.** 12 rms. High season $55 double. Low season $25 double.

The "Tired Frog" is one of the most simply pleasant inns in the village, though it's a bit overpriced in high season. Behind an elegant hacienda-style wall and handsome iron gate, the plainly furnished but neat and clean rooms face an inner courtyard that has a small snack bar under a large thatched palapa. Hammocks are strung on the covered porch outside the row of rooms. Some rooms have concrete ceilings and oth- ers a thatched roof, and all have well-screened doors and windows. New rooms were on the drawing board as well as a small pool and breakfast service. Trade paperbacks are available at the front desk, and manager John Swartz is very accommodating with tips on seeing the area. It's a block and a half inland from the beach. To find it from the main plaza, walk 5 blocks north on Avenida 5 and turn left on Calle 10; the hotel is on the left.

✪ **Treetops.** Calle 8 s/n, 77710 Playa del Carmen, Q. Roo. ☎ and fax **987/3-0351.** E-mail: treetops@linux.pya.com.mx. 10 rms. AC or FAN. High season $45–$75 double. Low season $35– $55 double. Rates include continental breakfast.

Owners Sandy and Bill Dillon changed the name from Cuevo Pargo and added more rooms during their stem-to-stern cleaning and revamp. Set in a small patch of undisturbed jungle, with bungalows linked by stone pathways, this place is cooler than any in town and comes complete with its own cenote and swimming pool. The older bungalows (each a separate unit) are rustic but comfortable and come with small charms like thatched roofs and rock walls and unusual architecture— no two are alike. Two bungalows have kitchens. The new rooms, in a two-story fourplex, have a choice of air-conditioning or fan, refrigerators, and nice balconies or patios. The new air-conditioned Safari Restaurant is situated in the treetops above the pool. The restaurant offers a short menu of charcoal-broiled hot dogs and hamburgers (with U.S. beef), club sandwiches, homemade potato salad, Tex-Mex chili, and tacos. The Safari Bar, to the left after you enter, is a good place to go for an evening drink and to meet fellow travelers. The bar is open daily from 3pm to midnight. Happy hour is from 5 to 7pm. There's satellite TV broadcasting U.S.

channels in the reception area and bar. Additional rooms may be finished by the time you travel. From the Avenida Principal, walk 4 blocks north on Avenida 5, then turn right for half a block on Calle 8; the hotel is on the left, half a block from the beach.

WHERE TO DINE

Restaurants are constantly opening (and closing) in Playa, so besides these listed below, you may find many new ones to consider. Make your own delicious doughnut breakfast and savor aromatic Chiapan coffee at **Daily Doughnuts,** on Avenida 5, between Calles 8 and 10 (☎ 987/3-0396). It's open Monday through Saturday from 7am to 9pm.

EXPENSIVE

✪ **Flippers.** Av. 5 at Calle 4. No phone. Grilled specialties $7–$17; seafood platter $22. Daily 3–10:30pm. MEXICAN/GRILLED MEATS.

There's almost always a crowd at Flippers, which is noticeable from the street for its nautical theme, created by fishnets and ropes under a thatched palapa. There's an extensive bar list as well as a varied menu that includes grilled specialties from sea and land plus hamburgers, poc chuc, and beef tampiqueña. Happy hour, when drinks are two for the price of one, runs from 5 to 11pm, and live music springs forth between 7 and 10pm most evenings.

La Parrilla. Av. 5 at Calle 8. ☎ 987/3-0687. Breakfast specials $3–$4.50; main courses $5.25–$14. Daily 7am–1am. MEXICAN/GRILLED MEATS.

The Rincón del Sol plaza is one of the prettiest buildings in Playa, and now it houses one of the most popular restaurants in town. The dining room is set in two levels above the street with the open kitchen in back. The aroma of grilling meat permeates the air. The huge chicken fajitas come with plenty of homemade tortillas and beans, and if you want to splurge on lobster, this is the place to do it. The tables fill quickly in the evening, but there are smaller bar tables set out in the plaza's courtyards, where you can wait.

MODERATE

✪ **El Chino.** Calle 4 at Av. 15. ☎ 987/3-0015. Breakfast $2.25–$3.50; main courses $4–$9. Daily 8am–11pm. YUCATECAN/MEXICAN.

Despite its name, there's nary a Chinese dish on the menu. But locals highly recommend this place, as do I. Though slightly off the popular Avenida 5 row of restaurants, it has its own clean, cool ambience, with tile floors and plastic-covered polished wood tables set below a huge palapa roof with whirring ceiling fans. A side patio is open-air with uncovered tables that are good for evening meals. The standard breakfast menu applies, plus you can order fresh blended fruit drinks. Main courses include such regional favorites as poc chuc, chicken pibil, and Ticul-style fish, plus shrimp-stuffed fish and beef, chicken, and shrimp brochettes. Other selections are lobster and shrimp crepes, fajitas, and ceviche.

✪ **Media Luna.** Av. 5, corner of Calle 8. No phone. Breakfast $3.50–$4.75; main courses $4–$9. Tues–Sun 7:30am–3pm and 6:30–11:30pm. INTERNATIONAL.

Few restaurants have such mouthwatering aromas coming from the kitchen. When you read the menu you'll know why. The spinach-and-mushroom breakfast crepes arrive with fabulous herb-, onion-, and garlic-flavored potatoes. Other crepes are filled with fresh fruit. For dinner there are savory Greek salads, black bean quesadillas, grilled shrimp salads, fresh grilled fish, and pastas with fresh herbs and sauces, plus other entrees featuring Indian, Italian, Mexican, and Chinese specialties. Decorated in textiles from Guatemala, it's a casual, inviting place, with soft, taped guitar music in the background.

Pelicano Inn. On the beach, at Calle 6. ☎ **987/3-0997.** Buffet breakfast $6; main courses $3–$30. Buffet breakfast daily 7–11am; lunch daily 11:30am–6pm (happy hour noon–1pm and 4–6pm). MEXICAN/AMERICAN.

Located on the beach, this is a good place to meet Americans who live here and while away some hours munching and people-watching. The food is dependably good. The breakfast buffet is an "all-you-can-eat" affair, so arrive hungry. Apart from breakfast, you have a choice of peel-your-own, cajun-flavored shrimp with U.S.-style tartar and shrimp sauce, hamburgers, hot dogs, quesadillas, pastries, ice cream, beer, wine, and coffee. From Avenida Principal, walk 4 blocks north on Avenida 5, turn right a half block on Calle 8 to a marked Pelican Inn pathway, and turn right, or go to the beach and turn right. The hotel/restaurant is on the beach.

INEXPENSIVE

Sabor. Av. 5 between calles 2 and 4. No phone. Yogurt and granola $1.50–$2.75; sandwiches $2–$3; vegetarian plates $2.25–$4; pastries 95¢–$1.50. Daily 8am–11pm. BAKERY/HEALTH FOOD.

The patio full of patrons—it's always full—attests to the popularity of this modest restaurant. The list of hot and cold drinks has expanded to include espresso and cappuccino, café frappe, hot chocolate, tea, and fruit and vegetable drinks. Sabor now has Blue Bell ice cream (a favorite of Texans) and light vegetarian meals. Try a cup of something with a slice of pie and watch village life stroll by.

El Tacolote. Av. Juárez. ☎ **987/3-0066.** Main courses $3.25–$13. Daily 11am–3am. (Shortened hours in low season.) GRILLED MEATS/SEAFOOD.

There's a good selection of tacos, hamburgers, and mixed brochettes offered here. The "vegetarian plate" is grilled shrimp with peppers; the "gringas plate" comes with flour tortillas, grilled pork, and cheese. The restaurant faces the main plaza and has expanded to fill up half the block, but there's also a cool patio in back. Marimbas and mariachis play on weekend nights in high season.

✪ **Tarraya Restaurant/Bar.** Calle 2 Norte at the beach. No phone. Main courses $4–$7; whole fish $5.75. Daily noon–9pm. SEAFOOD.

"THE RESTAURANT THAT WAS BORN WITH THE TOWN," proclaims the sign. This is also the restaurant locals recommend as the best for seafood. Since it's right on the beach, with the water practically lapping at the foundations, and since the owners are fishermen, the fish is so fresh it's practically still wiggling. The wood hut doesn't look like much, but you can have fish fixed almost any way imaginable. If you haven't tried the Yucatecan specialty, tik-n-xic fish, this would be a good place. It's on the beach opposite the basketball court.

PLAYA DEL CARMEN AFTER DARK

It seems like everyone in town is out on Avenida 5 or Juárez across from the square until 10 or 11pm. There's pleasant strolling, meals and drinks at streetside cafes, huskers to watch and listen to, and shops to duck into. Later in the evening your choices diminish: a **Señor Frog's** down by the ferry dock, dishing out its patented mix of thumping dance music, Jell-O shots, and frat-house antics; **Karen's Pizza** on Avenida 5, with live entertainment nightly; the **Safari Bar** at the Treetops hotel always has a congenial crowd gathered around the bar and television until midnight; and then there's the beachside bar at the **Blue Parrot,** which seems to draw most of the European and American expatriate community, has swings for barstools, and stays open late (somewhere around 2 to 3am). *Caution:* Ladies—stay clear of Playa's unusual number of would-be gigolos—they're slick. And lately there have been a few reports of drug involvement in tourist robberies—don't do drugs in Mexico, and don't flash money.

5 Highway 307 from Xcaret to Xel-Ha

This section of the mainland coast—between Playa del Carmen and Tulum—is right on the front lines of the Caribbean coast's transformation from idyllic backwater to developing tourist destination. South of Playa del Carmen along Highway 307 is a succession of new planned resorts and nature parks, commercially developed beaches, and—for now, anyway—a few rustic beach hideaways and unspoiled coves. From north to south, this section will cover Xcaret, Paamul, Xpuha, Puerto Aventuras, Akumal, and Xel-Ha. Puerto Calica, the new cruise ship pier, is $2^1/2$ miles south of Xcarct and 8 miles south of Playa del Carmen.

Of the fledgling resorts south of Playa del Carmen, **Akumal** is one of the most developed, with moderately priced hotels and bungalows scattered among the graceful palms that line the beautiful, soft beach and gorgeous bay. **Puerto Aventuras** is a privately developed, growing resort city aimed at the well-heeled traveler and private-condo owner. **Paamul** and **Xpuha** offer inexpensive inns on gorgeous beaches $2^1/2$ miles apart. If the offbeat beach life is what you're after, grab it now before it disappears. (Other little-known and inexpensive getaways can be found on the **Punta Allen Peninsula** south of Tulum, and the **Majahual Peninsula** south of Felipe Carillo Puerto; see the next section for details.) You'll also enjoy a swim in the nearby lagoon of **Xel-Ha,** one of the coast's prettiest spots. And the new parklike development of **Xcaret** will appeal to some for an all-day excursion.

EN ROUTE SOUTH FROM PLAYA DEL CARMEN   Bus transportation from Playa del Carmen south is no longer as chancy as it used to be, but it's still not great. There are four bus companies in Playa; buses depart fairly frequently for Chetumal, stopping at every point of interest along the way. There's even bus service to and from Cobá three times a day. Though buses originate here, you may be told you can't buy tickets ahead of time. If you choose to hire a car and driver, be sure to find a driver you like and whose English is good—remember, you'll be with him all day.

XCARET: A DEVELOPED NATURE PARK

Six and a half miles south of Playa del Carmen (and 50 miles south of Cancún) is the turnoff to Xcaret (*ish*-car-et), a heavily commercialized, specially-built tourist destination that promotes itself as a 150-acre ecological park. Prior to development, this was a heavenly, little-visited cove and lagoon hidden in the jungle; it looked nothing like it does today. Meant as a place to spend the day, it's open Monday through Saturday from 8:30am to 8:30pm and Sunday from 8:30am to 5:30pm. Without exaggeration, everywhere you look in Cancún are signs advertising Xcaret, or someone handing you a leaflet about it. They even have their own bus terminal to take tourists from Cancún at regular intervals, and they've added an evening extravaganza.

Xcaret may celebrate mother nature, but its builders rearranged quite a bit of her handiwork in completing it. If you're looking for a place to escape the commercialism of Cancún, this may not be it. It's expensive and contrived and may even be very crowded, thus diminishing the advertised "natural" experience. Children, however, seem to love it, and the jungle setting and palm-lined beaches are beautiful. Once past the entry booths (built to resemble small Maya temples), you'll find pathways that meander around bathing coves, the snorkeling lagoon, and the remains of a group of Maya temples. You'll have access to swimming beaches with canoes and pedal boats; limestone tunnels to snorkel through; marked palm-lined pathways; a wild bird breeding aviary; a charro exhibition; horseback riding; scuba diving; botanical garden and nursery; a sea turtle nursery where the turtles are released after their first year; a pavilion showcasing regional butterflies; a tropical aquarium where visitors can touch underwater creatures such as manta rays, starfish, and octopi; and a "Dolphinarium" where visitors swim with the dolphins—for a hefty extra charge. There is also a visitor's center with lockers, first aid, and gifts. Visitors aren't allowed to bring in food or drinks, so you're at the mercy of the high-priced restaurants. Personal radios are a no-no, as is use of suntan lotion if you swim in the lagoon; chemicals in lotion will poison the lagoon habitat.

The price of $35 per person entitles you to all the facilities—boats, life jackets, and snorkeling equipment for the underwater tunnel and lagoon, and lounge chairs and other facilities. Other attractions, such as horseback riding, scuba diving and the Dolphinarium, cost extra. However, there may be more visitors than equipment (such as beach chairs), so bring a beach towel and your own snorkeling gear. Travel agencies in Cancún offer Xcaret as a day-trip that includes transportation and admission. You can also buy a ticket to the park at the **Xcaret Terminal** (☎ **987/83-0654,** 987/83-0743, or 987/83-3143) next to the Hotel Fiesta Americana Coral Beach on Cancún Island. Xcaret's nine colorfully painted buses haul people to and from Cancún. From Cancún the price including transportation and admission is $50 for adults and $36 for children age 6 and older. "Xcaret Night" costs $80 for adults and $70 for children and includes round-trip transportation from Cancún, a *charreada* festival, lighted pathways to Maya ruins, dinner, and folkloric show. Xcaret buses leave its terminal at 9 and 10am daily.

PAAMUL: A BEACH HIDEAWAY

About 10 miles south of Xcaret, 16 miles south of Cozumel, 62 miles southwest of Cancún, and half a mile east of the highway is Paamul (also written Pamul), which in Maya means "a destroyed ruin." Turn when you see the Minisuper (a place to pick up reasonably priced snacks and drinks), which is also owned by the Cabañas Paamul (see below). At Paamul you can enjoy a beautiful beach and a safe cove for swimming; it's a delightful place to leave the world behind. Thirty years ago the Martin family gave up coconut harvesting on this wide stretch of land—which includes a large, shallow bay—gained title to the land, and established this comfortable out-of-the-way respite. They plan to soon build more rooms on the unoccupied portion of the bay.

Mark and Lester Willis established their PADI- and SSI-certified fully equipped dive shop here a few years ago and opened **Scuba Max** (☎ **987/3-0667;** fax 987/4-1729), next to the cabañas. Using three 38-foot boats, they take guests on dives 5 miles in either direction. If it's too choppy, the reefs in front of the hotel are also excellent. The cost per dive is $25–$45 if you have your own equipment or $35–$65 if you rent. The snorkeling is excellent in this protected bay and the one next to it. They were establishing an office at the Hotel La Jungla in Playa del Carmen when I checked.

WHERE TO STAY & DINE

○ **Cabañas Paamul.** Km 85 Carretera Cancún–Tulum (Apdo. Postal 83), 77710 Playa del Carmen, Q. Roo. ☎ **99/25-9422** in Mérida. Fax 99/25-6913. Reservations: Av. Colón

501-C, Depto. D-211 x 6 y 62, 97000 Mérida, Yuc. 10 bungalows; 140 trailer spaces (all with full hookups). FAN. July–Aug and Dec–Feb $60 double. March–June and Sept–Nov $50 double. RV space with hookups $16 per day, $360 per month.

When you reach this isolated, relaxing hotel you'll see an extremely tidy lineup of mobile homes and beyond them a row of coral-and-white beachfront bungalows with covered porches, just steps away from the Caribbean. Despite the number of mobile homes (which are occupied more in winter than any other time), there's seldom a soul on the beautiful little beach. I eagerly anticipate reaching Paamul, for the bit of peace it provides during hectic days of travel writing. Each bungalow contains two double beds, tile floors, rattan furniture, ceiling fans, hot water, and 24-hour electricity. A new, large, breezy, palapa-topped restaurant serves delicious food at more than reasonable prices. On Saturdays the happy hour starts at 6pm with country music, and Sundays at 6pm there's a buffet dinner. Try the pescado Paamul or shrimp Paamul; both are wonderful baked medleys devised by the gracious owner Eloiza Zapata. For stays longer than a week, ask for a discount, which can sometimes be as much as 10%. The trailer park isn't what you might expect—some trailers have decks or patios and thatched palapa shade covers. Trailer guests have access to 12 showers and separate baths for men and women. Laundry service is available nearby. Turtles nest here June through September. The Paamul turnoff is clearly marked on the highway; then it's almost a mile on a straight, narrow, paved-but-rutted road to the bungalows. Visitors not staying here are welcome to use the beach, though the owners request that they not bring in drinks and food and use the restaurant instead.

PUERTO AVENTURAS: A RESORT COMMUNITY

About 2¹/₂ miles south of Paamul (65 miles southwest of Cancún), you'll come to the new city-size development of Puerto Aventuras on Chakalal Bay. Though it's on 900 oceanfront acres, you don't see the ocean unless you walk through one of the three hotels. A complete resort, it includes a state-of-the-art marina, hotels, several restaurants, and multitudes of fashionable condominiums winding about the grounds and around the marina. The golf course has nine holes open for play. I don't recommend this resort for a vacation at this time because it's so far from anything. And, if you're touring this part of the world you won't see much of it by staying here. Architecturally sophisticated, it's like being on the island of Cancún without the crowds or nightlife. It's aimed more at well-heeled Mexicans who've purchased condominiums here than at foreign tourists who've come to experience the Yucatecan culture.

Even if you don't stay here, the **Museo CEDAM** on the grounds is worth a stop. CEDAM stands for Center for the Study of Aquatic Sports in Mexico, and the museum houses displays on the history of diving on this coast from pre-Hispanic times to the present. Besides dive-related memorabilia, there are displays of pre-Hispanic pottery, figures, copper bells found in the cenotes of Chichén-Itzá, shell fossils, and sunken ship contents. It's supposed to be open daily from 10am to 1pm and 2 to 6pm. Donations are requested.

If you're hungry, there's a restaurant opposite the museum.

XPUHA: ANOTHER BEACH HIDEAWAY

Almost 3 miles beyond Paamul, east of the highway, is an area known as Xpuha (ish-poo-*hah*) consisting of an incredibly beautiful, wide bay and a fine stretch of sand. Before October 1995's Hurricane Roxanne, tall palms leaned over the beach, but, unfortunately, the storm destroyed the trees and toppled the encroaching jungle, revealing the seamier side of Xpuha. Some of this heavenly beach is junked with trashy-looking abodes and tacky restaurants, with the all-inclusive Robinson Club at the far southern end. If you're looking for something totally offbeat, clean, but not at all posh, then consider two of the humble inns on this beach. These are on a nicely-kept part of the beach (comparatively speaking), where you can still enjoy its uninhabited appeal. Finding them can be confusing, since from Highway 307 several crude signs mark entry down even cruder, narrow, rutted roads cutting through the jungle. To get to these hotels and the best portion of beach, take the one marked VILLAS XPUHA.

The **restaurant** of the Villas Xpuha offers home-style cooking with a simple-but-varied menu and several fish entrees to choose from. It's open daily from 7am to 8pm. It's ideal for day-trippers who want to spend the day on the beach and have restaurant facilities, too; they request that visitors not bring food. As long as you use the restaurant of the Villas Xpuha, there's no charge for the two public baths and showers. Besides the beach, a huge lagoon is within walking distance, and the reef is not far offshore.

WHERE TO STAY & DINE

Villas del Caribe Xpuha. Km 88 Carretera Cancún–Tulum, 77710 Playa del Carmen, Q. Roo. No phone. 9 rms. High season $35 double. Low season double $26.

Not quite as nice as its neighbor (see "Villas Xpuha," below), this inn is still a good choice. The two stories of rooms face the beach, with communal porches for lounging. Rooms have blue tile floors and matching blue walls, and each comes with one or two double beds, an all-tile bath, and windows facing the beach; one room has a kitchen. There's 24-hour electricity and hot water here, too. The management has radio communication with the Hotel Flores in Cozumel (☎ **987/2-1429**), so if you're there, you can reserve a room ahead (or vice versa).

۞ Villas Xpuha and Restaurant. Km 88 Carretera Cancún–Tulum (Apdo. Postal 115), 77710 Playa del Carmen, Q. Roo. No phone. 5 rms. FAN. High season $40 double. Low season $32 double.

The five rooms here line up in a row of blue buildings; four have a porch area on the beach and ocean, and one is an island-style wooden structure. The rooms are plain but clean, each with nice tile floors, two windows, two single beds, two plastic chairs, hammock hooks, and a place for a suitcase—but no closet. A single bare bulb in the center of each ceiling provides light. Count on 24-hour electricity and hot water. The hotel has a dive shop offering diving and snorkeling trips and kayak rentals.

AKUMAL: RESORT ON A LAGOON

Continuing south on Highway 307 a short distance, you'll come to Akumal, a resort development built around and named after a beautiful lagoon. It's one of those places foreigners discover, explore, fall in love with, and return to live. Signs point the way in from the highway, and the white arched Akumal gateway is less than half a mile toward the sea. The resort complex here consists of five distinct establishments sharing the same wonderful, smooth, palm-lined beach and the adjacent Half Moon Bay and Yalku Lagoon. The hotel's signs and white entry arches are clearly visible from Highway 307.

You don't have to be a guest to enjoy the **beach,** swim in the beautiful clear bay, and eat at the restaurants. It's an excellent place to spend the day while on a trip down the coast. Besides the excellent snorkeling, ask at the reception desk about **horseback rides on the beach.** Equipment rental for snorkeling and windsurfing are readily available. For **scuba diving,** two completely equipped dive shops with PADI-certified instructors serve the hotels and bungalows in this area. Both are located between the two hotels. There are almost 30 dive sites in the region (from 30 to 80 feet), and two-tank dives cost around $65. Both shops offer resort courses as well as complete certification. **Lagoon snorkeling** is best on the left side of the lagoon—the side by the big circular restaurant and a bit farther out. **Fishing trips** can also be arranged through the dive shops. You're only 15 minutes from good fishing. Two hours (the minimum period) costs $100, and each additional hour is $35 for up to four people with two fishing lines.

WHERE TO STAY

Hotel-Club Akumal Caribe Villas Maya. Km 63 Carretera Cancún–Tulum (Hwy. 307). ☎ **987/3-0596.** Reservations: P.O. Box 13326, El Paso, TX 79913; ☎ **800/351-1622** in Texas, or 915/584-3552 in the U.S. outside Texas, or 800/343-1440 in Canada. 73 rms. A/C TEL. High season $95 bungalow; $110 hotel room; $130–$375 villa/condo. Low season $85 bungalow; $100 hotel room; $110–$210 villa.

The white arches you drive under and the entry are not impressive, but the lodging varieties here are. The 41 spacious **Villas Maya Bungalows** have beautiful tile floors and comfortable, nice furniture, all with fully equipped kitchens. The 21 rooms in the new three-story **beachfront hotel** are similarly furnished but with small kitchens (no stove), a king-size or two queen-size beds, pale tile floors, and stylish Mexican accents. The **Villas Flamingo** are four exquisitely designed and luxuriously (but comfortably) furnished two-story homes facing Half Moon Bay. Each has one, two, or three bedrooms; large living, dining, and kitchen areas; and a lovely furnished patio just steps from the beach. The hotel has its own pool separate from other facilities on the grounds. Akumal's setting is truly relaxing and there's a restaurant facing the beach and lagoon, plus a **grocery store** with all the common necessities. If you're traveling with children, ask about the **children's program** that functions during specific times of the year.

A CAVERN TOUR/SCUBA DIVING OPERATOR

On the right side of the road (if you're coming from Cancún) about $11^1/2$ miles south of Xcacel (and about 9 miles north of Tulum) is **Divers of the Hidden Worlds** (☎ **98/74-4081;** it's a cellular phone in Cancún). Experienced divers lead certified divers, snorkelers, and hikers on a variety of unusual trips. Some require hiking in the jungle to dry caves, others to caves where divers penetrate the underground world of watery caves with glass-clear water. Snorkelers investigate the *cenotes* (sinkholes leading to underground caves). Some dives are for more advanced divers, and some trips last all day, while others consume half a day. They also offer reef dives, resort courses, and cave diving certification. They'll provide transportation from Cancún.

XEL-HA: SNORKELING & SWIMMING

The Caribbean coast of the Yucatán is carved by the sea into hundreds of small *caletas* (coves) that form the perfect habitat for tropical marine life, both flora and fauna. Many caletas remain undiscovered and pristine along the coast, but Xel-Ha, 8 miles south of Akumal, is enjoyed daily by throngs of snorkelers and scuba divers who come to luxuriate in its warm waters and swim among its brilliant fish. Xel-Ha (pronounced shell-*hah*) is a swimmers' paradise, with no threat of undertow or pollution. It's a beautiful, completely calm cove that's a perfect place to bring kids for their first snorkeling experience (experienced snorkelers may be disappointed—the crowds here seem to have driven out the living coral and a lot of the fish; you can find more abundant marine life and avoid an admission charge by going to Akumal, among other spots).

The entrance to Xel-Ha is half a mile in from the highway. You'll be asked to pay a "contribution" to the upkeep and preservation of the site of $10 per adult and $7 for children ages 5 to 12. It's open daily from 8am to 4:30pm.

Once in the park, you can rent snorkeling equipment and an underwater camera—but it's much cheaper to bring your own. You can also buy an outrageously priced drink or a meal, change clothes, take showers, and count lizards—the place is teeming with iguanas and other species. When you swim, be careful to observe the SWIM HERE and NO SWIMMING signs. (The greatest variety of fish can be seen right near the ropes marking off the no swimming areas and near any groups of rocks.)

Just south of the Xel-Ha turnoff on the west side of the highway, don't miss the **Maya ruins** of ancient Xel-Ha. You'll likely be the only one there as you walk over limestone rocks and through the tangle of trees, vines, and palms. There is a huge, deep, dark cenote to one side and a temple palace with tumbled-down columns, a jaguar group, and a conserved temple group. A covered palapa on one pyramid guards a partially preserved mural. Admission is $2.50.

Xel-Ha is close to the ruins at Tulum—it's a good place for a dip when you've finished clambering around the Maya ruins. You can make the short 8-mile hop north from Tulum to Xel-Ha by bus. When you get off at the junction for Tulum, ask the restaurant owner when the next buses come by—otherwise you may have to wait as much as two hours on the highway. Most tour companies in Cancún and Cozumel include a trip to Tulum and a swim at Xel-Ha in the same journey.

6 Tulum, Punta Allen & Sian Ka'an

Tulum (80 miles southwest of Cancún) and the Punta Allen Peninsula (110 miles southwest of Cancún at its tip) are the southernmost points many travelers reach in their wanderings down the Caribbean coast (although there is more to discover farther on). The walled Maya city of Tulum—a large Postclassic Maya site that dramatically overlooks the Caribbean—is a natural beacon to visitors to Quintana Roo, and from Cancún it's within a two-hour drive. Tour companies and public buses make the trip regularly from Cancún and Playa del Carmen. And for those who want to leave the modern world a long, long way behind, Punta Allen (which can take between 1¹/₂ to 3 hours to reach from Tulum, depending on how miserable the road's condition is) may be the ultimate. It's a place without the crowds, frenetic pace, or the creature comforts of the resorts to the north—down here, the generator shuts down at 10pm (if there is one). What you will find is great fishing and snorkeling, the natural and archaeological riches of the Sian Ka'an Biosphere Reserve, and a chance to rest up at what truly feels like the end of the road. A few beach cabañas now offer reliable power, telephones, and hot showers.

ESSENTIALS

When traveling south of Highway 307, get your bearings on Tulum by thinking of it as several distinct areas: First, on your left will be the junction of Highway 307 and the old access road to the Tulum ruins (it no longer provides access); here you'll find two small hotels, two restaurants, and a Pemex gas station. Next, a few feet south of the old road on Highway 307, also on the left, is the new Tulum ruins access road, leading to a large parking lot. And a few feet farther along 307 is the left turn onto the road leading to the hotels and campgrounds south of the ruins.

This last road is the road south along the narrow **Punta Allen Peninsula** to **Boca Paila,** a portion of the **Sian Ka'an Biosphere Reserve,** and **Punta Allen,** a lobstering/fishing village at the tip's end. Though most of this 30-mile-long peninsular stretch of sandy, potholed road is uninhabited, there are several rustic inns along a fabulous beach south of the ruins.

Across the highway from the turnoff to the Punta Allen Peninsula on Highway 307 is the road to Cobá, another fascinating Maya city 40 miles inland. See "Cobá," below, for details.

Finally, south of the Punta Allen road on Highway 307 is the **village of Tulum.** The highway here is lined with businesses, including the bus stations, auto repair shops, markets, and pharmacies. The village of Tulum, by the way, increasingly has the look of an up-and-coming place, with sidewalks and restaurants it's never sported before.

EXPLORING THE TULUM ARCHAEOLOGICAL SITE

Located 8 miles south of Xel-Ha, Tulum is a Maya fortress overlooking the Caribbean. At the end of the Classic period, in A.D. 900, Maya civilization began to decline and most of the large ceremonial centers were deserted. During the Postclassic period (A.D. 900 to the Spanish Conquest), small rival states developed with a few imported traditions from north central Mexico. Tulum is one such walled city-state. Built in the 10th century, it functioned as a seaport. Aside from the spectacular setting, Tulum is not an impressive city when compared to Chichén-Itzá or Uxmal. There are no magnificent pyramidal structures as are found in the Classic Maya ruins. The stone carving is crude, and the site looks as though it was put together in a hurry or by novice apprentices rather than skilled masters. The primary god here was the diving god, depicted on several buildings as an upside-down figure above doorways. Seen at the Palace at Sayil and Cobá, this curious, almost comical figure is also known as the bee god.

The most imposing building in Tulum is the large stone structure on the cliff called the **Castillo** (castle), actually a temple as well as a fortress, once covered with stucco and painted. In front of the Castillo are several unrestored palacelike buildings partially covered with stucco. On the **beach** below, where the Maya once came ashore, tourists frolic, combining a visit to the ruins with a dip in the Caribbean.

The **Temple of the Frescoes,** directly in front of the Castillo, contains interesting 13th-century wall paintings inside the temple, but entrance is no longer permitted. Distinctly Maya, they represent the rain god Chaac and Ixchel, the goddess of weaving, women, the moon, and medicine. On the cornice of this temple is a relief of the head of the rain god. If you get a slight distance from the building you'll see the eyes, nose, mouth, and chin. Notice the remains of the red-painted stucco on this building—at one time all the buildings at Tulum were painted a bright red.

Much of what we know of Tulum at the time of the Spanish Conquest comes from the writings of Diego de Landa, third bishop of the Yucatán. He wrote that Tulum was a small city inhabited by about 600 people, who lived in dwellings situated on platforms along a street and who supervised the trade traffic from Honduras to the Yucatán. Though it was a walled city, most of the inhabitants probably lived outside the walls, leaving the interior for governors, priestly hierarchy, and religious ceremonies. Tulum survived about 70 years after the Conquest, when it was finally abandoned.

Because of the excessive number of visitors this site receives, it is no longer possible to climb the ruins. Visitors are asked to remain behind roped-off areas to view them.

In late 1994 a new entrance to the ruins was constructed about a 10-minute walk from the archaeological site. Cars and buses enter a large parking lot; some of the public buses from Playa del Carmen go directly to the visitor's center, where there are artisans' stands, a bookstore, a museum, a restaurant, several large rest rooms, and a ticket booth for Inter-Playa buses, which depart for Playa del Carmen and Cancún frequently between 7:40am and 4:40pm. After walking through the center, visitors pay the admission fee to the ruins, and another fee to ride an open-air shuttle to the ruins and, if you're driving, another fee to park. You can easily walk, however. Admission is $3.50; free on Sunday. There's an additional charge of $4 for a permit

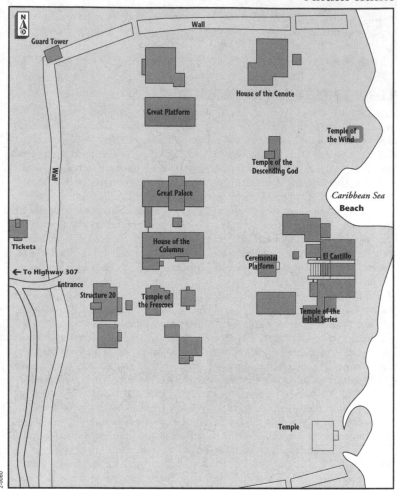

Map labels: Wall · Guard Tower · N · House of the Cenote · Great Platform · Temple of the Wind · Temple of the Descending God · Wall · Great Palace · Caribbean Sea · Beach · Tickets · House of the Columns · Ceremonial Platform · El Castillo · ← To Highway 307 · Entrance · Structure 20 · Temple of the Frescoes · Temple of the Initial Series · Temple

2-0060

to use a video camera at the site. Licensed guides have a stand by the path to the ruins and charge $20 for a 45-minute tour in English, French, or Spanish for up to four persons. They will point out many architectural details you might otherwise miss, but their history information may not be up-to-date.

WHERE TO STAY & DINE IN TULUM

Two motels, the **Motel Crucero** and **Hotel Acquario** at the old crossroads entrance to Tulum, have **restaurants** and the Acquario also offers a **grocery store.** I prefer the Motel Crucero restaurant where the food is inexpensive and excellent and the service is good. The motel rooms, while inexpensive, are quite basic. Rooms at the Acquario are much better and cost more, but they suffer from erratic maintenance and indifferent management. Both, however, are good to know about in case you need a place for the night before continuing south. Better lodgings on the Punta Allen Peninsula face the beach just a few miles south of this crossroads and are worth a detour if you're in the area. (See "The Punta Allen Peninsula," below, for details.)

THE PUNTA ALLEN PENINSULA

About 3 miles south of the Tulum ruins on the Punta Allen Road, the pavement ends and the road becomes narrow and sandy, with many potholes during the rainy season. Beyond this point is a 30-mile-long peninsula called Punta Allen, split in two at a cut called Boca Paila, where a bridge connects the two parts of the peninsula and the Caribbean enters a large lagoon on the right. It's part of the far eastern edge of the 1.3-million-acre **Sian Ka'an Biosphere Reserve** (see below). Along this road you'll find several cabaña-type inns, all on beautiful beaches facing the Caribbean. Taxis from the ruins can take you to most of these; then you can find a ride back to the junction at the end of your stay.

EXPLORING THE PUNTA ALLEN PENINSULA

The natural environment is the peninsula's marquee attraction, whether your tastes run to relaxing on the beaches or going on bird-watching expeditions (these are available between June and August, with July being best). Sea turtles nest on the beaches along here from May to October. The turtles lumber ashore at night, usually between 10pm and 3am. *A note about provisions:* Since the Punta Allen Peninsula is rather remote and there are no stores, handy provisions to bring along include a flashlight, mosquito repellent, mosquito coils, water, and snacks. Most hotels along here charge for bottled water in your room and for meals. From October through December winds may be accompanied by nippy nights, so come prepared—the hotels don't have blankets.

Lodgings here vary in quality—some are simple but quite comfortable, while others are a lot like camping out. One or two have electricity for a few hours in the evening—but shut it off around 10pm—and there are no electrical outlets; most don't have hot water. The first one is half a mile south of the ruins, and the farthest is 30 miles down the peninsula.

The following hotels are listed in the order you'll find them as you drive south on the Punta Allen road (from Tulum). To reach the first one you'll need to take the Punta Allen exit from Highway 307, then turn left when it intersects the coastal road. The rest of the hotels are to the right.

Cabañas Zazil Kin Don Armando. Apdo. Postal 44, 77780 Tulum, Q. Roo. ☎ **987/4-3856.** 30 bungalows (none with bath). $10 bed with hammock; $15 double with two beds. $10 deposit for bedding, key, and flashlight. Free unguarded parking.

Casual accommodations on a big, beautiful beach, these stick-walled bungalows are spread over the large stretch of sand, mingled with clotheslines flapping with guests' laundry and a restaurant that's notably good. Each of these basic bungalows has a bed on a concrete slab, sheets, a blanket, and occasional mosquito netting, but there's electricity only in the restaurant. (Bring your own soap, towel, and mosquito netting.) Some of the bungalows have no windows or ventilation, except through the cracks, unless the door is open. There are separate shared-bath facilities for men and women. The friendly English-speaking owners also run the restaurant. An average meal costs $3 to $6. At night Don Armando's restaurant is *the* place to be while you're in the area, offering the best food, service, and conviviality among guests.

From here you can arrange taxi service to and from the Tulum ruins and to the Cancún airport. It's half a mile south of the Tulum ruins; the sign on the right as you drive toward the ruins says ZAZIL KIN.

Restaurant y Cabañas Ana y José. Punta Allen Peninsula, km 7 Carretera Punta Allen (Apdo. Postal 15), 77780 Tulum, Q. Roo. ☎ **98/80-6022** in Cancún. Fax 98/80-6021 in Cancún. E-mail: anayjose@cancun.rce.com.mx. 16 rms (all with bath). High season $60–$70 double. Low season $50–$60 double. Free unguarded parking.

The Sian Ka'an Biosphere Reserve

Down the peninsula a few miles south of the Tulum ruins, you'll pass the guard-house of the Sian Ka'an Biosphere Reserve, 1.3 million acres set aside in 1986 to preserve tropical forests, savannas, mangroves, coastal and marine habitats, and 70 miles of coastal reefs. The area is home to jaguars; pumas; ocelots; margays; jagua-rundis; spider and howler monkeys; tapirs; white-lipped and collared peccaries; manatees; brocket and white-tailed deer; crocodiles; and green, loggerhead, hawks-bill, and leatherback sea turtles. It also protects 366 species of birds—you might catch a glimpse of an ocellated turkey, a great curassow, a brilliantly colored par-rot, a toucan or trogon, a white ibis, a roseate spoonbill, a jabiru (or wood stork), a flamingo, or one of 15 species of herons, egrets, and bitterns.

The park is separated into three parts: a "core zone," restricted to research; a "buffer zone," where visitors and families already living there have restricted use; and a "cooperation zone," outside the reserve but vital to its preservation. If you drive on Highway 307 from Tulum to an imaginary line just below the Bahía (bay) de Espíritu Santo, all you see on the Caribbean side is the reserve; but except at the ruins of Muyil/Chunyaxche, there's no access. At least 22 archaeological sites have been charted within Sian Ka'an. The best place to sample the reserve is the Punta Allen Peninsula, part of the "buffer zone." The inns were already in place when the reserve was created. Of these, only the Cuzan Guest House (see "Exploring the Punta Allen Peninsula") offers trips for birding. But bring your own binoculars and birding books and have at it—the birdlife anywhere here is rich. At the Boca Paila bridge you can often find fishermen who'll take you into the lagoon on the landward side, where you can fish and see plenty of birdlife; but it's unlikely the boatman will know bird names in English or Spanish. Birding is best just after dawn, especially during the April through July nesting season.

Day-trips to the Sian Ka'an are led by the **Friends of Sian Ka'an** from the Restau-rant y Cabañas Ana y José just south of the Tulum ruins on Monday, Tuesday, Friday, and Saturday for $50 per person using their vehicle, or $40 per person if you drive yourself. Trips start from the Cabañas at 9:30am and return there around 2:30pm. For reservations, contact Amigos de Sian Ka'an (☎ **98/84-9583;** fax 98/87-3080) in Cancún. Or you may be able to book the tour once you've arrived at the Restaurant y Cabañas Ana y José if the tour, which is limited to 19 people, isn't full.

This place started as a restaurant and blossomed into a comfortable inn on the beach. All rooms have tiled floors, one or two double beds, baths with cold-water showers, patios or balconies, and electricity between 5:30 and 10:30pm. The rock-walled cabañas in front are a little larger, and some face the beautiful wide beach just a few yards off, but these are also the most expensive rooms. New rooms have been added on a second level in back. The only drawback is the lack of cross-ventilation in some of the lower rooms in the back section, which can be extremely uncomfortable at night without electricity to power fans. The inn also offers bicycle and kayak rent-als, trips through Maya canals and to little-known ruins, snorkeling, and dive trips. Biologist-led boat excursions, organized by the Friends of Sian Ka'an headquartered in Cancún, to the Sian Ka'an Biosphere Reserve begin here at 9:30am Monday, Tues-day, Friday, and Saturday (weather permitting) for $50 per person. (See "The Sian

Ka'an Biosphere Reserve" box, above, and chapter 5, "Road Trips from Cancún," for details on making reservations for the Biosphere Reserve trip.)

The excellent, screened-in restaurant, with sand floors under the palapa, offers modest prices and is open daily from 8am to 9pm. The hotel is 4 miles south of the Tulum ruins. Reservations are a must in high season, or arrive very early in the day before it fills up.

Cabañas Tulum. Punta Allen Peninsula, km 7 Carretera Tulum (Apdo. Postal 63), 77780 Tulum, Q. Roo. No phone. 18 rms (all with bath). FAN. High season $38 double. Low season $28 double.

Next door to Ana y José's (above) is a row of bungalows facing a heavenly stretch of ocean and beach. Each bungalow includes a cold-water shower, two double beds, screens on the windows, a table, one electric light, a nice-size tiled bathroom, and a veranda where you can hang a hammock. Mattresses, which rest on a cement platform, are too thin to cushion against the hard surface. Flat topsheets, which are also used as bottom sheets, immediately work off the mattress, leaving guests either wrestling with them all night or giving up to settle in on the bare mattress. The electricity is on from 5:30 to 10pm only, so bring candles or a flashlight. A small restaurant serves beer, soft drinks, and all three meals for reasonable prices—just don't expect a gourmet meal. In fact, for any meal other than breakfast, you're better off taking meals at Ana y José or at the above-mentioned Zazil Kin. The cabañas are often full between December 15 and Easter, and July and August, so arrive early or make reservations. It's 4 miles south of the ruins.

Boca Paila Fishing Lodge. Apdo. Postal 59, 77600 Cozumel, Q. Roo. ☎ and fax **987/ 2-5944.** Reservations: Frontiers, P.O. Box 959, 100 Logan Rd., Wexford, PA 15090; ☎ 800/ 245-1950 or 412/935-1577 in the U.S.; fax 412/935-5388. 8 cabañas. FAN. High season (Dec 3–June 2) $2,000 per person double. Low season $1,600 per person double. Rates for 6 days and 7 nights, including all meals and a private boat and bonefishing guide for each cabaña. Ask about prices for a nonangler sharing a double with an angler. Nonfishing drop-in prices July–Sept, $200 per person double with three meals; $275 one or two people for day of fishing with lunch but no overnight.

Easily a top contender for the nicest spot along this road, the white-stucco cabañas offer friendly beachside comfort. Spread out on the beach and linked by a pleasant walkway, each individual unit has a mosquito-proof palapa roof, large tiled rooms comfortably furnished with two double beds, rattan furniture, hot water in the bathrooms, wall fans, 24-hour electricity, and comfortable screened porch. The Boca Paila attracts a clientele that comes for saltwater fly-fishing in the flats, mostly for bonefish. Prime fishing months are March through June. But when occupancy is low, nonfishing guests can be accommodated with advance notice. Overnight non-fishing rates are priced high as a discouragement to drop-ins. The lodge is about midway down the Punta Allen Peninsula, just before the Boca Paila bridge.

✪ **Cuzan Guest House.** Punta Allen. Reservations: Apdo. Postal 24, 77720 Felipe Carrillo Puerto, Q. Roo. ☎ **983/4-0358** and fax 983/4-0383 in Felipe Carrillo Puerto. 8 rms (all with bath). $90–$110 double. All inclusive 7-day fly-fishing package $1,499. Rates include all meals.

About 30 miles south of the Tulum ruins is the end of the peninsula and Punta Allen, the Yucatán's best-known lobstering and fishing village planted on a palm-studded beach. Isolated and rustic, it's part Indiana Jones, part Robinson Crusoe, and certainly the most laid-back end of the line you'll find for a while. The small town has a lobster cooperative, a few streets with modest homes, and a lighthouse at the end of a narrow sand road dense with coconut palms and jungle on both sides. So it's a welcome sight to see the beachside Cuzan Guest House and its sign in English that reads STOP HERE FOR TOURIST INFORMATION. A stay here could well be the highlight of your trip, provided you're a flexible traveler.

Two rooms are simply furnished Maya-style oval stucco buildings with thatched roofs, concrete floors, hammocks, private bathrooms, and a combination of single and king beds with mosquito netting. Six more comfortable and spacious wooden huts, with thatched roofs and private bathrooms, offer ocean views from hammocks on the porch. These have two double beds each. A few other rooms or houses elsewhere in the village are sometimes available for rent as well, but these don't offer that special Cuzan experience and may suffer from loud village noises at night. Unfortunately, Cuzan's delightful thatched teepees disappeared during Hurricane Roxanne. There's solar-powered electricity at night and plenty of hot water. The real charmer here is the sand-floored restaurant run by co-owner Sonja Lilvik, a Californian who makes you feel right at home. If it's lobster season, you may have lobster at every meal, always prepared with a deliciously different recipe. But you might also be treated to a pile of heavenly stone crabs or some other gift from the sea.

Sonja arranges fly-fishing trips for bone, permit, snook, and tarpon to the nearby saltwater flats and lagoons of Ascension Bay. The $25-per-person boat tour of the coastline that she offers is a fascinating 3 hours of snorkeling, slipping in and out of mangrove-filled canals for bird watching, and skirting the edge of an island rookery loaded with frigate birds. November through March is frigate mating season and the male frigate shows off his big, billowy red breast pouch to impress potential mates. The all-day Robinson Crusoe Tour costs $100 per person and includes a boat excursion to remote islands, beaches, reefs, jungles, lagoons, and bird-watching areas. Or you can also go kayaking along the coast or simply relax in a hammock on the beach.

7 Cobá

105 miles SW of Cancún

From the turnoff at the Tulum junction, you travel inland an hour or so to arrive at these mystical ruins jutting up from the forest floor.

The impressive Maya ruins at Cobá, deep in the jungle, are a worthy detour from your route south. You don't need to stay overnight to see the ruins, but there are a few hotels. The village is small and poor, gaining little from the visitors who pass through to see the ruins. **Used clothing** (especially for children) would be a welcome gift.

ESSENTIALS
GETTING THERE & DEPARTING

BY BUS   From Playa del Carmen there are three buses to Cobá. Two buses leave Valladolid for Cobá, but they may fill early, so buy tickets as soon as possible.

Several buses a day leave Cobá: At 6:30am and 3pm a bus goes to Tulum and Playa del Carmen, and at noon and 7pm there's a bus to Valladolid. To double-check this bus schedule, check at the Restaurant and Hotel El Bocadito mentioned below.

BY CAR   The road to Cobá begins in Tulum, across Highway 307 from the turnoff to the Punta Allen Peninsula. Turn right when you see the signs to Cobá and continue on that road for 40 miles. When you reach the village, proceed straight until you see the lake; when the road curves right, turn left. The entrance to the ruins is at the end of that road past some small restaurants. Cobá is also about a 3-hour drive south from Cancún.

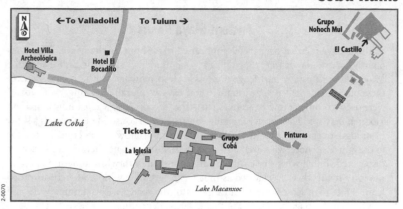

ORIENTATION

The highway into Cobá becomes one main paved street through town, which passes El Bocadito restaurant and hotel on the right (see "Where to Stay & Dine," below) and goes a block to the lake. If you turn right at the lake you reach the Villas Arqueológicas a block farther. Turning left will lead past a couple of informal/ primitive restaurants on the left facing the lake, and to the ruins, straight ahead, the equivalent of a block.

EXPLORING THE COBÁ RUINS

The Maya built many breathtaking cities in the Yucatán, but few were grander in scope than Cobá. However, much of the 42-square-mile site, on the shores of two lakes, is unexcavated. A 60-mile-long *sacbe* (a pre-Hispanic raised road or causeway) through the jungle linked Cobá to Yaxuná, once a large and important Maya center 30 miles south of Chichén-Itzá. It's the Maya's longest-known sacbe, and there are at least 50 or more shorter ones from here. An important city-state, Cobá, which means "water stirred by the wind," flourished between A.D. 632 (the oldest carved date found here) until after the founding of Chichén-Itzá, around 800. Then Cobá slowly faded in importance and population until it was finally abandoned. Scholars believe Cobá was an important trade link between the Yucatán Caribbean coast and inland cities.

Once in the site, keep your bearings—it's very easy to get lost on the maze of dirt roads in the jungle. Bring your bird and butterfly books; this is one of the best places to see both. Branching off from every labeled path you'll notice unofficial narrow paths into the jungle, used by locals as shortcuts through the ruins. These are good for scouting for birds, but be careful to remember the way back.

The **Grupo Cobá** boasts a large, impressive pyramid, the **Temple of the Church** (La Iglesia), which you'll find if you take the path bearing right after the entry gate. While walking to it, notice the unexcavated mounds on the left. Though the urge to climb the temple is great, the view is better from El Castillo in the Nohoc Mul group farther back at the site.

From here, return back to the main path and turn right. You'll pass a sign pointing right to the ruined *juego de pelota* (ball court), but the path is obscure.

Continuing straight ahead on this path for 5 to 10 minutes, you'll come to a fork in the road. To the left and right you'll notice jungle-covered, unexcavated pyramids, and at one point you'll cross a raised portion crossing the pathway—this is the

Ancient Maya Roads

Scholars have puzzled over the elegant raised roads built by the Maya: Were they mainly ceremonial or were they the lanes of commerce? One thing is for sure, the Maya did not possess knowledge of the wheel, so vehicular traffic is out. Many of these raised roads, called *sacbe* (singular) and *sacbeob* (plural), meaning "white road," were used to connect towns. Some, such as the 60-mile-long sacbe lining Cobá and Yaxuná, may well have been originally constructed to consolidate power as a show of strength over rival cities. At Chichén-Itzá, visitors follow a broad tree-lined sacbe to the famous cenote, where remains of animals, humans, and their possessions were discovered. Filled with stone rubble and smoothed with white limestone plaster, the lofty roadbeds were elevated as much as 3 feet. The widths of sacbeob varied from 9 feet to at least 60 feet, and support of the roads, with retaining walls and culverts for drainage and access to them, varied depending on the terrain.

visible remains of the *sacbe* (ancient Maya road) to Yaxuná. Throughout the area, intricately carved *stela* (tall, curved stone) stand by pathways, or lie forlornly in the jungle underbrush. Though protected by crude thatched roofs, most are so weatherworn as to be indiscernible.

The left fork leads to the **Nohoch Mul Group,** which contains **El Castillo,** the tallest pyramid in the Yucatán (rising even higher than the great El Castillo at Chichén-Itzá and the Pyramid of the Magician at Uxmal). So far, visitors are still permitted to climb to the top. From this magnificent lofty position you can see unexcavated jungle-covered pyramidal structures poking up through the forest all around. The right fork (more or less straight on) goes to the **Conjunto Las Pinturas.** Here, the main attraction is the **Pyramid of the Painted Lintel,** a small structure with traces of the original bright colors above the door. You can climb up to get a close look. Though maps of Cobá show ruins around two lakes, there are really only two excavated buildings to see after you enter the site.

Note: Because of the heat, visit Cobá in the morning or after the heat of the day has passed. Mosquito repellent, drinking water, and comfortable shoes are imperative.

Admission is $2; children under 12 enter free daily, and Sunday and holidays it's free for everyone. Camera permits are $4 for each video camera. The site is open daily from 8am to 5pm.

WHERE TO STAY & DINE

El Bocadito. Calle Principal, Cobá, Q. Roo. No phone. Reservations: Apdo. Postal 56, 97780 Valladolid, Yuc. 8 rms. FAN. $16–$21 double. Free unguarded parking.

El Bocadito, on the right as you enter town, could take advantage of being the only game in town besides the much more expensive Villas Arqueológicas—but it doesn't. Next to the hotel's restaurant of the same name, the rooms are arranged in two rows facing an open patio. They're simple, each with tile floors, two double beds, no bedspreads, a ceiling fan, and a washbasin separate from the toilet and cold-water shower cubicle. It's agreeable enough and always full by nightfall, so to secure a room, arrive no later than 3pm.

The clean open-air restaurant offers good meals at reasonable prices, served by a friendly, efficient staff. Busloads of tour groups stop here at lunch (always a sign of approval). I enjoy the casual atmosphere of El Bocadito, and there's a bookstore and gift shop adjacent to the restaurant.

✪ **Villas Arqueológicas Cobá.** Cobá, Q. Roo. ☎ **800/258-2633** in the U.S., or 5/203-3086 in Mexico City. 44 rms. A/C. $90 double. Rates include all charges and taxes. Free guarded parking.

Operated by Club Med but nothing like a Club Med Village, this lovely lakeside hotel is a 5-minute walk from the ruins. The hotel has a French polish, and the restaurant is top-notch, though expensive. A room rate including meals is available. The rooms, built around a plant-filled courtyard and beautiful pool, are stylish and soothingly comfortable. The hotel also has a library on Mesoamerican archaeology (with books in French, English, and Spanish). Make reservations—this hotel fills with touring groups.

To find it, drive through town and turn right at the lake; the hotel is straight ahead on the right.

8 En Route to Felipe Carrillo Puerto: Muyil & Chunyaxche

From Tulum you continue along the main Highway 307 past the Cobá turnoff; it heads southwest through Tulum village. About 14 miles south of Tulum village are the ruins of **Muyil** (ca. A.D. 1–1540) at the settlement of **Chunyaxche,** on the left side. Although archaeologists have done extensive mapping and studies of the ruins, only a few of the more than 100 or so buildings, caves, and subterranean temples have been excavated; it's actually more historically significant than it is interesting, and for most people it may not be worth the time or admission price. Birding in the early morning, however, is quite worthwhile. New excavations take place off and on, so keep checking the progress. One of the objects of this research is to find evidence of an inland port, since canals link the site to the Caribbean 9 miles east of the Boca Paila cut.

Note: The mosquito and dive-bombing fly population is fierce, but this is one of the best places along the coast for birding—go early in the morning.

Admission is $2; free for children under 12 and free for everyone on Sunday and festival days. It's open daily from 8am to 5pm.

The **Friends of Sian Ka'an** in Cancún (see the box, "The Sian Ka'an Biosphere Reserve," above) organizes trips through the canals from Boca Paila. The Restaurant y Cabañas Ana y José south of the Tulum ruins (see the listing under "Exploring the Punta Allen Peninsula," above) also guides visitors here through the lagoons and canals.

After Muyil and Chunyaxche, Highway 307 cuts through 45 miles of jungle to Felipe Carrillo Puerto.

9 Felipe Carrillo Puerto

134 miles SW of Cancún

Felipe Carrillo Puerto (pop. 47,000) is a busy crossroads in the jungle along the road to Ciudad Chetumal. It has gas stations, a market, a small ice plant, a bus terminal, and a few modest hotels and restaurants.

Since the main road intersects the road back to Mérida, Carrillo Puerto is the turning point for those making a "short circuit" of the Yucatán Peninsula. Highway 184 heads west from here to Ticul, Uxmal, Campeche, and Mérida.

As you pass through, consider its strange history: This was where the rebels in the War of the Castes took their stand, guided by the "Talking Crosses." Some remnants of that town (named Chan Santa Cruz) are still extant. Look for signs in town pointing the way.

ESSENTIALS

Coastal Highway 307 from Cancún leads directly here. There's frequent bus service south from Cancún and Playa del Carmen. The highway goes right through the town, becoming **Avenida Benito Juárez** in town. Driving in from the north, you'll pass a traffic circle with a bust of the great Juárez. The town **market** is here. Small hotels and good restaurants are located on the highway through town.

The directions given above assume you'll be driving. If you arrive by bus, the **bus station** is right on the plaza. From there it's a 10-minute walk east down Calle 67, past the cathedral and banks, to Avenida Juárez. Turn left onto Juárez to find restaurants and hotels and the traffic circle I use as a reference point.

The telephone **area code** is **983. Banks** here don't exchange foreign currency. *Important note:* This is the only place to buy **gasoline** between Tulum and Chetumal.

10 Majahual, Xcalak & the Chinchorro Reef

Within the last year, a tremendous amount of commercial attention has been focused on this remote part of Quintana Roo, with resorts rumored to be forthcoming both north of the Majahual turnoff and in the tiny village of Xcalak itself. Several small inns have also opened between Majahual and Xcalak since the last edition. But the peninsula is still a little-known area—at least for the moment. A roll-with-the-punches kind of traveler will savor its rustic and remote appeal—especially those preferring this coast's offbeat offerings, divers looking for new underwater conquests, bird lovers seeking an abundance of colorful tropical birdlife, and anyone looking for quiet, beachfront relaxation. Your destination is the **Costa de Cocos Dive Resort** and the nearby fishing village of **Xcalak** near the end of the peninsula. Offshore reefs and the little-known Chinchorro Reef offer great diving possibilities. The village of Xcalak once had a population as large as 1,200 before the 1958 hurricane; now it has only 200 inhabitants. You'll pass many down-and-out places on the way, so the clean Costa de Cocos will stand out when you see it.

ESSENTIALS

Driving south from Felipe Carrillo Puerto, you'll come to the turnoff (left) onto Highway 10, 1¹/₂ miles after Limones, then it's a 30-mile drive to the coastal settlement of Majahual (mah-*hah*-wahl), and another 35 miles to the end of the peninsula and the tiny fishing village of Xcalak (eesh-*kah*-lahk). To orient you further, the turnoff from Highway 307 is 163 miles southwest of Cancún and 88 miles southwest of Tulum.

Driving from the turnoff at Highway 307 to Xcalak takes around two hours. At Majahual, where you turn right (south), there's a military guard station. Tell the guard your destination and continue on the sandy, sometimes potholed road for 35 more miles—about an hour. *Slow down at settlements. Residents aren't expecting much traffic, and dogs and children play on the road.*

Public transportation note: From Chetumal, two full-size **buses** daily go to Xcalak from Chetumal's bus station. There's combi (minivan) transportation too, from behind the Holiday Inn, but they cram in twice as many passengers as will fit comfortably and may carry a pig or goat on top as well.

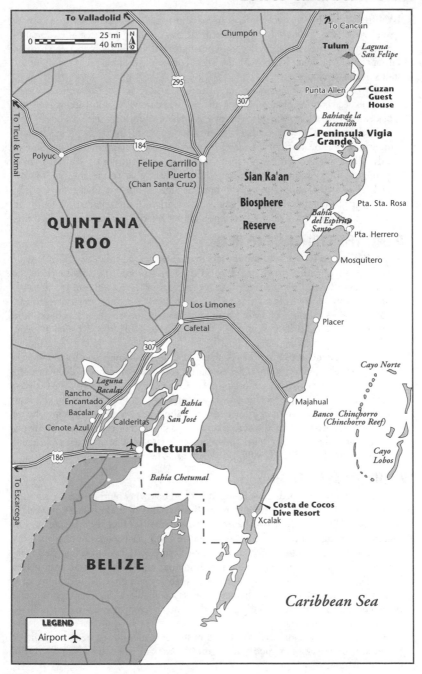

Lower Caribbean Coast

To Valladolid

To Cancún

Chumpón

Tulum

Laguna San Felipe

0   25 mi
    40 km

N

295

307

Punta Allen

Cuzan Guest House

Bahía de la Ascensión

Peninsula Vigía Grande

To Ticul & Uxmal

Polyuc

184

Felipe Carrillo Puerto
(Chan Santa Cruz)

Sian Ka'an

Biosphere

Reserve

Bahía del Espíritu Santo

Pta. Sta. Rosa

Pta. Herrero

QUINTANA ROO

Mosquitero

Los Limones

Cafetal

Placer

307

Cayo Norte

Laguna Bacalar

Rancho Encantado

Bacalar

Cenote Azul

Calderitas

Bahía de San José

Majahual

Banco Chinchorro (Chinchorro Reef)

Cayo Lobos

✈ **Chetumal**

186

Bahía Chetumal

To Escárcega

Costa de Cocos Dive Resort

Xcalak

BELIZE

Caribbean Sea

LEGEND
Airport ✈

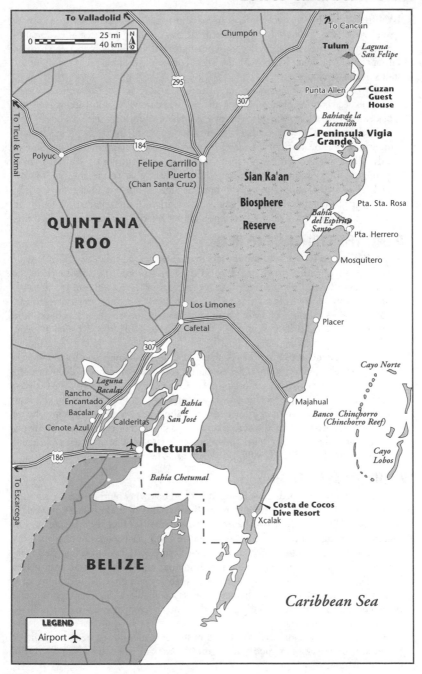

BY FERRY   When I checked, ferry docks and two 20-car ferries (with passenger space) were being prepared to ply Chetumal Bay running between the capital of Chetumal and the village of Xcalak, eliminating the tedious road trip through Limones and Majahual. Check with the State Tourism Office in Chetumal about the status of this service.

Important note about provisions: Since this is a remote part of the world, travelers should expect inconveniences. When things break down or food items run out, replacements are a long way off. You might arrive to find that the dive boat's broken, or that there's no beer, or that the generator powering the water pumps, toilets, and electricity is off for hours or days. Needless to say, a flashlight might come in handy. Bring a large quantity of strong mosquito repellent with DEET as a main ingredient—the mosquitoes are undaunted by anything else. You might want to stow a package or two of mosquito coils to burn at night. Your last chance for gas is at Felipe Carrillo Puerto, although if you're desperate, the tire repairman's family in Limones might sell you a liter or two. Look for the big tire leaning against the fence.

DIVING THE CHINCHORRO REEF

The **Chinchorro Reef Underwater National Park** is a 24-mile-long, 8-mile-wide oval-shaped reef with a depth of 3 feet on the reef's interior to 3,000 feet on the exterior. Locals claim it's the last virgin reef system in the Caribbean. It's invisible from the ocean side; one of its diving attractions is the number of shipwrecks—at least 30 of them—along the reef's eastern side. One is on top of the reef. Divers have counted 40 cannons at one wreck site. On the west side are walls and coral gardens, but it's too rough to dive there.

Aventuras Chinchorro is the fully equipped dive shop for Sandwood Villas and Villa Caracol (see below) as well as for other establishments in the area. Local diving just offshore costs $30 per diver for a two-tank dive. Chinchorro Reef diving costs between $25 and $65 per person, depending on how long you stay, how far you go, and how many divers are in the group. Fishing and snorkeling excursions and trips into Belize can also be arranged, as well as rental of kayaks and horses. For reservations for diving, or for rooms at the abovementioned inns, contact Aventuras Chinchorro, 812 Garland Ave., Nokomis, FL 34275 (☎ **800/480-4505** or 941/488-4505).

WHERE TO STAY & DINE

Besides the Costa de Cocos Dive Resort described below, two other small, cozy inns have opened about a half a mile from each other and near the village of Xcalak. **Sandwood Villas** are four two-bedroom apartments renting for $55 per person double; the **Villa Caracol,** where rooms rent for $65 per person double, is a four-room inn with air-conditioning, balconies, 24-hour electricity, hot water, free snorkeling and fishing equipment, and a beachside bar and grill. Rates at both places include breakfast and dinner, and lunch is available. Discounts are offered for stays of a week or more. Thirteen RV hookups are also available, at $15 per night for one or two people, but no camping is permitted. Contact **Aventuras Chinchorro,** listed above, for reservations.

Aside from those connected to the establishments mentioned here, a couple of restaurants in Xcalak offer good seafood meals—ask at your hotel which one is the current favorite.

Costa de Cocos Dive Resort. Km 52 Carretera Majahual–Xcalak, Q, Roo. Reservations: ☎ **800/443-1123** in the U.S., or 708/529-4473; fax 813/488-4505. 8 cabañas. FAN. High season $115 double with 1 or 2 beds. Low season $100 double. Dive rates and packages available. Three-night minimum stay with dive package. Rates includes breakfast and dinner.

Far and away the most sophisticated hostelry along this route, this place will seem a welcome respite. It's located in a palm grove just before the fishing village of Xcalak, which is a half mile farther at the end of the peninsula. The beautifully constructed thatch-roofed cabañas are fashioned after Maya huts but with sophisticated details like limestone walls halfway up, followed by handsomely crafted mahogany-louvered and screened windows, beautiful wood plank floors in the bedroom, large tile bathrooms, comfortable furnishings, shelves of paperback books, hot water, and mosquito netting. Nice as it is, it still won't hurt to inspect your shoes daily for hidden critters—this is the jungle, after all. All dive equipment is available and included in dive packages or rented separately for day guests. The resort operates a 40-foot dive boat for diving Chinchorro. Water-sports equipment for rent includes an ocean kayak and windsurf board. PADI open-water certification can be arranged also at an additional cost. Beer and soft drinks are sold at the resort, but bring your own liquor and snacks. The casual restaurant features home-style cooking, usually with a choice of one or two main courses at dinner, sandwiches at lunch, and regular breakfast fare in the morning.

Anytime the sea gets choppy, your planned dive at Chinchorro Reef (22 miles offshore) may be grounded. However, the diving 5 minutes offshore from the Costa de Cocos Resort is highly rewarding when weather prohibits Chinchorro diving.

11 Lago Bacalar

65 miles SW of Felipe Carrillo Puerto, 23 miles NW of Chetumal

If you can arrange it, staying in Bacalar sure beats staying in Chetumal or Felipe Carrillo Puerto. The crystal-clear spring-fed waters of Lake Bacalar, which is Mexico's second largest lake at slightly over 65 miles long, empty into the Caribbean. Known as the Lake of Seven Colors, mismanagement of the natural mixture of spring and seawater in recent years changed the characteristic varied deep blue colors. It's still beautiful to gaze upon, and the colors range from crystal clear and pale blue to deep blue-green and Caribbean turquoise. Spaniards fleeing coastal pirates used Maya pyramid stones to build a fort in Bacalar, which is now a modest museum. The area is very quiet—the perfect place to swim and relax. At least 130 species of birds have been counted in the area. If you're in a car, take a detour through the village of Bacalar and down along the lakeshore drive. To find the lakeshore drive, go all the way past town on Highway 307, where you'll see a sign pointing left to the lake. When you turn left, that road is the lakeshore drive. You can double back along the drive from there to return to the highway. The Hotel Laguna is on the lakeshore drive. From here it's a 30-minute drive to Chetumal and to the Corozol Airport in Belize. Besides its location on Lago Bacalar, this area is also perfect for launching excursions into the Río Bec ruin route, described below.

ESSENTIALS

Buses going south from Cancún and Playa del Carmen stop here, and there are frequent buses from Chetumal. Signs into Bacalar are plainly visible from Highway 307.

WHERE TO STAY

Hotel Laguna. Costera de Bacalar 143, 77010 Lago Bacalar, Q. Roo. ☎ **983/2-3517** in Chetumal. 30 rms, 4 bungalows. FAN. $30 double. $55 bungalow for 5 persons.

The Laguna is off the beaten path, so there are almost always rooms available—except in winter, when it's full of Canadians. Rooms overlook the pool and have a lovely view of the lake. The water along the shore is very shallow, but you can dive from the hotel's dock into 30-foot water. The hotel's restaurant offers main courses costing about $4 to $8. It's open daily from 8am to 8pm. To find it, go through town toward Chetumal. Just at the edge of town you'll see a sign pointing left to the hotel and lakeshore drive.

◊ Rancho Encantado Cottage Resort. Carretera Felipe Carrillo Puerto–Chetumal (Apdo. Postal 233), 77000 Chetumal, Q. Roo. ☎ and fax **983/8-0427.** Reservations: P.O. Box 1256, Taos, NM 87571. ☎ 800/505-MAYA in the U.S.; fax 505/776-2102. E-mail: mpstarr@laplaza.org. Web site: http://www.encantado.com. 12 casitas. FAN. Including continental breakfast and dinner, Dec–April $150 double; May–Nov. $120 double. Villa $1,100 week (discount for longer villa stays). Casita rates are $17.50 per person less without food.

What an Edenic, serene place in which to unwind! Rancho Encantado's immaculate white stucco individual casitas/cottages are spread out on a shady manicured lawn beside the smooth Lago Bacalar. Each spacious, sublimely comfortable, and beautifully kept room has mahogany-louvered windows, a shiny red-tile floor, mahogany dining table and chairs, a living room or sitting area, a porch with chairs, and hammocks strung between trees. Some have a handsome blue-tile kitchenette and others have a coffee area; coffeemakers and coffee are provided in each room. Some rooms have cedar ceilings and red-tiled roofs and others have thatched roofs. All are decorated with folk art, handsome Maya ruins–inspired murals, foot-loomed pastel-colored bedspreads, and Zapotec rugs from Oaxaca. The newest rooms are the four waterfront casitas (rooms 9 through 12) with white stucco walls, thatched roofs, and fabulous hand-painted murals inspired by those at Bonampak. Two of these have a striking large rust-colored plaster face resembling the faces at nearby Kohunlich. The owners' villa on the lake is also available several months a year.

A beautiful, open-air conference center, with a soaring palapa roof, sits next to the water and near the restaurant. The large palapa-topped restaurant overlooks the lake and serves all three meals. There's no beef on the menu, but plenty of chicken, fish, vegetables, and fresh fruit. The honey here is from Rancho hives. You can swim from the hotel's dock, and kayaks and canoes are available for guest use. Orange, lime, mango, sapote, ceiba, banana, palm, and oak trees, wild orchids, and bromiliads on the expansive grounds make great bird shelters, attracting flocks of chattering parrots, turquoise-browed motmots, toucans, and at least a hundred more species, many of which are easy to spot outside your room. Ask the manager, Luis Tellez, for a copy of the extensive birding list.

Tellez also keeps abreast of developments at the nearby archaeological sites and is the only source of current information before you reach the ruins. He's developed a lot of knowledge about the sites and leads several trips himself. Almost a dozen excursions are available through the hotel. Among them are day-trips to the Río Bec ruin route, an extended visit to Calakmul, a ruins visit and lunch with a local family (a guest favorite), outings to the Majahual Peninsula, and a riverboat trip to the Maya ruins of Lamanai deep in a Belizian forest. Mirabai Starr offers 8-day "Writing at the Ruins" workshops in January and June. *Note:* This is the only hotel offering guided trips to the Río Bec ruins, many of which are available only by special permit, which Tellez can obtain. Several ruins are easily reachable from the road, and others are so deep in the jungle that a guide is necessary to find them and a four-wheel-drive vehicle is a must. With advance notice, the hotel can arrange guides and the hotel has transportation. They also work with Río Bec specialist Serge Rìou (see "Touring the Ruins with a Guide," below). Excursions range in price from $55 to $115 per person, depending on the length and difficulty of the trip, and several have a three-person minimum. Groups interested in birding, yoga, archaeology, and the like are invited to bring a leader and use Rancho Encantado as a base. Special packages and excursions can be arranged in advance from the hotel's U.S.

office. To find the Rancho, look for the hotel's sign on the left about 1 mile before Bacalar.

WHERE TO EAT

Besides the lakeside restaurant of **Rancho Encantado** (see above), you may enjoy the **Restaurant Cenote Azul,** a comfortable open-air thatched-roof restaurant on the edge of the beautiful Cenote Azul. In both places, main courses cost from $5 to $12. To get to Restaurant Cenote Azul, follow the highway to the south edge of town and turn left at the restaurant's sign; follow that road around to the restaurant. At Rancho Encan-tado you can swim in Lago Bacalar, and at the Restaurant Cenote you can take a dip in placid Cenote Azul—but without skin lotion of any kind because it poisons the cenote.

12 West of Bacalar: The Río Bec Ruin Route

A few miles west of Bacalar begins the Yucatán's southern ruin route, generally called the Río Bec region, although other architectural styles are present. Until recently the region enjoyed little attention. However, all that is rapidly changing. Within the last several years, the Mexican government has spent millions of pesos to build a new highway, conserve previously excavated sites, and uncover heretofore unexcavated ruins. This is an especially ruin-rich but little-explored part of the peninsula. With the opening in late 1994 of **Dzibanché** (an extensive "new" site), paved-road access to **Calakmul** in 1994, and the **Museo de la Cultura Maya** in 1995 in Chetumal, together with other "new sites" and discoveries at existing ruins, the region is poised to become the peninsula's "newest" tourist destination. With responsible guides, other jungle-surrounded but difficult-to-reach sites may also be available soon. A new four-lane highway leads from close to Bacalar for several miles before it becomes two-lane again; construction crews are continuing to work widening the road even further. Touristic services (restaurants, hotels) are slowly being added along the route, informed guides must be arranged before you arrive, and there are no visitor's centers. Rancho Encantado trucks in water to the bathrooms at the ruins of Kohunlich, making them the only public rest rooms on the route. Part of what makes this area so special is the feeling of pioneering onto unmarked land—and with that comes a bit of inconvenience. However, this area is definitely worth watching and visiting now. And, finally, I must mention the richness of the bird and animal life along the whole route. Toucans flying across the highway and orioles are extremely common. Grey fox, wild turkey, tesquintle (a bushy-tailed plant-eating rodent), the raccoon relative coatimundi (with its long tapered snout and tail), and armadillos will surely cross your path. At Calakmul, a family of howler monkeys resides in the trees overlooking the parking area. To make the most of your visit, preparatory reading would include *A Forest of Kings: The Untold Story of the Ancient Maya* by Linda Schele and David Friedel (William Morrow, 1990), *The Blood of Kings: Dynasty and Ritual in Maya Art* by Linda Schele and Mary Ellen Miller (George Braziller, Inc., 1968), and *The Maya Cosmos* by David Freidel and Linda Schele (William Morrow, 1993). *Arqueológica Mexicana* magazine, which is written in Spanish, devoted its July–August 1995 issue to the Quintana Roo portion of the Río Bec ruin route. Lastly, though it lacks historic and cultural information, and many sites have expanded since it was written, Joyce Kelly's *An Archaeological Guide to Mexico's Yucatán Peninsula* (University of Oklahoma, 1993), is the best companion book to have. For a crash course, focus your learning on the meaning of the jaguar, Xibalba (the underworld), and the earth monster.

The route starts just 9 miles from the edge of Bacalar where there's the turnoff from Highway 307 to Highway 186, which leads to the Río Bec ruin route as well as to Escarcega, Villahermosa, and Palenque. *A reminder:* On your return, if you are going back to Bacalar (or north on Highway 307), the guards at the government inspection station at the Reforma intersection will ask to see your travel papers (birth certificate or passport) and Tourist Permit. It is the intersection you pass after turning from Highway 186 north on Highway 307 toward Bacalar. You can divide your sightseeing into several day-trips. If you get an early start, many of the ruins mentioned below can be easily visited in a day from Bacalar. These sites will be changing, though, since swarms of laborers are still busy with further exploration. Evidence shows that these ruins, especially Becán, were part of the trade route linking the Caribbean coast at Cobá to Edzná and the Gulf coast, and with Lamanai in Belize and beyond. Once this region was dense with Maya cities, cultivated fields, lakes, and an elaborate system of rivers that connected the region with Belize and Central America. Today many of these ancient cities hide under cover of jungle, which has overtaken the land from horizon to horizon.

There are no visitor facilities or refreshments at these sites, so bring your own water and food. However, in the village of Xpujil (just before the ruins of Xpujil), the **Restaurant Posada Calakmul** (☎ **983/2-3304**), under the watchful eye of Doña María Cabrera, serves excellent home-style food and caters to ruins enthusiasts—hung about the room are photos and descriptions of little-known sites written by Río Bec specialist Serge Rìou (see below). The new **hotel rooms** behind the restaurant cost $16 for a double and are clean and comfortable, with tile floors, private bathrooms with hot water, good beds, and a small porch. Near the entrance to the Chicanná ruins, on the north side of the road, is the new **Ramada Inn Eco Village,** km 144 Carretera Excarcega (☎ **983/2-8863**). Though the name suggests an ecological bent, approximately 20 acres of jungle were completely leveled to build an as yet unpaved parking lot for all the buses and cars that will one day come, a swimming pool, a restaurant, and 28 nicely furnished rooms in sets of two stories. Manicured lawns with flower beds and pathways link the rooms, which have a Polynesian architecture. There are no ecologically oriented tours. For the moment, the hotel attracts primarily bus tours and individual travelers. Electricity is generated between 6pm and 10am. Restaurant prices are high and don't include the 15% tax. A 15% service charge might also be added. Double rooms go for $100, including breakfast.

Luis Tellez at Rancho Encantado, at Bacalar (see "Where to Stay," under "Lago Bacalar," above), is the best source of information about the status of these sites and any new ones. Entry to each site is $2 to $4, and all are free on Sunday. Informational signs at each building within the sites are in Mayan, Spanish, and English. Wear loads of mosquito repellent. The following list of sites is in order if you're driving from Bacalar or Chetumal.

For a map of this area, consult the Yucatán Peninsula map in chapter 2.

TOURING THE RUINS WITH A GUIDE   If you're traveling to this part of the Yucatán specifically to see the Río Bec ruins, the services of Serge Rìou, "Maya Lowland Specialist," will probably be indispensable to you. Several years ago young Mr. Rìou visited the Río Bec ruin route on a vacation from France. He fell so in love with the culture, romance, and history of the ruins that he returned to live and learn all that was possible about these little-known ruins. Living in Xpujil, he hiked the forests daily in search of ruins, worked with archaeologists on the trail of new sites, photographed the ruins, attended conferences of Maya specialists, and read everything he could find on Mexican archaeology. Today his encyclopedic knowledge of the nearby ruins makes him the most informed guide. He speaks excellent English and Spanish and charges around $75 to $100 per person a day to guide up to three people to a variety of sites. The higher price is for Calakmul, the farthest site from Chetumal. He can arrange necessary permits to unopened sites. You can contact him directly (Apdo. Postal 238, 77000 Chetumal, Q. Roo; ☎ 983/2-9819 or 983/2-1251) or arrange for his services through **Rancho Encantado** at Lago Bacalar (see "Where to Stay & Dine," under "Lago Bacalar," above), which has all the necessary types of vehicles, or contact him through the **Holiday Inn** in Chetumal (see "Where to Stay & Dine," under "Chetumal," below).

DZIBANCHÉ

Dzibanché (or Tzibanché) means "place where they write on wood." Exploration began here in 1993, and it opened to the public in late 1994. Scattered over 26 square miles (though only a small portion is excavated), it's both a Preclassic and a Postclassic site (A.D. 300–900) that was occupied for around 700 years. Two enormous adjoining plazas have been cleared. The site shows influence from Río Bec, Petén, and Teotihuacán. The Temple of the Owl, on the Plaza de Xibalbá, has a miniature version of Teotihuacán-style *talud tablero* (slant and straight facade) architecture flanking the sides of the main stairway leading to the top with its lintel and entrance to an underground tomb. (Teotihuacán ruins are near Mexico City, but their influence was strong as far as Guatemala.) Despite centuries of an unforgiving wet climate, a wood lintel, in good condition and with a date carving, still supports a partially preserved corbeled arch on top of this building. Inside the temple, a tomb was discovered, making this the second known temple in Mexico built over an underground tomb (the first discovered was the Temple of Inscriptions at Palenque). A diagram of this temple shows interior steps leading from the top, then down inside the pyramid to ground level, just as at Palenque. The stairway is first reached by a deep, well-like drop that held remains of a sacrificial victim and which was sacked during pre-Hispanic times. Uncovered at different levels of the stairwell were a number of beautiful polychromed lidded vessels, one of which has an owl painted on the top handle, with its wings spreading onto the lid. White owls were messengers of the gods of the underworld in the Maya religion. This interior stairway isn't open to the public, but you can clearly see the lintel just behind the entrance to the tomb. Further exploration of the tomb awaits stabilization of interior walls.

Opposite the Temple of the Owl is the Temple of the Cormorant, so named after a polychromed drinking vessel found here picturing a cormorant. Here, too, archaeologists have found evidence of an interior tomb similar to the one in the Temple of the Owl, but excavations of it have not begun. Other magnificently preserved pottery pieces found during excavations include an incense burner with an almost three-dimensional figure of the diving god attached to the outside, and another incense burner with an elaborately dressed figure of the god Itzamná attached.

The site also incorporates another section of ruins called **Kinichná** (keen-eech-*nah*), which is about 1½ miles north and is reachable only by a rutted road that's impassable in the rainy season. There, an Olmec-style jade figure was found.

A formal road to these ruins had not yet been built, but there's a sign pointing to the right turn to Morocoy approximately 18 miles from the Highway 307 turnoff. You follow that paved road, which becomes an unpaved road, and pass the small settlement (not really a town) of Morocoy to another rough dirt road to the right (there's a sign to the ruins there), and follow it for about a mile to the ruin entrance. Ask at Rancho Encantado, near Bacalar (see "Where to Stay," under "Lago Bacalar," above), about the condition of the unpaved portion of road.

Maya Construction Styles

Río Bec Style Found particularly in the states of Campeche and Quintana Roo, and south in Guatemala, the style takes its name from the ruins of Río Bec, located south of Xpuhil off Highway 186 between Chetumal and Escarcega. Río Bec architecture is characterized by roofcombs, which adorn rooftops like latticework false fronts. Frequently, doorways are elaborate stonework mouths of Chaac, also called "monster mouths." Steep pyramids are frequently almost cone-shaped, with such narrow stairs leading to the top that they are difficult, if not impossible, to climb. Examples of the Río Bec style are at Xpuhil, Becán, Chicaná, and Calakmul. Away from the traditional Río Bec area, roofcombs also appear in several places such as Palenque, Uxmal, and Kabah.

Chenes Style The baroque examples of Maya architecture, Chenes buildings have facades that are elaborately embellished from top to bottom with separately cut stone pieces, often with many representations of Chaac, the Maya rain god. As with the Río Bec style, doorways are often open mouths of a fierce-looking Chaac with pointed teeth representing the "monster mouth" entrance to Xibalba, the Maya underworld. Though the Chenes heartland is in the states of Campeche and Quintana Roo, Yucatán's ruins also have excellent Chenes-style buildings. Good examples are the Nunnery Annex at Chichén-Itzá, and the high-up doorway on the Temple of the Magician at Uxmal, and at Kabah where 250 Chaac masks cover the stunning facade of the Codz Poop. Chenes, or "well country" style, is the name given to a region that contains many wells or that features this type of architecture.

Puuc Style The name Puuc refers to a region, a culture, and an architectural style. The Yucatán's only hilly area, south of Mérida, is known as the Puuc (Mayan for hills or mountains), and gives the architecture its name. Architecturally elaborate stonework, often mosaic-like, generally begins from the top of the doorline to the roofline and includes many masks of Chaac, appearing with an elephant trunk–like hook nose. In other places, these masks appear on the facade as well as ornamental corner ends of buildings. Puuc buildings are also embellished with a series of short stone columns, giving the buildings a beautiful, almost Greek appearance.

KOHUNLICH

Kohunlich (koh-*hoon*-leek), 26 miles from the intersection of Highways 186 and 307, dates from around A.D. 100 to 900. Turn left off the road, and the entrance is 5¹/₂ miles ahead. From the parking area you enter the grand parklike site, crossing a large and shady ceremonial area flanked by four large conserved pyramidal edifices. Continue walking, and just beyond this grouping you'll come to Kohunlich's famous **Pyramid of the Masks** under a thatched covering. The masks, actually enormous plaster faces, date from around A.D. 500 and are on the facade of the building. Besides an elongated face and undulating lips, the masks show vestiges of blue and red paint. Note the carving on the pupils, which show a cosmic connection, possibly with the night sun that illuminated the underworld. It's speculated that masks covered much of the facade of this building, which is built in the Río Bec style with rounded corners, a false stairway, and a false temple on the top. At least one theory is that the masks are a composite of several rulers at Kohunlich. During recent excavations of buildings immediately to the left after you enter, two intact pre-Hispanic skeletons and five decapitated heads were uncovered that were once probably used in a ceremonial rite. To the right after you enter (follow a shady path through the jungle) is another recently excavated plaza. It's thought to have housed elite citizens, due to the high quality of pottery found there and the fine architecture of the rooms. Scholars believe that Kohunlich became overpopulated, leading to its decline. The bathrooms here are the only ones at any site on the route.

CHACAN BACAN

Chacan Bacan (chah-*kahn* bah-*kahn*), which dates from around 200 B.C., was first discovered in 1980 with excavation beginning in 1995. It's scheduled to open sometime in 1998, with 30 to 40 buildings uncovered. Only one imposing 107-foot-high pyramid was being excavated when I was there. However, the discovery of huge Olmec-style heads on its facade can only lend excitement to future digs. The heads, showing from the middle of the skull forward, have helmet-like caps similar in style to the full multi-ton Olmec heads unearthed in Veracruz and Tabasco on Mexico's Gulf Coast, where the Olmecs originated. These heads are thought to be older than the figures at both Kohunlich and Balamkú. The exact size of the site hasn't been determined, but it's huge and is located in a densely forested setting, with thousands of tropical hardwood trees, plants, birds, and wild animals. This has been earmarked as an ecological/touristic center. Though not yet open to the public, it's about 50 miles and a 1¹/₂-hour drive from Bacalar. The turnoff (left) to it is at Caoba, where you follow a paved road for about 1¹/₂ miles, then turn left on an unmarked path. From the paved portion you can look left and see the uncovered pyramid protruding over the surrounding jungle. Ask Luis Tellez at Rancho Encantado at Lago Bacalar about the accessibility of this site.

XPUJIL

Xpujil (also spelled Xpuhil) means either "cattail" or "forest of kapok trees" and flourished between A.D. 400 and 900. Ahead on the left after you enter, you'll see a rectangular ceremonial platform 6¹/₂ feet high and 173 feet long holding three once-ornate buildings. These almost-conical edifices resemble the towering ruins of Tikal in Guatemala and rest on a lower building with 12 rooms. Unfortunately, they are so ruined you can only ponder how it might have been. To the right after you enter are two newly uncovered structures, one of which is a large acropolis. From the highway, a small sign on the right points to the site that is just a few yards off the highway and 49 miles from Kohunlich.

BECÁN

Becán (bay-*kahn*), about 4¹/₂ miles beyond Xpujil and once surrounded by a moat, means "canyon filled by water" and dates from Early Classic to Late Classic—600 B.C. to A.D. 1200. The moat, which isn't visible today, once had seven bridges leading to the seven cities that were pledged to Becán. Following jungle paths beyond the first visible group of ruins, you'll find at least two recently excavated acropoli. Though the site was abandoned by A.D. 850, ceramic remains indicate there may have been a population resurgence between A.D. 900 and 1000, and it was still used as a ceremonial site as late as A.D. 1200. Becán was a governmental and ceremonial center with political sway over at least seven other cities in the area, including Chicanná, Hormiguerro, and Payan. To really understand this site, you need a good guide. But for starters, the first plaza group you see after you enter was the center of grand ceremonies. From the highway you see the backside of a pyramid (temple 1) with two temples on top. From the highway you can see between the two pyramid-top temples to temple 4, which is opposite temple 1. When the high priest appeared through the mouth of the earth monster in the center of temple 4 (which he reached via a hidden side stairway that's now partly exposed), he was visible from what is now the highway. It's thought that commoners had to watch ceremonies from outside the ceremonial plaza; thus the site was positioned for good viewing purposes. The backside of temple 4 is believed to have been a civic plaza where rulers sat on stone benches while pronouncing judgments. The recently uncovered second plaza group dates from around A.D. 850 and has perfect twin towers on top, where there's a big platform. Under the platform are 10 rooms that are thought to be related to Xibalba (shee-*bahl*-bah), the underworld. Earth monster faces probably covered this building (and they appeared on other buildings as well). Remains of at least one ball court have been unearthed. Becán is about 4½ miles beyond Xpujil and is visible on the right side of the highway, about half a mile down a rutted road.

CHICANNÁ

Slightly over a mile beyond Becán, on the left side of the highway, is Chicanná, which means "house of the mouth of snakes." Trees loaded with bromeliads shade the central square surrounded by five buildings. The most outstanding edifice features a monster-mouth doorway and an ornate stone facade with more superimposed masks. As you enter the mouth of the earth monster, note that you are walking on a platform that functions as the open jaw of the monster with stone teeth on both sides.

CALAKMUL

This area is both a massive Maya archaeological zone with at least 60 sites and a 178,699-acre rain forest designated in 1989 as the Calakmul Biosphere Reserve, which includes territory in both Mexico and Guatemala.

THE ARCHAEOLOGICAL ZONE   Since 1982, archaeologists have been excavating the ruins of Calakmul, which dates from 100 B.C. to A.D. 900. It's the largest of the area's 60 known sites. Nearly 7,000 buildings have been discovered and mapped. At its zenith at least 60,000 people may have lived around the site, but by the time of the Spanish Conquest of Mexico in 1519, there were fewer than 1,000 inhabitants. Discoveries include more stelae than any other site. By building 13 is a stelae of a woman dating from A.D. 652. Of the buildings, temple 3 is the best preserved. In it were found offerings of shells, beads, and polychromed tripod pottery. The tallest, at 178 feet, is temple 2. From the top of it you can see the outline of the ruins of El Mirador, 30 miles across the forest in Guatemala. Temple 4 charts the line of the sun from June 21, when it falls on the left (north) corner, to September 21 and March 21, when it lines up in the east behind the middle temple on the top of the building, to December 21 when it falls on the right (south) corner. Numerous jade pieces, including spectacular masks, were uncovered here, most of which are on display in the **Museo Regional** in Campeche. Temple 7 is largely unexcavated except for the top, where in 1984 the most outstanding jade mask yet to be found at Calakmul was uncovered. In *A Forest of Kings*, Linda Schele and David Freidel tell of wars between Calakmul, Tikal, and Naranjo (the latter two in Guatemala) and how Ah-Cacaw, king of Tikal (75 miles south of Calakmul), captured King Jaguar-Paw in A.D. 695 and later Lord Ox-Ha-Te Ixil Ahau, both of Calakmul. From January to May the site is open Tuesday through Sunday from 7am to 7pm. The site is so wet during the rainy season from June through October that it's best not to go.

CALAKMUL BIOSPHERE RESERVE   Set aside in 1989, this is the peninsula's only high forest selva, a rain forest that annually records as much as 16 feet of rain. Among the plants are cacti, epiphytes, and orchids. Endangered animals include the white-lipped peccary, jaguar, and puma. So far more than 250 species of birds have been recorded. At the moment there are no guided tours in the reserve, and no overnight stays or camping are permitted. But a hint of the region can be seen around the ruins. Howler monkeys are often peering down on visitors as they park their cars near the entrance to the ruins.

The turnoff on the left for Calakmul is located approximately 145 miles from the intersection of highways 186 and 307, just before the village of Conhuas. There's a guard station where you pay to enter the road/site. From the turnoff it's a 1 1/2-hour drive on a newly paved, but very narrow and somewhat rutted road that may be difficult during the rainy season from May through October. *A driving caution:* Numerous curves in the road make seeing oncoming traffic (what little there is) difficult, and there have been head-on collisions. (I nearly had one.)

BALAMKÚ

Balamkú (bah-lahm-*koo*) was literally snatched from the incredibly destructive hands of looters by Instituto de Historia y Antropologia (INAH) archaeologist Florentino García Cruz in October 1990. Amateur archaeologist and guide Serge Rìou was close behind him to photograph the site before looters hit one last time, destroying the head of one of the figures. An uncharted site at the time, it was saved by García, who had been alerted by locals that looters were working there. Today it's open to the public, and though small, it's worth the time to see it since the facade of one building is among the most unusual on this route. When you reach the clearing, about 2 miles from the highway via a narrow dirt path through the jungle, there are two buildings, one on the right and one on the left. The right building is really three continuous, tall but narrow pyramids dating from around A.D. 700. The left building, which dates from around A.D. 400, holds the most interest because of the cross-legged figures resembling those found at Copan, in Honduras. Originally there were four of these regal figures (probably representing kings), seated on crocodiles or frogs above the entrance to the underworld, but looters destroyed two on each end and further disfigured the others. Still, enough remains to see the beauty. The whole concept of this building, with its molded stucco facade, is of life and death. On the head of each almost–three-dimensional figure are the eyes, nose, and mouth of a jaguar figure, followed by the full face of the human figure, then a neck formed by the eyes and nose of another jaguar, and an Olmeclike face on the stomach, its neck decorated by a necklace, then the crossed legs of the figure seated upon a frog or crocodile. The earth monster is represented by a half-snake, half-crocodile animal, all symbols of death, water, and life. The May 1992 issue of *Mexico Desconocido* features the discovery of Balamkú written by Florentino García Cruz.

13 Chetumal

85 miles S of Felipe Carrillo Puerto, 23 miles S of Lago Bacalar

Quintana Roo became a state in 1974, and Chetumal (pop. 170,000) is its capital. While Quintana Roo was still a territory, it was a free-trade zone to encourage trade and immigration between neighboring Guatemala and Belize. The old part of town, down by the river (Río Hondo), has a Caribbean atmosphere and wooden buildings, but the newer parts are modern Mexican. There is lots of noise and heat, so your best plan would be not to stay—it's not a particularly interesting or friendly town. It is, however, worth a detour to see the wonderful **Museo de la Cultural Maya,** especially if your trip involves seeing the Río Bec ruin route described above.

ESSENTIALS
GETTING THERE & DEPARTING

BY PLANE   **Aerocaribe** (Mexicana) has daily flights to and from Cancún and flights several times weekly between Chetumal and the ruins of Tikal in Guatemala. **Avio Quintana** (☎ 983/2-9692) flies Monday through Friday to Cancún in a 19-passenger plane for around $50 one-way. **Taesa** flies from Cancún and Cozumel.

BY BUS   The bus station of **Autotransportes del Caribe** (☎ 983/2-0740) is 20 blocks from the town center on Insurgentes at Niños Héroes. Buses go to Cancún, Tulum, Playa del Carmen, Puerto Morelos, Mérida, Campeche, Villahermosa, and Mexico City. **Caribe Express** (☎ 983/2-7889 or 983/2-8001) has deluxe buses to Mérida and Cancún. This service features a 28-seat bus with video movies, steward service, and refreshments. Sixteen second-class buses run to and from Bacalar daily.

   To Belize: Two companies make the run from Chetumal (through Corozal and Orange Walk) to Belize City. **Batty's Bus Service** runs 10 buses per day, and **Venus Bus Lines** (☎ 04/2-2132 in Corozal) has seven daily buses, the first at 11am; the 2pm bus is express, with fewer stops. Though it's a short distance from Chetumal to Corozal, it may take as long as 1 1/2 hours, depending on how long it takes the bus to pass through Customs and Immigration.

   To Limones, Majahual, and Xcalak: Two buses a day run between these destinations.

BY CAR   It's a 2 1/2-hour ride from Felipe Carrillo Puerto. If you're heading to Belize you'll need a passport and special auto insurance, which you can buy at the border. You can't take a rental car over the border, however.

   To get to the ruins of Tikal in Guatemala you must first go through Belize to the border crossing at Ciudad Melchor de Mencos.

BY FERRY   The docks are ready, but the new ferry was too big and ferry service has been delayed between Chetumal and the Xcalak/Majahual Peninsula. However, check at the State Tourism Office to see if it's running by the time you travel. If it is, the service will make that once-tedious road trip much shorter.

VISITOR INFORMATION

The State Tourism Office (☎ 983/2-0266 or 983/2-0855; fax 983/2-5073 or 983/2-6097) is at Avenida Hidalgo 22, corner of Carmen Ochoa.

ORIENTATION

The telephone **area code** is **983.** Chetumal has many "no left turn" streets, with hawk-eyed traffic policemen at each one. Be alert—they love to nail visitors and may even motion you into making a traffic or pedestrian violation, then issue a ticket, or take a bribe instead.

   You'll arrive following Obregón into town. Niños Héroes is the other main cross street. When you reach it, turn left to find the hotels mentioned below.

A MUSEUM NOT TO MISS

Chetumal is really the gateway to Belize or to the Río Bec ruins, and not a touristically interesting city. But it's worth a detour to Chetumal to see the **Museo de la Cultura Maya.** If you can arrange it, see the museum before you tour the Río Bec ruins, since it will all make more sense after getting it in perspective here.

Museo de la Cultura Maya. Av. de los Héroes s/n. ☎ **983/2-6838.** Admission $1; children 50¢. Tues–Thurs 9am–7pm, Fri and Sat 9am–8pm, Sun 9am–2pm. It's on the left between Colón and Primo de Verdad, 8 blocks from Avenida Obregón, past the Holiday Inn.

Sophisticated, impressive, and informative, this new museum unlocks the complex world of the Maya. Push a button and an illustrated description appears explaining the medicinal and domestic uses of plants with their Maya and scientific names, another describes the five social classes of the Maya by the way they dress, and yet another shows how the beauty signs of cranial deformation, crossed eyes, and facial scarification were achieved. An enormous screen flashes moving pictures taken from an airplane flying over more than a dozen Maya sites from Mexico to Honduras. Another large television shows the architectural variety of Maya pyramids and how they were probably built. Then a walk on a glass floor takes you over representative ruins in the Maya world, clearly showing the variety of pyramidal shapes and particular sites. And, finally, one of the most impressive sections is the three-story stylized sacred ceiba tree, which the Maya believed represented the underworld (Xibalba) (on the bottom floor of the museum), earth (the middle floor of the museum), and the 13 heavens (the third floor of the museum). From this you'll have a better idea of the significance of the symbolism on the pyramids in the Maya world. Plan no less than 2 hours here. Even then, especially if your interest is high, you may want to take a break and return with renewed vigor—there's a lot to see and learn. What a museum!

WHERE TO STAY & DINE

Hotel Holiday Inn Caribe. Niños Héroes 171, 77000 Chetumal, Q. Roo. ☎ **800/465-4329** in the U.S., or 983/2-1100. Fax 983/2-1676. 75 rms. A/C TV TEL. $60–$85 double. Free parking.

This modern hotel (formerly the Hotel Continental) across from the central market was remodeled in 1995 and became a Holiday Inn. The hotel has a good-size pool (a blessing in muggy Chetumal) and a good restaurant. The hotel is only two blocks from the Museo de la Cultura Maya. You can contact Río Bec specialist Serge Rìou (see "Touring the Ruins with a Guide," above) through the travel agency here. To find it as you enter the town on Obregón, turn left on Niños Héroes, go 6 blocks and look for the hotel on the right, opposite the market.

Hotel Nachacan. Calz. Veracruz 379, 77000 Chetumal, Q. Roo. ☎ **983/2-3232.** 20 rms. A/C TV. $26 double.

Opposite the new market, this nice hotel offers rooms that are plain, but clean and comfortable. A restaurant is off the lobby. It's relatively convenient to the bus station, but not close enough to walk if you arrive by bus. It is, however, within walking distance of the Museo de la Cultura Maya. To find it from Avenida Obregón, turn left on Calzada Veracruz and follow it for at least 10 blocks; the hotel will be on the right.

ONWARD FROM CHETUMAL

From Chetumal you have several choices. You can go south to Belize and Guatemala (though not in a rental car); the Maya ruins of Lamanai are an easy day-trip into Belize if you have transportation. You can explore the Río Bec ruin route north of the city. North of Bacalar you can cut diagonally across the peninsula to Mérida or retrace your steps to Cancún. You can take Highway 186 west to Escarcega, Villahermosa, and Palenque, but I don't recommend it and neither does the U. S. State Department: It's a long, hot, and lonely trip on a highway that is often riddled with potholes after you cross into Campeche state. Permanent ZONA DE DESLAVE signs warn motorists that parts of the roadbed are missing entirely or are so badly dipped they might cause an accident. Road conditions improve from time to time, but annual rains cause constant problems. And from time to time bandits have robbed travelers. At the Campeche state line there's a military guard post with drug-sniffing dogs; every vehicle is searched. A military guard post at the Reforma inter-section just before Bacalar requires motorists to present the identification you used to enter Mexico (birth certificate or passport), plus your Tourist Permit. Other photo identification may be required, as well as information on where you are staying or where you are headed. The whole procedure should take only minutes.

Mérida & the Maya Cities 6

Mérida and its environs in Campeche and Yucatán states in the western Yucatán Peninsula are abundantly endowed with the qualities that can make a Mexican vacation something to remember. The area is rich in living pre-Hispanic traditions—you'll find clothing, crafts, and village life that hearken back to Maya ways of 10 centuries ago. And there are plenty of the more traditional reminders of the past—the ruins of spectacular Maya cities such as Chichén-Itzá, Uxmal, and others, along with the walled Spanish colonial city of Campeche. The western half of the Yucatán also offers the budget-minded traveler a wide choice of economical lodgings, and you'll enjoy the relaxed pace of Yucatecan life and the warm, friendly people.

EXPLORING THE YUCATÁN'S MAYA HEARTLAND

The cultural center of the Yucatán, beautiful Mérida is a natural launching pad for trips to the Yucatán's major archaeological sites, to interior rock-walled villages inhabited by the Maya, to the Gulf coast, and to the Yucatán's northern coast. This part of the Yucatán Peninsula is among the best places in Mexico to take a driving tour—there are no mountains; roads, though only two-lane, are fairly well-maintained; traffic is light; and stops in the many rock-walled Maya villages are delightful. In fact, those who've traveled from Cancún or the Costa Turquesa haven't really seen what the Yucatán is all about until they've ventured into its heartland south of Mérida. Heading to the interior of the peninsula is where visitors and local Maya finally meet; most foreigners depart with warm memories of the many friendly Maya people they encountered. The inland villages are just that—villages—made by and for the Maya, and except for the two-lane highway through them, they show few traces of the modern world—no shopping centers, tourist shops, or tourist-oriented restaurants. Their neat homes, made of mud and sticks or whitewashed plaster over cement, are often oval-shaped like the *nah* the Maya inhabited before the Spanish arrived and have a traditional thatched roof. In these villages, you'll find small grocery stores or village markets where you can stock up on water, bread, fruit, snacks, and canned goods. A few commercial centers, such as Valladolid and Oxkutzkab, have a more Spanish-colonial look and stores with modern merchandise, but even there, you'll see traditional Maya homes sprinkled about on the side streets. Because the Maya are rather shy, they may not quickly strike up a conversation with a stranger. However, if they come to their door to see what you're doing, that's an open invitation to chat (or gesture, since they speak only Yukatek Maya). The friendliness of the lowland Maya is in contrast to the more withdrawn and somewhat unfriendly nature of the highland Maya of Chiapas, described in chapter 7.

CELESTÚN NATIONAL WILDLIFE REFUGE: A WETLANDS RESERVE

This flamingo sanctuary and offbeat sand-street fishing village on the Gulf coast is a 1½-hour drive from Mérida. Plan a long day—with a very early start—for the 7am flamingo trip. However, people looking for solitude might find this a welcome respite for a week.

DZIBILCHALTÚN: MAYA RUINS

This Maya site, now a national park, is located 9 miles north of Mérida along the Progreso Road. Here you'll find a number of pre-Hispanic structures, nature trails, and the new Museum of the Maya. Make this one a half-day trip in the cool of the morning.

PROGRESO: GULF COAST CITY

A modern city and Gulf coast beach escape 21 miles north of Mérida, Progreso has a beautiful oceanfront drive and a vast beach lined with coconut palms that's popular on the weekends. Plan a full day trip if you like beaches, but there's not a lot else to do.

UXMAL: SPECTACULAR MAYA RUINS

The best way to visit the splendid archaeological zone of Uxmal (oosh-mahl; it's about 50 miles to the south of Mérida) is to rent a car, stay 2 nights in a hotel at Uxmal or a less expensive hotel in Ticul, and allow for 2 to 3 full days of sightseeing. It's also possible—though a bit rushed—to see Uxmal and the quartet of ruins south of there on a day-trip by special excursion bus from Mérida. Sunday is a good day to go, since admission to the archaeological sites is free.

CAMPECHE: WALLED COLONIAL CITY

A pretty colonial city with a relaxed pace, Campeche is also somewhat off the main tourist path. It's about 3 hours southwest of Mérida. Two nights and a full day should give you enough time to see Campeche's architectural highlights and museums, especially the **Museo Regional de Campeche,** housing the clay and jade objects taken from the freshly excavated southern Campeche ruins of Calakmul.

CHICHÉN-ITZÁ & VALLADOLID

From Mérida, it's 75 miles to the famed ruins of **Chichén-Itzá** and 100 miles to the sleepy town of **Valladolid.** The ruins at Chichén-Itzá are so vast that you'll want to spend the better part of 2 days, taking your time in the heat, to see this site. The colonial city of Valladolid offers an inexpensive alternative to staying at Chichén-Itzá.

1 Mérida: Gateway to the Maya Heartland

900 miles NE of Mexico City, 200 miles W of Cancún

Mérida, capital of the state of Yucatán, has been the major city in the area since the mid-1500s, when the Spanish founded it on the site of the defeated Maya city of Tihó. Although it's a major tourist crossroads—within range of both the peninsula's archaeological ruins and its glitzy coasts, this modern city of one million inhabitants is easygoing. The friendliness of its people remains its trademark.

Downtown Mérida is full of fine examples of colonial-style architecture. Vestiges of the opulent 19th-century era of the Yucatán's henequen boom remain in the ornate mansions sprinkled throughout the city.

ESSENTIALS

GETTING THERE & DEPARTING

BY PLANE   For carriers serving Mérida from the United States, see chapter 3, "Planning a Trip to the Yucatán." **Mexicana** (☎ **99/24-6633** or 99/24-6910) flies in from Mexico City. **Aeroméxico** (☎ **99/27-9000** or 99/27-9544) flies to and from Cancún and Mexico City. **Aerocaribe,** a Mexicana affiliate (☎ **99/28-6786**), provides service to and from Cozumel, Cancún, Oaxaca, Tuxtla Gutiérrez, Veracruz, Villahermosa, and points in Central America. **Taesa** (☎ **99/46-1826** at the airport) flies in from Monterrey and Mexico City. **Aviateca** (☎ **99/26-9131** or 99/26-9164) flies in from Guatemala City. **Aviacsa** (☎ **99/26-9087**) provides service from Cancún, Monterrey, Villahermosa, Tuxtla Gutiérrez, Tapachula, Oaxaca, and Mexico City. Taxis to and from the city to the airport are expensive.

Arriving in Mérida   Mérida's airport is 8 miles from the city center on the southwestern outskirts of town where Highway 180 enters the city. The airport has desks for renting a car, reserving a hotel room, and getting tourist information. *A note of caution:* Customs inspectors at the Mérida airport have been known to hassle tourists by confiscating and refusing to return the legal, legitimate, and allowable contents of their luggage. Upon arrival at all airports in Mexico passengers receive a customs statement with all allowable items listed. If you are within your rights according to that list and you are hassled, tell the officials that you are reporting them to SEDOCAM (say-doh-kahm), which is the Comptroller and Administrative Development Secretariat (☎ **01-800/0-0148** in Mexico). Of course, their idea is to relieve you of your possessions, but threatening to go over their heads to their superiors *may* save you further discussion. The allowable items per person include a portable computer, a video camera, two still cameras, personal clothing, and used fishing equipment for one person.

Taxi tickets to town are sold outside the airport doors under the covered walkway. A colectivo (group van or minibus) ticket is the least expensive, but you have to wait for a group of five to assemble. Private taxis cost about double the price.

City bus no. 79 ("Aviación") operates between the town center and the airport, but the buses do not have frequent service. Other city buses run along Avenida Itzáes, just out of the airport precincts, heading for downtown.

BY BUS   The second-class Central Camionera is 7 blocks southwest of Plaza Mayor at Calle 68, between Calles 69 and 71. The new first-class station, CAME, is directly behind it on Calle 70, between Calles 69 and 71. A separate station for travelers to Progreso is at Calle 62 no. 524, between Calles 65 and 67.

To/From Uxmal: Autotransportes del Sur buses depart at 6 and 9am, noon, and 2:30pm; return trips are at 2:30, 3:30, and 7:30pm. The same company also offers one bus daily on the Mérida–Uxmal–Kabah–Sayil–Labná–Xlapak route. The trip costs $12; it departs Mérida at 8am and returns at 4pm. The driver allows passengers to spend approximately 2 hours at Uxmal and 30 minutes at each of the other archaeological sites before returning. There is no evening departure for the sound-and-light show at Uxmal.

To/From Chichén-Itzá: There are first-class **ADO** buses at 7:30am and 3:30pm, leaving from the CAME. If you're planning a day-trip (something I don't recommend because you'll want more time to see the impressive ruins), take the 7:30am bus and reserve a seat on the 3:30pm return bus.

To/From Pisté/Chichén-Itzá: ADO runs second-class buses every hour from 5am till midnight, and a luxury bus at 11am.

To/From Valladolid and Cancún: Expresso de Oriente offers deluxe service—video, rest room, and refreshments—to Cancún (a 4- to 5-hour trip) 19 times daily between 6am and 11:15pm. The line also has eight deluxe buses daily to Valladolid between 6am and 11:45pm. **Caribe Express** runs at least nine deluxe buses daily to Cancún between 7:15am and 10pm. **Autotransportes del Caribe** goes to Cancún three times daily, and **ADO** runs three buses daily to Valladolid.

To/From Playa del Carmen, Tulum, and Chetumal: Three deluxe **ADO** buses go to Valladolid and on to Playa del Carmen between 7:30am and midnight. ADO also has deluxe buses to Chetumal twice daily. **Caribe Express** buses to Playa del Carmen and Tulum depart at 6:15am and 11pm; Caribe Express buses depart for Chetumal five times. **Autotransportes Peninsulares** offers Servicio Plus deluxe service to Chetumal at 8:30am and 6pm.

To/From Campeche: Autotransportes Peninsulares offers deluxe service to Campeche at 8am and 3pm. **ADO** has first-class service to Campeche every half hour between 6am and 10pm; **Autotransportes del Sur** buses leave every 45 minutes from 6am to 11:30pm.

To/From Palenque and San Cristóbal de las Casas: ADO has first-class service to Palenque twice daily. **Autotransportes del Sureste** offers second-class service to Palenque and San Cristóbal de las Casas at 6pm.

To/From Progreso, Dzibilchaltún, and Celestún: Buses depart from the Progreso Station at Calle 62 no. 524, between calles 65 and 67.

BY CAR Highway 180 from Cancún, Chichén-Itzá, or Valladolid leads into Calle 65 past the market and within 1 block of the Plaza Mayor. Highway 261 from Uxmal (via Muna and Uman) becomes Avenida Itzáes (if you arrive by that route, turn right on Calle 63 to reach the Plaza Mayor). If you arrive from Uxmal via Ticul and the ruins of Mayapán, the road passes through Kanasín before joining Highway 180 into Mérida. The free, two-lane, Highway 180 is in good shape and passes through many picturesque villages.

A traffic loop encircles Mérida, making it possible to skirt the city and head for a nearby city or site. Directional signs are generally good into the city, but going around the city on the loop requires constant vigilance to spot appropriate directional signs.

The eight-lane toll (*cuota*) highway (*autopista*) between Mérida and Cancún was completed in 1993 and shaved the driving between the two cities by about 1 hour; the drive from Cancún to Mérida takes about 4 hours on the autopista. The highway begins about 35 miles east of Mérida at Kantuníl, intersecting with Highway 180. It ends at Nuevo Xcan, which is about 50 miles before Cancún. One-way tolls cost about $20. See "En Route to Uxmal," below, at the end of the Mérida section, for suggested routes from Mérida.

ORIENTATION

VISITOR INFORMATION The most convenient source of information is the downtown branch of the **State of Yucatán Tourist Information Office,** in the hulking edifice known as the Teatro Peón Contreras, on Calle 60 between calles 57 and 59 (☎ **99/24-9290** or 99/24-9389). It's open Monday through Sunday from 8am to 8pm, as are the information booths at the **airport** (☎ **99/24-6764**), the bus station, and on Calle 62 next to the Palacio Municipal. **Yucatán Information Office,** P.O. Box 140681, Coral Gables, FL 33114-0681, is a nonprofit service of the Mesoamerica Foundation. They offer helpful information about the Yucatán, such as the current cost of admission to archaeological sites, reports on new museums, and updates on customs scams.

CITY LAYOUT   As in many colonial Mexican cities, Mérida's streets were originally laid out in a grid: **Even-numbered streets** run north–south; **odd-numbered streets** run east–west. In the last few decades the city has expanded well beyond the grid, and several grand boulevards have been added on the outskirts to ease traffic flow.

When looking for an address, you'll notice that street numbers progress very slowly because of the many unnumbered dwellings and the addition of letters (A, B, C, and so on) to numbered dwellings. For example, the distance between 504 to 615D on Calle 59 is 12 blocks.

The center of town is the very pretty **Plaza Mayor** (sometimes called the Plaza Principal), with its shady trees, benches, vendors, and a social life all its own. Around the Plaza Mayor are the massive cathedral, the Palacio de Gobierno (state government headquarters), the Palacio Municipal, and the Casa de Montejo. Within a few blocks are several smaller plazas, the University of Yucatán, and the sprawling market district.

Mérida's most fashionable address is the broad, tree-lined boulevard called **Paseo de Montejo** and the surrounding neighborhood. The Paseo de Montejo begins 7 blocks northwest of the Plaza Mayor and is home to Yucatán's anthropological museum, several upscale hotels, and the U.S. Consulate. New high-rise deluxe hotels are opening just off the Paseo on **Avenida Colón,** another shaded boulevard containing some of the city's finest old mansions. Within the next few years, this neighborhood will become Mérida's more exclusive tourism zone, with fine restaurants and boutiques catering to the travelers drawn to the new hotels.

GETTING AROUND

BY BUS   Bus travel within the heart of downtown isn't necessary since everything is within walking distance of the main plaza. However, to get to the large, shady Parque Centenario on the western outskirts of town, a bus is available. Look for a bus of the same name ("Centenario") on Calle 64. Most buses on Calle 59 go to the zoo or to the Museum of Natural History. "Central" buses stop at the bus station, and any bus marked "Mercado" or "Correo" (post office) will take you to the market district.

BY TAXI   As in most Mexican cities, taxis are found in abundance. But Mérida taxi drivers are beginning to overcharge tourists in Mérida the way they do in Mexico City. Be sure to set a price in advance, and be sure you're both talking pesos, not dollars. The Yucatán generally isn't known for scams, but in Mérida, taxi drivers love to confuse passengers with the words *dos* meaning two and *doce* meaning twelve or some other confusing numeral. Write the price down, if necessary, and say pesos.

BY CAR   A car is handy for exploring Mayapán, Uxmal, and Kabah, but you don't need one to get around Mérida or to reach Chichén-Itzá or Cancún. Rental cars are expensive, averaging $48 to $75 per day for a VW Beetle. As you scour the city for a rental-car deal, be sure the price quoted includes tax, insurance, and unlimited mileage, and get deductible information before settling the deal. For tips on saving money on car rentals by renting in advance from your home country see "Getting Around" in chapter 3. Also, you may want to look into the free car rental (you pay for insurance) offered by Mayaland Tours if you stay at their hotels at Chichén-Itzá and Uxmal. Ask about pick-up or drop-off in Cancún if your trip starts or ends there. For information contact Mayaland Resorts, Av. Colón 502, 97000 Mérida, Yuc.; ☎ **800/235-4079** in the U.S., or 99/25-2122; fax 99/25-7022.

BY FOOT   Most tourist attractions are within walking distance of the Plaza Mayor.

FAST FACTS: Mérida

Area Code   The telephone **area code** is **99.**

Bookstore   The Librería Dante, Calle 60 at Calle 57 (☎ **99/24-9522**), has a selection of English-language cultural-history books on Mexico. It's open Monday through Friday from 8am to 9:30pm, Saturday from 8am to 2pm and 5 to 9pm, and Sunday from 10am to 2pm and 4 to 8pm.

Climate   From November through February the weather can be chilly, windy, and rainy. You'll need a light jacket or sweater for occasional cool winter weather and thin, light clothes for summer days. Light rain gear is suggested for the brief showers in late May, June, and July, but there's a chance of rain year-round in the Yucatán.

Complaints   Tourists experiencing difficulties with public officials such as police officers can call ☎ **91-800/0-0148** in Mexico to report incidents. If you have difficulties with customs officials at the airport, report them to SEDOCAM (*say*-doh-kahm), which is the Comptroller and Administrative Development Secretariat (☎ **91-800/0-0148** in Mexico).

Consulates   The British Vice-Consulate is at Calle 58 no. 498 (☎ **99/28-6152**). Though in theory it's open Monday through Friday from 9:30am to 1pm, you may find no one there. The vice-consul fields questions about travel to Belize as well as British matters.

Currency Exchange   Banamex, in the Palacio Montejo on the Plaza Mayor, usually provides a better rate of exchange than other banks, but the lines are often maddeningly long. Exchange hours are Monday through Friday from 9:30am to 1:30pm. Another option is the money-exchange office just as you enter the bank gates, and more banks are located on and off Calle 65 between calles 62 and 60.

Hospitals   Hospital O'Horan is on Avenida Itzáes at Calle 59A (☎ **99/24-8711**), north of the Parque Centenario.

Post Office   Mérida's main post office (correo) is located in the midst of the market at the corner of calles 65 and 56. A branch office is located at the airport. Both are open Monday through Friday from 8am to 5pm and Saturday from 8am to 2pm.

Seasons   There are two high seasons—one in July and August when the weather is very hot and humid and when Mexicans most commonly take their vacations, and one between November 15 and Easter Sunday when the northerners flock to the Yucatán to escape winter weather and when weather in the Yucatán is cooler.

Spanish Classes   Maya scholars, Spanish teachers, and archaeologists from the United States are among the students at the **Centro Idiomas del Sureste,** Calle 14 no. 106 at Calle 25, Colonia México, 97000 Mérida, Yuc. (☎ **99/26-1155;** fax 99/26-9020). The school has two locations: in the Colonia México, a northern residential district, and on Calle 66 at Calle 57 in the downtown area. Students live with local families or in hotels; sessions running 2 weeks or longer are available for all levels of proficiency and areas of interest. For brochures and applications, contact Chloe Conaway de Pacheco, Directora.

Telephones   There are long-distance *casetas* at the airport and the bus station. Look also for the blue-and-silver Ladatel phones appearing in public places all over Mexico. Also see "Telephone/Fax" in "Fast Facts: Mexico," in chapter 3. *Important note:* Telephone numbers are being changed throughout the city, so if you have difficulty reaching a number, ask the telephone operator for assistance.

EXPLORING MÉRIDA

Most of the city's attractions are within walking distance of each other in the downtown area.

FESTIVALS & EVENTS

On the evening of the **first Friday** of each month, Dennis LaFoy of the Yucatán Trails Travel Agency (☎ 99/28-2582) invites the English-speaking community to a casual get-together. They usually gather at the Hotel Mérida Misión Park Plaza on Calle 60, across from the Hotel Casa del Balam, but call Dennis to confirm the location.

Many Mexican cities offer weekend concerts in the park, but Mérida surpasses them with almost-daily high-quality public events, most of which are free.

Sunday   Each Sunday from 9am to 9pm there's a fair called **Domingo en Mérida** (Sunday in Mérida). The downtown area, blocked off from traffic for the day, bustles with activity; there are children's art classes, antiques vendors, and food stands, as well as concerts of all kinds. At 11am in front of the Palacio del Gobierno, musicians play everything from jazz to classical and folk music. Also at 11am the police orchestra performs Yucatecan tunes at the Santa Lucía park. At 11:30am, marimba music brightens the Parque Cepeda Peraza (Parque Hidalgo) on Calle 60 at Calle 59. At 1pm in front of the Palacio Municipal on the Plaza Mayor, folk ballet dancers reenact a typical Yucatecan wedding. All events are free.

Monday   The **City Hall Folklore Ballet** and the **Police Jaranera Band** perform at 8pm in front of the Palacio Municipal. The music and dancing celebrate the Vaquerías feast, which occurs after the branding of cattle on Yucatecan haciendas. Among the featured performers are dancers with trays of bottles or filled glasses on their heads—a sight to see. Admission is free.

Tuesday   The theme for the Tuesday entertainment, held at 9pm in Parque Santiago, on Calle 59 at Calle 72, is **Musical Memories.** Tunes range from South American and Mexican to North American from the 1940s. Admission is free. Also at 9pm in the Teatro Peón Contreras on Calle 60 at Calle 57, the **University of Yucatán Folklore Ballet** presents "Yucatán and Its Roots." Admission is $5.

Wednesday   The **University of Yucatán Folklore Ballet,** along with guitarists and poets, performs at 8pm at the Mayab Culture House on Calle 63, between calles 64 and 66. Admission is free.

Thursday   Typical Yucatecan music and dance are presented at the **Serenata** in Parque Santa Lucía at 9pm. Admission is free.

Friday   At 9pm in the patio of the University of Yucatán, Calle 60 at Calle 57, the **University of Yucatán Folklore Ballet** often performs typical regional dances from the Yucatán. Admission is free.

WALKING TOUR
Mérida

Start: Plaza Mayor.
Finish: Palacio Cantón.
Time: Allow approximately 2 hours, not counting time for browsing or refreshment.
Best Times: Wednesday through Sunday before noon.
Worst Time: Monday, when the Anthropology Museum is closed; Tuesday when the Museo de Arte Contemporáneo is closed.

Downtown Mérida is a visitor's visual delight, with several tree-shaded parks and most of the finest examples of both colonial and late 19th-century architecture the city has to offer. The downtown is within an easy stroll of the:

1. **Plaza Mayor.** Flanked east and west by calles 61 and 63 and north and south by calles 60 and 62, the plaza began its history as the Plaza de Armas—a training field for Montejo's troops. It was renamed Plaza de la Constitución in 1812 and then Plaza de la Independencia in 1821 before assuming its current name. Other common names for it include Plaza Grande, Plaza Principal, and the zócalo. Today this beautiful town square, shaded by topiary laurel trees, is decked out with manicured shrubs and lawns with iron benches. Numerous entertainment events open to the public take place here throughout the year. On the east side of the plaza stands the:

2. **Cathedral.** Built between 1561 and 1598, it looks like a fortress, as do many other early churches in the Yucatán. (For several centuries, defense was actually one of the functions of such churches, as the Maya did not take kindly to European domination.) Much of the stone in the cathedral's walls came from the ruined buildings of Tihó, the former Maya city. Inside, decoration is sparse, with altars draped in fabric colorfully embroidered like a Maya woman's shift. The most notable feature is a picture over the right side door of Ah Kukum Tutul Xiú visiting the Montejo camp.

To the left of the main altar is a smaller shrine with a curious statue of Jesus recovered from the church in the town of Ichmul, which burned down. The figure was carved by a local artist in the 1500s from a miraculous tree that was hit by lightning and burned but did not char. The figure, along with the church, broke out in blisters as the flames enveloped it, but the figure survived the fire. It was moved to the cathedral in Mérida in 1645. The local people named it Cristo de las Ampollas (Christ of the Blisters). Also take a look in the side chapel (open from 8 to 11am and 4:30 to 7pm), which contains a lifesize diorama of the Last Supper. The Mexican Jesus is covered with prayer crosses brought by supplicants asking for intercession.

To the right (south) of the cathedral is the:

3. **Museo de Arte Contemporáneo Ateneo de Yucatán (MACAY) (☎ 99/ 28-3258),** the city's exquisite contemporary art museum in the former Seminary and site of the archbishop's palace. The palace was torn down during the Mexican Revolution in 1915, but the remaining building is a stately architectural gem. Inside its two stories, built around a patio, seventeen exhibition rooms show works by contemporary artists from the Yucatán and around the world. Nine of the rooms hold the museum's permanent collection, while eight rooms showcase changing exhibits. One area includes a display of the building's history and Yucatecan embroidery. It's open Wednesday through Monday from 10am to 6pm (closed Tuesday). Admission $3; free Sunday. On the south side of the Plaza Mayor is the:

4. **Palacio Montejo,** also called the Casa de Montejo. Started in 1542 by Francisco Montejo *el mozo* (the Younger, in other words, the first Montejo's natural son), it was occupied by Montejo descendants until the 1970s. It now houses a Banamex bank branch, which means you can get a look at parts of the palace just by wandering in during banking hours: Monday through Friday from 9am to 1:30pm. Note the coat of arms of the Spanish kings and of the Montejo family on the plateresque facade, along with figures of the conquistadores standing on the heads of "barbarians." Look closely and you'll find the bust of Francisco Montejo the Elder, his wife, and his daughter. Facing the cathedral across the Plaza Mayor (on the west side) is the:

Walking Tour—Mérida

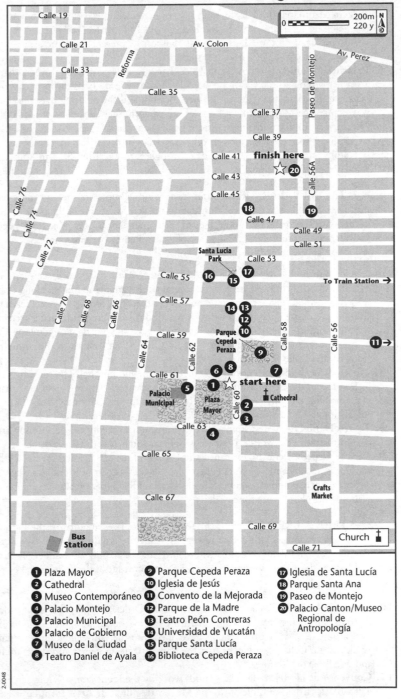

1 Plaza Mayor
2 Cathedral
3 Museo Contemporáneo
4 Palacio Montejo
5 Palacio Municipal
6 Palacio de Gobierno
7 Museo de la Ciudad
8 Teatro Daniel de Ayala
9 Parque Cepeda Peraza
10 Iglesia de Jesús
11 Convento de la Mejorada
12 Parque de la Madre
13 Teatro Peón Contreras
14 Universidad de Yucatán
15 Parque Santa Lucía
16 Biblioteca Cepeda Peraza
17 Iglesia de Santa Lucía
18 Parque Santa Ana
19 Paseo de Montejo
20 Palacio Canton/Museo Regional de Antropología

2-0048

5. **Palacio Municipal** (City Hall), with its familiar clock tower. It started out as the *cabildo*—the colonial town hall and lockup—in 1542. It had to be rebuilt in the 1730s and again in the 1850s, when it took on its present romantic aspect. On the north side of the Plaza Mayor is the:

6. **Palacio de Gobierno,** dating from 1892. Large murals painted by the Meridiano artist Fernando Pacheco Castro between 1971 and 1973 decorate the interior walls. Scenes from Maya and Mexican history abound, and the painting over the stairway depicts the Maya spirit with ears of sacred corn, the "sunbeams of the gods." Nearby is a painting of the mustachioed benevolent dictator Lázaro Cárdenas, who in 1938 expropriated 17 foreign oil companies and was hailed as a Mexican liberator. The palace is open Monday through Saturday from 8am to 8pm and Sunday from 9am to 5pm.

☕ **TAKE A BREAK**   Revive your motor with a cup of coffee and some pan dulce or a bolillo from the **Pan Montejo** on the southwest side of the plaza on the corner of calles 63 and 62. Add a glass of fresh orange or papaya juice from **Jugos California** next door, take a seat at the plaza, and enjoy the morning sun.

Exploring Calle 60

Continuing north from the Plaza Mayor up Calle 60, you'll see many of Mérida's old churches and little parks. Several stores catering to tourists along Calle 60 sell gold-filigree jewelry, pottery, and folk art. A stroll along this street leads to the Parque Santa Ana and continues to the fashionable boulevard Paseo de Montejo and its Museo Regional de Antropología. On your right as you leave the northeast corner of the Plaza, turn right on Calle 61 for a block to the corner of Calle 61 and Calle 58 and the:

7. **Museo de la Ciudad**, occupying a former convent and hospital. The museum collection relates the city's past in the form of photographs, drawings, and dioramas. It's open Tuesday through Saturday from 9am to 8pm, Sunday 9am to 1pm. Admission is $2. Backtrack to Calle 60; ahead on your right is the:

8. **Teatro Daniel de Ayala,** which offers a continuous schedule of performing artists from around the world. A few steps beyond and across the street is the:

9. **Parque Cepeda Peraza** (also called the Parque Hidalgo). Named for the 19th-century general Manuel Cepeda Peraza, the *parque* was part of Montejo's original city plan. Small outdoor restaurants front hotels on the *parque,* making it a popular stopping-off place at any time of day.

☕ **TAKE A BREAK**   Any of the several outdoor restaurants on the Parque Cepeda Peraza makes an inviting respite. My favorite is **Giorgio,** where you can claim a table and write postcards while bartering for hammocks, amber jewelry, and baskets displayed by wandering artisans. It's in front of the Gran Hotel.

Bordering Parque Cepeda Peraza across Calle 59 is the:

10. **Iglesia de Jesús,** or El Tercer Órden (the Third Order), built by the Jesuit order in 1618. The entire city block on which the church stands was part of the Jesuit establishment, and the early schools developed into the Universidad de Yucatán. Walk east on Calle 59, 5 blocks past the Parque Cepeda Peraza and the church, and you'll see the former:

11. **Convento de la Mejorada,** a late-1600s work by the Franciscans. While here, go half a block farther on Calle 59 to the **Museo Regional de Artes Populares** (see "More Attractions," below). Backtrack to Calle 60 and turn north. Just beyond the church (Iglesia de Jesús) is the:

12. **Parque de la Madre** (also called the Parque Morelos), which contains a modern statue of the Madonna and Child. The statue is a copy of the work by Renoir that stands in the Luxembourg Gardens in Paris. Beyond the Parque de la Madre and across the pedestrian way is:

13. **Teatro Peón Contreras,** an enormous beige edifice designed by Italian architect Enrico Deserti in the early years of this century. In one corner you'll see a branch of the State Tourist Information Office facing the Parque de la Madre. The main theater entrance, with its Carrara marble staircase and frescoed dome, is a few steps farther. Domestic and international performers appear here frequently. On the west side of Calle 60, at the corner of Calle 57, is the:

14. **Universidad de Yucatán,** founded in the 19th century by Felipe Carrillo Puerto with the help of General Cepeda Peraza. The founding is illustrated by a fresco (1961) by Manuel Lizama.

    A block farther on your left, past the Hotel Mérida Misión Park Inn, is the:

15. **Parque Santa Lucía.** Surrounded by an arcade on the north and west sides, the *parque* once was where visitors first alighted in Mérida after arriving in their stage-coaches. On Sunday, Parque Santa Lucía holds a used-book sale and small swap meet, and several evenings a week it hosts popular entertainment. On Thursday nights performers present Yucatecan songs and poems. A block west from the *parque* on Calle 55 at the corner of Calle 62 is:

16. **Biblioteca Cepeda Peraza,** a library founded by the general in 1867. Head back to the Parque Santa Lucía. Facing the *parque* is the ancient:

17. **Iglesia de Santa Lucía** (1575). To reach Paseo de Montejo, continue walking north on Calle 60 to the:

18. **Parque Santa Ana,** 4 blocks up Calle 60 from the Parque Santa Lucía. Turn right here on Calle 47 for 1¹/₂ blocks; then turn left onto the broad, busy boulevard known as the:

19. **Paseo de Montejo,** a broad tree-lined thoroughfare with imposing banks, hotels, and several 19th-century mansions erected by henequen barons, generals, and other Yucatecan potentates. It's Mexico's humble version of the Champs-Elysées.

☕ **WINDING DOWN**   Before or after tackling the Palacio Cantón (see below), stop for a break at the **Dulcería y Sorbetería Colón,** on Paseo de Montejo 1 block north of the Palacio between calles 39 and 41. Far grander than its sister cafe at the Plaza Mayor, this bakery/ice-cream shop/candy shop has a long glass counter displaying sweet treats. Unfortunately, coffee and tea are not available.

At the corner of Calle 43 is the:

20. **Palacio Cantón** (entrance on Calle 43), which houses the **Museo Regional de Antropología** (Anthropology Museum; ☎ 99/23-0557). Designed and built by Enrico Deserti, the architect who designed the Teatro Peón Contreras, this is the most impressive mansion on Paseo de Montejo and the only one open to the public. It was constructed between 1909 and 1911 during the last years of the Porfiriato as the home of General Francisco Cantón Rosado. The general enjoyed his palace for only 6 years before he died in 1917. The house was converted into a school and later became the official residence of the governor of the Yucatán.

    This is an interregional museum covering not only the state but also the rest of the peninsula and Mexico. Its exhibits include cosmology, pre-Hispanic time computation and comparative timeline, musical instruments, weaving examples and designs, and stone carving from all over the country.

On the right as you enter is a room used for changing exhibits, usually featuring "the piece of the month." After that are the permanent exhibits with captions mostly in Spanish. Starting with fossil mastodon teeth, the exhibits take you through the Yucatán's history, paying special attention to the daily life of its inhabitants. You'll see how the Maya tied boards to babies' skulls in order to reshape their heads, giving them the slanting forehead that was then a mark of great beauty, and how they filed teeth to sharpen them or drilled teeth to implant jewels. Enlarged photos show the archaeological sites, and drawings illustrate the various styles of Maya houses and how they were constructed. The one of Mayapán, for instance, clearly shows the city's ancient walls. Even if you know only a little Spanish, the museum provides a good background for explorations of Maya sites. The museum is open Tuesday through Saturday from 8am to 8pm and Sunday from 8am to 2pm. Admission is $3; free on Sunday. There's a museum bookstore on the left as you enter.

HORSE-DRAWN CARRIAGE TOURS

For a tour by horse-drawn carriage, look for a line of *coches de caleta* near the cathedral and in front of the Hotel Casa del Balam. Haggle for a good price.

ECOTOURS & ADVENTURE TRIPS

Companies that organize nature and adventure tours of the Yucatán Peninsula are just beginning to establish themselves. **Ecoturismo Yucatán,** Calle 3 no. 235, Col. Pensiones, 97219 Mérida, Yuc. (☎ 99/25-2187; fax 99/25-9047), is run by Alfonso and Roberta Escobedo. Alfonso has been guiding adventure tours for more than a dozen years, and Roberta runs the office with professional efficiency. The various tours emphasize remote ruin sites and culture in the Yucatán, Campeche, Chiapas, Tabasco, Oaxaca, Belize, and Guatemala. Customized tours are available.

Another specialty tour agency is **Yucatán Trails,** Calle 62 no. 482 (☎ 99/28-2582). Canadian Dennis LaFoy, well-known and active in the English-speaking community, is a font of information and can arrange a variety of individualized tours.

Roger Lynn at **Casa Mexilio Guest House** (☎ 99/28-2505), mentioned in "Where to Stay," below, arranges a variety of specialized trips. Concentrating on nature, Yucatán train trips, and haciendas, these are among the most unique trips in the area.

SHOPPING

Mérida is known for hammocks, guayaberas (short-sleeve, lightweight men's shirts that are worn untucked), and Panama hats. And there are good buys in baskets made in the Yucatán and pottery, as well as crafts from all over Mexico, especially at the central market. Mérida is also the place to pick up prepared achiote— a pastelike mixture of ground achiote, oregano, garlic, masa, and other spices used in Yucatecan cuisine. When mixed with vinegar to a soupy consistency, it makes a great marinade, especially on grilled meat and fish. It's also the sauce that makes baked chicken and cochinta pibil. On occasion, achiote is also found bottled and already mixed with juice of the sour orange. I don't leave the Yucatán without some achiote, which travels well if you double-bag it in plastic. If wrapped well, it lasts for years in the freezer.

Mérida's bustling **market district,** bounded by calles 63 to 69 and calles 62 to 54, is a few blocks southeast of the Plaza Mayor. The streets surrounding the market can be as interesting and crowded as the market itself. Heaps of prepared achiote are sold in the food section.

I love 0-800-99-0011
in the springtime.

**All you need for the
fastest, clearest connections home.**

Every country has its own AT&T Access Number which makes calling from France and other countries really easy. Just dial the AT&T Access Number for the country you're calling from and we'll take it from there. And be sure to charge your calls on your AT&T Calling Card. It'll help you avoid outrageous phone charges on your hotel bill and save you up to 60%.* 0-800-99-0011 is a great place to visit any time of year, especially if you've got these two cards. So please take the attached wallet card of worldwide AT&T Access Numbers.

Crafts

Casa del Las Artesanías. Calle 63 no. 513, between calles 64 and 66. ☎ **99/23-5392.**

This beautiful restored monastery houses an impressive selection of crafts from throughout Mexico. Stop by here before going to the various crafts markets to see what high-quality work looks like. The monastery's back courtyard is used as a gallery, with rotating exhibits on folk and fine arts. It's open Monday through Saturday from 8am to 8pm.

Crafts Market. In a separate building of the main market, Calle 67 at Calle 56.

Look for a large pale-green building behind the post office. Climb the steps and wade into the clamor and activity while browsing for leather goods, hammocks, Panama hats, Maya embroidered dresses, men's formal guayabera shirts, and craft items of all kinds.

Museo Regional de Artes Populares. Calle 59 no. 441, between calles 50 and 48. No phone.

A branch of the Museo Nacional de Artes y Industrías Populares in Mexico City, this museum displays regional costumes and crafts in the front rooms. Upstairs is a large room full of crafts from all over Mexico, including filigree jewelry from Mérida, folk pottery, baskets, and wood carving from the Yucatán. Open Tuesday through Saturday from 8am to 8pm and Sunday from 9am to 2pm. Admission is free.

Guayaberas

T-shirts, polo shirts, dress shirts, and the like can be horrendously hot and uncomfortable in Mérida's soaking humidity. For this reason, businessmen, politicians, bankers, and bus drivers alike don the guayabera—a loose-fitting button-down shirt worn outside pants. Mérida could well be called the hotbed of guayaberas, which can be purchased for under $10 at the market or for over $50 custom-made by a tailor. A guayabera made of Japanese linen can set you back about $65. The most comfortable shirts are made of light, breathable cotton, though polyester is surprisingly common, despite its tendency to seal in perspiration against the skin. Several guayabera shops are located along Calle 59; most display ready-to-wear shirts in several price ranges.

Jack Guayaberas. Calle 59 no. 507A. ☎ **99/28-6002.**

The tailors at Jack's, known for their craftsmanship since the mid-1950s, can make you the guayabera of your dreams in 3 hours. Connoisseurs have very definite opinions on color, the type of tucks that will run down the front, and the embroidery that will swirl around the buttons. Check out the shirts on the racks for your first guayabera or perhaps a blouse or dress. The shop is open daily from 9am to 1pm and 4 to 8pm.

Hammocks

The comfortable Yucatecan fine-mesh hammocks (*hamacas*) are made of string woven from silk, nylon, or cotton. Silk is extremely expensive and only for truly serious hammock sleepers. Nylon is long-lasting. Cotton is attractive, fairly strong, and inexpensive, but it wears out sooner than nylon. Here's how to select a hammock: Hold the hammock loosely and make sure the space between the weave is no larger than the size of your little finger. Grasp the hammock at the point where the wide part and the end strings meet and hold your hand level with the top of your head. The body should touch the floor; if not, the hammock is too short for you.

Hammocks are sold as *sencillo* (single); *doble* (double); and *matrimonial* (larger than double). The biggest hammock of all is called *matrimonial especial*. Buy the biggest hammock you can afford—the bigger ones take up no more room than smaller ones and are more comfortable, even for just one person.

Street vendors selling hammocks will approach you at every turn, "*¿Hamacas, señor, señorita?*" Their prices will be low, but so is the quality of their merchandise. If you buy from these vendors, be sure to examine the hammock carefully. Booths in the market have a larger selection and offer hammocks at only slightly higher prices.

La Poblana. S.A., Calle 65 no. 492, between calles 60 and 58. No phone.

La Poblana has been well recommended for years. Prices are marked, so don't try to bargain. Upstairs there's a room hung wall-to-wall with hammocks where you can give your prospective purchase a test-drive. La Poblana sells ropes and mosquito nets for hammocks, as well as Maya women's dresses and men's guayaberas. The store is open Monday through Saturday from 8am to 7pm.

Panama Hats

Another very popular item is these soft, pliable hats made from the palm fibers of the jipijapa in several towns along Highway 180, especially Becal, in the neighboring state of Campeche. There's no need to journey all the way to Campeche, however, as Mérida sells the hats in abundance. Just the thing to shade you from the fierce Yucatecan sun, the hats can be rolled up and carried in a suitcase for the trip home. They retain their shape quite well.

Jipi hats come in three grades determined by the quality (pliability and fineness) of the fibers and closeness of the weave. Hats with the coarser, more open weave of fairly large fibers cost a few dollars. The middle grade should be a fairly fine, close weave of good fibers. The finest weave, truly a beautiful hat, is easy to see in comparison with others.

WHERE TO STAY

Mérida is easier on the budget than other Yucatán cities. Most hotels offer at least a few air-conditioned rooms, and a few of the places also have pools. You may find every room taken in July and August, when Mexicans vacation in Mérida.

VERY EXPENSIVE

✪ **Hyatt Regency Mérida.** Calle 60 no. 344, 97000 Mérida, Yuc. ☎ **800/228-9000** in the U.S., 99/25-6722, or 99/42-0202. Fax 99/25-7002. 300 rms and suites. A/C MINIBAR TV TEL. Weekday $110–$125 double. Weekend $60–$70 double. Ask about "supersaver rates."

One of the most luxurious hotels in town, this 17-story hotel far surpasses the services and style to which Mérida is accustomed. The large, modern rooms have channels on satellite TV, 24-hour room service, direct-dial long-distance phone service, and personal safes. Regency Club rooms take up two floors of the hotel; guests here receive complimentary continental breakfast, evening cocktails, and hors d'oeuvres; special concierge service; and private lounges and boardrooms. The hotel is at the intersection of Calle 60 and Avenida Colón.

Dining/Entertainment: Several restaurants and bars.

Services: Complete business center, travel agency, and shops.

Facilities: Pool with swim-up bar.

EXPENSIVE

✪ **Casa del Balam.** Calle 60 no. 48, 97000 Mérida, Yuc. ☎ **800/624-8451** in the U.S., or 99/24-8844. Fax 99/24-5011. 54 rms, 2 suites. A/C MINIBAR TV TEL. $95 double; $115 suite. Free parking.

One of Mérida's most popular and centrally located hotels, the Casa del Balam is built around a lush interior courtyard. In two sections of three and six stories respectively, the colonial-style rooms are accented with Mexican textiles, folk art, dark furniture, iron headboards, and tile floors with area rugs. It's hard to top this place for location

Maquech—The Legendary Maya Beetle

One of the most unusual items for sale in the Yucatán is the live maquech beetle. Storekeepers display bowls of the large dusty-brown insects with long black legs and backs sprinkled with multicolored glass "jewels" attached to small gold chains. The chain hooks to a small safety pin and behold—you have a living brooch to wear.

One version of the maquech legend goes that a Maya princess became the forbidden love object of a Maya prince. Without her knowledge, he crept into her garden one night, and just as they met, he was captured by the princess's guards. To save the prince, a sorceress turned him into a beetle and put him on a decaying tree near where he was captured. When the princess recovered from her faint, she looked for the prince where she had last seen him and found the bejeweled beetle instead; in an instant she knew it was the prince. Using a few strands of her long hair, she harnessed the beetle and kept it over her heart forever. Another version has it that the prince asked a sorceress to put him close to the heart of his beloved princess, and because he was very rich, she turned him into a bejeweled beetle pin.

No matter which legend you believe, a purchased beetle comes with a piece of its favorite wood, a nice little box with air holes to carry it in, and a chain and safety pin. U.S. Customs, however, doesn't permit the beetle to cross the border, so plan to find it a home before you leave Mexico.

and comfort. There's a travel agency and a rental-car agency in the lobby, as well as a popular restaurant and bar with trio entertainment in the evenings. The tables scattered around the courtyard have become a favorite romantic spot for evening cocktails and appetizers.

The owners also run the **Hacienda Chichén-Itzá** hotel, at the entrance to the ruins of Chichén-Itzá, so you can make arrangements here to stay there. To find the hotel, walk 3 blocks north of the Plaza Mayor.

✪ **Hotel Misión Park Inn.** Calle 60 no. 491, 97000 Mérida, Yuc. ☎ **800/448-8355** in the U.S., or 99/23-9500. Fax 99/23-7665. 73 rms and suites. A/C TV TEL. $80 double; $90–$115 suite.

The Misión Park Inn is actually a large, modern addition grafted onto a gracious older hotel. The location is excellent—right across the street from the university and the Teatro Peón Contreras, and only 2 short blocks from the Plaza Mayor. Enter the hotel's cool lobby from the noisy street, and you'll find yourself in an oasis complete with bubbling fountain, high ceilings, and a nice little swimming pool. Though the public rooms are colonial in style, the guest units are Spartan in a modern way with blond furniture, tile floors, drapes and shutters, and two double beds in most rooms. Some of the suites have small kitchens and separate living-room areas.

Dining/Entertainment: One restaurant serves all meals. La Trova Bar has live piano entertainment Monday through Saturday evenings.

Services: Laundry and room service, and a travel agency.

MODERATE

✪ **Casa Mexilio Guest House.** Calle 68 no. 495, 97000 Mérida, Yuc. ☎ **800/538-6802** in the U.S., or ☎ and fax 99/28-2505. 8 rms. $55–$65 double. Rates include breakfast. Parking on street.

Roger Lynn, part owner and host, has created the atmosphere of a private home rather than that of a hotel in this 19th-century town house. Guests have the run of this three-story home built around indoor and outdoor patios. Each room is unique, and throughout the house pleasant decorative use is made of Mexican crafts. On the back patio are a small pool and whirlpool. The hotel is connected with the Turquoise Reef Group, which runs inns on Mexico's Caribbean coast between Cancún and Chetumal. You can make reservations here for those inns and sign up for a variety of trips in the Yucatán (see "Ecotours & Adventure Trips," above).

To find the hotel from the Plaza Mayor, walk 1 block north on Calle 62. Turn left on Calle 59 and walk for 3 blocks. Turn right on Calle 68; the hotel is half a block down on the left.

Hotel Caribe. Calle 59 no. 500, 97000 Mérida, Yuc. ☎ **99/24-9022.** Fax 99/24-8733. 18 rms, 38 suites. A/C (18) or FAN (38) TV TEL. $35–$45 double; $55 suite for two with A/C. Free guarded parking.

Step inside the entry of this small, two-story, central hotel and discover a well-located, comfortable jewel. Well-coordinated colonial-style furnishings accent new pastel tile floors. Comfortable sitting areas along the three stories of covered, open-air walkways are like extended living rooms offering a cozy respite at any time of day. From the top floor, where there's a small pool and sundeck, are great views of the cathedral and town. Rooms with air-conditioning are the most expensive. The interior restaurant is arranged around a quiet central courtyard, while the hotel's sidewalk cafe, El Mesón, is set out in front in the shady Parque Cepeda Peraza. To get to the hotel from the Plaza Mayor, walk a half block to the Parque Cepeda Peraza. The hotel is in the back right corner of the park.

INEXPENSIVE

✪ **Hotel Dolores Alba.** Calle 63 no. 464, 97000 Mérida, Yuc. ☎ **99/28-5650.** Fax 99/28-3163. E-mail: asanchez@yucatan.com.mx. 40 rms. A/C or FAN. $24 double. Free, guarded parking.

The Sánchez family converted this Spanish colonial residence into this charming, recently remodeled hotel. It boasts a large open court and a smaller courtyard with a nice clean pool, sundeck, and gardens. The rooms, half of which have air-conditioning, are decorated with local crafts and antiques and all have showers. The highest prices are for rooms with air-conditioning. A small dining room opens for breakfast between 7 and 9am. The hospitable Sánchez family also operates the **Hotel Dolores Alba** outside Chichén-Itzá, so you can make reservations at one hotel for another. To find this hotel from the Plaza Mayor, walk east on Calle 63 for 3¹/₂ blocks; it's between calles 52 and 54.

✪ **Hotel Mucuy.** Calle 57 no. 481, 97000 Mérida, Yuc. ☎ **99/28-5193.** Fax 99/23-7801. 22 rms. FAN. $12 double.

One of the most hospitable budget hotels in the country, the Mucuy is named for a small dove said to bring good luck to places where it alights. You'll see doves fluttering about the flower-filled interior courtyard. Owners Alfredo and Ofelia Comin strive to make guests feel welcome with conveniences such as a communal refrigerator in the lobby, and, for a small extra charge, the use of a washer and dryer. Outside there are comfortable tables and chairs. Inside, two floors of freshly painted rooms with window screens, showers, and ceiling fans face the courtyard. Señora Comin speaks English. To find the hotel from the Plaza Mayor, walk 2 blocks north on Calle 60, then turn right on Calle 57 and go a block and a half; it's between calles 56 and 58.

Hotel Santa Lucía. Calle 55 no. 508, 97000 Mérida, Yuc. ☎ **99/24-6233.** Fax 99/28-2662. 51 rms. A/C or FAN TV TEL. $30–$35 double. Free guarded parking nearby.

This small hotel opened in 1990. The rooms are in a three-story building with windows facing the inner hallways or the courtyard, which contains a long, inviting pool.

The highest rates are for rooms with air-conditioning. The management is very helpful, providing information on tours, restaurants, and sights. They also run the Hotel San Clemente in Valladolid. To find the hotel from the Santa Lucía Park, walk west on Calle 55; the hotel is on the left less than half a block down, between calles 60 and 62.

Hotel Trinidad Galería. Calle 60 no. 456, 97000 Mérida, Yuc. ☎ **99/23-2463.** Fax 99/ 24-2319. 31 rms, 1 suite. A/C or FAN. $27 double; $24–$30 suite with A/C and TV. Limited free parking.

Once an enormous home, this rambling hotel offers its guests a small shaded pool, a communal refrigerator, a shared dining room, oodles of original art and antiques, and lots of relaxing nooks with comfortable furniture. Upstairs, a covered porch decorated with antiques and plants runs the length of the hotel, providing yet another place to read or converse. Rooms are rather dark and simply furnished, and most don't have windows, but the overall ambience of the hotel is comparable to that of more expensive inns. To find the hotel from the Plaza Mayor, walk 5 blocks north on Calle 60; it's at the corner of Calle 51, 2 blocks north of the Santa Lucía Park.

Posada Toledo. Calle 58 no. 487, 97000 Mérida, Yuc. ☎ **99/23-1690.** Fax 99/23-2256. 21 rms, 2 suites. A/C (16) or FAN (7) TEL. $35–$40 double, $40 suite. Free parking next door.

This colonial inn was once a private mansion. It's now a cross between a garden dripping with vines and a fading museum with beautifully kept antique furnishings. Two of the grandest rooms have been remodeled into a suite with ornate cornices and woodwork. Most rooms have no windows, but high ceilings and appropriately creaky hardwood floors are standard. The highest rates are for air-conditioned rooms. The rooftop lounge area is excellent for viewing the city. Five rooms have TVs. To find the inn from the Plaza Mayor, walk 2 blocks north on Calle 60, then right 1 block on Calle 57 to Calle 58; it's on the left.

WHERE TO DINE

Calle 62 between the Plaza Mayor and Calle 57 contains a short string of small, budget food shops. To make your own breakfast, try the **Panificadora Montejo,** at the corner of calles 62 and 63 on the southwest corner of the Plaza Mayor. For those who can't start a day without fresh orange juice, **juice bars** have sprouted up all over Mérida, and several are on or near the Plaza Mayor.

EXPENSIVE

✪ **Alberto's Continental.** Calle 64 no. 482. ☎ **99/28-5367.** Reservations recommended. Main courses $8–$19. Daily 11am–11pm. LEBANESE/YUCATECAN/ITALIAN.

Created from a fine old town house, the large, elegantly furnished rooms are built around a plant- and tree-filled patio that's framed in Moorish arches. Cuban floor tiles from a bygone era and antique furniture and sideboards create an Old World mood. The eclectic menu features Lebanese, Yucatecan, and Italian specialties. There's a sampler plate of four Lebanese favorites, plus traditional Yucatecan specialties, such as pollo pibil and fish Celestún (bass stuffed with shrimp). Polish off your selections with Turkish coffee. Alberto's is at the corner of calles 57 and 64.

Le Gourmet. Perez Ponce 109. ☎ **99/27-1970.** Main courses $10–$30. Daily noon–midnight. INTERNATIONAL.

Behind stained-glass windows and sporting marble floors and art-filled walls, this elegant restaurant is a favorite of Mérida's upper crust. While the specialty here is seafood (try the pompano in puff pastry), there are almost as many beef selections to choose from but only a few chicken dishes. It's well known for the excellent steaks, so you can indulge that desire with confidence. The chef's daily suggestions are posted on the menu.

MODERATE

✪ **Los Almendros.** Calle 50A no. 493. ☎ **99/28-5459.** Main courses $4–$9; daily special $5–$8. Daily 9am–11pm. YUCATECAN.

The original Los Almendros is located in Ticul, deep in the Maya hinterland, but the branch in Mérida has become a favorite spot to sample local delicacies. The colorful chairs and tables will put you in a festive mood. Ask to see the menu with color photographs of the offerings accompanied by descriptions in English. Their famous poc chuc—a marinated and grilled pork dish created at the original restaurant in Ticul some years ago—is a must. To reach the restaurant from the Parque Cepeda Peraza, walk east on Calle 59 for 5 blocks, then left on Calle 50A; it's half a block on the left facing the Parque de Mejorada.

✪ **La Casona.** Calle 60 no. 434. ☎ **99/23-8348.** Reservations recommended. Pasta courses $4–$9; meat courses $5–$12. Daily 1pm–midnight. CONTINENTAL/ITALIAN.

A gracious old Mérida house and its lush interior garden make a charming and romantic restaurant. The cuisine is Yucatecan and continental, especially Italian, so you can choose among such dishes as *pollo pibil,* filet mignon with brandy and cream, linguine with mushrooms, and lasagna. It's also a fine place to wind up the day sipping espresso or cappuccino. To find it from the Plaza Mayor, walk north on Calle 60 for 6 blocks and it's at the corner of Calle 47.

✪ **Restaurante Portico del Peregrino.** Calle 57 no. 501. ☎ **99/28-6163.** Reservations recommended. Main courses $6–$10. Daily noon–11pm. MEXICAN/INTERNATIONAL.

This romantic restaurant captures the spirit of 19th-century Mexico with its patio dining on the side of the street and outdoor patio dining in back. Inside is an air-conditioned dining room decorated with antique mirrors and elegant sideboards. The extensive menu offers soup, fish fillet, grilled gulf shrimp, spaghetti, *pollo pibil,* baked eggplant with chicken and cheese, and coconut ice cream topped with Kahlúa. To find it from the Plaza Mayor, walk $2^1/2$ blocks north on Calle 60, turn left on Calle 57, and it's half a block down on the right before Calle 62.

INEXPENSIVE

Café Alameda. Calle 58 no. 474. ☎ **99/28-3635.** Breakfast $2.75–$3.25; main courses $3–$8. Mon–Sat 8am–10pm. YUCATECAN/MIDDLE EASTERN.

At about 10am on weekdays, the Alameda is filled with businesspeople all eating the same late breakfast—a shish kebab of marinated beef, a basket of warm pita bread, and coffee. If eggs are more your style, order them with beans; otherwise, you'll get a small plate with a little pile of eggs. Vegetarians can choose from tabbouleh, hummus, cauliflower, eggplant or spinach casseroles, and veggie tamales. The umbrella-shaded tables on the back patio are pleasant places to eat. To find the cafe from the Plaza Mayor, walk east on Calle 61 for 1 block, then turn left on Calle 58 and walk 3 blocks north, near the corner of Calle 55.

Café Amaro. Calle 59 no. 507. ☎ **99/28-2451.** Breakfast $2.75–$3.50; main courses $3–$4.50. Mon–Sat 8am–11pm. REGIONAL/VEGETARIAN.

This pleasant, small restaurant serves guests in an open courtyard to the accompaniment of soft background music. Their *crema de calabacitas* soup is delicious, as is the apple salad. The avocado pizza is terrific. There is also a limited menu of meat and chicken dishes. To find it from the Plaza Mayor, walk 1 block north on Calle 60 and turn left on Calle 59.

El Louvre. Calle 62 no. 499. ☎ **99/24-5073.** Main courses $2.75–$4; comida corrida $3.75. Daily 24 hours (comida corrida served 1–5pm). MEXICAN.

This big, open restaurant feeds everybody from farm workers to townspeople. There's also an English menu. The comida corrida might include beans with pork on Monday, pork stew on Tuesday, and so on, plus there are sandwiches, soups, and other full meals. From the Palacio Municipal, cross Calle 61 and walk north on Calle 62 a few steps; it's near the corner of Calle 61.

Restaurante Los Amigos. Calle 62 no. 497. ☎ **99/23-1957.** Comida corrida $3. Tues–Sun noon–midnight. MEXICAN.

This place serves a comida corrida of Yucatecan specialties that includes soup, a main course, and dessert. It's not classy, but the price is right. To find it from the Palacio Municipal (which faces the Plaza Mayor), walk north on Calle 62 half a block; it's on the left between calles 61 and 59.

Vito Corleone. Calle 59 at Calle 60. ☎ **99/28-5777.** Pizza $3–$7; spaghetti $3; beer $1.45. Daily 9:30am–11:30pm. PIZZA/SPAGHETTI.

Aside from the food, the most impressive aspect of this tiny pizza parlor is the interesting use of *ollas* (clay pots) embedded in the wall above the hand-painted tile oven. The oven's golden yellow tiles are as handsome as those that decorate church domes. The tables by the sidewalk are the only bearable places to sit when it's warm, since the oven casts incredible heat. Another section upstairs in the back is also tolerable. The thin-crusted pizzas taste smoky and savory, and on Thursdays there's a two-for-one pizza special. To find it from the Plaza Mayor, walk north on Calle 60 1 block and turn left on Calle 59; it's half a block ahead.

MÉRIDA AFTER DARK

For a full range of free or low-cost evening entertainment, as well as daily public events in Mérida, see "Festivals & Events," above.

Teatro Peón Contreras, at calles 60 and 57, and the **Teatro Ayala,** on Calle 60 at Calle 61, both feature a wide range of performing artists from around the world. Stop in and see what's showing.

The scenes at the hotel bars, lounges, and discos depend on the crowd of customers presently staying at each hotel. Most of Mérida's downtown hotels, however, are filled with tour groups whose members prefer to rest after an exhausting day of sightseeing.

ROAD TRIPS FROM MÉRIDA
CELESTÚN NATIONAL WILDLIFE REFUGE: FLAMINGOS & OTHER WATERFOWL

This flamingo sanctuary and offbeat sand-street fishing village on the Gulf coast is a 1¹/₂-hour drive from Mérida. To get here, take Highway 281 (a two-lane road) past numerous old henequen haciendas. Around 10 **Autobuses de Occidente** buses leave Mérida for Celestún from the terminal at calles 50 and 67 daily between 6am and 6:30pm.

One **telephone** at the Hotel Gutiérrez (☎ **99/28-0419**) serves as the public phone for the entire village. You'll find a bank, two gas stations (but no unleaded gas), and a grocery store. Bus tickets are purchased at the end of the row of market stalls on the left side of the church. Celestún hotels don't furnish drinking water, so bring your own or buy it in town.

December 8 is the Feast Day of the Virgen de Concepción, the patron saint of the village. On the Sunday that falls nearest to **July 15,** a colorful procession carries Celestún's venerated figure of the Virgen de Concepción to meet the sacred figure of the Virgen de Asunción on the highway leading to Celestún. Returning to Celestún, they float away on decorated boats and later return to be ensconced at the church during a mass and celebration.

Seeing the Waterfowl

The town is on a narrow strip of land separated from the mainland by a lagoon. Crossing over the lagoon bridge, you'll find the 14,611-acre **wildlife refuge** spreading out on both sides without visible boundaries. You'll notice small boats moored on both sides waiting to take visitors to see the flamingos. In addition to flamingos, you may see frigate birds, pelicans, cranes, egrets, sandpipers, and other waterfowl feeding on shallow sandbars at any time of year. Of the 175 bird species that come here, some 99 are permanent residents. At least 15 duck species have also been counted. Flamingos are found here all year; some nonbreeding flamingos remain year-round, even though the larger group takes off around April to nest on the upper Yucatán Peninsula east of Río Lagartos.

A $1^1/_2$- to 2-hour **flamingo-sighting trip** costs around $25 for four persons or twice that much if you stay half a day. The best time to go is around 7am, and the worst is mid-afternoon, when sudden storms come up. Be sure not to allow the boatmen to get close enough to frighten the birds; they've been known to do it for photographers, but it will eventually cause the birds to permanently abandon the habitat. Your tour will take you a short distance into the massive mangroves that line the lagoon to a sulfur pool, where the boatman kills the motor and poles in so you can experience the stillness and density of the jungle, feel the sultry air, and see other birds.

Where to Stay

To find restaurants and hotels, follow the bridge road a few blocks to the end. On the last street, Calle 12, paralleling the oceanfront, you'll find restaurants and hotels, all of which have decent rooms but marginal housekeeping standards. Always try to bargain for lower rates, which can go down by as much as 30% in the off-season.

Hotel María del Carmen. Calle 12 no. 111, 97367 Celestún, Yuc. ☎ **99/28-0152.** 9 rms (all with bath). FAN. $14 double.

New in 1992, this three-story hotel on the beach is a welcome addition to Celestún's modest accommodations lineup. Spare but clean and large, each room has terrazzo floors, two double beds with sheets but no bedspread, screened windows (check screens for holes), and a small balcony or patio facing the ocean. Best of all, there's hot water in the baths (not necessarily a hallmark of other Celestún hotels), but not always toilet seats. Lorenzo Saul Rodríguez and María del Carmen Gutiérrez own the hotel and are actively involved in local conservation efforts, particularly in protecting the sea turtles that nest on the beach in early summer. Look for the sign for Villa del Mar, the hotel's restaurant; the rooms are behind it across the parking area.

WHERE TO DINE

Calle 12 is home to several rustic seafood restaurants aside from the place listed below. All have irregular hours of operation.

✪ **Restaurant Celestún.** Calle 12, on the waterfront. No phone. Main courses $3.75–$7. Daily 10am–6pm (sometimes). SEAFOOD/MEXICAN.

I highly recommend this ocean-view restaurant, owned by Elda Cauich and Wenseslao Ojeda; the service is friendly and swift. Tables and chairs fill a long room that stretches from Calle 12 to the beach. The house specialty is a super-delicious shrimp, crab, and squid omelet (called a *torta*). But if you're a fan of stone crabs (*manitas de cangrejo* on the menu), this is definitely the place to chow down. Trapped in the gulf by Celestún fishermen, they come freshly cooked and seasoned with lime juice. Also popular during the fall season is *pulpo* (octopus). Other local specialties include *liza* (mullet) and caviar de Celestún (mullet eggs). To find the restaurant, follow the bridge road to the waterfront (Calle 12); turn left and the restaurant is immediately on the right.

DZIBILCHALTÚN: MAYA RUINS

This Maya site, now a national park located 9 miles north of Mérida along the Progreso road and 4¹/₂ miles east off the highway, is worth a stop. Though it was founded about 500 B.C. and flourished around A.D. 750, Dzibilchaltún was in decline long before the coming of the conquistadores. It may have been occupied until A.D. 1600—almost a hundred years after the arrival of the Spaniards. Since its discovery in 1941, more than 8,000 buildings have been mapped. The site, which was probably a center of commerce and religion, covers an area of almost 10 square miles with a central core of almost 65 acres. At least 12 *sacbeob* (causeways), the longest of which is 4,200 feet, have been unearthed. Dzibilchaltún means "place of the stone writing," and at least 25 stelae have been found, many of them reused in buildings constructed after the original ones were covered or destroyed.

Today, the most interesting buildings are grouped around the **Cenote Xlacah,** the sacred well, and include a complex of buildings around structure 38; the **Central Group** of temples; the raised **causeways;** and the **Seven Dolls Group,** centered on the **Temple of the Seven Dolls.** It was beneath the floor of the temple that seven weird little dolls (now in the museum) showing a variety of diseases and birth defects were discovered. The Yucatán State Department of Ecology has added nature trails and published a booklet (in Spanish) of birds and plants seen at various points along the mapped trail. The booklet tells where in the park you are likely to see specific plants and birds.

The federal government has spent over a million pesos for the **Museum of the Maya** on the grounds of Dzibilchaltún. The museum, which opened in 1995, is a replica of a Maya village of houses, called *na,* staffed by Maya demonstrating traditional cooking, gardening, and folk-art techniques.

To get to Dzibilchaltún by bus from Mérida, go to the Progreso bus station at Calle 62 no. 524, between calles 65 and 67. There are five buses per day Monday through Saturday at 7:10 and 9am and 1, 2, and 3:20pm to the pueblo of Chanculob; it's a 1-kilometer walk to the ruins from there. On Sunday there are only three buses to Chanculob—at 5:40 and 9am and 2pm. The return bus schedule is posted at the ticket window by the ruins. The last bus is at 4:15pm.

The site and nature trails are open daily from 8am to 5pm. Admission is $4, free on Sunday; video camera use costs $4.

PROGRESO: GULF COAST CITY

For another beach escape, go to Progreso, a modern city facing the gulf less than an hour from Mérida. Here, the Malecón, a beautiful oceanfront drive, borders a vast beach lined with coconut palms that's popular on the weekends. A long pier, or *muelle* (pronounced mu-*weh*-yeh), extends 5 miles out into the bay to reach water deep enough for oceangoing ships. Progreso is part-time home to many Americans and Canadians who come to escape northern winters and also to many Meridianos who want to escape Mérida.

Along or near the Malecón are several of the more desirable restaurants and hotels.

From Mérida, buses to Progreso leave the special bus station at Calle 62 no. 524, between calles 65 and 67, every 15 minutes during the day, starting at 5am. The trip takes 45 minutes.

In Progreso, the bus station is about 4 blocks south of Calle 19, or Malecón, which runs along the beach.

EN ROUTE TO UXMAL

There are two routes to Uxmal, about 50 miles south of Mérida. The most direct is Highway 261 via Uman and Muna. Your second choice is a scenic but meandering trip down State Highway 18. Additional details on this latter route are provided in "The Ruins of Mayapán & Village of Ticul," below.

HIGHWAY 261: YAXCOPOIL & MUNA   Ten miles beyond Uman along Highway 261 is Yaxcopoil (yash-koh-poe-*eel*), the tongue-twisting Maya name of a fascinating 19th-century hacienda on the right side of the road between Mérida and Uxmal. It's difficult to reach by bus.

This hacienda, dating from 1864, was originally a cattle ranch comprising over 23,000 acres. Around 1900, it was converted to growing henequen (for the manufacture of rope). Take half an hour to tour the house (which boasts 18-foot ceilings and original furniture), factory, outbuildings, and museum. You'll see that such haciendas were the administrative, commercial, and social centers of vast private domains; they were almost little principalities carved out of the Yucatecan jungle. It's open Monday through Saturday from 8am to 6pm and Sunday from 9am to 1pm.

From Mérida via Uman, it's 20 miles to the Hacienda Yaxcopoil and 40 miles to Muna on Highway 261. Uxmal is 10 miles from Muna.

HIGHWAY 18: KANASÍN, ACANCEH, MAYAPÁN & TICUL   Taking Calle 67 east, head out of Mérida toward Kanasín (kahn-ah-*seen*) and Acanceh (ah-*kahn*-keh), for about 12 miles. When Calle 67 ends, bear right, then go left at the next big intersection. Follow the wide divided highway with speed bumps. At Mérida's periférico (the road that circles the city), you'll see signs to Cancún. You can either cross the periférico and go straight into Kanasín or turn and follow the Cancún signs for a short distance and then follow the signs into Kanasín. In **Kanasín,** watch for signs that say CIRCULACIÓN or DESVIACIÓN. As in many Yucatán towns, you're being redirected to follow a one-way street through the urban area. Go past the market, church, and the main square on your left and continue straight out of town. The next village you come to, at km 10, is **San António Tehuit,** an old henequen hacienda. At km 13 is **Tepich,** another hacienda-centered village, with those funny little henequen-cart tracks crisscrossing the main road. After Tepich comes **Petectunich** and finally **Acanceh.**

Across the street from and overlooking **Acanceh's** church is a partially restored pyramid. From Acanceh's main square, turn right (around the statue of a smiling deer) and head for **Tecoh** with its huge crumbling church ($5^1/_2$ miles farther along Highway 18) and **Telchaquillo** (7 miles farther). This route takes you past several old Yucatecan haciendas, each with a big house, chapel, factory with smokestack, and workers' houses.

Shortly after the village of Telchaquillo, a sign on the right side of the road will point to the entrance of the ruins of Mayapán.

2 The Ruins of Mayapán & Village of Ticul

THE RUINS OF MAYAPÁN

30 miles S of Mérida, 25 miles NE of Ticul, 37 miles NE of Uxmal

Founded, according to Maya lore, by the man-god Quetzalcoatl (Kukulkán in Maya) in about A.D. 1007, Mayapán ranked in importance with Chichén-Itzá and Uxmal and covered at least 2¹/₂ square miles. For more than 2 centuries, it was the capital of a Maya confederation of city-states that included Chichén and Uxmal. But before the year 1200 the rulers of Mayapán ended the confederation by attacking and conquering Chichén and by forcing the rulers of Uxmal to live as vassals in Mayapán. Eventually a successful revolt by the captive Maya rulers brought down Mayapán, which was abandoned during the mid-1400s.

Though ruined, the main pyramid is still impressive. Next to it is a large cenote (a natural limestone cavern used as a well), now full of trees, bushes, and banana plants. Beside it is a small temple with columns and a fine high-relief mask of Chaac, the hook-nosed rain god. Jungle paths lead to other small temples, including El Caracol, with its circular tower. These piles of stones do not reflect the grandeur of the walled city of Mayapán in its heyday. Supplied with water from 20 cenotes, it had over 3,000 buildings in its enclosed boundaries of several square miles. Today, all is covered in dense jungle. However, new excavations may clear the jungle and reveal something of why this city was so powerful.

The site is open daily from 8am to 5pm. Admission is $2; free on Sunday; use of a personal video camera is $4.

FROM MAYAPÁN TO TICUL   The road is a good one, but directional signs through the villages are almost nonexistent. Stop and ask directions frequently. From Mayapán, continue along Highway 18 to **Tekit** (5 miles), turn right and go to **Mama** on a road as thrilling as a roller-coaster ride (4¹/₃ miles), then turn right again for **Chapab** (8 miles).

If you're ready for a break, take time out to visit the **tortilla factory** in Chapab. Turn left when you see a building named Centro Educativo Comunitario Chapab, and the factory will be a couple of blocks farther on the left. As you came into town, you probably noticed young Maya girls, masa dough up to their elbows, carrying large pans and buckets of it atop their heads. They're returning from the daily ritual of corn grinding, and they'll use the masa to make their own tortillas at home. Other youngsters are carrying large stacks of finished tortillas hot off the press. The Matos Sabino family owns the factory, and they don't mind if you stop in and watch the action, which goes on daily from 8am to around 3pm. Better yet, buy some tortillas; fill them with avocados, tomatoes, and cheese; and have a picnic on the lawn across the street. After Chapab you reach **Ticul** (6¹/₄ miles), the largest town in the region.

TICUL

12 miles E of Uxmal, 53 miles SE of Mérida

Many of the 27,000 inhabitants of this sprawling town make their living embroidering *huipiles* (the Maya women's shiftlike dress), weaving straw hats, making shoes and gold-filigree jewelry, and shaping pottery. Workshops and stores featuring most of these items are easy to find, especially in the market area.

ESSENTIALS

GETTING THERE & DEPARTING   There are frequent buses from Mérida. The Ticul bus station is near the town center on Calle 24 between calles 25 and 25A. Buses return to Mérida daily at 7 and 10am and 5:30 and 7pm. Also check with the drivers of the minivans that line up across from the bus station. Buses run twice hourly to Muna, where you can change for a bus to Uxmal. For car information, see "En Route to Uxmal," above.

ORIENTATION   The market, most hotels, and Los Almendros, Ticul's best-known restaurant, are on the main street, **Calle 23,** also called Calle Principal. The **telephone area code** is 997. Since cars, buses, trucks, bicycles, and tricycles all compete for space on the narrow potholed streets, **parking and driving** have become difficult. Consider parking several streets away from the center of town and walking around from there. Directional signs that allow drivers to bypass the most congested part of town are beginning to appear.

EXPLORING TICUL

Ticul's **annual festival**—complete with bullfights, dancing, and carnival games—is held during the first few days of April.

SHOPPING

Ticul is best known for the cottage industry of *huipil* embroidery and for the manufacture of ladies' dress shoes. It's also a center for large-size, commercially produced pottery. Most of the widely sold sienna-colored pottery painted with Maya designs comes from Ticul. If it's a cloudy, humid day, the potters may not be working since part of the process requires sun drying, but they still welcome visitors to purchase finished pieces.

Arte Maya. Calle 23 no. 301, Carretera Ticul Muna. ☎ **997/2-1095.** Fax 997/2-0334.

Owned and operated by Luis Echeverría and Lourdes Castillo, this shop and gallery produces museum-quality art in alabaster, stone, jade, and ceramics. Much of the work is done as it was in Maya times; soft stone or ceramic is smoothed with the leaf of the siricote tree, and colors are derived from plant sources. If you buy from them, hang onto the written description of your purchase—their work looks so authentic that U.S. customs have delayed entry of people carrying their wares, thinking that they're smuggling real Maya artifacts into the States.

WHERE TO STAY

Only 12 miles northeast of Uxmal, Ticul is an ideal spot from which to launch regional sightseeing trips and to avoid the high cost of hotels in Uxmal.

Hotel Bougambillias Familiar. Calle 23 no. 291A, 97860 Ticul, Yuc. ☎ **997/2-0761.** 20 rms (all with bath). FAN. $12 double, one bed; $15 double, two beds. Free parking; secure.

Ticul's nicest inn is more like a motel, with parking outside the rooms. The half-circle drive into the arched entrance is lined with plants and pottery from the owner's local factory. Ceiling-height windows don't let in much light, the rooms have saggy beds, and bathrooms come without shower curtains and toilet seats. But the cool tile floors and ready hot water are attractions. In back is the hotel's pretty restaurant, Xux-Cab, but it has a limited menu. To find the hotel, follow Calle 23 through Ticul on the road to Muna. It's on the right before you leave town, past the Santa Elena turnoff.

WHERE TO DINE

Decent restaurants in Ticul are few. The busy market on Calle 23 is a good place to mingle with chatty Maya women while you select fresh fruit or grab a bite at one of the little market fondas.

✪ **Los Almendros.** Calle 23 no. 207. ☎ **997/2-0021.** Main courses $4–$7. Daily 9am–7pm. YUCATECAN.

Set in a big old Andalusian-style house with interior-courtyard parking, this is the first of a chain that now has branches in Mérida and Cancún. The Maya specialties include papadzules (sauce-covered, egg-filled tortillas) poc chuc (which originated here), and the spicy pollo ticuleño; as in Mérida, the quality of the food can vary. Ask for the illustrated menu in English (also Spanish and French) that explains the dishes in detail. To find it, walk 1½ blocks west of the plaza/church on Calle 23; it's on the left.

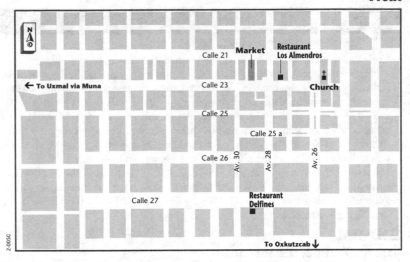

Restaurant Los Delfines. Calle 27 no. 216. No phone. Main courses $4–$5. Daily 8am–6pm. MEXICAN.

A favorite, although I've often found it closed, the Restaurant Los Delfines is in a beautiful garden setting near the center of town. The menu offers chiles rellenos stuffed with shrimp, *carne raja asada* with achiote, pork, garlic-flavored fish, and other seafood. The filling complimentary *botanas* (appetizers) are a refreshing treat. You can park off the street in the courtyard. If the restaurant appears to be closed, just bang on the large metal doors and someone will open them. To find the restaurant from the corner of calles 23 and 26 (by the church), go 2 blocks west on Calle 23 to Calle 28; turn left (south) and go 3 blocks to Calle 27, then right half a block. It's on the left.

A SIDE TRIP: SPELUNKING IN THE YAXNIC CAVES

Just outside the village of Yotolín (also spelled Yohtolín), between Ticul and Oxkutzcab (along Highway 184), are some impressive caves called **Yaxnic** (yash-*neek*) on the grounds of the old, private Hacienda Yotolín. Virtually undeveloped and full of colored stalactites and stalagmites, the caves are visited by means of a perilous descent in a basket let down on a rope.

Arranging this spelunking challenge takes time, but the thrill may be worth it. Here's the procedure: Several days (or even weeks or months) before your intended cave descent, go to Yotolín and ask for the house of the *comisario,* a village elder. He will make the proper introductions to the hacienda owners, who in turn will tell you how to prepare for the experience.

FROM TICUL TO UXMAL

From Ticul to Uxmal, follow the main street (Calle 23) west through town. Turn left at the sign to **Santa Elena.** It's 10 miles to Santa Elena; then, at Highway 261, cut back right for about 2 miles to Uxmal. The easiest route to follow is via Muna, but it's also longer and less picturesque. To go this way drive straight through Ticul 14 miles to Muna. At Muna, turn left and head south on Highway 261 to Uxmal, 10 miles away.

3 The Ruins of Uxmal

50 miles SW of Mérida, 12 miles W of Ticul, 12 miles S of Muna

One of the highlights of a vacation in the Yucatán, the ruins of Uxmal, noted for their rich geometric stone facades, are the most beautiful on the peninsula. Remains of an agricultural society indicate that the area was occupied possibly as early as 800 B.C. However, the great building period took place a thousand years later, between A.D. 700 and 1000, during which time the population probably reached 25,000. Then Uxmal fell under the sway of the Xiú princes (who may have come from the Valley of Mexico) after the year 1000. In the 1440s, the Xiú conquered Mayapán, and not long afterward the glories of the Maya ended when the Spanish conquistadores arrived.

Close to Uxmal, four other sites—Sayil, Kabah, Xlapak, and Labná—are worth visiting. With Uxmal, these ruins are collectively known as the Puuc route, for the Puuc hills of this part of the Yucatán. See the "Puuc Maya Sites" section below if you want to explore these sites.

ESSENTIALS

GETTING THERE & DEPARTING

BY BUS   See "Getting There & Departing" in Mérida, above, for information about bus service between Mérida and Uxmal. To return, wait for the bus on the highway at the entrance to the ruins. There is no evening departure from Mérida for the sound-and-light show at Uxmal.

BY CAR   Two routes to Uxmal from Mérida—via Highway 261 or via State Highway 18—are described in "En Route to Uxmal," at the end of the Mérida section, above. *Note:* There's no gasoline at Uxmal, so top off the tank in Mérida, Muna, or Ticul before continuing.

ORIENTATION

Uxmal consists of the archaeological site and its visitor center, four hotels, and a highway restaurant. The visitor center—open daily from 8am to 9pm—has a restaurant (with good coffee); toilets; a first-aid station; and shops selling soft drinks, ice cream, film, batteries, and books. There are no phones except at the hotels. Restaurants at hotels near Uxmal and at the visitor center are expensive, so if you're coming for the day, bring a lunch. Most public buses pick up and let off passengers on the highway at the entrance to the ruins. The site itself is open daily from 8am to 5pm. Admission to the archaeological site of Uxmal is $5, but a Sunday visit will save money since admission is free to Uxmal and other recommended sites nearby. There's a $4 charge for each video camera you bring in (save your receipt; it's good for other area sites on the same day). Parking costs $1.

Guides at the entrance of Uxmal give tours in a variety of languages and charge $20 for one person or a group. The guides frown on an unrelated individual joining a group (presumably a group is people traveling together). They'd rather you pay as a single entity, but you can hang around the entrance and ask other English speakers if they would like to join you in a tour and split the cost. As at other sites, the guides' information is not up-to-date, but you'll see areas and architectural details you might otherwise miss.

A 45-minute **sound-and-light show** is staged each evening in Spanish for $2 at 7pm and in English for $3 at 9pm. The bus from Mérida is scheduled to leave near the end of the Spanish show; confirm the exact time with the driver. If you stay for the English show, the only return to Mérida is via an expensive taxi. After the impressive show, the chant *"Chaaac, Chaaac"* will echo in your mind for weeks.

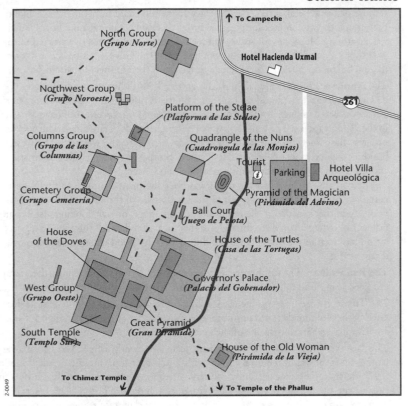

Uxmal Ruins

↑ To Campeche

North Group
(Grupo Norte)

Hotel Hacienda Uxmal

Northwest Group
(Grupo Noroeste)

Platform of the Stelae
(Platforma de las Stelae)

Columns Group
(Grupo de las Columnas)

Quadrangle of the Nuns
(Cuadrongula de las Monjas)

Tourist

Parking

Hotel Villa Arqueológica

Cemetery Group
(Grupo Cemetería)

Pyramid of the Magician
(Pirámide del Advino)

Ball Court
(Juego de Pelota)

House of the Doves

House of the Turtles
(Casa de las Tortugas)

West Group
(Grupo Oeste)

Governor's Palace
(Palacio del Gobenador)

South Temple
(Templo Sur)

Great Pyramid
(Gran Pirámide)

House of the Old Woman
(Pirámida de la Vieja)

To Chimez Temple ↓

↓ To Temple of the Phallus

2-0049

A TOUR OF THE RUINS

The Pyramid of the Magician   As you enter the ruins, note the *chultún* (cistern) inside the entrance to the right. Besides the natural underground cisterns (such as cenotes) formed in the porous limestone, chultúns were the principal source of water for the Maya.

Just beyond the chultún, Uxmal's dominant building, the Pyramid of the Magician (also called the Soothsayer's Temple) with its unique rounded sides, looms majestically on the right as you enter. The name comes from a legend about a mystical dwarf who reached adulthood rapidly after being hatched from an egg and who built this pyramid in one night. Beneath it are five temples, since it was common practice for the Maya to build new structures atop old ones as part of a pre-scribed ritual.

The pyramid is unique because of its oval shape, height, steepness, and odd door-way on the opposite (west) side near the top. The doorway's heavy ornamentation, a characteristic of the Chenes style, features 12 stylized masks of the rain god Chaac, and the doorway itself is a huge open-mouthed Chaac mask.

The tiring and even dangerous climb to the top is worth it for the view. From on top you can see Uxmal's entire layout. Next to the Pyramid of the Magician, to the west, is the Nunnery Quadrangle, and left of it is a conserved ball court, south of which are several large complexes. The biggest building among them is the Governor's Palace, and behind it lies the partially restored Great Pyramid. In the distance is the Dovecote

(House of the Doves), a palace with a lacy roofcomb (false front) that looks like the perfect apartment complex for pigeons. From this vantage point, note how Uxmal is special among Maya sites for its use of broad terraces or platforms constructed to support the buildings; look closely and you'll see that the Governor's Palace is not on a natural hill or rise but on a huge square terrace, as is the Nunnery Quadrangle.

The Nunnery Quadrangle   The 16th-century Spanish historian Fray Diego López de Cogullado gave the building its name because it resembled a Spanish monastery. Possibly it was a military academy or a training school for princes, who may have lived in the 70-odd rooms. The buildings were constructed at different times: The northern one was first, then the southern, then the eastern, then the western. The western building has the most richly decorated facade, composed of intertwined stone snakes and numerous masks of the hook-nosed rain god Chaac.

The corbeled archway on the south was once the main entrance to the Nunnery complex; as you head toward it out of the quadrangle to the south, look above each doorway in that section for the motif of a Maya cottage, or *nah,* looking just like any number of cottages you'd see throughout the Yucatán today. All this wonderful decoration has been restored, of course—it didn't look this good when the archaeologists discovered it.

The Ball Court   The unimpressive ball court is conserved to prevent further decay, but keep it in mind to compare with the magnificent restored court at Chichén-Itzá.

The Turtle House   Up on the terrace south of the ball court is a little temple decorated with a colonnade motif on the facade and a border of turtles. Though it's small and simple, its harmony is one of the gems of Uxmal.

The Governor's Palace   In size and intricate stonework, this is Uxmal's masterwork—an imposing three-level edifice with a 320-foot-long mosaic facade done in the Puuc style. Puuc means "hilly country," the name given to the hills nearby and thus to the predominant style of pre-Hispanic architecture found here. Uxmal has many examples of Puuc decoration, characterized by elaborate stonework from door tops to the roofline. Fray Cogullado, who named the Nunnery, also gave this building its name. The Governor's Palace may have been just that—the administrative center of the Xiú principality, which included the region around Uxmal. It probably had astrological significance as well. For years, scholars pondered why this building was constructed slightly turned from adjacent buildings. Originally they thought the strange alignment was because of the *sacbe* (ceremonial road) that starts at this building and ends 11 miles distant at the ancient city of Kabah. But recently scholars of archaeoastronomy (a relatively new science that studies the placement of archaeological sites in relation to the stars), discovered that the central doorway, which is larger than the others, is in perfect alignment with Venus.

Before you leave the Governor's Palace, note the elaborately stylized headdress patterned in stone over the central doorway. As you stand back from the building on the east side, note how the 103 stone masks of Chaac undulate across the facade like a serpent and end at the corners where there are columns of masks.

The Great Pyramid   A massive, partially restored nine-level structure, it has interesting motifs of birds, probably macaws, on its facade, as well as a huge mask. The view from the top is wonderful.

The Dovecote   It wasn't built to house doves, but it could well do the job in its lacy roofcomb—a kind of false front on a rooftop. The building is remarkable in that roofcombs weren't a common feature of temples in the Puuc hills, although you'll see one (of a very different style) on El Mirador at Sayil.

The Serpent Motif

Throughout Mesoamerica, the serpent motif appears embellished in stone, on murals, ceramics, shell, and in gold. Through its connection to water and land, the serpent represented fertility to the native cultures. Life depended on the land's production, so it is no wonder that this visually striking motif was so frequently represented.

It's memorable as much for the repetition of it throughout Mesoamerica as it is for the fabulous artistry required to produce it. A stone rattlesnake undulates across the facade of the Nunnery complex at Uxmal. The Governor's palace there projects 103 Chaac masks rising and falling across its facade like a slithering serpent. Light and shadow during the summer and winter solstices at Chichén-Itzá's El Castillo create the body of a serpent on the stairway. At Chichén-Itzá's Temple of the Warriors and other places, a human head often appears emerging from the wide open mouth of a serpent.

This motif appeared in the Yucatán before Toltec influence. Quetzalcoatl, the legendary god/king of the Toltec, was characterized as a serpent wearing the feathers of the quetzal bird, as was Kukulkán (the Maya representation of Quetzalcoatl). Vision serpents, yet another form of the plumed serpent, appear in Maya carvings often in association with bloodletting (induced to produce hallucinations).

WHERE TO STAY

Unlike Chichén-Itzá, which has several classes of hotels from which to choose, Uxmal has (with one exception) only one type: comfortable but expensive. Less expensive rooms are also available in nearby Ticul, but you'll need a car—bus service is limited.

MODERATE

✪ **Hotel Hacienda Uxmal.** Km 80 Carretera Mérida–Uxmal, 97840 Uxmal, Yuc. ☎ and fax **99/49-4754.** Reservations: Mayaland Resorts, Av. Colón 502, 97000 Mérida, Yuc; ☎ 800/235-4079 in the U.S., or 99/25-2122; fax 99/25-7022. 75 rms. A/C (21) or FAN (54). High season $120 double. Low season $110 double. Free guarded parking.

One of my favorites, this is also the oldest hotel in Uxmal. Located on the highway across from the ruins, it was built as the headquarters for the archaeological staff years ago. Rooms are large and airy, exuding an impression of a well-kept yesteryear, with patterned tile floors, heavy furniture, and well-screened windows. All rooms have ceiling fans, and TVs are being added. Guest rooms surround a handsome central garden courtyard with towering royal palms, a bar, and a pool. Other facilities include a dining room and gift shop. A guitar trio usually plays on the open patio in the evenings. Checkout time is 1pm, so you can spend the morning at the ruins and take a swim before you hit the road again.

Mayaland Resorts, owners of the hotel, offers tour packages that include free car rental for the nights you spend in its hotels. Although car rental is free, there's a daily insurance charge, which for a manual-shift Volkswagen Beetle is $18 per day. They also have Ford Escorts at a higher price. Mayaland also has a transfer service between the hotel and Mérida for about $30 one-way.

✪ **Villa Arqueológica.** Ruinas Uxmal, 97844 Uxmal, Yuc. ☎ **800/258-2633** in the U.S., or **99/49-6284.** Fax 99/49-5961. 40 rms and 3 suites. A/C. High season $85 double. Low season $70 double. Free guarded parking.

Operated by Club Med, the Villa Arqueológica offers a beautiful two-story layout around a plant-filled patio and a pool. At guests' disposal are a tennis court, a library, and an audiovisual show on the ruins in English, French, and Spanish. Each of the serene rooms has two oversize single beds. French-inspired meals are a la carte only. It's easy to find—follow the signs to the Uxmal ruins, then turn left to the hotel just before the parking lot at the Uxmal ruins.

INEXPENSIVE

Rancho Uxmal. Km 70 Carretera Mérida–Uxmal, 97840 Uxmal, Yuc. No local phone. Reservations: Sr. Macario Cach Cabrera, Calle 26 #156, 97860 Ticul, Yuc; ☎ **997/2-0277** or 99/23-1576. 20 rms. A/C or FAN. $18–$24 double; $4 per person campsite. Free guarded parking.

This modest little hotel is an exception to the high-priced places near Uxmal, and it gets better every year. Air-conditioning has been added to 10 of the rooms, all of which have good screens, hot-water showers, and 24-hour electricity. The restaurant is good; a full meal of poc chuc, rice, beans, and tortillas costs about $5, and breakfast is $2.25 to $3. It's a long hike to the ruins from here, but the manager may help you flag down a passing bus or combi or even drive you himself if he has time. A primitive campground out back offers electrical hookups and use of a shower. The hotel is 2¼ miles north of the ruins on Highway 261.

WHERE TO DINE

Besides the hotel restaurants mentioned above and the restaurant at the visitor's center, there are few other dining choices.

Café-Bar Nicte-Ha. In the Hotel Hacienda Uxmal, across the highway from the turnoff to the ruins. ☎ **997/24-7142.** Soups and salads $2–$5; main courses $5–$8; fixed-price lunch $9. Daily 1–8pm. MEXICAN.

This small restaurant attached to the Hotel Hacienda Uxmal is visible from the crossroads entrance to the ruins. The food is decent, though the prices tend to be high. If you eat here, take full advantage of the experience and spend a few hours by the pool near the cafe—use is free to customers. This is a favorite spot for bus tours that fill the place to overcrowding, so come early.

Las Palapas. Hwy. 261. No phone. Breakfast $3; comida corrida $3.75; soft drinks $1. Daily 9am–6pm (comida corrida served 1–4pm). MEXICAN/YUCATECAN.

Three miles north of the ruins on the road to Mérida you'll find this pleasant restaurant with open-air walls and a large thatched palapa roof. The amiable owner, María Cristina Choy, has the most reasonable dining prices around. Individual diners can sometimes become lost in the crowd if a busload of tourists arrives, but otherwise the service is fine and the food quite good. There's also a small gift shop with regional crafts and a few books.

THE PUUC MAYA ROUTE & VILLAGE OF OXKUTZCAB

South and east of Uxmal are several other Maya cities worth exploring. Though smaller in scale than either Uxmal or Chichén-Itzá, each has gems of Maya architecture. The facade of masks on the Palace of Masks at **Kabah,** the enormous palace at **Sayil,** and the fantastic caverns of **Loltún** may be among the high points of your trip. Also along the way are the **Xlapak** and **Labná** ruins and the pretty village of **Oxkutzcab.**

Note: All these sites are currently undergoing excavation and reconstruction, and some buildings may be roped off when you visit. And for photographers: You'll find afternoon light the best. The sites are open daily from 8am to 5pm. Admission is $2 each for Sayil, Kabah, and Labná; $1.25 for Xlapak; and $3 for Loltún. All except the caves of Loltún are free on Sunday. Use of a video camera at any time costs $4, but if you're visiting Uxmal in the same day, you pay only once for video permission and present your receipt as proof at each ruin. The sites are open daily from 8am to 5pm.

Kabah is 17 miles southeast of Uxmal. From there it's only a few miles to Sayil. Xlapak is almost walking distance (through the jungle) from Sayil, and Labná is just a bit farther east. A short drive beyond Labná brings you to the caves of Loltún. And Oxkutzcab is at the road's intersection with Highway 184, which can be followed west to Ticul or east all the way to Felipe Carillo Puerto.

If you are driving, between Labná and Loltún you'll find a road and a sign pointing north to Tabi. A few feet west of this road is a narrow dry-weather track leading into the seemingly impenetrable jungle. A bit over a mile up this track, the jungle opens to the remains of the fabulous old henequen-producing **Hacienda Tabí.** The hewed-rock, two-story main house extends almost the length of a city block, with the living quarters above and storage and space for carriages below. In places it looks ready to collapse. Besides the house, you'll see the ruined chapel, remnants of tall chimneys, and broken machinery. Though not a formal public site, the caretaker will ask you to sign a guestbook and allow you to wander around the hulking ruins—without climbing to the second story.

If you aren't driving, a daily bus from Mérida goes to all these sites, with the exception of Loltún and Tabí. (See "By Bus" under "Getting There & Departing," in Mérida, above, for more details.)

PUUC MAYA SITES

KABAH If you're off to Kabah, head southwest on Highway 261 to Santa Elena (8½ miles), then south to Kabah (8 miles). The ancient city of Kabah is on both sides along the highway. Make a right turn into the parking lot.

The most outstanding building at Kabah is the huge **Palace of Masks,** or Codz Poop ("rolled-up mat"), named for a motif in its decoration. You'll notice it first on the right up on a terrace. Its outstanding feature is the Chenes-style facade, completely covered in a repeated pattern of 250 masks of the rain god Chaac, each one with curling remnants of Chaac's elephant trunklike nose. There's nothing like this facade in all of Maya architecture. For years stone-carved parts of this building lay lined up in the weeds like pieces of a puzzle awaiting the master puzzlemaker to put them into place. Now workers are positioning the parts, including the broken roofcomb, in place. Sculptures from this building are in the museums of anthropology in Mérida and Mexico City.

Once you've seen the Palace of Masks, you've seen the best of Kabah. But you should take a look at the other buildings. Just behind and to the left of the Codz Poop is the **Palace Group** (also called the East Group), with a fine Puuc-style colonnaded facade. Originally it had 32 rooms. On the front you see seven doors, two divided by columns, a common feature of Puuc architecture. Recent restoration has added a beautiful L-shaped colonnaded extension to the left front. Further restoration is under way at Kabah, so there may be more to see when you arrive.

Across the highway, a large, conical, dirt-and-rubble mound (on your right) was once the **Great Temple,** or Teocalli. Past it is a **great arch,** which was much wider at one time and may have been a monumental gate into the city. A sacbe (ancient Maya road) linked this arch to a point at Uxmal. Compare this corbeled arch to the one at Labná (below), which is in much better shape.

SAYIL Just about 3 miles south of Kabah is the turnoff (left, which is east) to Sayil, Xlapak, Labná, Loltún, and Oxkutzcab. And 2½ miles along this road are the ruins of Sayil (which means "place of the ants").

Sayil is famous for **El Palacio,** the tremendous 100-plus-room palace that's a masterpiece of Maya architecture. Impressive for its simplistic grandeur, the building's facade, stretching three terraced levels, is breathtaking. Its rows of columns give it a Minoan appearance. On the second level, notice the upside-down stone figure of the diving god of bees and honey over the doorway; the same motif was used at Tulum several centuries later. From the top of El Palacio there is a great view of the Puuc hills. Sometimes it's difficult to tell which are hills and which are unrestored pyramids, since little temples peep out at unlikely places from the jungle. The large circular basin on the ground below the palace is an artificial catch basin for a chultún (cistern) because this region has no natural cenotes (wells) to catch rainwater.

In the jungle past El Palacio is **El Mirador,** a small temple with an oddly slotted roofcomb. Beyond El Mirador, a crude **stela** (tall, carved stone) has a phallic idol carved on it in greatly exaggerated proportions.

XLAPAK   Xlapak (shla-pahk) is a small site with one building; it's 3¹/₂ miles down the road from Sayil. The **Palace at Xlapak** bears the masks of the rain god Chaac.

LABNÁ   Labná, which dates to between A.D. 600 and 900, is 18 miles from Uxmal and only 1³/₄ miles past Xlapak. Like other archaeological sites in the Yucatán, it's also undergoing significant restoration and conservation. Descriptive placards fronting the main buildings are in Spanish, English, and German.

The first thing you see on the left as you enter is **El Palacio,** a magnificent Puuc-style building much like the one at Sayil but in poorer condition. There is an enormous mask of Chaac over a doorway with big banded eyes, a huge snout nose, and jagged teeth around a small mouth that seems on the verge of speaking. Jutting out on one corner is a highly stylized serpent's mouth out of which pops a human head with a completely calm expression. From the front you can gaze out to the enormous, grassy interior grounds flanked by vestiges of unrestored buildings and jungle.

From El Palacio you can walk across the interior grounds on a newly reconstructed sacbe leading to Labná's **corbeled arch,** famed for its ornamental beauty and for its representation of what many such arches must have looked like at other sites. This one has been extensively restored, although only remnants of the roofcomb can be seen; it was part of a more elaborate structure, which is completely gone. Chaac's face is on the corners of one facade, and stylized Maya huts are fashioned in stone above the doorways.

You pass through the arch to **El Mirador,** or **El Castillo,** as the rubble-formed, pyramid-shaped structure is called. Towering on the top is a singular room crowned with a roofcomb etched against the sky.

There's a refreshment/gift stand with restrooms at the entrance.

LOLTÚN   The caverns of Loltún are 18¹/₂ miles past Labná on the way to Oxkutzcab, on the left side of the road. The fascinating caves, home of ancient Maya, were also used as a refuge and fortress during the War of the Castes (1847–1901). Inside you can examine statuary, wall carvings and paintings, chultúns (cisterns), and other signs of Maya habitation, but the grandeur and beauty of the caverns alone are impressive. In front of the entrance is an enormous stone phallus. The cult of the phallic symbol originated south of Veracruz and appeared in the Yucatán between A.D. 200 and 500.

Tours in Spanish lasting 1¹/₂ hours are given daily at 9:30 and 11am and 12:30, 2, and 3pm and are included in the admission price. Before going on a tour, confirm these times at the information desk at Uxmal.

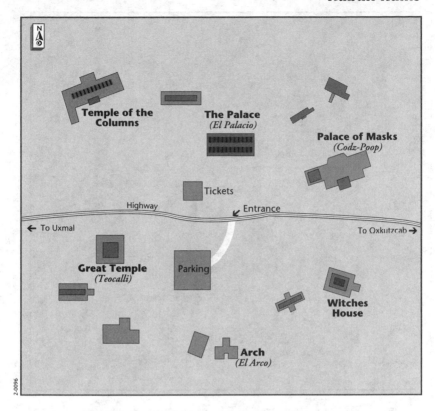

To return to Mérida from Loltún, drive the 4¹/₂ miles to Oxkutzcab and from there go northwest on Highway 184. It's 12 miles to Ticul and (turning north onto Highway 261 at Muna) 65 miles to Mérida.

OXKUTZCAB

Oxkutzcab (ohsh-kootz-*kahb*), 7 miles from Loltún, is the heartland of the Yucatán's fruit-growing region, particularly oranges. The tidy village of 21,000, centered around a beautiful 16th-century church and the market, is worth a stop if for no other reason than to eat at Su Cabaña Suiza (see below) before heading back to Mérida, Uxmal, or Ticul.

During the last week in October and the first week in November is the **Orange Festival,** when the village goes nuts with a carnival and orange displays in and around the central plaza.

A Good Place to Eat

✪ **Su Cabaña Suiza.** Calle 54 no. 101. ☎ **997/5-0457.** Main dishes $3.50; soft drinks or orange juice 75¢. Daily 7:30am–6:30pm. CHARCOAL-GRILLED MEATS/MEXICAN.

It's worth a trip from Loltún, Ticul, or Uxmal just to taste the delicious charcoal-grilled meat at this unpretentious restaurant dripping with colorful plants. Park in the gravel courtyard, then take a seat at one of the metal tables either under the palapa roof or outdoors where caged birds sing. Señora María Antónia Puerto de Pacho runs the spotless place with an iron hand, and family members provide swift, friendly

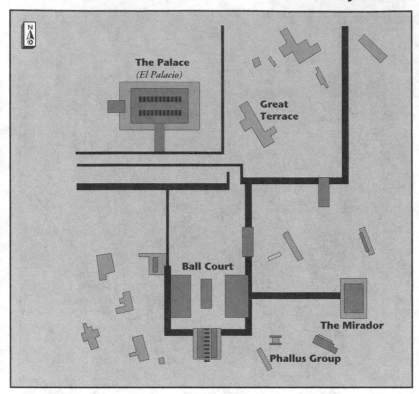

service. The primary menu items include filling portions of charcoal-grilled beef, pork, or chicken served with salad, rice, tortillas, and a bowl of delicious bean soup. But you can also find a few Yucatecan specialties, such as costillos entomatados, escabeche, queso relleno, and pollo pibil. The restaurant is between calles 49 and 51 in a quiet neighborhood 3 blocks south of the main square.

EN ROUTE TO CAMPECHE

From Oxkutzcab, head back 27 miles to Sayil, then drive south on Highway 261 to Campeche (78 miles). Along the way are several ruins and caves worth visiting.

XTACUMBILXUNA CAVES Highway 261 heads south for several miles, passing through a lofty arch marking the boundary between the states of Yucatán and Campeche. Continue on through Bolonchén de Rejón (Bolonchén means "nine wells").

About 1³/₄ miles south of Bolonchén, a sign points west to the Grutas de Xtacumbilxuna, though the sign spells it XTACUMBINXUNAN. Another sign reads: IT'S WORTH IT TO MAKE A TRIP FROM NEW YORK TO BOLONCHÉN JUST TO SEE XTACUMBILXUNA CAVES (JOHN STEPHENS—EXPLORER). The caves are open whenever the guide is around, which is most of the time. Follow him down for the 30- or 45-minute tour in Spanish, after which a $1 to $3 tip is customary.

Legend has it that a Maya girl escaped an unhappy love affair by hiding in these vast limestone caverns, which wouldn't be hard to do, as you'll see. Unlike the fascinating caves at Loltún, which are filled with traces of Maya occupation, these have only the standard bestiary of limestone shapes: a dog, an eagle, a penguin, a Madonna and child, a snake, and so on—figments of the guide's imagination.

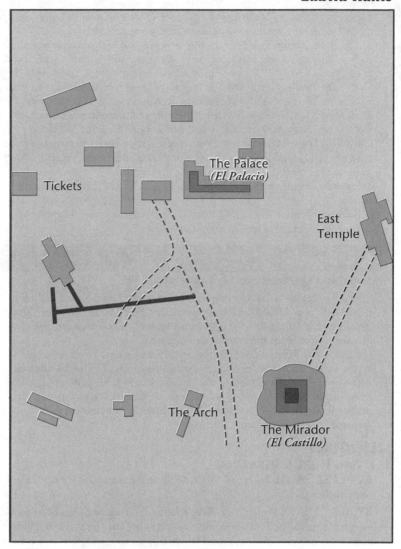

CHENES RUINS On your route south, you can also take a detour to see several unexcavated, unspoiled ruined cities in the Chenes style. You have to be adventurous for these; pack some food and water. When you get to Hopelchén, take the turnoff for Dzibalchén. When you get back to Dzibalchén (25½ miles from Hopelchén), ask for directions to Hochob, San Pedro, Dzehkabtún, El Tabasqueño, and Dzibilnocac.

EDZNÁ From Hopelchén, Highway 261 heads west, and after 26 miles you'll find yourself at the turnoff for the ruined city of Edzná, 12 miles farther along to the south.

Founded probably between 600 and 300 B.C. as a small agricultural settlement, it developed into a major ceremonial center during the next 1,500 years. Archaeologists estimate that to build and maintain such a complex center must have required a population in the tens of thousands. Once a network of Maya canals criss-crossed this entire area, making intensive cultivation possible.

The **Great Acropolis** is a unique five-level pyramid with a temple complete with roofcomb on top. Edzná means "house of wry faces," which undoubtedly there were at one time. Though the buildings at Edzná were mostly in the heavily baroque Chenes, or "well-country" style, no vestige of these distinctive decorative facades remains at Edzná. Several other buildings surround an open central yard. Farther back, new excavations have revealed the **temple of the stone mask,** a structure with several fine stucco masks similar to those of Kohunlich in the Río Bec region near Chetumal. The site takes only 30 minutes or less to see and is perhaps not worth the price of entry, especially if you've seen many other sites in the Yucatán. (*Note:* The afternoon light is better for photographing the temple.)

It's open daily from 8am to 5pm. Admission costs $3, plus $4 to use your video camera.

Back on Highway 261, it's 12 miles to the intersection with Highway 180, then another 26 miles to the very center of Campeche.

4 Campeche

157 miles SW of Mérida, 235 miles NE of Villahermosa

Campeche, capital of the state bearing the same name, is a pleasant, beautifully kept coastal city (pop. 172,000) with a leisurely pace. You'll be able to enjoy this charming city without the crowds because many tourists bypass Campeche on their way to Mérida in favor of the road via Kabah and Uxmal.

Founded by Francisco de Córdoba in 1517 and claimed for the Spanish Crown by the soldier Francisco de Montejo the Elder in 1531, Campeche was later abandoned and refounded by Montejo the Younger in 1540. To protect it against pirates who pillaged the gulf coastal towns, the townspeople built a wall around the city in the late 1600s. Remnants of this wall, called *baluartes* (bulwarks), are among the city's proudest links with the past.

ESSENTIALS
GETTING THERE & DEPARTING

BY PLANE **Aeroméxico** (☎ 981/6-6656 at the airport) flies once daily to and from Mexico City.

BY BUS The **Camioneros de Campeche** line runs second-class buses to Mérida every half hour for the 2- to 3-hour trip. There are first-class direct buses to Mérida three times a day and to Uxmal at 7 and 11am and 5pm, and buses to Edzná at 8am and 2:30pm (this bus drops you off and picks you up 1 km from the ruins). These tickets are sold on the Calle Chile side of the bus station at the Camioneros de Campeche ticket booth. **ADO,** in the front of the station, offers a first-class de paso bus to Palenque at 11pm and buses to Mérida every hour or less from 5:30am to midnight. **Caribe Express** has direct deluxe service to and from Mérida and Cancún. Their office and bus yard is on the north side of the Centro Comercial Ah Kin Pech, Local 304.

BY CAR Highway 180 goes south from Mérida, passing near the basket-making village of Halacho and near Becal, known for Panama-hat weavers. At Tenabo, take the shortcut (right) to Campeche rather than going farther to the crossroads near Chencoyí. The longer way from Mérida is along Highway 261 past Uxmal. From Uxmal, Highway 261 passes near some interesting ruins and the Xtacumbilxuna caves (see "En Route to Campeche" in the preceding section).

When driving the other direction, toward Celestún and Mérida, use the Vía Corta (short route) by going north on Avenida Ruíz Cortínez, bearing left to follow the water (this becomes Avenida Pedro Sainz de Baranda, but there's no sign). Follow the road as it turns inland to Highway 180, where you turn left (there's a gas station at the intersection). The route takes you through Becal and Halacho. Stores in both villages close between 2 and 4pm.

If you're leaving Campeche for Edzná and Uxmal, go north on either Cortínez or Gobernadores and turn right on Madero, which becomes Highway 281. To Villahermosa, take Cortínez south; it becomes Highway 180.

ORIENTATION

ARRIVING The **airport** is several miles northeast of the town center, and you'll have to take a taxi into town. The **ADO bus station,** on Avenida Gobernadores, is 9 long blocks from the Plaza Principal. Turn left out the front door and walk 1 block. Turn right (Calle 49) and go straight for 5 blocks to Calle 8. Turn left here, and the Plaza Principal is 3 blocks ahead. Taxis are readily available outside the station.

INFORMATION The **State of Campeche Office of Tourism** (☎ **981/6-6767;** fax 981/6-6068) is in the Baluarte Santa Rosa on the south side of town on Circuito Baluartes, between calles 12 and 14. It's open Monday through Friday from 9am to 9pm, Saturday and Sunday from 9am to 1pm.

CITY LAYOUT Most of your time in Campeche will be spent within the confines of the old city walls. The administrative center of town is the modernistic **Plaza Moch-Couoh** on Avenida 16 de Septiembre near the waterfront. Next door to the plaza rises the modern office tower called the Edificio Poderes or Palacio de Gobierno, headquarters for the state of Campeche. Beside it is the futuristic Cámara de Diputados or Casa de Congreso (state legislature chamber), which looks like an enormous square clam. Just behind it, the **Parque Principal** (central park) on Calle 8 will most likely be your reference point for touring.

Campeche's systematic street-numbering plan can be both clear-cut and confusing. Streets in the primary grid of downtown Campeche are all called "Calle" regardless of which way they run—that's the confusing part. The easy part is that those running roughly north to south have even numbers, and those running east to west have odd numbers. In addition, the streets are numbered so that numbers ascend toward the south and west. After walking around for 5 minutes you'll have the system down pat.

GETTING AROUND Most of the recommended sights, restaurants, and hotels are within walking distance of the Parque Principal. Campeche isn't easy to negotiate by bus, so I recommend taxis for the more distant areas.

FAST FACTS: CAMPECHE

American Express Local offices are at Calle 59 no. 4–5 (☎ **981/1-1010**), in the Edificio Belmar, a half block toward town from the Ramada Hotel. They're open Monday through Friday from 9am to 2pm and 5 to 7pm and Saturday from 9am to 1:30pm. They do not cash traveler's checks.

Area Code The telephone **area code** is **981.**

Post Office The post office (Correo) is in the Edificio Federal at the corner of Avenida 16 de Septiembre and Calle 53 (☎ **981/6-2134**), near the Baluarte de Santiago; it's open Monday through Saturday from 7:30am to 8pm. The telegraph office is here as well.

EXPLORING CAMPECHE

With its city walls, clean brick-paved streets, friendly people, easy pace, and orderly traffic, Campeche is a lovely city worthy of at least a day on your itinerary. Besides taking in the museums built into the city walls, you'll want to stroll the streets (especially calles 55, 57, and 59) and enjoy the typical Mexican colonial-style architecture. Look through large doorways to glimpse the colonial past—high-beamed ceilings, Moorish stone arches, and interior courtyards.

INSIDE THE CITY WALLS

As the busiest port in the region during the 1600s and 1700s, Campeche was a choice target for pirates. The Campechanos began building impressive defenses in 1668, and by 1704, the walls, gates, and bulwarks were in place. Today three of the seven remaining baluartes are worth visiting.

A good place to begin is the pretty zócalo, or **Parque Principal,** bounded by calles 55 and 57 running east and west and calles 8 and 10 running north and south. Construction of the church on the north side of the square began in 1650 and was finally completed a century and a half later.

For a good introduction to the city, turn south from the park on Calle 8 and walk 5 blocks to the Museo de la Ciudad (city museum).

Baluarte de San Carlos/Museo de la Ciudad. Circuito Baluartes and Av. Justo Sierra. No phone. Free admission. Tues–Sat 8am–8pm; Sun 8am–2pm.

This museum features a permanent exhibition of photographs and plans about the city and its history. The model of the city shows how it looked in its glory days and gives a good overview for touring within the city walls. There are several excellent ship models as well.

Baluarte de la Soledad. Calle 57 and Calle 8, opposite the Plaza Principal. No phone. Free admission. Tues–Sat 8am–8pm, Sun 8am–1pm.

This bastion houses the Sala de Estelas, or **Chamber of Stelae,** a display of Maya votive stones brought from various sites in this ruin-rich state. Many are badly worn, but the excellent line drawings beside the stones allow you to admire their former beauty. Three additional rooms also have interesting artifacts; each room is dedicated to a different Maya scholar.

Baluarte de Santiago. Av. 16 de Septiembre and Calle 49. No phone. Free admission. Tues–Fri 8am–3pm and 6–8:30pm, Sat–Sun 9am–1pm.

The **Jardín Botánico Xmuch'haltun** grows in a jumble of exotic and common plants within the stone walls of this baluarte. More than 250 species of plants and trees share what seems like a terribly small courtyard. Some are identified and, if the projector is working, a film explains the garden.

Museo de Arte de Campeche. Calles 10 and 63. ☎ **981/6-1424.** Admission 50¢. Tues–Fri 9am–1pm and 4–8pm.

To glimpse colonial glitter and a touch of modern art, visit this museum, which is actually the restored Templo de San José (1640). The museum displays traveling exhibits of Mexican art. The temple also holds the library for the university next door, and students' paintings and photographs are displayed in the gallery space. Peer around corners and behind shelves at the walls. Don't miss the large mural of the Virgin of Guadalupe. The temple is 1 block inland from the Museo de la Ciudad (see above).

Museo Regional de Campeche. Calle 59 no. 36, between calles 14 and 16. ☎ **981/6-9111.** Admission $3. Tues–Sat 8am–8pm, Sun 8am–1pm.

Campeche

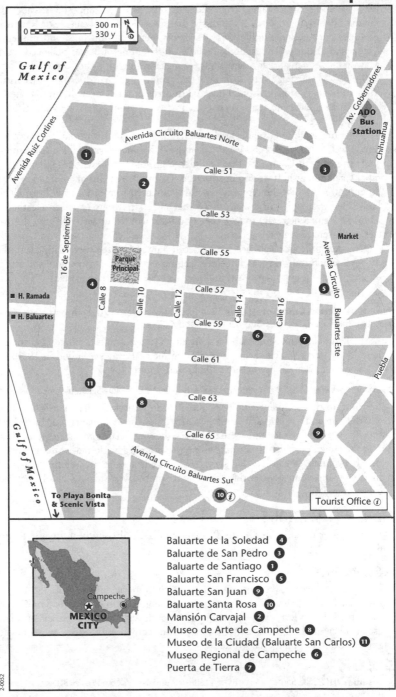

Baluarte de la Soledad ④
Baluarte de San Pedro ③
Baluarte de Santiago ①
Baluarte San Francisco ⑤
Baluarte San Juan ⑨
Baluarte Santa Rosa ⑩
Mansión Carvajal ②
Museo de Arte de Campeche ⑧
Museo de la Ciudad (Baluarte San Carlos) ⑪
Museo Regional de Campeche ⑥
Puerta de Tierra ⑦

2-0052

Just 2¹/₂ blocks farther inland from the Museo de Arte de Campeche (see above) is the city's best museum. Housed in the former mansion of the Teniente de Rey (royal governor), it features original Maya artifacts, pictures, drawings, and models of Campeche's history. The exhibit on the skull-flattening of babies practiced by the Maya includes actual deformed skulls. Another highlight is the Late Classic (A.D. 600–900) Maya stelae carved in a metamorphic rock that does not exist in the Yucatán but was brought from a quarry hundreds of miles away. Many clay figures show scarified faces and tools, such as manta ray bones, obsidian, and jade, used for cutting the face.

Other unusual pre-Hispanic artifacts include clay figures with movable arms and legs, as well as jade masks and jewelry from pre-Hispanic Maya tombs at Calakmul— a site in southern Campeche that is undergoing study and excavation. Among the other Calakmul artifacts found in structure VII are the remains of a human between 30 and 40 years old; the remains show the burial custom of partially burning the body, then wrapping it in a woven straw mat and cloth. Beans, copal, and feathers— all items deemed necessary to take the person through the underworld after death— were discovered in pottery vessels.

A model of the archaeological site at Becán shows Maya society in daily life. Other displays demonstrate Maya architecture; techniques of water conservation; and aspects of their religion, commerce, art, and considerable scientific knowledge. There's a bookstore on the left as you enter.

Puerta de Tierra (Land Gate). Calle 59 at Circuito Baluartes/Av. Gobernadores. No phone. Museum, free; show, $3. Tues–Sun 8am–2pm and 4–8pm.

At the Land Gate there's a small museum displaying portraits of pirates and the city founders. The 1732 French 5-ton cannon in the entryway was found in 1990. On Tuesday and Friday at 8pm there's a light-and-sound show.

Mansión Carvajal. Calle 10 no. 584. No phone. Free admission. Mon–Sat 9am–2pm and 4–8pm.

Restoration was completed in 1992 on this early 20th-century mansion, originally the home of the Carvajal family, owners of a henequen plantation. In its latest transformation, the blue-and-white Moorish home contains government agencies. Join the crowd purposefully striding along the gleaming black-and-white tile and up the curving marble staircase. No signs mark the entrance to the building—look for fresh blue-and-white paint inside the entrance on the west side of Calle 10 between calles 53 and 51.

MORE ATTRACTIONS

If you're looking for a **beach,** the Playa Bonita is 4 miles south of town; it's often dirty.

A SCENIC VISTA

For a dramatic view of the city and gulf, go south from the tourism office on Avenida Ruíz Cortínez and turn left on Ruta Escénica, winding up to the **Fuerte San Miguel.** Built in 1771, this fort was the most important of the city's defenses. Santa Anna later used it when he attacked the city in 1842. It is currently being used as a museum with a recent exhibit of pirate-related items.

SHOPPING

Artesanías DIF. Calle 55 no. 25 (between calles 12 and 14). ☎ **981/6-9088.**

This newly opened store in a restored mansion features quality textiles, clothing, and locally made furniture. DIF is the family-assistance arm of the government, and proceeds support government programs. It's open Monday through Friday from 9am to 1:30pm and 5 to 8pm, Saturday from 9am to 1:30pm.

WHERE TO STAY

Campeche's tourist trade is small and there are relatively few good places to stay. If you're driving, there are a few motels on the waterfront road, but you don't get a lot for the money.

EXPENSIVE

❖ **Ramada Inn.** Av. Ruíz Cortínez 51 (Apdo. Postal 251), 24000 Campeche, Camp. ☎ **800/ 272-6234** in the U.S., 981/6-2233 or 981/6-4611. Fax 981/6-1618. 120 rms. A/C TV TEL. $85 double. Parking free.

Extensively remodeled in 1990, the handsomely furnished rooms at the Ramada Inn all have tile floors and balconies facing the Gulf of Mexico. The restaurant, bar, and coffee shop are popular with local citizens—always a good recommendation. There's a large swimming pool, a discotheque, and a fenced parking lot behind the hotel. It's on the main oceanfront boulevard, 2 blocks west of the Plaza Principal and next to the Hotel Baluartes.

MODERATE

Hotel Baluartes. Av. Ruíz Cortínez 61, 24000 Campeche, Camp. ☎ **981/6-3911.** Fax 981/ 6-2410. 100 rms. A/C TV TEL. $55 double. Parking free.

Opposite the Gulf of Mexico and next door to the Ramada Inn, this was the city's original luxury hotel. It's still a nice place but not refurbished and modern like the Ramada. Many of the rooms have a Gulf view. A restaurant and bar are on the first floor, plus the swimming pool is refreshing after a day of touring. You're close to all the major museums and restaurants. The Baluartes is at the corner of Calle 61, 2 blocks west of the Plaza Principal.

INEXPENSIVE

Hotel América. Calle 10 no. 252, 24000 Campeche, Camp. ☎ **981/6-4588.** 52 rms. FAN TV. $19 double. Free guarded parking 3 blocks away.

This centrally located hotel is a choice only if La Posada del Angel is full. It is old and worn, semi-clean, and gets no high marks for maintenance. The three stories of rooms (no elevator) have one, two, or three double beds and come with tile floors. Corner rooms are quieter than those with windows on the street. To find the hotel from the Parque Principal, walk south on Calle 10 for $2^1/_2$ blocks; it's on the right between calles 61 and 63.

La Posada del Angel. Calle 10 no. 307, 24000 Campeche, Camp. ☎ **981/6-7718.** 14 rms. FAN A/C. $16–$19 double.

Rooms, with windows opening onto the dim narrow hall, are a little dark in this three-story hotel, but they are clean and freshly painted, and each comes with either two double beds or a single and a double. Carpeted halls in the upper two stories cut down on noise. To find the hotel from the Parque Principal, walk north on Calle 10 (with the cathedral on your left); the hotel is opposite the cathedral's right wall, a half block north of the Plaza Principal.

WHERE TO EAT

For regional food, try *colados,* which are delicious regional tamales, *tacos de salchicha* (an unusual pastry), *cazón de Campeche* (a tasty shark stew), and *pan de cazón* (another shark dish for those with more adventurous palates).

MODERATE

✪ **La Pigua.** Av. Miguel Alemán no. 197A. ☎ **981/1-3365.** Main courses $4–$7. Daily noon–6pm. SEAFOOD/MEXICAN.

You can easily pass the entire afternoon in this jungle-like dining room with glass walls between the diners and the trees. The most filling meal on the menu (in a sharkskin folder) is the plateful of rice with octopus and shrimp; the most unusual is chiles rellenos stuffed with shark. The *cangrejo* (stone crab) is a house specialty. To reach La Pigua from the Plaza Principal, walk north on Calle 8 for 3 blocks. Cross the Avenida Circuito by the botanical garden, where Calle 8 becomes Miguel Alemán. The restaurant is 1¹/₂ blocks north, on the east side of the street.

Restaurant Miramar. Calle 8 no. 293 (corner of Calle 61). ☎ **981/6-2883.** Main courses $3.75–$6. Mon–Fri 8am–midnight, Sat 8am–1am, Sun 11am–7pm. SEAFOOD/MEXICAN.

One of the best choices in Campeche, this restaurant has airy and pleasant decor with light-colored stone arches, dark wood, and ironwork. The menu offers typical Campeche seafood dishes, including lightly fried breaded shrimp (ask for *camarones empanizados*); *arroz con mariscos* (shellfish and rice); and *pargo poc chuc*. For dessert there's *queso napolitana*, a very rich, thick flan. Ask about the changing daily specials. To find the restaurant from the Plaza Principal, walk 2 blocks south on Calle 8; it's near the corner of Calle 61.

INEXPENSIVE

Panificadora Nueva España. Calle 10 no. 256. ☎ **981/6-2887.** All items 50¢–$2. Mon–Sat 6:30am–9:30pm. BAKERY.

A block and a half south of the Parque Principal is Campeche's best downtown bakery. Besides the usual assorted breads and pastries, you can stock up on food for the road—mayonnaise, catsup, cheese, butter, yogurt, and fruit drinks. This is the place to try the unusual *tacos de salchicha,* also called *feite.* Fresh breads come out of the oven at 5pm. A second location is on Calle 12 between calles 57 and 59.

La Parroquia. Calle 55 no. 9. ☎ **981/6-8086.** Breakfast $1–$3; main courses $2.75–$5; comida corrida $3.50. Daily 24 hours (comida corrida served 1–4pm). MEXICAN.

La Parroquia, a popular local hangout, has friendly waiters and offers excellent, inexpensive fare. Here, you can enjoy great breakfasts and colados, the delicious regional tamal. Selections on the comida corrida might include pot roast, meatballs, pork or fish, rice or squash, beans, tortillas, and fresh-fruit–flavored water.

La Perla. Calle 10 no. 345. ☎ **981/6-4092.** Breakfast $2.25; main courses $2.75–$4; sodas 75¢. Mon–Sat 7am–10pm. MEXICAN.

A popular student lounge (the Instituto Campechano is down the street near the Templo San José), La Perla has a youthful clientele with prices to match student budgets. The *arroz con camarones,* a filling meal of rice and shrimp, is a great bargain, and the *licuados,* made with purified water and fresh pineapple or cantaloupe, are refreshing. The coffee is instant, not brewed! At times, La Perla is noisy, but sometimes just a few customers are scattered about, seriously reading textbooks. To find the lounge from the Art Museum (at Calle 63 and Calle 10), walk 1 block north.

5 The Ruins of Chichén-Itzá & Village of Pisté

112 miles SW of Cancún, 75 miles SE of Mérida

The fabled pyramids and temples of Chichén-Itzá are the Yucatán's best-known ancient monuments. You must go, since you can't say you've *really* seen the Yucatán until you've gazed at the towering El Castillo, seen the sun from the Maya observatory called El Caracol, or shivered on the brink of the gaping cenote that may have served as the sacrificial well.

This post-Classic Maya city was established by Itzáes perhaps sometime during the 9th century A.D. Linda Schele and David Friedel, in *A Forest of Kings* (Morrow, 1990), have cast doubt on the legend that Kukulkán (called Quetzalcoatl by the Toltecs—a name also associated with a legendary god) came here from the Toltec capital of Tula, and, along with Putún Maya coastal traders, built a magnificent metropolis that combined the Maya Puuc style with Toltec motifs (the feathered serpent, warriors, eagles, and jaguars). Not so, say Schele and Friedel. Readings of Chichén's bas-reliefs and hieroglyphs fail to support that legend, they say, and instead show that Chichén-Itzá was a continuous Maya site which was influenced by association with the Toltecs but not by an invasion. Kukulkán's role in the Yucatán is once again in question. Not all scholars, however, embrace this new thinking, so the idea of a Toltec invasion still holds sway.

Though it's possible to make a round-trip from Mérida to Chichén-Itzá in 1 day, it will be a long, tiring, and very rushed day. Try to spend at least 1 night at Chichén-Itzá (you'll actually stay in the nearby village of Pisté), or two if you can. Take your time seeing the ruins in the cool of the morning or the afternoon after 3pm; take a siesta during the midday heat. The next morning, get to the ruins early; when the heat of the day approaches, catch a bus to your next destination. This may involve paying the admission fee more than once (unless you're there on a Sunday, when it's free), but the experience is worth it. Day-trip groups generally arrive when it's beginning to get hot, rushing through this marvelous ancient city in order to catch another bus or have lunch.

ESSENTIALS
GETTING THERE & DEPARTING
BY PLANE   Day-trips on charter flights from Cancún and Cozumel can be arranged by travel agents in the United States or in Cancún or Cozumel.

BY BUS   From Mérida, first-class **ADO buses** leave at 7:30am and 3:30pm. If you go round-trip in a day (a 2¹/₂-hour trip one way), take the 8:45am bus and reserve a seat on the return bus. There are direct buses to Cancún at 11:15am and 6pm and to Mérida at 3pm. De paso buses to Mérida leave hourly day and night, as do those to Valladolid and Cancún.

BY CAR   Chichén-Itzá is on the main Highway 180 between Mérida and Cancún.

ORIENTATION
ARRIVING   You'll arrive in the village of Pisté, at the bus station next to the Pirámide Inn. From Pisté there's a sidewalk to the archaeological zone, which is a mile or so east of the bus station.

CITY LAYOUT   The small town of **Pisté,** where most hotels and restaurants are located, is about a mile and a half from the ruins of Chichén-Itzá. Public buses from Mérida, Cancún, Valladolid, and elsewhere discharge passengers here. A few hotels are at the edge of the ruins, and one, the **Hotel Dolores Alba** (see "Where to Stay," below), is out of town about 1¹/₂ miles from the ruins on the road to Valladolid.

AREA CODE   The telephone **area code** is **985.**

EXPLORING THE RUINS
The site occupies 4 square miles, and it takes a strenuous full day (from 8am to noon and 2 to 5pm) to see all the ruins, which are open daily from 8am to 5pm. Service areas are open from 8am to 10pm. Admission is $4, free for children under 12, and

free for all on Sunday and holidays. A permit to use your own video camera costs an additional $4. Parking costs extra. *You can use your ticket to reenter on the same day, but you'll have to pay again for another day.* Chichén-Itzá's light-and-sound show was completely revamped in 1993 and is well worth seeing. The Spanish version is shown nightly at 7pm and costs $3.50; the English version is at 9pm and costs $4. The show may be offered in French and German as well. Ask at your hotel.

The huge visitor center, at the main entrance where you pay the admission charge, is beside the parking lot and consists of a museum, an auditorium, a restaurant, a bookstore, and rest rooms. You can see the site on your own or with a licensed guide who speaks either English or Spanish. These guides are usually waiting at the entrance and charge around $30 for one to six people. Although the guides frown on it, there's nothing wrong with your approaching a group of people who speak the same language and asking if they would like to share a guide with you. The guide, of course, would like to get $30 from you alone and $30 each from other individuals who don't know one another and still form a group. Don't believe all the history they spout—some of it is just plain out-of-date, but the architectural details they point out are enlightening.

There are actually two parts of Chichén-Itzá (which dates from around A.D. 600 to 900). There's the northern (new) zone, which shows distinct Toltec influence, and the southern (old) zone, which is mostly Puuc architecture.

El Castillo As you enter from the tourist center, the beautiful 75-foot El Castillo pyramid (also called the Pyramid of Kukulkán) will be straight ahead across a large open area. It was built with the Maya calendar in mind. There are 364 stairs plus a platform to equal 365 (days of the year), 52 panels on each side (which represent the 52-year cycle of the Maya calendar), and nine terraces on each side of the stairways (for a total of 18 terraces, which represents the 18-month Maya solar calendar). If this isn't proof enough of the mathematical precision of this temple, come for the spring or fall equinox (March 21 or September 21 between 3 and 5pm). On those days, the seven stairs of the northern stairway and the serpent-head carving at the base are touched with sunlight and become a "serpent" formed by the play of light and shadow. It appears to descend into the earth as the sun hits each stair from the top, ending with the serpent head. To the Maya this was a fertility symbol: The golden sun had entered the earth, meaning it was time to plant the corn.

El Castillo was built over an earlier structure. A narrow stairway entered at the western edge of the north staircase leads into the structure, where there is a sacrificial altar-throne—a red jaguar encrusted with jade. The stairway is open at 11am and 3pm and is claustrophobic, usually crowded, humid, and uncomfortable. A visit early in the day is best. No photos of the figure are allowed.

Main Ball Court (Juego de Pelota) Northwest of El Castillo is Chichén's main ball court, the largest and best preserved anywhere, and only one of nine ball courts built in this city. Carved on both walls of the ball court are scenes showing Maya figures dressed as ball players decked out in heavy protective padding. The carved scene also shows a headless player kneeling with blood shooting from the neck; the player is looked upon by another player holding the head.

Players on two teams tried to knock a hard rubber ball through one or the other of the two stone rings placed high on either wall, using only their elbows, knees, and hips (no hands). According to legend, the losing players paid for defeat with their lives. However, some experts say the victors were the only appropriate sacrifices for the gods. Either way, the game must have been exciting, heightened by the marvelous acoustics of the ball court.

The North Temple Temples are at both ends of the ball court. The North Temple has sculptured pillars and more sculptures inside, as well as badly ruined murals. The

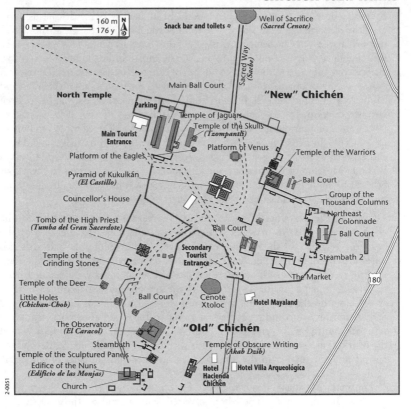

Chichén-Itzá Ruins map showing: Snack bar and toilets, Well of Sacrifice (Sacred Cenote), Sacred Way (Sacbe), North Temple, Main Ball Court, "New" Chichén, Parking, Temple of Jaguars, Temple of the Skulls (Tzompantli), Main Tourist Entrance, Platform of Venus, Temple of the Warriors, Platform of the Eagles, Ball Court, Pyramid of Kukulkán (El Castillo), Group of the Thousand Columns, Councellor's House, Northeast Colonnade, Tomb of the High Priest (Tumba del Gran Sacerdote), Ball Court, Ball Court, Temple of the Grinding Stones, Secondary Tourist Entrance, Steambath 2, Temple of the Deer, The Market, Little Holes (Chichan-Chob), Ball Court, Cenote Xtoloc, Hotel Mayaland, The Observatory (El Caracol), "Old" Chichén, Steambath 1, Temple of Obscure Writing (Akab Dzib), Temple of the Sculptured Panels, Edifice of the Nuns (Edificio de las Monjas), Hotel Hacienda Chichén, Hotel Villa Arqueológica, Church. Scale 0–160 m / 176 y. Road 180.

acoustics of the ball court are so good that from the North Temple a person speaking can be heard clearly at the opposite end about 450 feet away.

Temple of Jaguars   Near the southeastern corner of the main ball court is a small temple with serpent columns and carved panels showing warriors and jaguars. Up the flight of steps and inside the temple, a mural was found that chronicles a battle in a Maya village.

Temple of the Skulls (Tzompantli)   To the right of the ball court is the Temple of the Skulls with rows of skulls carved into the stone platform. When a sacrificial victim's head was cut off, it was stuck on a pole and displayed in a tidy row with others. As a symbol of the building's purpose, the architects provided these rows of skulls. Also carved into the stone are pictures of eagles tearing hearts from human victims. The word *Tzompantli* is not Maya but came from central Mexico. Reconstruction using scattered fragments may add a level to this platform and change the look of this structure by the time you visit.

Platform of the Eagles   Next to the Tzompantli, this small platform has reliefs showing eagles and jaguars clutching human hearts in their talons and claws, as well as a head coming out of the mouth of a serpent.

Platform of Venus   East of the Tzompantli and north of El Castillo near the road to the Sacred Cenote is the Platform of Venus. In Maya-Toltec lore, Venus was represented by a feathered monster or a feathered serpent with a human head in its mouth. It's also called the tomb of Chaac-Mool because a Chaac-Mool figure was discovered "buried" within the structure.

Sacred Cenote   Follow the dirt road (actually an ancient sacbe) that heads north from the Platform of Venus, and after 5 minutes you'll come to the great natural well that may have given Chichén-Itzá (the Well of the Itzáes) its name. This well was used for ceremonial purposes, not for drinking water, and according to legend, sacrificial victims were drowned in this pool to honor the rain god Chaac. Anatomical research done early this century by Ernest A. Hooten showed that bones of both children and adults were found in the well. Judging from Hooten's evidence, they may have been outcasts, diseased, or feeble-minded.

Edward Thompson, American consul in Mérida and a Harvard professor, bought the ruins of Chichén early this century, explored the cenote with dredges and divers, and exposed a fortune in gold and jade. Most of the riches wound up in Harvard's Peabody Museum of Archaeology and Ethnology. Later excavations in the 1960s brought up more treasure, and studies of the recovered objects show offerings from throughout the Yucatán and even farther away.

Temple of the Warriors (Templo de los Guerreros)   Due east of El Castillo is one of the most impressive structures at Chichén—the Temple of the Warriors—named for the carvings of warriors marching along its walls. It's also called the **Group of the Thousand Columns** for the many columns flanking it. During the recent restoration, hundreds more of the columns were rescued from the rubble and put in place, setting off the temple more magnificently than ever. Climb up the steep stairs at the front to reach a figure of Chaac-Mool and several impressive columns carved in relief to look like enormous feathered serpents. South of the temple was a square building that archaeologists called the **Market** (mercado). Its central court is surrounded by a colonnade. Beyond the temple and the market in the jungle are mounds of rubble, parts of which are being reconstructed.

The main Mérida–Cancún highway once ran straight through the ruins of Chichén, and though it has now been diverted, you can still see the great swath it cut. South and west of the old highway's path are more impressive ruined buildings.

Tomb of the High Priest (Tumba del Gran Sacerdote)   Past the refreshment stand to the right of the path is the Tomb of the High Priest, which stood atop a natural limestone cave in which skeletons and offerings were found, giving the temple its name.

This building has been reconstructed, and workers are unearthing other smaller temples in the area. As the work progresses, some buildings may be roped off and others will open to the public for the first time. It's fascinating to watch the archaeologists at work, meticulously numbering each stone as they take apart what appears to be a mound of rocks and then reassembling the stones into a recognizable structure.

Temple of the Grinding Stones (Casa de los Metates)   This building, the next one on your right, is named after the concave corn-grinding stones used by the Maya.

Temple of the Deer (Templo del Venado)   Past the House of Metates is this fairly tall though ruined building. The relief of a stag that gave the temple its name is long gone.

Little Holes (Chichan-chob)   This next temple has a roofcomb with little holes, three masks of the rain god Chaac, three rooms, and a good view of the surrounding structures. It's one of the older buildings at Chichén, built in the Puuc style during the Late Classic period.

The Maya Calendar

To understand Chichén-Itzá fully, you need to know something about the unique way in which the Maya kept time on several simultaneous calendars.

Although not more accurate than our own calendar, the intricate Maya calendar systems begin, according to many scholars, in 3114 B.C.—before Maya culture existed. From that date, the Maya could measure time—and their life cycle—to a point 90 million years in the future! They conceived of world history as a series of cycles moving within cycles.

The Solar Year   The Maya solar year measured 365.24 days. Within that solar year there were 18 "months" of 20 days each, for a total of 360 days, plus a special 5-day period.

The Ceremonial Year   A ceremonial calendar, completely different from the solar calendar, ran its "annual" cycle at the same time, but this was not a crude system like the Gregorian calendar, which has saints' days, some fixed feast days, and some movable feasts. It was so intricate that the ordinary Maya depended on the priests to keep track of it. Complex and ingenious, the ceremonial calendar system consisted of 13 "months" of 20 days; but within that cycle of 260 days were another of 20 "weeks" of 13 days. The Maya ceremonial calendar interlaced exactly with the solar calendar. Each date of the solar calendar had a name, and each date of the ceremonial calendar also had a name; therefore, every day in Maya history has two names, which were always quoted together.

The Double Cycle   After 52 solar years and 73 ceremonial "years," during which each day had its unique, unduplicated double name, these calendars ended their respective cycles simultaneously on the very same day, and a brand-new, identical double cycle began. Thus, in the longer scheme of things, a day would be identified by the name of the 52-year cycle, the name of the solar day, and the name of the ceremonial day.

Mystic Numbers   As you can see, several numbers were of great significance to the system. The number 20 was perhaps most important, as calendar calculations were done with a number system with base 20. There were 20 "suns" (days) to a "month," 20 years to a katun, and 20 katuns (20 times 20, or 400 years) to a baktun.

The number 52 was of tremendous importance, for it signified, literally, the "end of time," the end of the double cycle of solar and ceremonial calendars. At the beginning of a new cycle, temples were rebuilt for the "new age," which is why so many Maya temples and pyramids hold within them the structures of earlier, smaller temples and pyramids.

The Maya Concept of Time   The Maya considered time not as "progress" but as the wheel of fate, spinning endlessly, determining one's destiny by the combinations of attributes given to days in the solar and ceremonial calendars. The rains came on schedule, the corn was planted on schedule, and the celestial bodies moved in their great dance under the watchful eye of Maya astronomers and astrologers. *The Blood of Kings* (see "Recommended Books & Recordings" in chapter 2) has an especially good chapter on the Maya calendar.

As evidence of the Maya obsession with time, Chichén's most impressive structure, El Castillo, is an enormous "timepiece."

Observatory (El Caracol)   Construction of the Observatory, a complex building with a circular tower, was carried out over a long period of time. Without a doubt, the additions and modifications reflected the Maya's increasing knowledge of celestial movements and their need for increasingly exact measurements. Through slits in the tower's walls, Maya astronomers could observe the cardinal directions and the approach of the all-important spring and autumn equinoxes, as well as the summer solstice. The temple's name, which means "snail," comes from a spiral staircase, now closed off, within the structure.

On the east side of El Caracol, a path leads north into the bush to the **Cenote Xtoloc,** a natural limestone well that provided the city's daily water supply. If you see any lizards sunning there, they may well be *xtoloc,* the lizard for which the cenote is named.

Temple of Panels (Templo de los Tableros)   Just to the south of El Caracol are the ruins of a **steambath** (*temazcalli*) and the Temple of Panels, named for the carved panels on top. This temple was once covered by a much larger structure, only traces of which remain.

Edifice of the Nuns (Edificio de las Monjas)   If you've visited the Puuc sites of Kabah, Sayil, Labná, or Xlapak, the enormous nunnery here will remind you at once of the "palaces" at the other sites. Built in the Late Classic period, the new edifice was constructed over an older one. Suspecting that this was so, Le Plongeon, an archaeologist working earlier in this century, put dynamite in between the two and blew part of the newer building to smithereens, thereby revealing part of the old. You can still see the results of Le Plongeon's indelicate exploratory methods.

On the eastern side of the Edifice of the Nuns is an annex (Anexo Este) constructed in highly ornate Chenes style with Chaac masks and serpents.

The Church (La Iglesia)   Next to the annex is one of the oldest buildings at Chichén, ridiculously named the Church. Masks of Chaac decorate two upper stories. Look closely and you'll see among the crowd of Chaacs an armadillo, a crab, a snail, and a tortoise. These represent the Maya gods called *bacab,* whose job it was to hold up the sky.

Temple of Obscure Writing (Akab Dzib)   This temple is along a path east of the Edifice of the Nuns. Above a door in one of the rooms are some Maya glyphs, which gave the temple its name, since the writings have yet to be deciphered. In other rooms, traces of red handprints are still visible. Reconstructed and expanded over the centuries, this building has parts that are very old; it may well be the oldest building at Chichén.

Old Chichén (Chichén Viejo)   For a look at more of Chichén's oldest buildings, constructed well before the time of Toltec influence, follow signs from the Edifice of the Nuns southwest into the bush to Old Chichén, about half a mile away. Be prepared for this trek with long trousers, insect repellent, and a local guide. The attractions here are the **Temple of the First Inscriptions** (Templo de los Inscripciones Iniciales), with the oldest inscriptions discovered at Chichén, and the restored **Temple of the Lintels** (Templo de los Dinteles), a fine Puuc building.

WHERE TO STAY

It's difficult to reach Chichén and Pisté by phone; however, many hotels have reservation services in Mérida or in Mexico City.

EXPENSIVE

Hacienda Chichén-Itzá. Zona Arqueológica, 97751 Chichén-Itzá, Yuc. ☎ **985/6-2513** or 985/6-2462. Reservations: Casa del Balam, Calle 60 no. 48, 97000 Mérida, Yuc; ☎ 800/624-

8451 in the U.S., or 99/24-8844. Fax 99/24-5011. 18 rms. FAN. $80–$110 double. Closed off-season.

A romantic hotel a short walk from the back entrance to the ruins, the Hacienda Chichén-Itzá consists of bungalows built years ago for those who were excavating the ruins. Each cottage is named for an early archaeologist working at Chichén. There's a pool open to those who drop in for lunch. The dining room is outside under the hacienda portals overlooking the grounds. But any meal is expensive.

The hacienda is closed from May through October, though the owners were reconsidering this policy, and it may be open year-round. It's often booked solid in the high season; advance reservations are strongly recommended.

○ **Hotel Mayaland.** Zona Arqueológica, 97751 Chichén-Itzá, Yuc. ☎ **985/6-2777.** Reservations: Mayaland Resorts, Av. Colón 502, 97000 Mérida, Yuc; ☎ 800/235-4079 in the U.S., or 99/25-2122; Fax 99/25-7022. 164 rms. A/C or FAN TV. High season $165 double. Low season $120 double. Free guarded parking.

In operation since the 1930s, this is a longtime favorite by the ruins. No other hotel quite captures the feel of a ruins experience, with the front doorway framing El Caracol (the observatory) as you walk outside from the lobby. Rooms in the main building, connected by a wide, tiled veranda, have air-conditioning and TV, tiled baths (with tubs), and colonial-style furnishings. Romantic oval Maya huts with beautifully carved furniture, palapa roofs, and mosquito netting are tucked around the wooded grounds. The grounds are gorgeous, with huge trees and blossoming ginger plants. There's a long pool and lounge area, and a restaurant that serves only fair meals at fixed prices. Mayaland has a shuttle service between the hotel and Mérida for about $35 each way.

The Hotel Mayaland is a great bargain if you take advantage of their rental-car deal. If you stay at one of their hotels and rent a car through their office in Mérida or Cancún, your car rental is free with no minimum stay. There is a charge for car insurance, however.

○ **Hotel Villa Arqueológica.** Zona Arqueológica, 97751 Chichén-Itzá, Yuc. ☎ **800/258-2633** in the U.S., or 985/6-2830. 32 rms. A/C. High season $110 double. Low season $70 double.

Operated by Club Med, the Villa Arqueológica is almost next to the ruins and built around a swimming pool. The very comfortable rooms are like those at Uxmal and Cobá, each with two oversize single beds. There are tennis courts, and the hotel's rather expensive restaurant features French and Yucatecan food.

MODERATE

Pirámide Inn. Km 117 Carretera Mérida–Valladolid, 97751 Pisté, Yuc. ☎ and fax **985/1-0059.** 44 rms. A/C. $35–$40 double.

Less than a mile from the ruins at the edge of Pisté, this hospitable inn has large motel-like rooms equipped with two double beds or one king-size bed; but do check your mattress for its sag factor before accepting the room. Hot water comes on between 5 and 9am and 5 and 9pm. Water is purified in the tap for drinking. There is a pool in the midst of landscaped gardens, which include the remains of a pyramid wall. Try to get a room in the back if street noise bothers you. If you're coming from Valladolid, it's on the left, and from Mérida look for it on the right.

Stardust Inn. Calle 15A no. 34A, Carretera Mérida–Valladolid, 97751 Pisté, Yuc. ☎ and fax **985/1-0122.** Reservations: Calle 81A no. 513, 97000 Mérida, Yuc; ☎ 99/84-0072. 53 rms. AC TV. $35–$40 double. Free guarded parking.

The two-story Stardust Inn is built around a pool and a shaded courtyard. Each of the comfortable rooms has a tile floor, a shower, nice towels, and one or two double beds or three single beds; check the condition of your mattress before selecting a room. During high season there's a video bar/disco on the first floor; it's open during other times of the year if there are groups. If tranquillity is one of your priorities, ask if the disco is functioning before you rent a room. The very nice air-conditioned restaurant adjacent to the lobby and facing the highway serves all three meals and is open from 7:30am to 9:30pm.

INEXPENSIVE

Hotel Dolores Alba. Km 122 Carretera Mérida–Valladolid, 97751 Pisté, Yuc. No phone. Reservations: Hotel Dolores Alba, Calle 63 no. 464, 97000 Mérida, Yuc; ☎ **99/28-5650;** fax 99/28-3163. E-mail: asanchez@yucatan.com.mx. 30 rms. A/C or FAN. $20–$25 double. Free unguarded parking.

You'll be a mile from the back entrance to the ruins and about 2 miles from Pisté if you stay at the Dolores Alba. The nice rooms are clean with matching furniture, tile floors and showers, and well-screened windows. Plus you can cool off after a day clambering around the ruins in the refreshing pool in front of the restaurant. The restaurant serves good meals at moderate prices. Free transportation is provided to the ruins and the Caves of Balanche during visiting hours, but you'll have to get back on your own. Taxis are also available at the ruins and in Pisté for around $4 one-way. The Dolores Alba in Mérida, also recommended, is owned by the same family, so either hotel will help you make reservations. The hotel is 1¹/₂ miles past the ruins on the road going east to Cancún and Valladolid.

Posada Chac Mool. Carretera Mérida–Valladolid, 97751 Pisté, Yuc. No phone. 8 rms. FAN. $12 double. Limited free, unguarded parking.

Clean and plain, this no-frills, single-story motel opened in 1990. The basically furnished rooms have new mattresses on the beds, red-tile floors, and well-screened windows. Little tables and chairs outside each room on the covered walkway make a pleasant place to read or enjoy a self-made meal. The motel is located at Calle 15, next to the Restaurant Las Mestizas, and almost opposite Hotel Misión.

Posada Novelo. Carretera Mérida–Valladolid, 97751 Pisté, Yuc. ☎ and fax **985/1-0122.** 11 rms. FAN. $10 double. Free parking in front.

Operated by the Stardust Inn next door, this very basic hotel may serve you well if your budget is more important than a status address. Rooms, attached in a row and linked by a covered walkway, all have one or two beds and are sparsely furnished but clean. Hot water is a rarity.

WHERE TO DINE

Reasonably priced meals are available at the restaurant in the visitor's center at the ruins and at the better hotels in Pisté. Hotel restaurants near the ruins are more expensive. In Pisté, however, most of the better spots cater to large groups, which converge on them for lunch after 1pm.

Cafetería Ruinas. In the Chichén-Itzá visitors' center. No phone. Breakfast $4; sandwiches $4–$5; main courses $5–$8. Daily 9am–5pm. MEXICAN/ITALIAN.

Though it has the monopoly on food at the ruins, this cafeteria actually does a good job with such basic meals as enchiladas, spaghetti, and baked chicken. Eggs are cooked to order, as are burgers, and their coffee is very good. Sit outside at the tables farthest from the crowd and relax.

La Fiesta. Carretera Mérida–Valladolid, Pisté. No phone. Main courses $4–$6; comida corrida $6.50. Daily 7am–9pm (comida corrida served 12:30–5pm). REGIONAL/MEXICAN.

With Maya motifs on the wall and colorful decorations, this is one of Pisté's long-established restaurants catering especially to tour groups. Though expensive, the food is very good. You'll be quite satisfied unless you arrive when a tour group is being served, in which case service to individual diners may suffer. Going toward the ruins, La Fiesta is on the west end of town.

Puebla Maya. Carretera Mérida–Valladolid, Pi_sté. No phone. Fixed-price lunch buffet $7. Daily 1–5pm. MEXICAN.

Opposite the Pirámide Inn, the Puebla Maya looks just like its name, a Maya town with small white huts flanking a large open-walled palapa-topped center. Inside, however, you cross an artificial lagoon, planters drip with greenery, and live musicians play to the hundreds of tourists filling the tables. Service through the huge buffet is quick, so if you've been huffing around the ruins all morning, you have time to eat and relax before boarding the bus to wherever you're going. You can even swim in a lovely landscaped pool.

Restaurant Bar "Poxil." Calle 15 s/n, Carretera Mérida–Valladolid, Pi_sté. ☎ **985/1-0123.** Breakfast $3–$4; main courses $3–$5. Daily 7am–8pm. MEXICAN/REGIONAL.

A *poxil* is a Mayan fruit somewhat akin to a guanabana. Although this place doesn't serve them, what is on the menu is good, though not gourmet, and the price is right. You will find the Poxil near the west entrance to town on the south side of the street.

A SIDE TRIP TO THE GRUTAS (CAVES) DE BALANKANCHE

The Grutas de Balankanche are $3^1/_2$ miles from Chichén-Itzá on the road to Cancún and Puerto Juárez. Taxis will make the trip and wait, but they are also usually on hand when the tours let out. The entire excursion takes about half an hour, and the walk inside is hot and humid. The natural caves became wartime hideaways for the Mayas. You can still see traces of carving and incense burning, as well as an underground stream that served as the sanctuary's water supply. Outside, take time to meander through the botanical gardens, where most of the plants and trees are labeled with their common and scientific names.

The caves are open daily. Admission is $5; free on Sunday. Use of your video camera will cost an additional $4. Children under 6 are not admitted. Guided tours in English are at 11am and 1 and 3pm, and in Spanish, at 9am, noon, and 2 and 4pm. Tours go only if there are a minimum of 6 people and take up to 30 people at a time. Double-check these hours at the main entrance to the Chichén ruins.

6 Valladolid

25 miles E of Chichén-Itzá and Pisté, 100 miles SW of Cancún

The somewhat sleepy town of Valladolid (pronounced *bye*-ah-doh-*leet*), 25 miles east of Pisté/Chichén-Itzá, is an inexpensive alternative to staying in Pisté, which is near the ruins of Chichén. You can get an early bus from Mérida, spend the day at the ruins, then travel another hour to Valladolid to overnight.

ESSENTIALS
GETTING THERE & DEPARTING
BY BUS   Buses leave almost hourly from Mérida, passing through Pisté and Chichén-Itzá on the way to Valladolid and Cancún. There are also regular buses from Cancún and at least six daily buses from Playa del Carmen. Because of the frequency of buses to Mérida and Cancún, advance purchase of tickets isn't usually necessary.

Autotransportes Oriente offers de paso buses to Pisté (the town nearest the Chichén-Itzá ruins) every hour from 2am to midnight; these same buses go on to Mérida. De paso buses on this same line go to Cobá at 4:30am and 1pm. Buses to

Centuries of Conflict: Spanish & Maya in the Yucatán

Though Spanish conquerors landed in Yucatán as early as 1511, the conquest of Yucatán began in 1526, 5 years after the completion of the conquest of Mexico in 1521. The Maya were fervid in their opposition to the Spaniards and so the Yucatán conquest took 20 years. It was finally achieved by three men, all with the same name: Francisco de Montejo, the Elder (also called El Adelantado, the pioneer), who started the process; his son, Francisco Montejo, the Younger (known as El Mozo, the lad); and a cousin. Montejo the Elder sailed from Spain in 1527 with 400 soldiers and landed at Cozumel but was forced to relaunch his campaign from the western coast, where he could more easily receive supplies from New Spain (Mexico).

From Mexico, he conquered what is now the state of Tabasco (1530), pushing onward to the Yucatán. But after 4 difficult years (1531–35) he was forced to return to Mexico penniless and exhausted. In 1540, Montejo the Younger and his cousin (another Francisco de Montejo) took over the cause, successfully establishing a town at Campeche and another at Mérida (1542); by 1546, virtually all of the peninsula was under their control.

A few weeks after the founding of Mérida, the greatest of the several Mayan leaders, Ah Kukum Xiú, head of the Xiú people, offered himself as Montejo's vassal and was baptized, giving himself the name Francisco de Montejo Xiú. With the help of Montejo's troops, Montejo the Younger and his cousin then accomplished their objective, the defeat of the Cocoms. By allying his people with the Spaniards, Xiú triumphed over the Cocoms but surrendered the freedom of the Yucatecan Maya. In later centuries warfare, disease, slavery, and emigration all led to the decline of the peninsula's population. Fray Diego de Landa, second bishop of Yucatán, destroyed much of the history of the Maya culture when he ordered the mass destruction of the priceless Maya codices, or "painted books," at Maní in 1562; only three survived.

The Yucatán struggled along under the heavy yoke of Spanish colonial administration until the War of Independence (begun in 1810) liberated Mexico and the Yucatán in 1821. In that same year, the Spanish governor of the Yucatán resigned, and the Yucatán, too, became an independent country. Though the Yucatán decided to join in a union with Mexico 2 years later, this period of sovereignty is testimony to the Yucatecan spirit of independence. That same spirit arose again in 1846 when the Yucatán seceded from Mexico.

Tizimin leave every hour from 5am to 10pm. **Expresso de Oriente** buses go to Mérida six times daily, to Playa del Carmen six times daily, and to Cancún five times daily. **Autobuses del Centro del Estado** offers five daily buses to Tinum and several other small towns on the way to Mérida.

BY CAR   From Valladolid, there are frequent signs directing you via the toll road (*cuota*) to Mérida, Chichén-Itzá, or Cancún. No signs point you to the free (*libre*) road, but don't despair. To take the free road to Pisté/Chichén-Itzá and Mérida, take Calle 39, a one-way street going west on the north side of the Parque Cantón (the main plaza); this becomes the free Highway 180. Calle 41, a one-way east-bound street on the south side of the zócalo, becomes the free highway to Cancún.

Highway 180 links Valladolid with both Cancún and Mérida. It's a good, well-marked road and goes right past the main square in town. If you come from the toll road, the exit road leads to the Parque Cantón (the main plaza).

After the war, sugarcane and henequen cultivation were introduced on a large scale, organized around vast landed estates called haciendas, each employing hundreds of Maya virtually as slaves. During the war for secession, weapons were issued to the Maya to defend independent Yucatán against attack from Mexico or the United States. The Maya turned these same weapons on their local oppressors, setting off the **War of the Castes** in 1847.

The Maya ruthlessly attacked and sacked Valladolid and strengthened their forces with guns and ammunition bought from British merchants in Belize (British Honduras). By June 1848, they held virtually all the Yucatán except Mérida and Campeche—and Mérida's governor had already decided to abandon the city.

Then followed one of the strangest occurrences in Yucatecan history. It was time to plant the corn, and the Maya fighters dropped their weapons and went off to tend the fields. Meanwhile, Mexico sent reinforcements in exchange for the Yucatán's resubmission to Mexican authority. Government troops took the offensive, driving many of the Maya to the wilds of Quintana Roo, in the southeastern reaches of the peninsula.

Massed in southern Quintana Roo, the Maya, seeking inspiration in their war effort, followed the cult of the Talking Crosses, which was started in 1850 by a Maya ventriloquist and a mestizo "priest," who carried on a tradition of "talking idols" that had flourished for centuries in several places, including Cozumel. The "talking cross" first appeared at Chan Santa Cruz (today's Felipe Carrillo Puerto), and soon several crosses were talking and inspiring the Maya.

The Yucatecan authorities seemed content to let the rebels and their talking crosses rule the southern Caribbean coast, which they did with only minor skirmishes until the late 1800s. The rebel government received arms from the British in Belize, and in return allowed the British to cut lumber in rebel territory.

At the turn of the century, Mexican troops with modern weapons penetrated the rebel territory, soon putting an end to this bizarre, if romantic, episode of Yucatecan history.

The town of Chan Santa Cruz was renamed in honor of a Yucatecan governor, Felipe Carrillo Puerto, and the Yucatán was finally a full and integral part of Mexico, although the eastern side was sparsely inhabited and a sort of no-man's land.

ORIENTATION

VISITOR INFORMATION   There is a small tourism office in the Palacio Municipal that will furnish you with some good information and maps. Señora Tete Mendoza B. is extremely helpful and knows her city and its history.

CITY LAYOUT   All hotels and restaurants are within walking distance of Valladolid's pretty **main square,** the **Parque Francisco Cantón Rosado.** The Valladolid **bus station** is at the corner of calles 37 and 57, 10 very long blocks from the parque and too far to haul heavy luggage. Taxis are usually in front of the station.

AREA CODE   The telephone area code is **985.**

EXPLORING VALLADOLID

Valladolid was founded in 1543 on the shore of a lagoon near the coast. As it lacked good agricultural land, 2 years later it was moved to its present location on the site of a Maya religious center called Zací (meaning "white hawk"). The Franciscans built an impressive monastery here, the **Convento de San Bernardino de Siena** (1552); the town boasts another half-dozen colonial churches, including the Templo de Santa Ana built in the 1500s originally for the exclusive use of the Maya. Two **cenotes,** one only 2 blocks east of the Parque Cantón, supplied water during colonial times. A small park—with a restaurant, a small bowl for the performing arts, and three Maya-style stick-and-thatched-roof houses—has been created around the cenote Zací. These houses are meant to depict a typical Maya settlement, and inside are some old photographs of Valladolid and a few arts and crafts for sale. **El Parroquia de San Servasio** (1545), the parish church, is on the south side of the main square, and the **Palacio Municipal** (Town Hall) is on the east.

SHOPPING

Embroidered Maya dresses can be purchased at the **Mercado de Artesanías de Valladolid** at the corner of calles 39 and 44 and from women around the main square. The latter also sell—of all things—Barbie-doll-size Maya dresses! Just ask "¿Vestidos para Barbie?" and out they come.

The **food market** is on Calle 32 between calles 35 and 37. Though it's open other days, the main market time is Sunday morning, when it's most active.

WHERE TO STAY

Hotels (and restaurants) here are less crowded and less expensive than the competition in Chichén.

Hotel El Mesón del Marqués. Calle 39 no. 203, 97780 Valladolid, Yuc. ☎ **985/6-3042** or 985/6-2073. Fax 985/6-2280. 38 rms. A/C FAN TV TEL. $37 double; $47 suite. Free interior parking; secure.

This comfortable colonial-era mansion-turned-hotel offers rooms in both the original 200-year-old mansion and a new addition built around a pool in back. There is always hot water, and most of the rooms are sheltered from city noise. On the first floor there's a travel agency, gift shop, and restaurant (see "Where to Dine," below). It's on the north side of the Parque Cantón opposite the church.

Hotel María de la Luz. Calle 42 no. 195, 97780 Valladolid, Yuc. ☎ and fax **985/6-2071.** 33 rms. A/C FAN TV. $18 double. Free parking; secure.

The two stories at the María de la Luz are built around an inner swimming pool and a lobby restaurant. The freshly painted rooms have been refurbished with new tile floors and baths and new mattresses. A couple of rooms have balconies overlooking the square. The wide interior covered walkway to the rooms is a nice place to relax in comfortable chairs. The hotel is on the west side of the Parque Francisco Cantón Rosado (the main square) between calles 39 and 41.

WHERE TO DINE

The lowest restaurant prices are found in the Bazar Municipal, a little arcade of shops beside the Hotel El Mesón del Marqués (see "Where to Stay," above) right on the Parque Cantón. The cookshops open at mealtimes, when tables and chairs are set in the courtyard. You won't find many printed menus, let alone one in English, but a quick look around will tell you what's cooking, and you can order with a discreetly pointed finger. Ask the price beforehand so you won't be overcharged.

Hostería del Marqués. Calle 39 no. 203. ☎ **985/6-2073.** Breakfast $3–$5; main courses 3.50–$7. Daily 7am–11:30pm. MEXICAN/YUCATECAN.

This place is part of the Hotel El Mesón del Marqués, facing the main square. Its patrons often spill out of the air-conditioned dining room onto the hotel's open *portales* on the interior courtyard, where tables have fresh flowers and are festively decorated in hot pink and turquoise. It's definitely a popular place, often crowded at lunch. The guacamole is great.

SIDE TRIPS FROM VALLADOLID
CENOTE DZITNUP

The Cenote Dzitnup (also known as Cenote Xkeken), 2¹/₂ miles west of Valladolid off Highway 180, is worth a visit, especially if you have time for a dip. Descend a short flight of rather perilous stone steps, and at the bottom, inside a beautiful cavern, is a natural pool of water so clear and blue it's like something from a dream. If you decide to take a swim, be sure you don't have creams or other chemicals on your skin, as they damage the habitat for the small fish and other organisms living there. Also, no alcohol, food, or smoking is allowed after you enter the cavern.

Admission is $1. The cenote is open daily from 8am to 5pm.

EKBALAM: NEWLY EXCAVATED MAYA RUINS

About 21 miles northeast of Valladolid is Ekbalam (which in Maya means "star jaguar"), a newly opened archaeological site. Excavations of these ruins, which date from 100 B.C. to A.D. 1200, are ongoing.

To get here from Valladolid, go north on Highway 295 for 11 miles. Watch for the sign pointing right to the village of **Hunuku** and turn right there, following the road for 8¹/₂ miles. When you reach Hunuku, a small village, ask someone to point to the dirt road that leads about 1¹/₂ miles to the ruins. Caretaker Felipe Tuz Cohuo or willing young children can point out the highlights (the children have absorbed a lot of information during the years the ruins have been excavated). A tip to the caretaker is greatly appreciated. Pencils or ballpoint pens are good gifts for the children.

To really get a lot out of this site, you should be prepared to climb up the mountain-like pyramids with sides made of loose dirt and even looser rocks. Some of the important parts can also be seen from the pathway, but climbing is much more rewarding.

You can park at the entry sign and walk from there. Located on 2,500 wooded acres, the buildings are grouped closely around a large central area; along 350 feet of the perimeter are the remains of two low walls. The largest building, called **structure 1**, or the **Tower**, is impressive for its dimensions—it's 100 feet high, 517 feet long, and 200 feet wide. From the top you can see the tallest building of Cobá, 30 miles southeast as the crow flies. Scholars believe that Ekbalam was the center of a vast agricultural region. From this lofty vantage point, all around you can see fertile land that still produces corn, cotton, and honey.

Structure 3, also called the **Palace of the Nuns**, has a row of corbel-arched rooms. Though greatly destroyed, this architecture resembles the Puuc style of other Yucatecan sites. A few badly weathered stela fragments are on display under flimsy thatched coverings. Structures show partial walls, some made of irregular rocks and others of carefully fitted and cut rock. Sacbeob (causeways) fan out in several directions, but so far none is thought to go farther than a mile or so. If you do any climbing at all, seeing the area will take a minimum of 2 hours.

The site is open daily from 8am to 5pm. Admission is $1.75; free on Sunday. A video camera permit costs $4.

Río Lagartos Nature Reserve: Nesting Flamingos

Some 50 miles north of Valladolid (25 miles north of Tizimin) on Highway 295 is Río Lagartos, a 118,000-acre refuge established in 1979 to protect the largest nesting population of flamingos in North America. Found in the park's dunes, mangrove swamps, and tropical forests are jaguars, ocelots, sea turtles, and at least 212 bird species (141 of which are permanent residents).

You can make the trip in one long day from Valladolid, but you'll have to leave by at least 5am to get to Río Lagartos by 7am, in time to arrange a trip to see the flamingos with one of the local boatmen. There's one poor-quality hotel in Río Lagartos, which I don't recommend. If you prefer to overnight closer to the refuge, then a good choice is **Tizimin** (pop. 50,000), 35 miles north of Valladolid. This pleasant city is the agricultural hub of the region. From Tizimin to Río Lagartos is about a 30-minute drive. Inexpensive hotels and restaurants are on or around Tizimin's main square.

SEEING THE RÍO LAGARTOS REFUGE   Río Lagartos is a small fishing village of around 3,000 people who make their living from the sea and from the occasional tourist who shows up to see the flamingos. Colorfully painted homes face the Malecón (the oceanfront street), and brightly painted boats dock along the same half-moon–shaped port. While Río Lagartos bird-watching is interesting, if you have time for only one flamingo foray, make it in Celestún (west of Mérida). I've seen more flamingos and other kinds of birds at Celestún.

Plan to arrive in Río Lagartos around 7am and go straight to the dock area. There, boatmen will offer to take you on an hour-long trip to the flamingo lagoons for around $30 for up to six people in a motor-powered wooden boat. Ask around for Filiberto Pat Zem, a reliable boatman who takes the time to give a good tour.

Although thousands of flamingos nest near here from April to August, it is prohibited by law to visit their nesting grounds. Flamingos need mud with particular ingredients (including a high salt content) in order to multiply, and this area's mud does the trick. On your boat tour you'll probably see flamingos wading in the waters next to Mexico's second-largest salt-producing plant—the muddy bottom is plenty salty here. Flamingos use their special bills to suck up the mud, and they have the ability to screen the special contents they need from it. What you see on the boat trip is a mixture of flamingos, frigates, pelicans, herons in several colors, and ducks. Don't allow the boatman to frighten the birds into flight for your photographs; it causes the birds to eventually leave the habitat permanently.

Tabasco & Chiapas 7

Technically not part of the Yucatán Peninsula, though adjacent to it, these two states, along with the Yucatán Peninsula, complete **Mexico's Maya route.** Travelers to the Yucatán frequently continue their journey by venturing into the completely different geography and culture of the states of Tabasco and Chiapas. Conversely, those beginning in Chiapas often top off their Chiapas and Tabasco travels by heading to the peninsula for further ruins exploration combined with lazing on one of Mexico's famous Caribbean beaches.

These neighbor states span the distance from the Gulf of Mexico to the Pacific Ocean. **Tabasco** and its cities have profited from the oil trade along its coast; the state is also noted for its production of tobacco and cacao. And Tabasco, because of the oil trade, is more affected by the modern world than Chiapas, which is hemmed in by majestic mountains and an undeveloped coast. **Chiapas** produces cacao too, and some of the best coffee in Mexico. Both states boast important indigenous influences. The famous Olmec site of La Venta is in Tabasco state; the contents of that site have been removed to the famous **Museo Olmeca de la Venta** in **Villahermosa,** which showcases the Olmec civilization, a precursor to the Maya civilization. Tabasco's lowland Maya are less obvious, since they've primarily adopted western clothing, though they still speak Cholan, a Maya language. Villahermosa is also a main route to the ruins of **Palenque** and an important gateway to **San Cristóbal de las Casas,** both in the state of Chiapas. The Maya of highland Chiapas, on the other hand, are quite evident by their everyday use of indigenous clothing, their customs, festivals, villages, and four primary languages—Cholan, Tojolobal, Tzotzil, and Tzeltal. The latter two languages are often heard around San Cristóbal de las Casas, which is surrounded by indigenous villages, each of which has unique language, cultural, and craft traditions.

EXPLORING TABASCO & CHIAPAS

There are several ways to access the Tabasco-Chiapas region. Some people arrive at Villahermosa from Campeche, Mérida, Cancún, or Mexico City and go inland by bus to Palenque and San Cristóbal, and onward by bus to Tuxtla Gutiérrez to leave the region. This works well if you are coming from or going to Oaxaca, Mexico City, or Cancún, since there are direct flights from Tuxtla to these major cities. Villahermosa, too, is a major airline hub, and access to it may be more convenient than to Tuxtla. Bus travel is also an option. Others take the opposite approach, beginning at Mexico City, Cancún, or Oaxaca and flying to Tuxtla Gutiérrez, and from there traveling by bus to San Cristóbal, Palenque, and Villahermosa where they continue their journey by air or bus. This works well if you'll be moving on to the Yucatán Peninsula.

Palenque and San Cristóbal de las Casas are the two stellar attractions in the Tabasco-Chiapas area. You might budget your time in the following manner: Spend 1 day in Villahermosa and no less than a day (2 nights) at Palenque. You'll want at least 2 days amid San Cristóbal's captivating culture and another 2 days to visit the outlying villages—try to spend at least 4 days there. I've spent much longer in Palenque and as much as 2 weeks in San Cristóbal without running low on something to do and especially to see. And finally, for those of you with a love of birds, tote your bird books, for the creatures abound, especially around Palenque.

1 Villahermosa

89 miles NW of Palenque, 293 miles SW of Campeche, 100 miles N of San Cristóbal de las Casas

Villahermosa (pop. 265,000), the capital of the state of Tabasco, is right at the center of Mexico's oil boom, but it's off-center from just about everything else. Were it not for oil, the city's proximity to the ruins of Palenque, and several good museums, visitors would have little reason to come here. Nevertheless, oil wealth has helped transform this dowdy provincial town into a more attractive and obviously prosperous modern city, making it a comfortable crossroads in your Mexican journeys.

Prosperity has recently brought the city a number of developments, including a beautiful park surrounding the Parque-Museo de la Venta; a high-class business, residence, and hotel development called Tabasco 2000 (containing gleaming office buildings, a convention center, golf course, and exclusive residences); the CICOM development, with theaters and the **Museo Regional de Antropología Carlos Pellicer Camara;** and the pedestrians-only shopping area along Avenida Benito Juárez. You really shouldn't miss the **Parque-Museo de la Venta,** which contains the Olmec remains found at La Venta northwest of Villahermosa.

ESSENTIALS
GETTING THERE & DEPARTING

BY PLANE   Because it's a business center, Villahermosa is unusually well-connected by air with most major places in Mexico. **Mexicana** (☎ **93/16-3785** or 93/16-3132; at the airport 93/12-1164) flies to Villahermosa from Mexico City, Tuxtla Gutiérrez, and Guadalajara. **Aeroméxico** (☎ **93/12-1528;** at the airport 93/14-1675) flies from Mexico City, Guadalajara, Mérida, Acapulco, and U.S. gateways. **Aviación de Chiapas (Aviacsa)** (☎ **93/14-5770** or 93/14-5780; at the airport 93/14-4755) flies to and from Mérida, Mexico City, Tuxtla Gutiérrez, and Oaxaca. **AeroLitoral,** another regional airline and a subsidiary of Aeroméxico, is at the airport (☎ **93/ 12-6991**) and serves the route to and from Veracruz, Tampico, Minatitlán, Ciudad del Carmen, and Monterrey. **Aerocaribe** (☎ **93/16-5046;** fax 93/16-5047), a Mexicana affiliate, serves Cancún, Cozumel, Tuxtla Gutiérrez, Oaxaca, and Mérida.

BY BUS   The two bus stations in Villahermosa are about 5 blocks apart. The first-class **ADO** station is at Mina and Merino, 3 blocks off Highway 180. This nice bus station has a clean waiting area, luggage storage, souvenir shops, and snack bars. Buses for most destinations leave from here, and the station houses many lines. Most ticket booths offer computerized ticketing, and you can look at the computer screen and select your seat. Eight first-class ADO buses leave for Palenque (3 hours) between

6am and 7:45pm. Deluxe service to Palenque (2 hours) leaves at 8am and 1:30pm. Additional first-class buses go to Mexico City and most major Gulf Coast cities. **Autotransportes Cristóbal Colón** has seven daily buses to Tuxtla Gutiérrez (passing through Palenque and San Cristóbal de las Casas), Tapachula, Oaxaca, and Mexico City. **UNO** runs luxury buses with 25 seats, smoking and no-smoking sections, self-service refreshments, video movies, and air-conditioning. They go to Mexico City, Veracruz, Puebla, and Mérida. You can reserve seats up to 2 days in advance.

The **Central Camionera de Segunda Clase** (second-class bus station) is on Highway 180/186, about 5 blocks from the ADO station. From the second-class bus station you go to Tuxtla, Campeche, and Mérida. **Servicio Somellera** (☎ 93/12-3973) goes to Comalcalco every 30 minutes. **Autobuses Unidos de Tabasco** travels to Veracruz and Mexico City. Be forewarned that this bus station is horrid and the buses are even worse.

BY CAR   Paved Highway 195 connects the Tabascan capital of Villahermosa with Tuxtla Gutiérrez, the capital of the state of Chiapas. Between these cities lie Palenque and San Cristóbal de las Casas. The road to Palenque is a good one, and the drive should take about 2 hours. Between Villahermosa and San Cristóbal de las Casas, the road, although paved, sometimes has stretches with many potholes. Often a portion of the roadway caves in and traffic slows to one lane to avoid it; these conditions occur more frequently during the rainy season between May and October. The trip to San Cristóbal takes a minimum of 5 hours from Villahermosa. The paved, mountainous (and very curvy) road between San Cristóbal and Tuxtla is in good condition, and the trip takes about 1 1/2 hours.

The drive between Villahermosa and Chetumal (about 350 miles) can seem interminable if the road is in poor condition. And vast parts of it are quite lonely; the U.S. State Department includes this road on its warning list due to car and bus hijackings. If you take it, one possible stopover between the two would be at Xpujil, 62 miles west of Chetumal. (See "West of Bacalar: The Río Bec Ruin Route" in chapter 5.) Another potential stopover is Francisco Escárcega, but only in an emergency. Once here, you're not too far from wherever you're going.

ORIENTATION

ARRIVING   Coming in from Villahermosa's airport, which is 6 1/2 miles east of town, you'll cross a bridge over the Río Grijalva; turn left to reach downtown. Both multi-passenger minibuses and private taxis are available for transportation into the city, with the minibus costing the least. However, don't linger in the terminal and expect a minibus to still be at the curb when you're ready. Minibuses leave when they fill up and only taxis will be available.

From the bus station, local buses marked "Mercad–C. Camionera" or simply "Centro" leave frequently for the center of town. Taxis are readily available in front of the station.

Parking downtown can be difficult, but there are several parking lots near the hotels I recommend below. Use one that's guarded around the clock.

VISITOR INFORMATION   The best source of information is at the **State Tourism Office** in the Tabasco 2000 complex, Paseo Tabasco 1504, SEFICOT Building, Centro Administrativo del Gobierno (☎ 93/16-3633 or 93/16-2890). Inconveniently located opposite the Liverpool department store and an enclosed shopping center on the second floor of the building, it's open Monday through Friday from 8am to 4pm. There are two other branches—the **airport office** is staffed daily from 10am to 5pm, and **La Venta Park** has an office open Tuesday through

Sunday from 10am to 5pm. The staff can supply rates and telephone numbers for the hotels, as well as useful telephone numbers for bus companies and airlines.

CITY LAYOUT   The hotels and restaurants I recommend are located off the main streets: **Madero, Pino Suárez,** the **Malecón,** and **Grijalva/Ruíz Cortinez.** Highway 180 skirts the city, so a turn onto Madero or Pino Suárez will take you into the center of town.

Your point of reference in town can be **Plaza Juárez,** or the main square, bounded by the streets Zaragoza, Madero, Sánchez, and Carranza. The plaza is just off the center of the downtown district, at the north end of the pedestrian zone, with the Río Grijalva to its east and Highway 186 to its north. Within this area is the **pedestrian zone,** with roads closed to traffic for 5 blocks. This zone is often called **Centro,** or **Zona Luz.** At the south end of the pedestrian zone is the **Plaza de Armas** bounded by 27 de Febrero, Guerrero, Maquiliz, and Independencia, and with the Palacio de Gobierno at its north end. Villahermosa's main thoroughfare is **Avenida Madero,** running south from Highway 186 past the Plaza Juárez to the river, where it intersects with the riverside avenue, the **Malecón.** I have used the Plaza Juárez, Plaza de Armas, and the popular Restaurant Galerías Madan as points of reference.

GETTING AROUND   All the **city buses** converge on Avenida Pino Suárez at the market and are clearly labeled for Tabasco 2000, Parque La Venta, and Centro.

Taxis from the center of town to main sites such as the Parque La Venta are inexpensive. If you're getting around **by car,** you'll be glad to know that Villahermosa's streets are well marked, with arrows clearly designating the direction of traffic.

FAST FACTS: VILLAHERMOSA   **American Express** is represented by Turismo Nieves, Bulevar Simón Sarlat 202 (☎ **93/14-1888**; fax 93/12-5130). The telephone **area code** is **93.**

EXPLORING VILLAHERMOSA

Major sights in Villahermosa include the Parque-Museo de la Venta, the Museo Regional de Antropología Carlos Pellicer Camara, the History of Tabasco Museum, and the Museum of Popular Culture (see below). You can hit the high points in a day.

If you need to shop for any necessities or luxuries, head for the indoor shopping mall at Tabasco 2000 or the shops lining Avenida Madero.

The most popular side trip from Villahermosa is to the archaeological site of Palenque, covered later in this chapter.

Parque-Museo de la Venta. Av. Ruíz Cortínez. ☎ **93/12-8910.** Museum $1; still camera free (no flash); no video. Archaeological Park $1; no video. Daily 9am–6pm. Take Paseo Tabasco northeast to Highway 180 and turn right; it's less than a mile down on your right next to the Exposition Park.

This recently refurbished park incorporates not only the fascinating outdoor La Venta Museum, but also the **regional zoo,** and the **Museo Olmeca de la Venta,** an exceptionally well-done explanation of the Olmec civilization.

La Venta was one of three major Olmec cities during the Preclassic period (2,000 B.C.–A.D. 300). The mammoth heads you see in the park were found when the ruins of La Venta were discovered in 1938. Today all that remains of the once-impressive city are some grass-covered mounds—once earthen pyramids—84 miles west of Villahermosa. All the gigantic heads and other important sculptures have been moved from the site to this interesting museum/park. Allow at least 2 hours to wander through the jungle-like sanctuary and to look at the 3,000-year-old sculpture and listen to the birds that inhabit the grounds. *Important note:* Mosquitoes can be thick during certain times of the year, so bring insect repellent.

Villahermosa Area

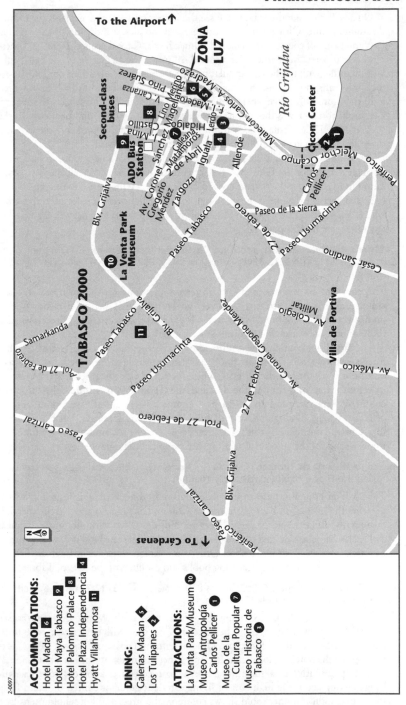

To the Airport ↑

ZONA LUZ

Río Grijalva

Qcom Center

Second-class buses

ADO Bus Station

La Venta Park Museum

TABASCO 2000

Second-class buses

Malecón Carlos A. Madrazo

Madero
V. Carranza
Lino Merino
Pino Suárez
J. Castillo
Hidalgo
Lerdo
Allende
Zaragoza
Iguala
2 de Abril
Matamoros
Galeana
Av. Coronel Sánchez Magallanes
Gregorio Méndez
Mina
J. M.

Paseo de la Sierra

Carlos Pellicer
Melchor Ocampo
Periférico

Blv. Grijalva

Paseo Tabasco

27 de Febrero

Paseo Usumacinta

César Sandino

Av. Colegio Militar

Villa de Portiva

Av. México

Samarkanda

Prol. 27 de Febrero

Paseo Tabasco

Blv. Grijalva

Paseo Usumacinta

Av. Coronel Gregorio Méndez

27 de Febrero

Prol. 27 de Febrero

Paseo Carrizal

Blv. Grijalva

Periférico

Paseo Carrizal

↓ To Cárdenas

N

2-0097

ACCOMMODATIONS:
Hotel Madan 6
Hotel Maya Tabasco 9
Hotel Palomino Palace 8
Hotel Plaza Independencia 4
Hyatt Villahermosa 11

DINING:
Galerías Madan 5
Los Tulipanes 2

ATTRACTIONS:
La Venta Park/Museum 10
Museo Antropolgía
Carlos Pellicer 1
Museo de la
Cultura Popular 7
Museo Historia de
Tabasco 3

On a walk through the park, you'll see the indoor museum that explains the Olmec throughout time; Olmec relics, sculptures, and mosaics; a mock-up of the original La Venta; and, of course, three colossal Olmec heads. Carved around 1000 B.C., these heads are 6¹/₂ feet high and weigh around 40 tons. The faces seem to be half-adult, half-infantile, with the fleshy, undulating lips characteristic of Olmec art. The basalt rock was transported from the nearest source, over 70 miles from La Venta, which is all the more impressive when you realize the sculptors had no wheels to move it. The multi-ton rock was thought to have been brought by raft from the quarry to the site. At least 17 heads have been found: four at La Venta, 10 at San Lorenzo, and three at Tres Zapotes—all Olmec cities on Mexico's east coast.

On your stroll through the park, notice the other fine stone sculptures and artistic achievements of the Olmecs, who are considered to have created the first civilization in Mexico and the first art style in Mesoamerica with their monumental works (chiseled without the use of metal). Their exquisite figurines in jade and serpentine, which can be seen in the Museo Regional de Antropología (see below), far exceeded any other craft of this period.

✪ **Museo Regional de Antropología Carlos Pellicer Camara.** CICOM Center, Av. Carlos Pellicer 511. ☎ **93/12-3200.** Admission $1.50. Daily 9am–6pm; gift shop, Tues–Sun 10am–4pm.

This museum, on the west bank of the river a mile south of the town center, is architecturally bold and attractive and very well organized. The pre-Hispanic artifacts on display include not only Tabascan finds (Totonac, Zapotec, and Olmec) but also those of other Mexican and Central American cultures.

The first floor contains the auditorium, bookstore, and gift shop; most of what interests visitors is on the upper floors, reached by an elevator or the stairs. The second floor is devoted to the Olmecs, while the third floor features artifacts relating to central Mexico, including the Tlatilco and Teotihuacán cultures; the Huasteca culture of Veracruz, San Luis Potosí, and Tampico states; and the west-coast cultures of Nayarit state. Photographs and diagrams provide vivid images, but the explanatory signs are mostly in Spanish. Look especially for the figurines that were found in this area and for the colorful *Codex* (an early book of pictographs).

Museo de Historia de Tabasco (Casa de los Azulejos). At the corner of 27 de Febrero and Av. Juárez. No Phone. Admission 75¢. Daily 10am–4pm.

Take half an hour and head to the pedestrian-only zone to see this museum, which presents the history of Tabasco from pre-Columbian times to the present through documents, artifacts, and pictures. Every room is decorated with tiles in the Spanish and Italian baroque style, and the building's blue-and-white–tiled exterior, with wrought iron balconies, is worth a snapshot. Only some explanations are in English. There's a nice gift shop off the lobby featuring books and products of the state of Tabasco.

Museo de Cultura Popular. Calle Zaragoza 810, at Juárez. ☎ **93/12-1117.** Free admission. Daily 10am–4pm; gift shop, daily 10am–4pm.

This museum is 3 blocks north and 4¹/₂ blocks west of the Museo de Historia (see above). As you enter, on the right there's a small gift shop with baskets, carved gourds, embroidered regional clothing, and chocolate from Tabasco. Displays in the next room show the state's regional clothing and dance costumes. In the back is a Chontal hut, complete with typical furnishings and a recorded conversation of two female villagers talking about the high cost of living. Student guides are often on hand for a free explanation. Another room shows ceremonial pottery and household utensils.

WHERE TO STAY

The area around the intersections of Avenidas Juárez and Lerdo, sometimes referred to as the "Zona Luz," is now one of the best places to stay; the streets are pedestrian malls closed to traffic. One drawback to this plan is parking, though there are guarded lots on the outskirts of the mall.

Room rates in Villahermosa are distressingly high, especially considering what you get. The price headings used below are for doubles during high season.

EXPENSIVE

✪ **Hyatt Villahermosa.** Av. Juárez 106, 86000 Villahermosa, Tab. ☎ **800/233-1234** in the U.S., or 93/15-1234. Fax 93/15-5808. 209 rms. A/C MINIBAR TV TEL. $80 double; $155 Regency Club room.

A quick taxi ride from the Parque La Venta, the Hyatt is a mainstay among travelers to Villahermosa. The beautifully furnished rooms are quiet and comfortable. Floors 6 through 10 hold the Regency Club, where guests receive special amenities such as separate check-in, daily newspaper, continental breakfast, and evening cocktails. There's also a business center and guests can rent cellular phones. The Hyatt is at Tabasco and Bulevar Grijalva.

Dining/Entertainment: Two restaurants and two bars cover dining needs from refined to cafe style.

Services: Laundry and room service, travel agency, car rental

Facilities: Pool, two tennis courts, boutiques, beauty shop, pharmacy, business center.

MODERATE

Hotel Maya Tabasco. Av. Ruíz Cortínez 907 (Apdo. Postal 131), 86000 Villahermosa, Tab. 8600. ☎ **800/221-6509** in the U.S., or 93/14-4466. Fax 93/12-1097. 156 rms. A/C TV TEL. $55 double.

You can't go wrong in this comfortable and busy hotel; consider it a value since it cost twice as much to stay here before the devaluation and the services are that of a more upscale hotel. It's not the Hyatt, however, but it's darn close for comfort and service. The large, carpeted rooms come with a choice of single, double, and king-size beds. Some rooms have individually controlled air-conditioning and some are centrally controlled. It's located on the main highway, convenient to the bus station, museums, and downtown.

Dining/Entertainment: Two restaurants, one formal and one informal cover all meals.

Services: Laundry and room service, travel agency, and car rental.

Facilities: Pool, pharmacy/gift shop.

INEXPENSIVE

Hotel Madan. Pino Suárez 105, 86000 Villahermosa, Tab. ☎ **93/12-1650.** Fax 93/14-3192. 20 rms. A/C TV TEL. $25 double. Free parking; secure.

The two-story Madan is another convenient downtown hotel within walking distance of the pedestrians-only zone and central-city museums. The pleasant rooms are clean and carpeted. On the second floor, you'll find a comfortable sitting room and cold-water dispenser. It's between Reforma and Lerdo, on the street behind the popular Restaurant Galerías Madan.

Hotel Palomino Palace. Av. Mina 222, 86000 Villahermosa, Tab. ☎ **93/12-8431.** 45 rms. FAN. $20 double. Free parking on the street.

Directly across from the first-class bus station, the Palomino is surprisingly clean and quiet. The rooms are small, with a couple of shelves for clothes, no closets, and blue-tiled baths with hot showers. Those overlooking Avenida Mina are the noisiest; there are a few rooms away from the street that should be your first choice. The restaurant off the lobby is open daily from 6am to midnight.

✪ **Hotel Plaza Independencia.** Independencia 123, 86000 Villahermosa, Tab. ☎ **93/ 12-7541** or 93/12-1299. Fax 93/14-4724. 90 rms. A/C TV TEL. $35 double. Free parking.

Of the many hotels in this price range, the Plaza Independencia is one of the best. The rooms, which are on six floors served by an elevator, contain avocado drapes and rugs and nice bamboo furnishings, including small desks. Some rooms have balconies, and from the top floor you can see the river. It's the only budget hotel with a pool and enclosed parking. There's an off-lobby restaurant and a bar. To find the hotel from the Plaza de Armas, face in the direction of the Malecón and walk to the right on Guerrero a half block to the corner of Macuiliz. Turn right and walk a block to Independencia and turn left; the hotel is a half block ahead on the right.

WHERE TO DINE

Just like other Mexican cities, Villahermosa is beginning to receive U.S.-franchise restaurants, such as Dunkin' Donuts, which is opposite the Museo de la Historia.

Galerías Madan. Madero 408. ☎ **93/12-1650.** Breakfast $1.95–$3.50; comida corrida $3.75; main courses $3–$6. Daily 7am–11:30pm (comida corrida served 1–4pm). MEXICAN.

Situated in a lobby of shops, this calm, soft pink, air-conditioned restaurant serves a comida corrida of soup, rice, a main course, vegetables, coffee, and dessert. The *empañadas de carne* (meat pies) are superior, and the tamales are just plain good. Large windows look onto the street, and the room has the feel of a hotel coffee shop where downtown shoppers and business types gather. It's between Lerdo de Tejada and Reforma.

✪ **Los Tulipanes.** CICOM Center, Periférico Carlos Pellicer Camara 511. ☎ **93/12-9209** or 93/12-9217. Seafood courses $7–$13; beef courses $8–$12. Daily 1–9pm. SEAFOOD/STEAKS.

Supremely popular with the local upper class, Los Tulipanes offers pricey but good food and excellent service. The staff seems to serve a full house with ease, and on busy days, a trio strolls and serenades. Since the restaurant is located by the Río Grijalva and the Pellicer Museum of Anthropology, you can combine a visit to the museum with lunch here. They may bring you a plate of *tostones de plátano*—a monster-size tortilla made of banana instead of corn. In addition to seafood and steaks, there are such Mexican specialties as chiles rellenos, tacos, and *rejelagarto* (something like gar) empañadas.

A SIDE TRIP TO CHOCOLATE PLANTATIONS & THE RUINS OF COMALCALCO

Fifty miles from Villahermosa is Comalcalco, the only pyramid site in Mexico made of kilned stone. Your route will take you through Tabasco's cacao (chocolate)-growing country, where you can visit plantations and factories to see the cacao from the pod on the tree to the finished chocolate bars.

You'll need a car to enjoy the cacao touring, but Comalcalco itself can be reached by bus from Villahermosa. Somellera line buses leave for the town of Comalcalco from the second-class bus station every 30 minutes; ADO has first-class buses twice daily. From the town of Comalcalo take a taxi or a VW minivan to the ruins, which are 2 miles farther. Travel agencies in Villahermosa offer a Comalcalco day-trip as well. Generally it leaves at 8am and returns around 5pm.

By car, the fastest route from Villahermosa is on Highway 190 west to Cárdenas then north on Highway 187. Along the road to Cárdenas are numerous banana plantations and roadside stands loaded with the yellow fruit, one of the primary cash crops of the region. As you come into Cárdenas, look for the Alteza chocolate factory of the cooperative **Industriador de Cacao de Tabasco (INCATAB).** There's a sales shop in front where you can buy boxes of chocolate in all its variations. The big boxes of chocolate they sell are actually filled with small, wrapped, two-bite bars—which make great gifts and snacks.

Cárdenas is the center of cacao processing, but the fruit itself is grown in plantations in a wide area west of Villahermosa as far south as Teapa and north to the coast. After you turn right at Cárdenas onto Highway 187, you'll begin passing trees laden with the heavy cacao pod, full of small beans.

Twelve miles before Comalcalco, in the village of Cunduacan, stop and ask for directions to the **Asociación Agricola de Productores de Cacao.** It's on the main street, but the sign isn't visible. Mornings are best for a tour during November through April when there's an abundance of cacao. Here the cacao beans are received from the growers and processing begins. First the beans are fermented in huge tubs for a little over a week and you see the beans in various stages of bubbling fermentation. Then they are mechanically dried for 16 hours. A fresh white cacao bean is slightly larger and fatter than a lima bean, but after roasting it's brown and bitter and smaller than a black-eyed pea. The roasted beans are sacked and sent to the INCATAB chocolate cooperative in Cárdenas.

Along this route are many mom-and-pop cacao plantations, where families grow and process their own cacao and sell it at local markets and roadside stands rather than to the cooperative. One of these is **Rancho La Pasadita,** 4^1/$_2$ miles before Comalcalco on the right. Look carefully for the sign (it's a bit obscured), but the sign on the pink-and-blue house says CHOCOLATE CASERO LA PASADITA. Here Aura Arellano has 19 acres of cacao trees that she planted in the 1950s. She will gladly take you out back where the trees grow, and if it's bean season (November through April) you'll more than likely see workers hacking open the football-shaped cantaloupe-size pods and dumping the contents in big wicker baskets. She ferments her beans the traditional way, in a hollowed-out, canoe-size wooden container. She dries and toasts the beans on a small *comal* (clay pan) over an open fire until they are hard like a nut, after which she grinds them to a powder, mixes it with sugar to cook and make into logs for hot chocolate that's *casera,* or homemade. These she sells in her living-room storefront. You see this type of chocolate for sale in shops in Villahermosa.

Comalcalco, 25 miles from Cárdenas, is a busy agricultural center with an interesting market where you can buy wicker baskets, like those used to ferment cacao and *pichanchas* (a gourd with multiple holes in it), used to strain flavor from fresh cacao beans for a refreshing drink.

The **ruins** of Comalcalco are about 2 miles on the same highway past the town; watch for signs to the turnoff on the right. Park in the lot and pay admission to the visitors center by the museum. The museum, with many pre-Hispanic artifacts, is small but interesting and worth the 20 minutes or so it takes to see it. Unfortunately, all the descriptions are in Spanish, but there's a history of the people who lived here, the Putún/Chongal Maya, a rough people who were traders, spoke fractured Maya, and were believed to be those who founded or greatly influenced Chichén-Itzá.

The neat, grass-covered site spreads out grandly as you enter, with pyramidal mounds left, right, and straight ahead. Comalcalco means "house of the comals" in Nahuatl. A comal is a round clay pan used for roasting and making tortillas. All about the grounds you see shards of kilned brick that are also evident on the sides of the pyramidal structures. These bricks were made with clay mixed with sand and ground oyster shell. Owing to the fragile nature of these ruins, there are many NO SUBIR signs warning visitors not to climb certain structures. Others have paths and arrows pointing to the top. From the **palace** there's a fabulous view of the whole site. On the **Acropolis,** under a protective covering, are remains of stucco and plaster masks in surprisingly good condition, although there are few of them. Seeing the ruins takes an hour or so. Admission is $2, and the site is open daily from 8am to 5pm. The afternoon light is great for photographs.

2 Palenque

89 miles SE of Villahermosa, 143 miles NE of San Cristóbal

The ruins of Palenque are one of the most spectacular of the Maya archaeological sites, with roof-combed temples ensconced in lush vegetation high above the savannas. The ruins, located on the edge of the jungle in the state of Chiapas, are part of a reserve known as the Parque Nacional Palenque. The flora of the surrounding countryside continues to encroach on the park, and it takes a team of machete wielders to hold the jungle back.

Were it not for the local ruins, the town of Palenque (pop. 16,000) would hardly exist. This slow-paced, somnolent village is accustomed to visitors passing through, but it pays them little heed.

ESSENTIALS
GETTING THERE & DEPARTING

BY PLANE   A new airport at San Cristóbal de las Casas is still under construction. It will handle smaller private and charter aircraft. Check with travel agencies in Villahermosa, Tuxtla Gutiérrez, and San Cristóbal de las Casas for information. Until the new airport was slated to open in San Cristóbal, the airport at Comitán (about 50 miles southeast of San Cristóbal de las Casas) served all Palenque charter flights; however, it was still closed when I checked.

BY BUS   Four bus stations serve Palenque, and all are within 3 blocks of the hospital on Avenida Juárez. Of these, the Transportes Cristóbal Colón and Transportes Rudolfo Figueroa (which share a building) should be the first choice when looking for transportation.

From Tuxtla Gutiérrez, with stops in San Cristóbal, both **Transportes Cristóbal Colón** and **Transportes Rudolfo Figueroa (TRF)** run several deluxe buses to Palenque—a 6-hour trip. When TRF buses reach San Cristóbal, passengers are dropped off on the highway near the central bus station and opposite the Figueroa terminal, which is across the highway from the central bus station. TRF buses are the most deluxe buses traveling this route, with movies, curtained windows, air-conditioning, heat, and a bathroom. From Mérida, the trip to Palenque takes around 9 hours. Twice daily, deluxe Cristóbal Colón buses make the trip with onboard bathroom, movies, snacks, and soft drinks.

From Villahermosa's first-class **ADO** station, there are at least eight buses to Palenque daily; the trip takes 2 hours. Military patrols may stop the bus and question the driver and/or visually scan the passengers. From San Cristóbal there are only three ADO buses to Villahermosa.

BY CAR   The 143-mile trip from San Cristóbal to Palenque takes 5 to 6 hours and passes through lush jungle and mountain scenery. Take it easy since potholes and other hindrances occur. Highway 186 from Villahermosa is in good condition, and the trip from there and on the Palenque turnoff should take about 2 hours. Expect military roadblocks and cursory inspection of your travel credentials and perhaps your vehicle.

ORIENTATION

ARRIVING   Most travelers reach Palenque by bus, which arrive 4 or 5 blocks from the zócalo. Taxis are either in front of the station or pass by frequently. Only those hotels surrounding the zócalo are within walking distance if you're carrying heavy luggage.

VISITOR INFORMATION   The **State Tourism Office** (☎ and fax **934/5-0356**) is located a block east of the zócalo on Jiménez. The office is open Monday through Saturday from 8am to 9pm.

CITY LAYOUT   The **ruins** are about 5 miles southwest of town. The road from Villahermosa forks just west of town at the impossible-to-miss Maya statue; the ruins are southwest of the statue, and the town lies to the east.

Palenque has three separate areas where tourists tend to congregate. The most central area is around the **main plaza,** bordered by Avenidas Hidalgo, 20 de Noviembre, Independencia, and Jiménez. **La Cañada** is a pleasant area located 5 very long blocks west of the main plaza on Merle Green, a partially paved road that runs through a tropical forest. Here, you'll find a few small hotels and restaurants and stands of artists who carve and paint. Aside from the main plaza area, this is the best location for travelers without cars, since the town is within a few blocks and the buses that run to the ruins pass by La Cañada. The third tourist zone is along the **road to the ruins,** where small hotels, RV parks, and campgrounds are tucked into the surrounding jungle. This is an ideal location for those with cars.

GETTING AROUND   The cheapest way to get back and forth from the ruins is on the Chambalu colectivo buses, which depart from the terminal at Avenidas Juárez and Allende every 10 minutes from 6am to 6pm. The buses pass La Cañada and hotels along the road to the ruins, but they may not stop if they're full. Chambalu also runs buses five times daily to Misol Ha and Agua Azul.

FAST FACTS: PALENQUE   The telephone **area code** is **934.** As for the **climate,** Palenque's constant humidity is downright oppressive in the summer, especially after rain showers. During the winter, the damp air can be chilly, especially in the evenings, so a jacket is a good idea. Rain gear is important any time of year. Concerning **safety,** you'll see military units garrisoned on the outskirts of town complete with rifles and sandbag bunkers. These were established as a precaution after the uprising in Chiapas. Personnel here stop all passing buses and cars, but usually make no more than a brief overview of passengers, or perhaps briefly question the driver, before waving vehicles on.

EXPLORING PALENQUE

The real reason for being here is the ruins, which can be toured in a morning; but many people savor Palenque for days. Despite the fame of the ruins, the village of Palenque remains rather uncommercialized, though more shops and restaurants are opening. There are no must-see sights in the town; if you have time to spare, sit on the main plaza and observe the goings-on. The La Cañada area west of town (see "City Layout," above) is a pleasant spot for a leisurely lunch and for browsing through Maya reproductions made by local artists.

PARQUE NACIONAL PALENQUE

The archaeological site of Palenque underwent several changes in 1994, which culminated in the opening of a new museum/visitors center on the highway to the

King Pacal's Tomb

The great stone hieroglyphic panels found inside the **Temple of the Inscriptions** contain the dynastic family tree of King Pacal (most of the panels are in the National Anthropological Museum in Mexico City). The temple is famous for the tomb, or crypt, of Pacal that archaeologist Alberto Ruz Lhuller discovered in its depths in 1952. Ruz's discovery of the tomb is considered by Mayanists (scholars who study the Maya) to be among a handful of great discoveries in the Maya world. Ruz's own gravesite is opposite the Temple of the Inscriptions, on the left as you enter the park.

Pacal began building the temple less than a decade before he died at age 80 in A.D. 683. It took Ruz and his crew four seasons of digging to clear out the rubble that was put there to conceal the crypt containing the remains of King Pacal. Ascending to the throne at age 12, Pacal reigned for 67 years. The crypt itself is 80 feet below the floor of the temple and was covered by a monolithic, sepulchral slab 12¹/₂ feet long and 7 feet wide, engraved with a depiction of Pacal falling backwards from the land of the living into the underworld. Five natives (four men and a woman) were left at the entrance to the crypt when it was sealed so they could accompany Pacal on his journey through the underworld. Unless you're claustrophobic, you should definitely visit the tomb. The way down is lighted, but the steps can be slippery due to condensed humidity. Carved inscriptions on the sides of the crypt (which visitors can't see) show the ritual of the funerary rites carried out at the time of Pacal's death and portray the lineage of Pacal's ancestors, complete with family portraits.

ruins. The complex includes a large parking lot, a refreshment stand serving snacks and drinks, and several shops. The **museum,** although not large, is worth the time it takes to see it; it's open Tuesday through Sunday from 10am to 5pm. It contains well-chosen and artistically displayed exhibits, including the jade contents of recently excavated tombs. (The museum was robbed in 1996, but most of the jade pieces have been recovered.) Explanatory texts, in both Spanish and English, describe the life and times of the magnificent city of Palenque. New pieces are constantly being added as they are uncovered in ongoing excavations.

The **main entrance,** about a mile beyond the museum, is at the top of a hill at the end of the paved highway. There, you'll find a large parking lot, a refreshment stand, a ticket booth, and several shops. Among the vendors selling souvenirs by the parking lot are Lacandón Indians wearing white tunics and hawking bows and arrows.

Admission to the ruins is $2; free on Sunday. There's a $4 charge for each video camera used. Parking at the main entrance and at the visitors center is free. The site and visitors center shops are open daily from 8am to 4:45pm; King Pacal's crypt is open daily from 10am to 4pm.

TOURING THE RUINS   Pottery found during the excavations shows that people lived in this area as early as 300 B.C. During the Classic Period (A.D. 300–900), the ancient Maya city of Palenque was a ceremonial center for the high priests; the civilization peaked at around A.D. 600 to 700.

When John Stephens visited the site in the 1840s, the cleared ruins you see today were buried under centuries of accumulated earth and a thick canopy of jungle. The dense jungle surrounding the cleared portion still covers yet unexplored temples,

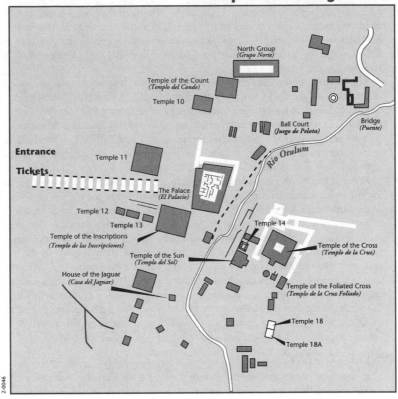

North Group
(Grupo Norte)

Temple of the Count
(Templo del Conde)

Temple 10

Ball Court
(Juego de Pelota)

Bridge
(Puente)

Entrance

Temple 11

Rio Otulum

Tickets

The Palace
(El Palacio)

Temple 12

Temple 14

Temple 13

Temple of the Cross
(Templo de la Cruz)

Temple of the Inscriptions
(Templo de las Inscripciones)

Temple of the Sun
(Templo del Sol)

House of the Jaguar
(Casa del Jaguar)

Temple of the Foliated Cross
(Templo de la Cruz Foliado)

Temple 18

Temple 18A

2-0046

which are easily discernible in the forest, even to the untrained eye. Of all the ruins in Mexico open to the public, this site is the most haunting because of its majesty and sense of the past. Scholars have unearthed names of the rulers and their family histories, putting visitors on a first-name basis with these ancient people etched in stone. Read about it in *A Forest of Kings,* by Linda Schele and David Friedel.

As you enter the ruins from the entrance, the building on your right is the **Temple of the Inscriptions,** named for the great stone hieroglyphic panels found inside. It's all described in *A Forest of Kings.*

Just to your right as you face the Temple of the Inscriptions is **Temple 13,** which is receiving considerable attention from archaeologists. Recently, the burial of another richly adorned personage was discovered here, accompanied in death by an adult female and an adolescent. These remains are still being studied, but the treasures are on display in the museum.

When you're back on the main pathway, the building directly in front of you will be the **Palace,** with its unique watchtower. A pathway between the Palace and the Temple of the Inscriptions leads to the **Temple of the Sun,** the **Temple of the Foliated Cross,** the **Temple of the Cross,** and **Temple 14.** This group of temples— now cleared and in various stages of reconstruction—was built by Pacal's son, Chan-Bahlum, who is usually shown on inscriptions as having six toes. Chan-Bahlum's plaster mask was found in Temple 14 next to the Temple of the Sun. Archaeologists have recently begun probing the depths of the Temple of the Sun in search of Chan-Bahlum's tomb. Little remains of this temple's exterior carving. Inside, however, behind a fence, a carving of Chan-Bahlum shows him ascending the throne in A.D. 690. The panels, which are still in place, depict Chan-Bahlum's version of his historic link to the throne.

The North Group, to the left of the Palace, is also undergoing restoration. Included in this area are the **Ball Court** and the **Temple of the Count,** so named because Count Waldeck camped there in the 19th century. Explorer John Stephens camped in the Palace when it was completely tree- and vine-covered, spending sleepless nights fighting off mosquitoes. At least three tombs, complete with offerings for the underworld journey, have been found here. The lineage of at least 12 kings has been deciphered from inscriptions left at this marvelous site.

Just past the North Group is a small building (once a museum) now used for storing the artifacts found during the restorations. It is closed to the public. To the right of the building, a stone bridge crosses the river, leading to a pathway down the hillside to the new **museum.** The path is lined with rocks and has steps in the steepest areas, leading past the **Cascada Motiepa,** a beautiful waterfall that creates a series of pools perfect for cooling weary feet. Benches are placed along the way as rest areas, and some small temples have been reconstructed near the base of the trail. In the early morning and evening, you may hear monkeys crashing through the thick foliage by the path; if you keep noise to a minimum, you may spot wild parrots as well. Walking downhill (by far the best way to go), it will take you about 20 minutes to reach the main highway. The path ends at the paved road across from the museum. The colectivos going back to the village will stop here if you wave them down.

WHERE TO STAY

The main hotel zones are near the fork in the road at La Cañada, in the village, and on the road to the ruins.

IN LA CAÑADA

✪ **Hotel Maya Tulipanes.** Calle Merle Green No. 6, 29960 Palenque, Chi. ☎ **934/5-0201.** Fax 934/5-1004. 34 rms. A/C or FAN. $37–$42 double. Free parking.

Maya statues, carvings, and paintings fill the hallways and public areas in this rambling, overgrown, but comfortable two-story hotel. Some of the windows are even shaped like the Maya corbeled arch. You definitely feel as if you're in the jungle here, and the dark shade is a cool respite from the sun's glare. Higher prices are for rooms in the new section. The hotel is 1 long block north of the Maya statue in La Cañada.

La Posada. Calle Inominada La Cañada, 29960 Palenque, Chi. ☎ **934/5-0437.** Fax 934/5-0193. 16 rms. FAN. $20 double.

Owner Lourdes Chávez de Grajales took over this hotel in 1993 and continues its tradition of budget-priced rooms in pleasant surroundings. The original rooms are basic; each has one cement-platform double bed, a portable fan, and a large tiled bath with hot showers. Room numbers are painted in Maya symbols. A second story has been added with eight new rooms, each with two beds, fans, and tiled baths. The rooms face a wide lawn where tables and chairs are set out for guests, and the owner reports that she has spotted howler monkeys in the nearby trees. Cold sodas, water, beer, and snacks are sold from a refrigerator in the lobby, near the Ping-Pong table. La Posada is off Merle Green on a dirt road just past the Hotel Maya Tulipanes.

Palenque Dining & Accommodations

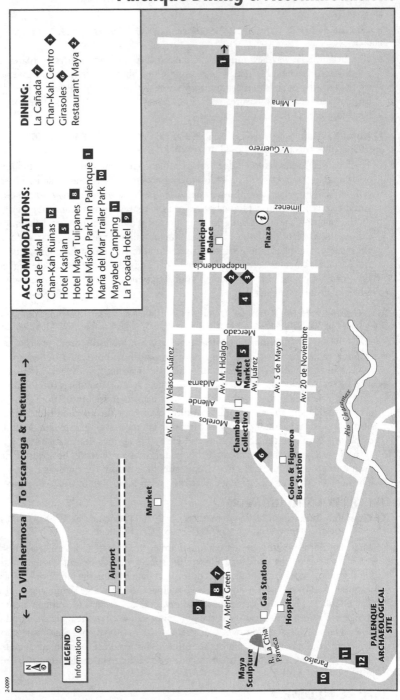

DINING:
La Cañada **7**
Chan-Kah Centro **3**
Girasoles **6**
Restaurant Maya **2**

ACCOMMODATIONS:
Casa de Pakal **4**
Chan-Kah Ruinas **12**
Hotel Kashlan **5**
Hotel Maya Tulipanes **8**
Hotel Misión Park Inn Palenque **1**
María del Mar Trailer Park **10**
Mayabel Camping **11**
La Posada Hotel **9**

← To Villahermosa   To Escarcega & Chetumal →

LEGEND
Information *i*

Airport

Market

J. Mina

V. Guerrero

Jimenez

Municipal Palace

Independencia

Plaza

Mercado

Av. M. Hidalgo

Crafts Market

Av. Juárez

Av. 5 de Mayo

Av. 20 de Noviembre

Aldama

Allende

Morelos

Chambalu Collectivo

Av. Dr. M. Velasco Suárez

Colon & Figueroa Bus Station

Av. Merle Green

Gas Station

Hospital

Maya Sculpture

R. La Chia Paneca

Paraíso

Río Chacamax

PALENQUE ARCHAEOLOGICAL SITE

2-0099

IN THE VILLAGE

Hotel Casa de Pakal. Av. Juárez 10, 29960 Palenque, Chi. ☎ **934/5-0443.** 15 rms. A/C. $22 double.

This bright, relatively new four-story hotel far surpasses most others on Juárez. Air-conditioning is a big plus here. The rooms are small but far brighter and cleaner than those at nearby establishments, and they come with either one double or one single bed covered with chenille spreads. A good restaurant is on premises. The hotel is a half block east of the main plaza.

✪ **Hotel Kashlan.** 5 de Mayo no. 105, 29960 Palenque, Chi. ☎ **934/5-0297.** Fax 934/5-0309. 58 rms. FAN (30 rms) A/C (28 rms). $20–$25 double.

You'll be well-located if you lodge in the Kashlan. The clean rooms have interior windows opening onto the hall, marble-square floors, nice bedspreads, tile baths, small vanities, and luggage racks. Show owner Ada Luz Navarro your *Frommer's* book and you'll receive a discount. Higher prices are for rooms with air-conditioning, but I should mention that the ceiling fans are powerful and even in sultry Palenque air-conditioning might not be needed. The hotel restaurant features vegetarian food. A video bar was in the planning stages. Trips around the region, including to Agua Azul and Misol Ha can also be arranged at the hotel. To find this hotel from the Figueroa/Cólon station, walk to the corner on your left, which is Juárez, and turn right; it's 4 blocks ahead on the left.

Hotel Misión Park Inn Palenque. Domicilio Conocido, Rancho San Martín de Porres, 29960 Palenque, Chi. ☎ **800/448-8355** in the U.S., or 934/5-0241. Fax 934/5-0300. $75 double.

Palenque's most luxurious hotel, this place is a 5-minute ride from town or a 20-minute walk. The views of the surrounding peaceful countryside—encompassing mountains and jungle—are beautiful. The spacious rooms, with high-beamed ceilings and cobalt-blue and white walls, are in long, two-story buildings overlooking the gardens; rooms near the restaurant must bear hearing music until 10pm. The beds are enormous and the bathrooms sparkling clean, but the air-conditioners are the noisiest I've ever heard. The pool is a blessing after a morning of pyramid climbing or playing tennis on the hotel's courts; there's a hot springs nearby for soaking your weary feet. The restaurant is remarkably good for one that serves busloads of European tour groups. The hotel's free shuttle goes to and from the ruins six times a day. The hotel is at the far eastern edge of town; go left at the end of Cinco de Mayo.

ON THE ROAD TO THE RUINS

✪ **Chan-Kah Ruinas.** Km 31 Carretera Palenque, 29960 Palenque, Chi. ☎ **934/5-01100.** Fax 934/5-0820. 70 rms. A/C (30 rms) FAN (40 rms). $55–$70 double.

These comfortable bungalows are about 5 miles from town and 2 miles before you reach the ruins on the same road. Rooms are spread out in a beautiful jungle setting. Sliding glass doors in the rooms open onto small patios facing the jungle or in a newer section linked by pathways and gardens. Facilities include a large swimming pool and a nice-looking restaurant that receives no raves. Taxis are hard to come by here and charge extra for picking you up at the hotel; instead, walk to the main road and flag down a colectivo or taxi to town. Christmas prices may be higher than those quoted here, and you may be quoted a higher price if you reserve a room in advance from the United States. The hotel is on the left side of the road to the ruins, 2^1/$_2$ miles northwest of the ruins.

WHERE TO DINE

Avenida Juárez is lined with many small restaurants, none of which is exceptional. Good options are the many markets and *panaderías* (bakeries) along Juárez.

Panificadora La Tehuanita, near the bus stations, has fresh baked goods, and **La Bodeguita** has a beautiful display of fresh fruit—just stick with those you can peel.

MODERATE

✪ La Chiapaneca. Carretera Palenque. ☎ **934/5-0363.** Main courses $7–$9. Daily 11am–10pm. MEXICAN.

Palenque's traditional "best" restaurant continues to serve top-notch regional cuisine in a pleasant tropical setting. Though it has a thatched roof, the dining room is large and refined. The *pollo Palenque* (chicken with potatoes in a tomato-and-onion sauce) is a soothing choice; save room for the flan. Mexican wines are served by the bottle. La Chiapaneca is about a 20-minute walk from the Maya statue toward the ruins.

INEXPENSIVE

La Cañada. Calle Merle Green s/n. ☎ **934/5-0102.** Main courses $3.25–$8. Daily 7am–10pm. MEXICAN.

This palapa-topped restaurant tucked into the jungle is said to be one of the best in town, though it never seems crowded. Though the dining room has a dirt floor, the place is spotless, the service attentive, and the food good—if not exceptional. Try one of the local specialties such as *pollo mexicano* or bean soup. Near the restaurant lies the two-story thatched disco, La Nuit, the most popular dance spot in town. This restaurant is in the Hotel La Cañada on the left, about midway down the road.

Chan-Kah Centro. Av. Independencia s/n. ☎ **934/5-0318.** Breakfast $1.50–$3; comida corrida $2.50–$3.25; main courses $1.50–$5.50. Daily 7am–11pm. MEXICAN.

This attractive hotel restaurant is the most peaceful place to eat. The waiters are extremely attentive, and the food is fairly well prepared (avoid the tough beef though). The second-story bar overlooks the main plaza and has live music on some weekend nights. It's on the east side of the main plaza at the corner of Independencia and Juárez.

Girasoles. Av. Juárez 189. ☎ **934/5-0383.** Comida del día $2.50; main courses $2.50–$3.75. Daily 7am–11pm. MEXICAN.

There's always a smattering of locals and foreigners here taking advantage of the good prices. The simple decor boasts cloth-covered tables, wicker lampshades on ceiling lights, and fans. It's a good place for resting your feet and watching the action, in addition to getting a good deal on the food. An upstairs section is cooler and offers a view. The menu covers the basics and has fish, poultry, and Mexican specialties, including decent tacos that are more like flautas. The freshly brewed coffee comes from Chiapas, and you can buy it ground by the kilo. Girasoles is on Avenida 5 de Mayo across from the ADO bus station.

✪ Restaurant Maya. Av. Independencia s/n. No phone. Breakfast $2–$3; main courses $3–$5. Daily 7am–10pm. MEXICAN/STEAKS/SEAFOOD.

The most popular place in town among tourists and locals, Restaurant Maya is opposite the northeast corner of the main plaza near the post office. Breezy and open, it's managed by a solicitous family. At breakfast, there are free refills of very good coffee. Try the tamales.

ROAD TRIPS FROM PALENQUE
AGUA AZUL & CASCADA DE MISOL HA: SPECTACULAR WATERFALLS

The most popular excursion from Palenque is a day-trip to the Misol Ha waterfall about 12 miles from Palenque off the road to Ocosingo. Patrons of this spot swim in the waters below the falls and scramble up slippery paths to smaller falls beside the large one, which drops about 90 feet before spraying its mist on the waters below. There's a small restaurant run by the ejido cooperative that owns the site. Entrance costs around $1.25. Approximately 22 miles beyond Misol Ha on the same road, and about 40 miles from Palenque, are the Agua Azul waterfalls, a truly spectacular series of beautiful cascades tumbling into a wide river. This is usually considered a full day trip. Visitors can picnic and relax (bring something to sprawl on), swim, or clamber over the slippery cascades and go upstream for a look at the jungle encroaching on the water. Cost to enter is around $3. Trips can be arranged through Shivalva Tours (see "Bonampak & Yaxchilán," below) or the Hotel Kashlan. Minivans from the Chambalu Colectivo Service (see "Getting Around," above) make the trip to Agua Azul and the Cascada de Misol Ha every day with two round-trips beginning at 10am; the last van departs Agua Azul for Palenque at 6:30pm. They may wait until six or eight people want to go, so check a day or two in advance of your proposed trip.

BONAMPAK & YAXCHILÁN: RUINS & RUGGED ADVENTURE

Intrepid travelers might consider the 2-day excursion to the Maya ruins of Bonampak and Yaxchilán. The ruins of Bonampak, southeast of Palenque on the Guatemalan border, were discovered in 1946. The mural discovered on the interior walls of one of the buildings is the greatest battle painting of pre-Hispanic Mexico. Reproductions of the vivid murals found here are on view in the Regional Archaeology Museum in Villahermosa.

You can fly or drive to Bonampak. Several tour companies offer a 2-day (minimum) tour by four-wheel-drive vehicle to within 4¹/₂ miles of Bonampak. You must walk the rest of the way to the ruins. After camping overnight, you continue by river to the extensive ruins of the great Maya city, Yaxchilán, famous for its highly ornamented buildings. Bring rain gear, boots, a flashlight, and bug repellent. All tours include meals but vary in price ($80 to $120 per person); some take far too many people for comfort (the 7-hour road trip can be unbearable).

Among the most reputable tour operators is **Viajes Shivalva,** Calle Merle Green 1 (Apdo. Postal 237), Palenque, Chi. 29960 (☎ **934/5-0411;** fax 934/5-0392). Office hours are Monday through Friday from 7am to 3pm. A branch office is now open a block from the zócalo (main plaza) at the corner of Juárez and Abasolo (across the hall from the State Tourism Office). It's open Monday through Saturday from 9am to 9pm (☎ 934/5-0822).

Information about **ATC Tours and Travel** can be obtained at their office in San Cristóbal de las Casas. This agency has a large number of clients (and thus the best chance of making a group) and offers a large number of tours. Among its offerings is a 1-day trip to the ruins of Tikal in Guatemala for five people; another tour takes in Yaxchilán, Bonampak, and Tikal with a minimum of four people. Though rustic, they have the only permanent overnight accommodations at Yaxchilán at their Posada del Río Usumacinta. Their headquarters are in San Cristóbal (see "San Cristóbal de las Casas," below). See also chapter 3, "Active Vacations in the Yucatán," for U.S. companies offering this trip.

An alternative way to reach Bonampak and Yaxchilán is via tours run by the **Chambalu Colectivo Service** at Juárez and Allende. But, be sure to ask plenty of questions about the conditions of travel, size of the van, meals, and sleeping accommodations. It's been known as a strenuous, no-frills trip without much in the way of service. Bring plenty of food and drink, a hammock and net, and a great deal of patience.

Recent road improvements should shorten the trip and may alter tour arrangements considerably.

3 San Cristóbal de las Casas

143 miles SW of Palenque, 50 miles E of Tuxtla Gutiérrez, 46 miles NW of Comitán, 104 miles NW of Cuauhtémoc, 282 miles E of Oaxaca

San Cristóbal is a colonial town set in a lovely valley—still nearly 7,000 feet high—where the centuries-old Maya civilization continues to flourish. Part of the town's name is derived from the 16th-century bishop Fray Bartolomé de las Casas, who sought to protect native peoples from exploitation. Nearly all the Indians in the immediate area speak Maya languages such as Tzotzil or Tzeltal. The town of 90,000 is the major market center for Maya Indians of various groups, who trek down from the surrounding mountains; but some groups, such as the Lacandóns (who number only about 450) don't come into town at all; they live so far off in the forests of eastern Chiapas that it takes 6 days on horseback to get to their territory.

Probably the most visible among the local indigenous groups are the **Chamula.** The men wear baggy thigh-length trousers and white or black serapes, while the women wear blue rebozos, gathered white blouses with embroidered trim, and black wool wraparound skirts.

Another local Indian group is the **Zinacantecan,** whose male population dresses in light-pink overshirts with colorful trim and tassels and sometimes short pants. Hat ribbons (now a rare sight) are tied on married men, while ribbons dangle loosely from the hats of bachelors and community leaders. The Zinacantecan women wear beautiful, brightly colored woven shawls along with black wool skirts. You may also see **Tenejapa** men clad in knee-length black tunics and flat straw hats and Tenejapa women dressed in beautiful reddish and rust-colored *huipils.* Women of all groups are barefooted, while men wear handmade sandals or cowboy boots.

There are several Indian villages within access of San Cristóbal by road—Chamula, with its weavers and non-Christian church; Zinacantán, whose residents practice a unique religion; Tenejapa, San Andrés, and Magdalena, known for brocaded textiles; Amatenango del Valle, a town of potters; and Aguacatenango, known for embroidery. Most of these "villages" consist of little more than a church and the municipal government building, with homes scattered for miles around and a general gathering only for church and market days (usually Sunday).

You'll hear the word *ladino* here—it refers to non-Indian Mexicans or people who have taken up modern ways, changed their dress, dropped their Indian traditions and language, and decided to live in town. It may be used derogatorily or descriptively, depending on who is using the term and how it's used.

Other local lingo you should know about includes *Jovel,* San Cristóbal's original name, used often by businesses, and *coleto,* meaning someone or something from San Cristóbal. You'll see signs for tamales coletos, coleto bread, and coleto breakfast.

In recent years, San Cristóbal has become more popular with Mexicans, not to mention North Americans and Europeans in search of a charming, "unspoiled" traditional town to visit. Evangelical Protestant missionaries recently have converted large numbers of indigenous peoples, and in some villages new converts find themselves expelled from their homelands—in Chamula, for example, as many as 30,000 people have been expelled. Many of these people, called *expulsados* (expelled ones), have taken up residence in new villages on the outskirts of San Cristóbal de las Casas. They still wear their traditional dress. Other villages, such as Tenejapa, allow the Protestant church to exist and villagers to attend it without prejudice.

San Cristóbal de las Casas

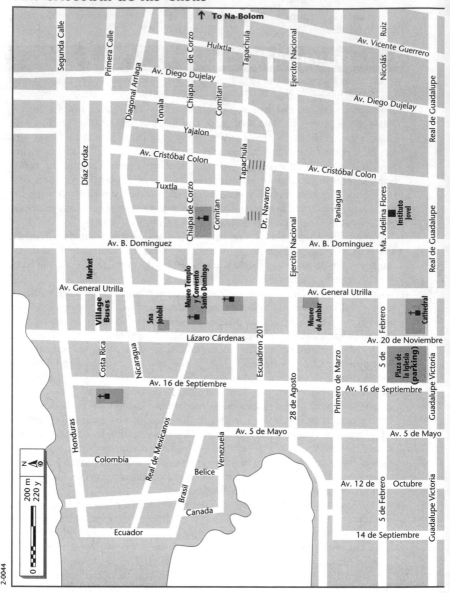

Although the influx of tourists is increasing and the influence of outsiders (including Mexicans) is inevitably chipping away at the culture, the Indians aren't really interested in being or looking like the foreigners in their midst. They may steal glances at tourists or even stare curiously, but mainly they pay little attention to outsiders. Just in case we think they are envious of our clothing, possessions, or culture, I'll repeat an interesting comment made one night during dinner at Na-Bolom with a Maya specialist living in San Cristóbal: "They think we are the remains of a left-over civilization and that we eat our babies."

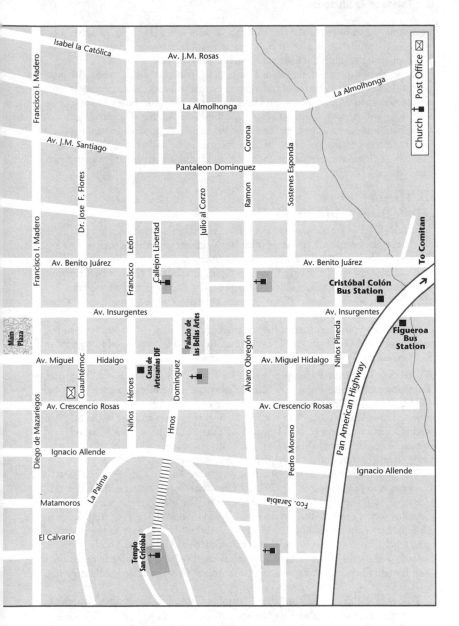

Important note: In January 1994, Indians from this area led a revolt against the *ladino*-led towns and Mexican government over the issues of health care, education, land distribution, and representative government. Finally, after 3 years of on-again-off-again negotiations, portions of the disagreement have been resolved. Discussions about remaining issues are ongoing and tension still exists in the area—tension that tourists are unlikely to discern. Hotels are often filled. Europeans didn't suspend travel to San Cristóbal during and after the crisis, but Americans did. But now even the Americans are back. Though I don't wish to diminish the gravity of the issues provoking the uprising, or the fact that people were killed during it, and that tourists were rightfully scared away, it is, however, possible that news reports today oversensationalize the subject; it does sell newspapers.

Rather than a town suffering from a siege, San Cristóbal appears to be more prosperous than ever, with new shops and a generally renewed appearance over all. If given the chance, I would go again to San Cristóbal tomorrow. Polite armed military personnel are still stopping traffic at several roadblocks on all highways leading to San Cristóbal. At these stops, travelers were required to present personal travel documents such as tourist permits, passports, or other identification and to state the purpose of their travel. Some vehicles are searched. None of these searches in any way inconvenienced me.

ESSENTIALS
GETTING THERE & DEPARTING

BY PLANE   For the status of services at a proposed new airport near San Cristóbal, check with the Municipal Tourism Office (see "Visitor Information," below) or ATC Travel (also below). Until the new airport is open, there are no commercial flights to San Cristóbal—only charter flights to Comitán. **Tuxtla Gutiérrez** is the only nearby airport with regularly scheduled flights. Tour agencies in Palenque and San Cristóbal can arrange charter flights between the two cities for a minimum of four people, but the flights are costly.

Charter-flight arrangements or flight changes on any airline in another city can be made through **ATC Tours and Travel,** across from El Fogón de Jovel Restaurant in San Cristóbal (☎ 967/8-2550; fax 967/8-3145).

BY BUS   To/From Palenque: From both Tuxtla Gutiérrez and Palenque, **Transportes Rudolfo Figueroa, Mundo Maya,** and **Autotransportes Cristóbal Colón** all have deluxe service several times a day. Seven first-class Cristóbal Colón buses go to Palenque daily, with the first leaving at 7:30am and the last at 6:30pm. Rudolfo Figueroa buses go to Palenque four times; buses leave from their office on the opposite side of the highway from the main bus station. In either city, buy your ticket the day before your planned departure to ensure a seat.

To/From Tuxtla Gutiérrez: The best way to get to San Cristóbal from Tuxtla Gutiérrez is to hop on one of the 12 direct **Cristóbal Colón** buses from the first-class Cristóbal Colón bus station for the 1¹/₂-hour trip. The road between Tuxtla and San Cristóbal is curvy and the buses cover it rapidly, so motion sickness is a consideration. The highway climbs to almost 7,000 feet in a matter of 50 miles, and the scenery is spectacular. To Tuxtla from San Cristóbal, **Cristóbal Colón** has hourly first-class buses (called locales) from 6:30am to 9pm originating in San Cristóbal; nine others pass through (de paso). There are a few deluxe "plus" Cristóbal Colón buses departing for Tuxtla.

To/From Villahermosa: One daily Cristóbal Colón bus leaves for Villahermosa at 3:25pm, and the trip takes 7 to 8 hours.

To/From Oaxaca: There's limited daily service on Cristóbal Colón to Oaxaca; be prepared for a 12-hour, windy, mountainous trip. The daytime trip will be safer than one driving through the mountains at night.

To/From Mérida: Deluxe "plus" Cristóbal Colón buses leave for Mérida twice daily (a 14-hour trip). For safety reasons, avoid the night bus. Purchase your ticket a day or two in advance.

BY TAXI   Taxis from Tuxtla Gutiérrez to San Cristóbal leave from the airport and the Cristóbal Colón bus station. See "Getting There & Departing" in "Tuxtla Gutiérrez," below, for details.

BY CAR From Tuxtla, a 1½-hour trip, the road winds through beautiful mountain country. The road between Palenque and San Cristóbal de las Casas is adventurous and provides jungle scenery, but portions of it may be heavily potholed, washed out, or have dangerous dips. The trip takes about 5 hours.

ORIENTATION

ARRIVING The first-class **Cristóbal Colón bus station** is on Highway 190 (Pan American Highway), which runs on the southern outskirts of San Cristóbal. The street that intersects the highway in front of the bus station is Avenida de los Insurgentes (which becomes Avenida General Utrilla after the main plaza). From the station, the main plaza is 9 blocks north along Insurgentes (a 10- or 15-minute walk).

Deluxe **Rudolfo Figueroa** buses traveling between Palenque and Tuxtla drop passengers on the side of the highway near the first-class bus station. To catch a cab or minibus, walk over to the station.

Urbano minibuses (see "Getting Around," below) pass by the station on Avenida Insurgentes/Avenida Utrilla headed toward the central plaza. Use these if you have only a small bag; if you have heftier luggage, take one of the taxis from in front of the station.

If you're arriving by car, when you see the bus station turn toward it and follow that street, which is Avenida Insurgentes/Avendia Utrilla, to the main plaza where you can get your bearings.

VISITOR INFORMATION The **Municipal Tourism Office** (☎ **967/8-0660,** ext. 126; fax 967/8-0135), on the main square in the town hall, across the street from the cathedral, is well organized and has a friendly, helpful staff. The office keeps especially convenient hours: Monday through Saturday from 9am to 8pm and Sunday from 9am to 2pm. Check the bulletin board here for apartments, shared rides, cultural events, and local tours.

CITY LAYOUT The cathedral marks the main plaza, where Avenida de los Insurgentes becomes Avenida General Utrilla. All streets crossing the plaza change their names here. The market is 9 blocks north along Utrilla, while the bus station is south. From the market, minibuses (colectivos) trundle to outlying villages.

Take note that this town has at least three streets named "Domínguez." There's Hermanos Domínguez, Belisário Domínguez, and Pantaleón Domínguez.

GETTING AROUND Most of the sights and shopping in San Cristóbal are within walking distance of the plaza.

Urbano buses are minibuses that take residents to and from town and the outlying neighborhoods. All buses pass by the market and central plaza on their way through town. Utrilla and Avenida 16 de Septiembre are the two main arteries; all buses use the market area as the last stop. Utrilla is one way going toward the market, and any bus on that street will take you to the market. "María Auxiliadora" buses pass by all the bus stations on the way to the distant barrio of the same name.

Colectivo buses to outlying villages depart from the public market at Avenida Utrilla. Buses late in the day are usually very crowded. Always check to see when the last or next-to-last bus returns from wherever you're going, then take the one before that—those last buses sometimes don't materialize, and you'll be stranded. I speak from experience!

As traffic increases in the city, it often seems quicker to walk to your destination than to grab a taxi. Taxis, however, are inexpensive. There is a taxi stand on the east side of the plaza.

Rental cars come in handy for trips to the outlying villages and may be worth the expense when shared by a group, but keep in mind that insurance is invalid on unpaved roads. There's a **Budget** rental-car office here at Av. Mazariegos 36 (☎ 967/8-3100). You'll save money by arranging the rental from your home country; otherwise, a day's rental with insurance will cost $62 for a VW Beetle with manual transmission, the cheapest car for rent. Office hours are Monday through Sunday from 8am to 1pm and 5 to 8pm.

Bicycles are another option for getting around the city; a day's rental is about $10. Bikes are available at **Rent a Bike,** Av. Insurgentes 57 (☎ 967/8-4157), and at some hotels.

FAST FACTS: San Cristóbal de las Casas

Area Code   The telephone area code is 967.

Books   *Living Maya* by Walter Morris, with photography by Jeffrey Fox, is the best book to read to understand the culture, art and traditions around San Cristóbal de las Casas. Though published in 1987, the Epilogue in this book gives insight to the same unsolved social, economic and political problems that gave rise to the 1994 Chiapas Indian uprising. *The People of the Bat: Mayan Tales and Dreams from Zinacantán* by Robert M. Laughlin is a priceless collection of beliefs from that village near San Cristóbal. Another good book with a completely different overview of today's Maya is *The Heart of the Sky* by Peter Canby, who traveled among the Maya to chronicle their struggles. Though written before the recent uprising in Chiapas, it nevertheless offers a unique insight into their lives.

Bookstores   For a good selection of books about local Indians and crafts, go to Librería Soluna, Real de Guadalupe 13B and Insurgentes 27. Another good bookstore is La Pared de las Casas, located in the Centro Cultural El Puente (Real de Guadalupe #55). Here you'll find a selection of both new and used books, as well as a collection of travel guides and postcards.

Bulletin Boards   Since San Cristóbal is a cultural crossroads for travelers from all over the world, several places maintain bulletin boards with information on Spanish classes, local specialty tours, rooms or houses to rent, rides needed, etc. These include boards at the Tourism Office, Cafe el Puente, Mi Tierra and Na Bolom.

Climate   San Cristóbal can be very cold day or night year-round, especially during the winter. Most hotels are not heated, although some have fireplaces. Come prepared to bundle up in layers that can be peeled off. I always bring heavy socks, gloves, long johns, and a wool jacket, except in June, July, and August, when I take only heavy socks and a medium-weight jacket or sweater. Some sort of rain gear is handy year-round as well, especially in summer, when rains can be torrential.

Currency   Exchange Banamex is on the main plaza opposite the municipal palace; it's open Monday through Friday from 9:30am to 1pm. However, the most convenient place to exchange money is the Lacantún Money Exchange on Real de Guadalupe 12A, half a block from the plaza and next to the Real del Valle Hotel. It's open Monday through Saturday from 9am to 2pm and 4 to 8pm, and Sunday from 9am to 1pm.

Homestays   Café el Puente (see "Where to Dine," below), besides being a gathering place, restaurant, and telephone center can also arrange homestays.

Parking   If your hotel does not have parking, use the underground public lot (*estacionamiento*) located in front of the cathedral, just off the main square on 16 de Septiembre. Entry is from Calle 5 de Febrero.

Photography   *Warning:* Photographers should be very cautious about when, where, and at whom or what they point their cameras. In San Cristóbal, taking a photograph of even a chile pepper can be a risky undertaking, partly because of the native belief that a photograph endangers the soul and partly because the native people are tired of being photographed. Especially in the San Cristóbal market, people who think they or their possessions are being photographed may angrily pelt photographers with whatever object is at hand—rocks, rotten fruit, etc. Be respectful and ask first. You might even try offering a small amount of money in exchange for taking a picture. Young handcraft vendors will sometimes offer to be photographed for money.

Important note: In villages outside of San Cristóbal, there are strict rules about photography. To ensure proper respect by outsiders, villages around San Cristóbal, especially Chamula and Zinacantán, require visitors to go to the municipal building upon arrival and sign an agreement (written in Spanish) not to take photographs. The penalty for disobeying these regulations is stiff—confiscation of your camera and perhaps even a lengthy stay in jail. They mean it!

Post Office   The post office (correo) is at Crecencio Rosas and Cuauhtémoc, half a block south of the main square. It's open Monday through Friday from 8am to 7pm for purchasing stamps and mailing letters, 9am to 1pm and 4 to 5pm for mailing packages, and Saturday and holidays from 9am to 1pm.

Spanish Classes   The Centro Bilingue, at the Centro Cultural El Puente, Real de Guadalupe 55, San Cristóbal de las Casas, Chi. 29250 (☎ 800/303-4983 in the U.S., ☎ and fax 967/8-3723), offers classes in Spanish. The Director, Roberto Rivas, customizes instruction, be it one-on-one or in a small group, and strongly recommends that students expand their study by lodging with a local family. The Instituto Jovel, María Adelina Flores 21 (Apdo. Postal 62), San Cristóbal de las Casas, Chi. 29250 (☎ and fax 967/8-4069) is another well-regarded center for learning Spanish. Living with a local family is also part of the learning experience.

Telephone   Centro del Puente at the Café el Puente, Real de Guadalupe 55 (☎ and fax 967/8-1911), functions as the tourist's phone away from home, offering telephone and fax service at reasonable prices. Besides sending faxes, they'll receive faxes and hold them for you. The telephone service is open Monday through Saturday from 9am to 2pm and 5 to 9pm.

EXPLORING SAN CRISTÓBAL

Although San Cristóbal, a mountain town, is hard to get to, it continues to draw more and more visitors who come to enjoy the scenery, air, and hikes in the mountains. However, the town's biggest attraction is its colorful, centuries-old indigenous culture. The Chiapan Maya, attired in their beautifully crafted native garb, surround tourists in San Cristóbal, but most travelers take at least one trip to the outlying villages for a truer vision of Maya life.

SPECIAL EVENTS

In nearby Chamula, **Carnaval,** the big annual festival which takes place days before Lent, is a fascinating mingling of the Christian pre-Lenten ceremonies and the ancient Maya celebration of the 5 "lost days" at the end of the 360-day Maya agricultural cycle. Around noon on Shrove Tuesday, groups of village elders run across patches of burning grass as a purification rite, and then macho residents run through the streets with a bull. During Carnaval, roads are closed in town and buses drop visitors at the outskirts.

Warning: No photography of any kind is allowed during the Chamula Carnaval celebrations.

Nearby villages (except Zinacantán) also have celebrations during this time, although they're perhaps not as dramatic. Visiting these villages, especially on the Sunday before Lent, will round out your impression of Carnaval in all its regional varieties. In Tenejapa, the celebrants are still active during the Thursday market after Ash Wednesday.

San Cristóbal explodes with lights, excitement, and hordes of visitors during **Easter** and the week after it, when the annual **Feria de Primavera** (Spring Festival) is held. Activities, which fill an entire week, include carnival rides, food stalls, handcraft shops, parades, and band concerts. Hotel rooms are scarce, and room prices rise accordingly.

Another spectacle is staged July 22–25, the dates of the annual **Fiesta of San Cristóbal,** honoring the town's patron saint. The steps up to San Cristóbal's church are lit with torches at night. Pilgrimages to the church begin several days earlier, and on the night of the 24th, there's an all-night vigil.

For the **Día de Guadalupe,** on December 12, honoring Mexico's patron saint, the streets are gaily decorated and food stalls line the streets leading to the church honoring her high on a hill.

ATTRACTIONS IN TOWN

✪ **Na-Bolom.** Av. Vicente Guerrero 3, 29200 San Cristóbal de las Casas, Chi. ☎ and fax **967/ 8-5586** for the cultural center; ☎ and fax 967/8-1418 for hotel reservations. Admission $2 individual tours; $3 group tour and film *La Reina de la Selva,* an excellent 50-minute film on the Bloms, the Lacandóns, and Na-Bolom. Individual tours (in Spanish) are available daily 11:30am– 1:30pm. The group tour and film *La Reina de la Selva* (in English) is offered Tues–Sun 4:30– 7:30pm. The extensive library devoted to Mayan studies is open Mon–Thurs 8am–3pm, and Friday 8–11am. The small gift shop is open Tues–Sun from 10am–2pm and 4:30–6:30pm. Leave the square on Real de Guadalupe, walk 4 blocks to Avenida Vicente Guerrero, and turn left; Na-Bolom is 5½ blocks up Guerrero, just past the intersection with Comitán.

If you're interested in the anthropology of this region, you'll want to visit this house-cum-museum and stay here if you can. The house, built as a seminary in 1891, became the headquarters of anthropologists Frans and Trudy Blom in 1951 and the gathering place of outsiders interested in studying the region. Frans Blom led many early archaeological studies in Mexico, and Trudy was noted for her photographs of the Lacandón Indians and her efforts to save them and their forest homeland. A room at Na-Bolom contains a selection of her Lacandón photographs, and postcards of the photographs are on sale in the gift shop. A tour of the home includes the displays of pre-Hispanic artifacts collected by Frans Blom, the cozy library with its numerous volumes about the region and the Maya, and the gardens Trudy Blom started for the ongoing reforestation of the Lacandón jungle. Trudy Blom died in 1993, but Na-Bolom continues to operate as a nonprofit public trust.

The 13 guest rooms, named for surrounding villages, are decorated with local objects and textiles. All rooms have fireplaces, a welcome gift on cold nights. But the sheets are thin and in a three-night stay, not changed once, and the towels are old and stiff. A tax-deductible donation to this worthy house of culture could go toward upkeep—or donate some new sheets and towels to the cause. Prices for rooms (including breakfast) are $28 single and $40 double.

Even if you're not a guest here you can come for a meal, usually a delicious assortment of vegetarian dishes. Just be sure to make a reservation and be on time. The colorful dining room has one large table; it's a gathering place for scholars, anthropologists, archaeologists, and the like, and the eclectic mix sometimes makes for interesting conversation. Breakfast costs $4, lunch and dinner $5 each. Following breakfast at 9am, tours to San Juan Chamula and Zinacantán are offered. (See "The Nearby Maya Villages and Countryside" below.)

Museo Templo y Convento Santo Domingo. Av. 20 de Noviembre. ☎ **987/8-1600.** Church, free. Museum, Tues–Sat $3; Sun and holidays free. Museum, Tues–Sun 10am–5pm.

Inside the front door of the carved-stone plateresque facade, there's a beautiful gilded wooden altarpiece built in 1560, walls with saints, and gilt-framed paintings. Attached to the church is the former Convent of Santo Domingo, which houses a small museum about San Cristóbal and Chiapas. The museum, housed on three floors, has changing exhibits and often shows cultural films. It's 5 blocks north of the zócalo.

Cathedral. 20 de Noviembre at Guadalupe Victoria. No phone. Free admission. Daily 7am–6pm.

San Cristóbal's main cathedral was built in the 1500s and boasts fine timberwork and a very fancy pulpit.

Palacio de las Bellas Artes. Av. Hidalgo, 4 blocks south of the plaza. No phone.

Be sure to check out this building if you are interested in the arts. It periodically hosts dance events, art shows, and other performances. The schedule of events is usually posted on the door if the Bellas Artes is not open. There's a public library next door.

Templo de San Cristóbal.

For the best view of San Cristóbal, climb the seemingly endless steps to this church and *mirador* (lookout point). Leave the zócalo on Avenida Hidalgo and turn right onto the third street (Hermanos Domínguez); at the end of the street are the steps you've got to climb. A visit here requires stamina. By the way, there are 22 more churches in town, some of which also require a strenuous climb.

Museo de Ambar. Plaza Sivan, Utrilla 10. ☎ **967/8-3507.** Free admission. Daily 9:30am–7pm. From the plaza, walk 2¹/₂ blocks north on Utrilla (going toward the market); the museum will be on your left.

Seen from the street, this place looks like just another store selling Guatemalan clothing, but pass through the small shop area and you'll find the long, narrow museum—a fascinating place to browse. It's the only museum in Mexico devoted to amber, a vegetable-fossil resin thousands of years old mined in Chiapas near Simojovel. Owner José Luís Coria Torres has assembled more than 250 sculpted amber pieces as well as a rare collection of amber with insects trapped inside and amber fused with fossils. Amber jewelry and other objects are also for sale.

HORSEBACK RIDING

The **Casa de Huespedes Margarita** and **Hotel Real del Valle** (see "Where to Stay," below) can arrange horseback rides for around $15 for a day, including a guide. Reserve your steed at least a day in advance. A horse-riding excursion might go to San Juan Chamula, to nearby caves, or just up into the hills.

THE NEARBY MAYA VILLAGES & COUNTRYSIDE

Na-Bolom (see "Attractions in Town," above) offers daily trips to San Juan Chamula and Zinacantán at 10am. Minivan transportation, and a knowledgeable guide are included in the $10 per person price. The tour returns to San Cristóbal between 2 and 3pm.

Another tour is led by a very opinionated mestiza woman, **Mercedes Hernández Gómez.** Mercedes, a largely self-trained ethnographer, is extremely well-informed about the history and folkways of the villages. She explains (in English) the religious significance of what you see in the churches, where shamans try to cure Indian patients of various maladies. She also facilitates tourists' firsthand contact with Indians. Her group goes by minivan to the village or villages she has selected; normally tours return to the plaza at about 2:30pm. You can meet her near the kiosk in the main plaza at 9am (she will be carrying an umbrella). The tour costs $10 per person.

Important note: Do not take photographs in the villages around San Cristóbal (see the photography warning in "Fast Facts: San Cristóbal de las Casas," above). During Carnaval in 1990, I met a French photographer who took one picture from a hill above Chamula, after which villagers hiding in the bushes wrestled him to the ground and seized his Nikon.

For excursions farther afield, see "Road Trips from San Cristóbal" at the end of this section.

CHAMULA & ZINACANTÁN   A side trip to the village of San Juan Chamula will really get you into the spirit of life around San Cristóbal. Sunday, when the market is in full swing, is the best day to go for shopping, but other days, when you'll be unimpeded by anxious children selling their crafts, are better for seeing the village and church. Colectivos (minibuses) to San Juan Chamula leave the municipal market in San Cristóbal about every half hour. Don't expect anyone in these vans to speak English or Spanish, and the driver may be around 11 or 12 years old and barely able to see over the steering wheel.

The village, 5 miles northeast of San Cristóbal, is the Chamula cultural and ceremonial center. Activity centers on the huge church, the plaza, and the municipal building. Each year, a new group of citizens is chosen to live in the municipal center as caretakers of the saints, settlers of disputes, and enforcers of village rules. As in other nearby villages, on Sunday local leaders wear their leadership costumes with beautifully woven straw hats loaded with colorful ribbons befitting their high position. They solemnly sit together in a long line somewhere around the central square. Chamula is typical of other villages in that men are often away working in the "hot lands" harvesting coffee or cacao, while women stay home to tend the sheep, the children, the cornfields, and the fires. It's almost always the women's and children's work to gather sticks for fires, and you see them along roadsides bent against the weight.

I don't want to spoil your experience of the interior of the Chamula church for the first time by describing it too much. Just don't leave Chamula without seeing it. As you step from bright sunlight into the candlelit interior, it will take a few minutes for your eyes to adjust. The tile floor is covered in pine needles scattered amid a meandering sea of lighted candles. Saints line the walls, and before them people are often kneeling and praying aloud while passing around bottles of Pepsi-Cola. Shamans are often on hand, passing eggs over sick people or using live or dead chickens in a curing ritual. The statues of saints are similar to those you might see in any Mexican Catholic church, but they take on another meaning to the Chamulas that has no similarity to the traditional Catholic saints other than in name. Visitors can walk carefully through the church to see the saints or stand quietly in the background and observe.

Carnaval, which takes place just before Lent, is the big annual festival. The Chamulas are not a very wealthy people as their economy is based on agriculture, but the women are the region's best wool weavers, producing finished pieces for themselves and for other villages.

In Zinacantán, a wealthier village than Chamula, you must sign a rigid form promising not to take any photographs before you are allowed to see the two side-by-side sanctuaries. Once permission is granted and you have paid a small fee, an escort will usually show you the church, or you may be allowed to see it on your own. Floors may be covered in pine needles here, too, and the rooms are brightly sunlit. The experience is an altogether different one from that of Chamula.

AMATENANGO DEL VALLE   About an hour's ride south of San Cristóbal is Amatenango, a town known mostly for its women potters. You'll see their work in San Cristóbal—small animals, jars, and large water jugs—but in the village, you can visit the potters in their homes. All you have to do is arrive and walk down the dirt streets. Villagers will lean over the walls of family compounds and invite you in to select from their inventory. You may even see them firing the pieces under piles of wood in the open courtyard or painting them with color derived from rusty iron water. The women wear beautiful red-and-yellow *huipils,* but if you want to take a photograph, you'll have to pay.

To get here, take a colectivo from the market in San Cristóbal, but before it lets you off, be sure to ask about the return-trip schedule.

AGUACATENANGO   Located 10 miles south of Amatenango, this village is known for its embroidery. If you've been in San Cristóbal shops before arriving here, you'll recognize the white-on-white or black-on-black floral patterns on dresses and blouses for sale. The locals' own regional blouses, however, are quite different.

TENEJAPA   The weavers of Tenejapa make some of the most beautiful and expensive work you'll see in the region. The best time to visit is on market day (Sunday and Thursday, though Sunday is best). The weavers of Tenejapa taught the weavers of San Andrés and Magdalena, which accounts for the similarity in their designs and colors. To get to Tenejapa, try to find a colectivo in the very last row of colectivos by the market or hire a taxi. On Tenejapa's main street, several stores sell locally woven regional clothing, and you can bargain for the price.

THE HUITEPEC CLOUD FOREST   **Pronatura,** a private nonprofit ecological organization, offers environmentally sensitive tours of the cloud forest. The forest is a haven for migratory birds, and over 100 bird species and 600 plant species have been discovered here. In the past, tours have been offered Tuesday, Thursday, and Saturday at 9:30am at a cost of $6 per person; these tours have been temporarily suspended because Pronatura has moved their office. Their office is at Adelina Flores 11. To reach the reserve on your own, drive on the road to Chamula; the turnoff is at km 3.5. The reserve is open Tuesday through Saturday from 9am to 5pm.

SHOPPING

Many Indian villages near San Cristóbal are noted for their weaving, embroidery, brocade work, leather, and pottery, making the area one of the best in the country for shopping. The craftspeople make and sell beautiful woolen shawls, indigo-died skirts, colorful native shirts, and magnificently woven *huipils* (women's long overblouses), all of which often come in vivid geometric patterns. In leather, they are artisans of the highest rating, making sandals and men's handbags. There's a proliferation of tie-dyed jaspe from Guatemala, which comes in bolts and is made into clothing, as well as other textiles from that country. There are numerous shops up and down the streets leading to the market. Calle Real de Guadalupe houses more shops than any other street.

CRAFTS

La Albarrada, Centro Desarrollo Comunitario DIF. Barrio María Auxiliadora. No phone.

At this government-sponsored school, young men and women from surrounding villages come to learn how to hook Persian-style rugs, weave fabric on foot looms, sew, make furniture, construct a house, cook, make leather shoes and bags, forge iron, and grow vegetables and trees for reforestation. Probably the most interesting crafts for the general tourist are the rugmaking and weaving. Artisans from Temoaya in Mexico State learned rugmaking from Persians, who came to teach this skill in the 1970s. The Temoaya artisans in turn traveled to San Cristóbal to teach the craft to area students, who have since taught others. The beautiful rug designs are taken from brocaded and woven designs used to decorate regional costumes. Visitors should stop at the entrance and ask for an escort. You can visit all the various areas and see students at work or simply go straight to the weavers. There's a small sales outlet at the entrance selling newly loomed fabric by the meter, leather bags, rugs, and baskets made at another school in the highlands. The rug selection is best here, but the Casa de Artesanías DIF in the town center (see "Textile Shops," below) features these crafts and more from around Mexico. La Albarrada is in a far southern suburb of the city off the highway to Comitán, to the right. To get here take the "María Auxiliadora" urbano bus from the market. Ask the driver to let you off at La Albarrada. The same bus makes the return trip, passing through the town center and ending its route at the market.

Central Market. Av. Utrilla. No phone.

The market buildings and the streets surrounding them offer just about anything you might need. The market in San Cristóbal is open every morning except Sunday (when each village has its own local market), and you'll probably enjoy observing the sellers as much as the things they sell. See "Photography" in "Fast Facts: San Cristóbal de las Casas," above, regarding photography here. The mercado is north of the Santo Domingo church, about 9 blocks from the zócalo.

El Encuentro. Calle Real de Guadalupe 63-A. ☎ 967/8-3698.

This place is tended by a pair of *dueñas muy simpáticas,* and you'll find some of your best bargains here—or at least you'll think the price is fair. The shop carries many regional ritual items, such as new and used men's ceremonial hats, false saints, and iron rooftop adornments, plus many *huipils* and other textiles. It's open Monday through Saturday from 9am to 8pm. It's between Dujelay and Guerrero.

La Galería. Hidalgo 3. ☎ 967/8-1547.

This lovely shop beneath a great cafe has a wonderful selection of paintings and greeting cards by Kiki, a German artist who has found her niche in San Cristóbal. There is also an extensive selection of Oaxacan rugs and pottery, plus unusual silver jewelry. Open daily from 10am to 9pm.

TEXTILE SHOPS

Casa de Artesanías DIF. Niños Héroes at Hidalgo. ☎ 967/8-1180.

Crafts made under the sponsorship of DIF (a governmental agency that assists families) are sold in a fine showroom in one of the city's old houses. Here you'll find such quality products as lined wool vests and jackets, bolts of foot-loomed fabrics, Persian-style rugs made at La Albarrada (see "Crafts," above), pillow covers, amber jewelry, and more. In back is a fine little museum showing costumes worn by villagers who live near San Cristóbal. Open Monday through Saturday from 9am to 2pm and 5 to 8pm.

Plaza de Santo Domingo. Av. Utrilla.

The plazas around this church and the nearby Templo de Caridad are filled with women in native garb selling their wares. Here you'll find women from Chamula weaving belts or embroidering, surrounded by piles of loomed woolen textiles from their village. More and more Guatemalan shawls, belts, and bags are included in their inventory. There are also some excellent buys in Chiapan-made wool vests, jackets, rugs, and shawls similar to those in Sna Jolobil (see below), if you take the time to look and bargain. Vendors arrive between 9 and 10am and begin to leave around 3pm.

Sna Jolobil. Av. 20 de Noviembre. No phone.

Meaning "weaver's house" in the Maya language, this place is located in the former convent (monastery) of Santo Domingo, next to the Templo de Santo Domingo between Navarro and Nicaragua. This cooperative store is operated by groups of Tzotzil and Tzeltal craftspeople and has about 3,000 members who contribute products, help in running the store, and share in the moderate profits. Their works are simply beautiful; prices are set and high—as is the quality. Be sure to take a look. Open Monday through Saturday from 9am to 2pm and 4 to 6pm; credit cards are accepted.

Tzontehuitz. Real de Guadalupe 74. ☎ and fax **967/8-3158.**

About 3¹/₂ blocks from the plaza, this shop is one of the best on Calle Real de Guadalupe, near the corner of Diego Dujelay. Owner Janet Giacobone specializes in her own textile designs and weavings. Some of her work is loomed in Guatemala, but you can also watch weavers using foot looms in the courtyard. Hours are Monday through Saturday from 9am to 2pm and 4 to 7pm.

Unión Regional de Artesanías de los Altos. Av. Utrilla 43. ☎**967/8-2848.**

Another cooperative of weavers, this one is smaller than Sna Jolobil (see above) but not necessarily any cheaper and not as sophisticated in its approach to potential shoppers. Also known as J'pas Joloviletic, it's worth looking around, and credit cards are accepted (though they weren't in the past). Open Monday through Saturday from 9am to 2pm and 4 to 7pm, and Sunday from 9am to 1pm.

WHERE TO STAY

Keep in mind that among the most interesting places to stay in San Cristóbal is an anthropologist's dream—the house/museum of **Na-Bolom.** See "Attractions in Town," above, for details.

For really low-cost accommodations, there are basic but acceptable *hospedajes* and *posadas,* which charge about $6 for a single and $8 to $12 for a double. Usually these places are unadvertised; if you're interested in a very cheap *hospedaje,* ask around in a restaurant or cafe, and you're sure to find one, or go to the tourist office, which often displays notices of new *hospedajes* on the metal flip rack in the office. Some of the best economical offerings are on Calle Real de Guadalupe, east of the main square.

MODERATE

✪ **Hotel Casa Mexicana.**28 de Agosto no. 1, 29200 San Cristóbal de las Casas, Chi. ☎**967/8-1348.** Fax 967/8-2627. E-mail: hcasamex@mail.internet.com.mx. 31 rms. TV TEL. $45 double. Free parking; secure.

This lovely hotel is a conveniently located deluxe addition to the San Cristóbal scene; at a beach location the price would be four times higher. Created from a large mansion with a grand exterior, the entry thrusts you into elegance, with refined pastel colors, handsome sitting areas, and the restaurant Los Magueys centered around a lovely courtyard and fountain with Zuniga sculpture. Tastefully designed, and decorated with a substantial art collection, talavera pottery, and antiques, the hotel is a bargain by any standard. The carpeted rooms have excellent reading lights, electric heaters for those chilly nights, and either one or two double beds with handsome carved headboards. Guests are welcome to use the sauna, and inexpensive massages can be arranged. The beautiful restaurant, with its handsome stained glass windows, is to the right of the entrance, and serves excellent regional and international food.

The hotel is owned by Kiki and her husband, who also own La Galeria Restaurant and shop. The hotel is 4 blocks north of the main plaza at the corner of Utrilla and Agosto/Eje Nacional.

✪ **Hotel Casavieja.** Ma. Adelina Flores 27, 29200 San Cristóbal de las Casas, Chi. ☎ and fax **967/8-5223** and 967/8-0385. 40 rms. TV TEL. $40 double. Free parking.

The Casavieja is undoubtedly one of the choice hotels in Mexico. Originally built in 1740, restoration and new construction have faithfully replicated the original design and detail, complete with wood beam ceilings. The size and beautiful furnishings of the carpeted rooms, plus the very welcome heaters, create an ideal, cozy nest. The hotel's stylish restaurant, Doña Rita, faces the interior courtyard with tables on the patio or inside and offers reasonable prices—but service is slow. Fifteen rooms across the street house the tour groups, which in the past have created lots of noise in this otherwise tranquil hotel. The hotel is 3¹/₂ blocks northeast of the plaza between Cristóbal Colón and Diego Dujelay.

✪ **Hotel Rincón del Arco.** Ejército Nacional 66, 29200 San Cristóbal de las Casas, Chi. ☎ **967/8-1313.** Fax 967/8-1568. 36 rms. TV TEL. $30 double. Free parking.

The original section of this former colonial-era home is built around a small interior patio and dates from 1650. Rooms in this part, with tall ceilings and carpet over hardwood floors, exude charm. No two rooms are alike in the adjacent new section, which faces a large grassy inner yard. They are nicely furnished and come with beds covered in thick, handsome bedspreads made in the family factory. Some are furnished in antiques, others in colonial style. Some have small balconies; all have fireplaces. In fact, if this hotel were a bit closer to the plaza, the cost of the rooms would be much more. Consider it a value. Owner José António Hernánz is eager to make your stay a good one. There's a restaurant just behind the lobby. The hotel offers special discounted prices to students, but make arrangements in advance and be able to show university identification. The hotel is 8 blocks northeast of the main plaza at the corners of Ejército Nacional and V. Guerrero.

INEXPENSIVE

Casa de Huespedes Margarita. Real de Guadalupe 34, 29200 San Cristóbal de las Casas, Chi. ☎ and fax **967/8-0957.** 25 rms (none with bath). $3.80 dorm bed; $5.50 single; $7.50 double; $9 triple.

Part hotel and part youth hostel, this establishment offers rooms arranged around a courtyard where the young backpackers congregate. The rooms have sagging mattresses and bare light bulbs hanging from the ceiling; the shared baths are only fair. The hotel's popular restaurant is filled with youths in the evening, and there is live music at 8pm. Margarita's also has horse rentals and offers tours to the nearby ruins and to the Sumidero Canyon near Tuxtla Gutiérrez. You'll find this lodging 1¹/₂ blocks east of the plaza between Avenida B. Domínguez and Colón.

Hotel Don Quijote. Colón 7, 29200 San Cristóbal de las Casas, Chi. ☎ and fax **967/8-0346.** 22 rms. TV. $15 double. Free parking; secure.

Upon entering this three-story hotel in a former residence built around a small patio, you'll see walls decorated with costumes from area villages. Throughout the hotel there are photos of old San Cristóbal and murals depicting Don Quixote. The small rooms are crowded with furniture and closets are small, but the rooms are carpeted and coordinated with warm, beautiful textiles foot-loomed in the family factory. All have two double beds with lamps over them, private tiled baths, and plenty of hot water. It's 2¹/₂ blocks east of the plaza, near the corner of Colón.

Hotel Palacio de Moctezuma. Juárez 16, 29200 San Cristóbal de las Casas, Chi. ☎ **967/ 8-0352** or 967/8-1142. Fax 967/8-1536. 42 rms. TV TEL. $20 double. Free parking; limited.

An excellent choice near the plaza, this three-story hotel is delightfully filled with bougainvillea and geraniums. Fresh-cut flowers tucked around tile fountains are a hallmark of this hotel. The rooms have lace curtains on French windows, nice co-ordinated drapes and bedspreads, red carpeting, and modern tiled showers. But alas, they are very cold in winter. Two suites have a TV and refrigerator. Overstuffed couches face a large fireplace in the lobby bar, and the cozy restaurant looks out on the interior courtyard. On the third floor is a solarium with comfortable tables and chairs and great city views. The hotel is 3¹/₂ blocks southeast of the main plaza at the corner of Juárez and León.

Hotel Plaza Santo Domingo. Utrilla 35, 29200 San Cristóbal de las Casas, Chi. ☎ **967/ 8-1927.** Fax 967/8-6514. 30 rms. TV TEL. $19 double. Limited parking.

New in 1992, this hotel is ideally situated close to the Santo Domingo Church, near the bustling market area. Behind the lobby and plant-filled entry courtyard are the nicely furnished, carpeted rooms. Each comes with a small closet and small desk below the TV, which is set high on the wall. Baths are trimmed in blue-and-white tile, and the sink area is conveniently placed outside the shower area. A large pleasant indoor dining room is off the lobby, along with a smaller patio dining area and a large bar. This is one of the few places near Santo Domingo and the market where you can get a good meal and use clean rest rooms.

Hotel Posada de los Angeles. Calle Francisco Madero 17, 29200 San Cristóbal de las Casas, Chi. ☎ **967/8-1173** or 967/8-4371. Fax 967/8-2581. 20 rms. TV TEL. $18 double.

With beautiful etched-glass doors opening to the street, this inn, which opened in 1991, deserves your attention. The vaulted ceilings and skylights make the three-story hotel seem much larger and brighter than many others in the city. Rooms have either two single or two double beds, and the baths are large, modern, and immaculately clean; windows open onto a pretty courtyard with a fountain. The rooftop sun deck is a great siesta spot. The hotel is a half block east of the plaza between Insurgentes and Juárez.

Hotel Real de Valle. Real de Guadalupe 14, 29200 San Cristóbal de las Casas, Chi. ☎ **967/ 8-0680.** Fax 967/8-3955. 36 rms. $17 double.

The helpful staff at the Real de Valle is quick to assist guests in any way possible. The 24 new rooms in the back three-story section have new baths, big closets, and a brown-and-cream decor. In addition to a rooftop solarium with chaise lounges, you'll find a small cafeteria and an upstairs dining room with a big double fireplace. Services include a travel agency offering personally guided tours, horse rental, laundry, Spanish-language study, and use of a fax and photocopy machine. To find the hotel from the plaza, walk a half block east of the central plaza on Real de Guadalupe.

Posada Jovel. Flavio Paniagua 28, 29200 San Cristóbal de las Casas, Chi. ☎ **967/8-1734.** 18 rms (9 with bath). $10.50 double without bath; $12 double with bath.

If you're low on funds and want to stay a while in cheery surroundings, then you may find this modest two-story inn to your liking. The bright, freshly painted rooms have tile floors and colorful blanket/bedspreads and *ixtle* (basket) lamps. Shelves and hooks hold belongings, and beds are firm. This place belongs to an association of posadas, so they'll recommend another budget lodging if they're full. The posada is between the market and main plaza, 2¹/₂ very long blocks east of Utrilla.

WHERE TO DINE

San Cristóbal is one of the country's best dining-out towns because of the quality of its food—not for luxury establishments. In addition to the restaurants mentioned below, most hotels have their own restaurants and serve good meals. Be sure to look for regional Chiapan food like large tamales, *butifarra* (a delicious sausage), and *pox* (pronounced posh, a local firewater similar to *aguardiente*). For baked goods, try the **Panadería Mercantil** at Mazariego 17, ☎ **967/8-0307.** It's open Monday through Saturday from 8am to 9:30pm, and Sunday from 9am to 9pm. Remember that you're about a mile and a half high here, and therefore you digest your food more slowly.

MODERATE

✪ **El Fogón de Jovel.** 16 de Septiembre no. 11. ☎ **967/8-1153.** Main courses $4–$8. Daily 1–5pm and 7–11pm. CHIAPAN.

This is one of my most favorite places to dine in San Cristóbal. If word-of-mouth doesn't lead you here, the lively sounds of marimba music will. Chiapan food is served at this handsome old town house, with dining under the portals and rooms built around a central courtyard. The waiters wear local costumes. Walls are hung with Guatemalan and Chiapan prints and folk art. Each dish and regional drink such as *posh* (a distilled sugar-and-corn drink) is explained on the menu, which is available in English. A basket of warm handmade tortillas with six filling condiments arrives before the meal. Among the specialties, the corn soup is delicious, as are the mole chiapaneca, pork or chicken adobado in a delicious chile sauce, and pepian, a savory chile and tomato sauce served over chicken. For a different dessert try the changleta, which is half of a sweetened baked chayote—so delicious you may want two. Cooking classes for small groups can be arranged, but make reservations well in advance. The restaurant is only a block northwest of the plaza at the corner of Guadalupe Victoria/Real de Guadalupe and 16 de Septiembre.

✪ **Madre Tierra.** Insurgentes 19. ☎ **967/8-4297.** Main courses $2–$5.50; comida corrida $5.50. Restaurant, daily 8am–9:45pm (comida corrida served 1–5pm); bakery, Mon–Sat 9am–8pm, Sun 9am–noon. MEXICAN/VEGETARIAN.

This restaurant satisfies the cravings of meat lovers and vegetarians alike. The bakery specializes in whole-wheat breads, pastries, pizza by the slice, quiche, grains, granola, and dried fruit. The restaurant serves the bakery's goods and other delicious fare in an old mansion with wood-plank floors, long windows looking onto the street, and tables covered in colorful Guatemalan *jaspe*. Classical music plays softly in the background. It's a good place for a cappuccino and pastry or an entire meal; the comida corrida is very filling, and I also recommend the chicken curry, lasagna, and fresh salads. Madre Tierra is on Insurgentes, $3^1/_2$ blocks south of the plaza.

INEXPENSIVE

Café el Puente. Real de Guadalupe 55. ☎ **967/8-2250.** Breakfast $1.75–$2.25; soups and salads $2–$3.50; pastries 75¢–$2. Mon—Sat 8am–10:30pm. MEXICAN.

Ex-Californian Bill English has turned a huge old mansion into a cafe/cultural center where tourists and locals can converse, take Spanish classes, arrange a homestay, leave a message on the bulletin board, and send and receive faxes. How's that for a one-stop place? The cafe takes up the main part of the building, and there are a weaver's shop and travel agency to the side. The Centro Bilingue language school is headquartered here as well, and movies, plays, and lectures are presented nightly in an interior patio and meeting room. It's the kind of place you return to often, for fresh waffles and coffee in the morning, for an inexpensive lunch or dinner of brown rice and veggies, or for good conversation at any time of day. Guests are welcome to post notices, messages, and advertisements on the long bulletin board, which is well worth checking out if you're looking for a ride, a place to stay, or information on out-of-the-way destinations. It's 2¹/₂ blocks east of the plaza between Dujelay and Cristóbal Colón.

Normita's II. Av. Juárez at F. Flores. No phone. Breakfast $1.25–$2.25; comida corrida $2.75–$3.50; pozole $2; tacos $1. Daily 8am–10pm (comida corrida served 1:30–3pm). MEXICAN.

This is the place for cheap, dependable, short-order Mexican mainstays. Everything is homemade—from the wood tables and checked tablecloths to the tacos and pozole. It's a very humble restaurant; the open kitchen takes up one corner of the room and tables are scattered in front of a large paper mural of a fall forest scene from some faraway place. It's 2 blocks southeast of the plaza at the corner of Flores and Juárez.

✪ Paris-Mexico Restaurant. Madero 20. ☎ **967/8-0695.** Crepes $1.75–$4; pizzas $3.75–$6.50; comida corrida $2.75–$3.25. Daily 7am–11pm. MEXICAN/FRENCH/ITALIAN.

Decorated with plain, nicely finished wood tables and chairs, the Paris-Mexico resembles a cozy neighborhood cafe. The food is wonderfully prepared. The comida corrida might consist of salad, grilled chicken breast, potatoes or rice, fruit salad, and coffee or tea. You can also choose from an endless list of crepes for breakfast, lunch, dinner, or dessert; pizza served 10 ways; five variations on spaghetti; or a small selection of beef and chicken dishes. The Paris-Mexico is on Madero half a block east of the plaza.

✪ Restaurant Tuluc. Insurgentes 5. ☎ **967/8-2090.** Breakfast $1.75–$2.50; main course $2–$3.25; comida corrida $3. Daily 7am–10pm (comida corrida served 1–5pm). MEXICAN.

This warm and inviting restaurant has lustrous wooden booths and tables with Guatemalan fabric. It's a cozy place for a cup of hot chocolate or espresso, but above all, the comida corrida is an exceptional value here. The house specialty is the *filete Tuluc*, a beef filet wrapped around spinach and cheese served with fried potatoes and green beans. The Chiapaneco breakfast is a filling quartet of juice, toast, two Chiapan tamales, and your choice of tea, coffee, cappuccino, or hot chocolate. The owner speaks seven languages. Tuluc is 1¹/₂ blocks south of the plaza between Cuauhtémoc and Francisco Leon.

COFFEEHOUSES

Since Chiapan-grown coffee is highly regarded, it's natural to find a proliferation of coffeehouses here. Most are concealed in the nooks and crannies of San Cristóbal's side streets.

Café Altura and Casa Naturista. Primero de Marzo no. 6C. ☎ **967/8-4038.** Soy burgers $1.75; salads $2; coffee 75¢–$1.25. Daily 7am–9pm. VEGETARIAN.

Café Altura specializes in organic vegetarian meals. Breakfasts include granola, yogurt, fruit, and whole-wheat breads. A variety of coffees is available all day. Grains, granola, teas, and coffee beans are sold in bulk. The cafe is 3 blocks north of the plaza near the corner of Primero de Marzo and 16 de Noviembre.

Café San Cristóbal. Cuauhtémoc 1. ☎ **967/8-3861.** Coffee 50¢–$1; cake 75¢–$2.50. Mon–Sat 9am–10pm, Sun 10am–2pm and 5–10pm. COFFEE/CAKE.

Not only is this a cafe, but it also sells coffee beans by the kilogram (2.2 lb.). Chess is the game of choice at the few tables and booths; men hunker over their chessboards for hours, drinking coffee and visiting with friends. A cup of coffee here provides a respite from the rush outside. The restaurant is 1 block south of the plaza near the corner of Cuauhtémoc and Insurgentes.

SAN CRISTÓBAL AFTER DARK

The cafes and restaurants of San Cristóbal are also home to the area's nightlife. The coffeehouses, with their international clientele, invite the pastime of conversation; you'll also see notices posted around town advertising live music, particularly in the cafes. One of the most popular of the cafes at night is **La Galería,** Av. Hidalgo 3, where there's live music nightly on the patio and movies inside—plus it's a full fledged restaurant.

ROAD TRIPS FROM SAN CRISTÓBAL

Several travel agencies in town offer excursions to nearby villages (see "The Nearby Maya Villages & Countryside," above) and those farther away. Strangely, except where noted otherwise, the cost of the trip includes a driver but does not necessarily include either a bilingual guide or guided information of any kind. You pay extra for those services, so if you want to be informed while taking a tour, be sure to ask if the tour is merely transportation or if it includes a knowledgeable guide as well.

RUINS OF TONINÁ

The Maya ruins of Toniná (which means "house of rocks") are 2 hours from San Cristóbal and 8¹/₂ miles east of Ocosingo. Dating from the Classic period, the terraced site covers an area of at least 9 square miles. Extensive excavations are under way here during the dry season.

As early as A.D. 350, Toniná emerged as a separate dynastic center of the Maya and has the distinction of having the last recorded date of the long count yet found (A.D. 909) on a small stone monument. The date signifies the end of the Classic period. Another stone, dated A.D. 711, discovered here depicts the captured King Kan-Xul of Palenque (the younger brother of Chan-Bahlum and the son of King Pacal); the portrait shows him with his arm tied by a rope but still wearing his royal headdress. Recently a huge stucco panel was unearthed picturing the Lord of Death holding Kan-Xul's head, confirming long-held suspicions that the king died at Toniná.

At the moment there are no signs to guide visitors through the site, so you're on your own. The caretaker can also show you around (in Spanish), after which a tip is appreciated. Ask at the Casa de Huespedes Margarita in San Cristóbal (see "Where to Stay," above) about guided trips to Toniná (four-person minimum). The trip includes the services of a bilingual driver, a tour of the site, lunch, and a swim in the river. From November through February you'll see thousands of swallows swarming near the ruins.

You can go on your own by bus to Ocosingo and from there take a taxi to the ruins, but have the taxi wait for your return. The ruins are open daily from 8am to 5pm; admission is $2.

PALENQUE, BONAMPAK & YAXCHILÁN

Many visitors to San Cristóbal want to visit the ruins of Palenque near Villahermosa and the Bonampak and Yaxchilán ruins on Mexico's border with Guatemala. A trip to Palenque can be accomplished in a long day-trip from San Cristóbal, but I don't recommend it because Palenque should be savored. Bonampak and Yaxchilán are easier to see from Palenque.

For arranging these trips from San Cristóbal, I highly recommend **ATC Tours and Travel,** located across from El Fogón restaurant, Calle 5 de Febrero no. 15 at the corner of 16 de Septiembre (☎ 967/8-2550; fax 967/8-3145). The agency has bilingual guides and good vehicles. See the "Palenque" section, above, for details on Bonampak and camping overnight at Yaxchilán; see "Active Vacations in the

Yucatán" in chapter 3 for other ATC regional tours focusing on birds and orchids, textiles, hiking, and camping.

If you're considering a day-trip to the archaeological site of Palenque using ATC (mentioned above) or a similar travel agency, here's how your tour will be arranged. You start at 7 or 8am and within 3 hours reach the Agua Azul waterfalls, where there's a 1½-hour stop to swim. From there it's another 1½-hour drive to Palenque. You'll have about 2 hours to see the site. If your group agrees, you can skip the swim and have more time at Palenque. It'll be a minimum 16-hour day and costs about $80 per person with a minimum of four people traveling.

CHINCULTIC RUINS, COMITÁN & MONTEBELLO NATIONAL PARK

Almost 100 miles southeast of San Cristóbal, near the border of Guatemala, is the Chincultic archaeological site and Montebello National Park, with 16 multicolored lakes and exuberant pine-forest vegetation. Forty-six miles from San Cristóbal is Comitán, a pretty hillside town of 40,000 inhabitants known for its flower cultivation and a sugarcane-based firewater called *comitecho*. It's also the last big town along the Pan American Highway before the Guatemalan border, and it's the location of the nearest airport to San Cristóbal.

The Chincultic ruins, a Late-Classic site, have barely been excavated, but the main acropolis, set high up against a cliff, is magnificent to see from below and worth the walk up for the vista. After passing through the gate, you'll see the trail ahead; it passes ruins on both sides. Steep stairs leading up the mountain to the acropolis are flanked by more unexcavated tree-covered ruins. From there, you can gaze upon distant Montebello Lakes and miles of cornfields and forest. The paved road to the lakes passes six lakes, all different colors and sizes, ringed by cool pine forests; most have car parks and lookouts. The paved road ends at a small restaurant. The lakes are best seen on a sunny day, when their famous, brilliant colors are optimal.

Most travel agencies in San Cristóbal offer a day-long trip that includes the lakes, the ruins, lunch in Comitán, and a stop in the pottery-making village of Amatenango del Valle. If you're driving, follow Highway 190 south from San Cristóbal through the pretty village of Teopisca and then through Comitán; turn left at La Trintaria, where there's a sign to the lakes. After the Trintaria turnoff and before you reach the lakes, there's a sign pointing left down a narrow dirt road to the Chincultic ruins.

4　Tuxtla Gutiérrez

51 miles W of San Cristóbal, 173 miles S of Villahermosa, 151 miles NW of Ciudad Cuauhtémoc on the Guatemalan border

Tuxtla Gutiérrez (alt. 1,838 ft.; pop. 300,000) is the boomtown capital of the wild, mountainous state of Chiapas. Long Mexico's coffee-growing center, the city has recently become an oil prospector's mecca. While Tuxtla is not exactly an unpleasant town, it hasn't been able to manage growth with any aesthetic considerations. To tourists, who are more of a footnote than a feature of interest to the town, Tuxtla Gutiérrez is a necessary crossroads for getting to San Cristóbal. If you have some time to spare, visit the Tuxtla Zoo and Sumidero Canyon.

ESSENTIALS
GETTING THERE & DEPARTING

BY PLANE **Aviación de Chiapas** (also known as Aviacsa, ☎ 961/2-6880 or 961/2-8081, fax 961/3-5029; at the airport 961/5-1011) connects Tuxtla to Cancún, Chetumal, Mérida, Mexico City, Guatemala City, Villahermosa, and Oaxaca. **Mexicana** (☎ 961/2-0020 or 961/2-5402; at the airport 961/3-4921) has daily flights from Mexico City, Cancún, Mérida, Oaxaca, and Villahermosa. Check with the local offices of Mexicana about van departures to the airport. They leave from the downtown office or will pick you up at your hotel if you reserve in advance. When the office is closed, the van departs from the plaza in front of the Gran Hotel Humberto. Vans leave about 2 hours before each scheduled departure from the Llano San Juan airport. **Aerocaribe** (☎ 961/1-1490, fax 961/2-2053; at the airport 961/5-1530), a Mexicana affiliate, flies between Tuxtla and Oaxaca from Tuxtla's small Aeropuerto Terán and to Cancún from the larger Llano San Juan airport. Aerocaribe and other commuter flights arrive at Tuxtla's downtown airport, a short taxi ride from the town center.

Tuxtla's large airport, Llano San Juan, about 40 minutes from town, is subject to closures and delays because of rain, high winds, and fog. If the weather looks bad, double-check your flight departure.

Important note: If you're flying on Aerocaribe and Aviacsa, be sure to clarify from which airport you'll be departing. Your ticket *may not* indicate the right airport or the right name of the airline, so check and double-check with the airline directly or a travel agent in Tuxtla.

BY BUS First-class **Omnibus Cristóbal Colón** (☎ 961/2-2624) goes every half hour to San Cristóbal (from 5am to 9:15pm). It also runs seven daily buses to Tuxtla from Villahermosa, as well as three to Oaxaca and many to Comitán and Ciudad Cuauhtémoc on the Guatemalan border. There are four "deluxe plus" buses to

Palenque between 7am and midnight. The first-class San Cristóbal buses are generally easy to book, unless it's a holiday; at such times, you may face a wait. **Transportes Rudolfo Figueroa** also provides deluxe service daily to and from San Cristóbal and Palenque.

BY CAR   From Oaxaca you enter Tuxtla by Highway 190. From Villahermosa or San Cristóbal, you'll enter at the opposite end of town on Highway 195. Eventually, you will end up at the big main square, Plaza Cívica.

From Tuxtla to Villahermosa, take Highway 195 to Villahermosa. To San Cristóbal, take Highway 190 out of town and look for the Highway 199 turnoff on the left, which leads to San Cristóbal. Because the road from Tuxtla to San Cristóbal and Villahermosa is mountainous and curvy, don't be in a hurry. It's in good repair to San Cristóbal, but there may be bad spots between San Cristóbal and Palenque. The trip from Tuxtla to Villahermosa takes 8 hours by car, and the scenery is beautiful.

BY TAXI   Taxi drivers solicit riders to San Cristóbal outside the bus station and airports. The going rate of $27 to $33 per car can be shared by up to four passengers. You'll have to wait for them to assemble, however, unless fewer than four agree to split the fare. I've used this service several times, and it's worked well. The drivers offering this service drive rather shabby taxis, but the service is generally congenial and efficient.

ORIENTATION

ARRIVING   From the international airport off Highway 190, it's a 40-minute ride to the center of town. The colectivo into town is inexpensive compared to a taxi. Upon arrival, don't linger inside the airport—the vans fill up and leave immediately, and taxis charge about five times the price of a colectivo for the same trip downtown.

The **Cristóbal Colón** bus terminal, 2a Avenida Norte and 2a Calle Poniente, is 2 blocks west of Calle Central.

For information about getting to San Cristóbal directly from the airport, see "Getting There & Departing: By Taxi," above.

VISITOR INFORMATION   The **tourist office** (☎ **961/2-5509** or 961/2-4535) is in the Secretaría de Fomento Económico building (previously called the Plaza de las Instituciones) on Avenida Central/Bulevar Domínguez, near the Hotel Bonampak Tuxtla. It's on the first floor of the plaza and is open Monday through Friday from 8am to 9pm. Most questions can be answered at the information booth in front of the office. There are also information booths at the international airport (staffed when flights are due) and at the zoo (open Tuesday through Sunday from 9am to 3pm and 6 to 9pm). Another kiosk (open the same hours as the one at the zoo) is located on Highway 190 about 3 miles west of town.

CITY LAYOUT   The city is divided by two "Central" streets: **Calle Central,** running north to south, and **Avenida Central** (also called Avenida 14 de Septiembre), running east to west. The main highway is Avenida Central (also named Bulevar Domínguez west of downtown). Streets are numbered from these central arteries, with the suffix *norte, sur, oriente, or poniente* designating the direction of progress from the central arteries.

GETTING AROUND   **Buses** to all parts of the city converge upon the Plaza Cívica along Calle Central. **Taxi** fares are higher here than in other regions.

FAST FACTS: TUXTLA GUTIÉRREZ   The local **American Express** representative is Viajes Marabasco, Plaza Bonampak, Loc. 4, Col. Moctezuma, near the tourist office (☎ **961/2-6998;** fax 961/2-4053). The **telephone area code** is 961.

TUXTLA'S MUSEUM & ZOO

The majority of travelers simply pass through Tuxtla on their way to San Cristóbal or Oaxaca. The excellent zoo and the Sumidero Canyon are the best places to spend time you have to spare.

Calzada de los Hombres Illustres. 1A Oriente Nte. at 5A Oriente Nte. Park and botanical garden, free. Museum, $2; free on Sunday. Museum, Tues–Sun 9am–4pm; botanical garden, daily 8:30am–5pm; children's area, Tues–Sun 8am–8pm. The park is 11 blocks northwest of the main plaza; catch a colectivo along Avenida Central or walk about 15 minutes west along Calle 5A Oriente Nte.

Tuxtla's cultural highlights are clustered in this area, once referred to as the Parque Madero. The park is one part of the area, which also includes the **Regional Museum of Anthropology,** a botanical garden, a children's area, and the city theater. The museum features exhibits on the lifestyles of the people of Chiapas and some artifacts from the state's archaeological sites. In one short stop you can learn about Chiapas's past civilizations, its flora, and its present-day accomplishments. It also has a FONART (government crafts) shop and cafeteria.

Miguel Alvarez del Toro Zoo (ZOOMAT). Bulevar Samuel León Brinois, southeast of downtown. Free admission; donations solicited. Tues–Sun 9am–5:30pm. The zoo is about 5 miles southeast of downtown; buses for the zoo can be found along Avenida Central and at the Calzada.

Located in the forest called El Zapotal, ZOOMAT is one of the best zoos in Mexico, and it's one of my personal favorites. The collection of animals and birds indigenous to this area gives the visitor a tangible sense of what the wilds of Chiapas are like. Jaguars, howler monkeys, owls, and many more exotic animals are kept in roomy cages that replicate their home terrain, and the whole zoo is so deeply buried in vegetation that you can almost pretend you're in a natural habitat. Unlike at other zoos I've visited, the animals are almost always on view; many will come to the fence if you make a kissing noise.

SHOPPING

The government-operated **Casa de las Artesanías,** Bulevar Domínguez 2035 (☎ 961/3-3478), is both a shop and gallery. The two stories of rooms feature a fine, extensive collection of crafts grouped by region and type from throughout the state of Chiapas. It's open Monday through Saturday from 9am to 2pm and 5 to 8pm, and Sunday from 9am to 1pm.

WHERE TO STAY

As Tuxtla booms, the center of the hotel industry has moved out of town, west to Highway 190. As you come in from the airport, you'll notice the new motel-style hotels, such as the Hotel Flamboyant, Palace Inn, Hotel Laganja, and La Hacienda. All of these are more expensive than those listed below, which are in the heart of town.

✪ **Hotel Bonampak Tuxtla.** Bulevar Domínquez 180, 29030 Tuxtla Gutiérrez, Chi. ☎ 961/3-2050. 70 rms. A/C TV TEL. $45 double.

This large, sprawling hotel has a swimming pool, tennis court, travel agency, boutique, coffee shop, and nice restaurant. The rooms facing the street are noisy, even with the air-conditioning on, but the interior rooms are blissfully quiet. The hotel's coffee shop, one of the best in town, is often packed with locals and tourists. The extensive menu includes an economical comida corrida. It's on the outskirts of downtown, where Avenida 14 de Septiembre becomes Bulevar Domínguez.

Gran Hotel Humberto. Av. Central 180, 29030 Tuxtla Gutiérrez, Chi. ☎ **961/2-2080.** Fax 961/2-9771. 112 rms. TV TEL. $32 double.

This older 10-story, inner-city hotel is your best budget bet in booming Tuxtla. It's clean and comfortable enough, with well-kept furnishings dating from the 1950s. However, it isn't always an oasis of peace and quiet, especially on weekends when church bells compete with the ninth-floor nightclub. The location is ideal—it's in the center of town half a block from Plaza Cívica restaurants and the Mexicana airline office and 1¹/₂ blocks from the Cristóbal Colón bus station.

Hotel Esponda. 1a Calle Poniente Nte. 142, 29030 Tuxtla Gutiérrez, Chi. ☎ **961/2-0080** or 961/2-9771. 50 rms. FAN TV TEL. $18 double. Free parking.

In a city where inexpensive rooms are hard to come by, the Esponda is an excellent choice. Its rooms are in a nondescript, five-story building with an elevator. The brown, green, and yellow decor is a bit unsettling, but the rooms are perfectly satisfactory—each has one, two, or three double beds; showers (without doors or curtains); big closets; and powerful ceiling fans. The hotel is conveniently located 1 block from the Plaza Cívica, near the Cristóbal Colón bus station.

WHERE TO DINE

Tuxtla's main plaza, the **Plaza Cívica** (Avenida Central at 1 Poniente), is actually two plazas separated by Avenida Central. Rimming the edges are numerous restaurants, many of which serve customers outdoors under umbrella-shaded tables. The restaurants change names with frequency, so I won't recommend one over another. Just stroll the area and pick one that looks interesting, clean, and reasonably priced.

Las Pichanchas. Av. Central Ote. 837. ☎ **961/2-5351.** Tamales $1.75–$2.25 each; main courses $4–$8. Daily 8am–11:30 (live marimba music 2:30–5:30pm and 8:30–11:30pm; patio dinner show Tues–Sun at 9pm). Closed New Year's Day and the 2 days following Easter. MEXICAN.

No trip to Tuxtla Gutiérrez is complete without a meal at this colorfully decorated restaurant devoted to the regional food and drink of Chiapas. Inverted *pichanchas* (pots full of holes used to make *nixtamal* masa dough) are hung on posts as lanterns. For a sampler plate, try the *platón de carnes frías* (cold meat platter that includes different local sausages, ham, cheese, and tortillas) or the *platón de botana regional* (a variety of hot tidbits). The cold meat platter and the especially tasty *butifarra* both feed two or three people nicely. Since Chiapan tamales are tastier and larger than those you may have eaten elsewhere, you must try at least one. From the Hotel Humberto in the center of town, walk 6 to 8 blocks south; you'll find the restaurant on the left.

ROAD TRIPS FROM TUXTLA GUTIÉRREZ
CHIAPA DE CORZO: HOME OF A LACQUER-PAINTING MUSEUM

The small town of Chiapa de Corzo is a 30-minute, 8-mile ride by bus from the main square (buses leave every 15 minutes in the morning, every 30 minutes in the afternoon), or a 10- to 15-minute ride by taxi. Those going on to San Cristóbal or over the mountains to the Yucatán will pass through this town on their way.

Chiapa de Corzo has a small **museum** on the main square dedicated to the city's lacquer industry; an interesting church; a colonial fountain; and a small **pyramid,** somewhat restored and visible from the road. In the museum, you can often see women learning the regional craft of lacquer painting, and sometimes mask makers give carving demonstrations and lessons.

EL SUMIDERO: AN AWESOME, SHEER-WALLED CANYON

Another, more spectacular trip is to the canyon of El Sumidero, 10 miles northeast of the center of town along a country road. Boat rides through the canyon can be arranged through some travel agencies and hotels in Tuxtla and through the Tuxtla office of **Transportes al Cañon** (☎ 961/3-3584). You can tour the canyon on your own by taking a bus or taxi to Chiapa de Corzo and negotiating a ride along the riverbed; the cost should be around $40 for five persons for a 2-hour ride. You can also go by bus to Cahuare from the main square and arrange for a boat under the Grijalva River Bridge; the rate may be somewhat lower here.

Appendix

A Telephones & Mail

USING THE TELEPHONES

Area codes and city exchanges are being changed all over the country. If you have difficulty reaching a number, ask an operator for assistance. Mexico does not have helpful recordings to inform you of changes or new numbers.

Most **public pay phones** in the country have been converted to Ladatel phones, many of which are both coin and card operated. Instructions on the phones tell you how to use them. When your time limit for local calls is about to end (about three minutes), you'll hear three odd-sounding beeps, and then you'll be cut off unless you deposit more coins. Ladatel cards come in denominations of 10, 20, and 30 New Pesos. If you're planning to make many calls, purchase the 30 New Peso card; it takes no time at all to use up a 10 peso card (about $1.65). They're sold at pharmacies, bookstores, and grocery stores near Ladatel phones. You insert the card, dial your number, and start talking, all the while watching a digital counter tick away your money.

Next is the *caseta de larga distancia* (long-distance telephone office), found all over Mexico. Most bus stations and airports now have specially staffed rooms exclusively for making long-distance calls and sending faxes. Often they are efficient and inexpensive, providing the client with a computer printout of the time and charges. In other places, often pharmacies, the clerk will place the call for you, then you step into a private booth to take the call. Whether it's a special long-distance office or a pharmacy, there's usually a service charge of around $3.50 to make the call, which you pay in addition to any call costs if you didn't call collect.

For **long-distance calls** you can access an English-speaking AT&T operator by pushing the star button twice and then 09. If that fails, try dialing 09 for an international operator. To call the United States or Canada, tell the operator that you want a collect call (*una llamada por cobrar*) or station-to-station (*teléfono a teléfono*) or person-to-person (*persona a persona*). Collect calls are the least expensive of all, but sometimes caseta offices won't make them, so you'll have to pay on the spot.

To make a long-distance call from Mexico to the United States or Canada, first dial 001, then dial the area code and the number you are calling.

To make a long-distance call from Mexico to anywhere else in the world, first dial 00, then dial the country code for the country you are calling, and then dial the city code and the number you want to call. The country code for Australia is 61; New Zealand, 64; the United Kingdom, 44.

To call long distance (abbreviated "lada") within Mexico, dial 01, the area code, then the number. Mexico's area codes (claves) may be one, two, or three numbers and are usually listed in the front of telephone directories. Area codes are listed before all phone numbers in this book.

To place a phone call to Mexico from your home country, dial the international service (011), Mexico's country code (52), then the Mexican area code (for Cancún, for example, that would be 98), then the local number. Keep in mind that calls to Mexico are quite expensive, even if dialed direct from your home phone.

Better hotels, which have more sophisticated tracking equipment, may charge for each local call made from your room. Budget or moderately priced hotels often don't charge, since they can't keep track. To avoid check-out shock, it's best to ask in advance if you'll be charged for local calls. These cost between 50¢ and $1 per call. In addition, if you make a long-distance call from your hotel room, there is usually a hefty service charge added to the cost of the call.

POSTAL GLOSSARY

Airmail **Correo Aéreo**
Customs **Aduana**
General Delivery **Lista de Correos**
Insurance (insured mail) **Seguros**
Mailbox **Buzón**
Money Order **Giro Postale**
Parcel **Paquete**
Post Office **Oficina de Correos**

Post Office Box
  (abbreviation) **Apdo. Postal**
Postal Service **Correos**
Registered Mail **Registrado**
Rubber Stamp **Sello**
Special Delivery,
  Express **Entrega Inmediata**
Stamp **Estampilla** or **Timbre**

B Basic Vocabulary

Most Mexicans are very patient with foreigners who try to speak their language; it helps a lot to know a few basic phrases.

I've included a list of certain simple phrases for expressing basic needs, followed by some common menu items.

ENGLISH–SPANISH PHRASES

English	Spanish	Pronunciation
Good day	**Buenos días**	*bway*-nohss-*dee*-ahss
How are you?	**¿Cómo está usted?**	*koh*-moh ess-*tah* oo-*sted?*
Very well	**Muy bien**	mwee byen
Thank you	**Gracias**	grah-see-ahss
You're welcome	**De nada**	day nah-dah
Goodbye	**Adiós**	ah-*dyohss*
Please	**Por favor**	pohr fah-*vohr*
Yes	**Sí**	see
No	**No**	noh
Excuse me	**Perdóneme**	pehr-*doh*-ney-may
Give me	**Déme**	*day*-may

Where is . . . ?	¿Dónde está . . . ?	*dohn*-day ess-*tah?*
the station	la estación	lah ess-tah-*seown*
a hotel	un hotel	oon oh-*tel*
a gas station	una gasolinera	oon-uh gah-so-lee-*nay*-rah
a restaurant	un restaurante	oon res-tow-*rahn*-tay
the toilet	el baño	el *bahn*-yoh
a good doctor	un buen médico	oon bwayn *may*-thee-co
the road to	el camino a/hacia	el cah-*mee*-noh ah/*ah*-see-ah
To the right	A la derecha	ah lah day-*reh*-chuh
To the left	A la izquierda	ah lah ees-ky-*ehr*-thah
Straight ahead	Derecho	day-*reh*-cho
I would like	Quisiera	key-see-*ehr*-ah
I want	Quiero	*kyehr*-oh
to eat	comer	ko-*mayr*
a room	una habitación	oon-nuh ha-bee tah-*seown*
Do you have?	¿Tiene usted?	tyah-nay oos-*ted?*
a book	un libro	oon *lee*-bro
a dictionary	un diccionario	oon deek-seown-*ar*-eo
How much is it?	¿Cuánto cuesta?	*kwahn*-to *kwess*-tah?
When?	¿Cuándo?	*kwahn*-doh?
What?	¿Qué?	kay?
There is (Is there . . . ?)	(¿)Hay (. . . ?)	eye?
What is there?	¿Qué hay?	kay eye?
Yesterday	Ayer	ah-*yer*
Today	Hoy	oy
Tomorrow	Mañana	mahn-*yawn*-ah
Good	Bueno	*bway*-no
Bad	Malo	*mah*-lo
Better (best)	(Lo) Mejor	(loh) meh-*hor*
More	Más	mahs
Less	Menos	*may*-noss
No smoking	Se prohíbe fumar	say pro-*hee*-bay foo-*mahr*
Postcard	Tarjeta postal	tar-hay-ta pohs-*tahl*
Insect repellent	Rapellante contra insectos	rah-pey-*yahn*-te *cohn*-trah een-*sehk*-tos

MORE USEFUL PHRASES

Do you speak English?	¿Habla usted inglés?	ah-blah oo-*sted* een-*glays*?
Is there anyone here who speaks English?	¿Hay alguien aquí qué hable inglés?	eye *ahl*-ghee-en kay *ah*-blay een-*glays*?
I speak a little Spanish.	Hablo un poco de español.	*ah*-blow oon *poh*-koh day ess-pah-*nyol*
I don't understand Spanish very well.	No (lo) entiendo muy bien el español.	noh (loh) ehn-tee-*ehn*-do myee bee-ayn el ess-pah-*nyol*
The meal is good.	Me gusta la comida.	may *goo*-sta lah koh-*mee*-dah
What time is it?	¿Qué hora es?	kay *oar*-ah ess?
May I see your menu?	¿Puedo ver el menú (la carta)?	*puay*-tho veyr el may-*noo* (lah *car*-tah)?

The check please.	**La cuenta por favor.**	lah *quayn*-tah pohr fa-*vorh*
What do I owe you?	**¿Cuánto lo debo?**	*Kwahn*-toh loh *day*-boh?
What did you say?	**¿Mande? (colloquial expression for American "Eh?")**	*Mahn*-day?
More formal:	**¿Cómo?**	*Koh*-moh?
I want (to see) a room	**Quiero (ver) un cuarto (una habitación). . .**	Key-*yehr*-oh vehr oon *kwar*-toh
for two persons	**para dos personas**	pahr-ah doss pehr-*sohn*-as
with (without) bath.	**con (sin) baño.**	kohn (seen) *bah*-nyoh
We are staying here only	**Nos quedamos aquí solamente . . .**	nohs kay-*dahm*-ohss ah-*key* sohl-ah-*mayn*-tay
one night.	**una noche.**	oon-ah *noh*-chay
one week.	**una semana.**	oon-ah say-*mahn*-ah
We are leaving tomorrow.	**Partimos (Salimos) mañana.**	Pahr-*tee*-mohss (sah-*lee*-mohss) mahn-*nyan*-ah
Do you accept traveler's checks?	**¿Acepta usted cheques de viajero?**	Ah-*sayp*-tah oo-*sted* *chay*-kays day bee-ah-*hehr*-oh?
Is there a laundromat near here?	**¿Hay una lavandería cerca de aquí?**	Eye oon-ah lah-*vahn*-day-*ree*-ah *sehr*-ka day ah-*key*?
Please send these clothes to the laundry.	**Hágame el favor de mandar esta ropa a la lavandería.**	*Ah*-ga-may el fah-*vhor* day mahn-*dahr ays*-tah *rho*-pah a lah lah-*vahn*-day-*ree*-ah

NUMBERS

1	**uno** (*ooh*-noh)	17	**diecisiete** (de-*ess*-ee-*syeh*-tay)
2	**dos** (dohs	18	**dieciocho** (dee-*ess*-ee-*oh*-choh)
3	**tres** (trayss)	19	**diecinueve** (dee-*ess*-ee-*nway*-bay)
4	**cuatro** (*kwah*-troh)	20	**veinte** (*bayn*-tay)
5	**cinco** (*seen*-koh)	30	**treinta** (*trayn*-tah)
6	**seis** (sayss)	40	**cuarenta** (kwah-*ren*-tah)
7	**siete** (*syeh*-tay)	50	**cincuenta** (seen-*kwen*-tah)
8	**ocho** (*oh*-choh)	60	**sesenta** (say-*sen*-tah)
9	**nueve** (*nway*-bay)	70	**setenta** (say-*ten*-tah)
10	**diez** (dee-ess)	80	**ochenta** (oh-*chen*-tah)
11	**once** (*ohn*-say)	90	**noventa** (noh-*ben*-tah)
12	**doce** (*doh*-say)	100	**cien** (see-en)
13	**trece** (*tray*-say)	200	**doscientos** (*dos*-se-en-tos)
14	**catorce** (kah-*tor*-say)	500	**quinientos** (*keen*-ee-ehn-tos)
15	**quince** (*keen*-say)	1000	**mil** (meal)
16	**dieciseis** (de-*ess*-ee-sayss)		

TRANSPORTATION TERMS

English	Spanish	Pronunciation
Bus	**Autobús**	ow-toh-*boos*
Bus or truck	**Camión**	ka-me-*ohn*
Lane	**Carril**	kah-*rreal*
Nonstop	**Directo**	dee-*reck*-toh

Baggage (claim area)	**Equipajes**	eh-key-*pah*-hays
Intercity	**Foraneo**	fohr-ah-*nay*-oh
Luggage storage area	**Guarda equipaje**	gwar-daheh-key-*pah*-hay
Arrival gates	**Llegadas**	yay-*gah*-dahs
Originates at this station	**Local**	loh-*kahl*
Originates elsewhere; stops if seats available	**De Paso**	day-pah-soh
First class	**Primera**	pree-*mehr*-oh
Second class	**Segunda**	say-*goon*-dah
Nonstop	**Sin Escala**	seen ess-*kah*-lah
Baggage claim area	**Recibo de Equipajes**	ray-see-boh day eh-key-*pah*-hay
Waiting room	**Sala de Espera**	*Saw*-lah day ess-*pehr*-ah
Toilets	**Sanitarios**	Sahn-ee-tahr-*ee*-oss
Ticket window	**Taquilla**	tah-*key*-lah

C Menu Glossary

Achiote   Small red seed of the annatto tree.

Achiote preparada   A prepared paste found in Yucatán markets made of ground achiote, wheat and corn flour, cumin, cinnamon, salt, onion, garlic, and oregano. Mixed with juice of a sour orange or vinegar and put on broiled or charcoaled fish (tikin chick) and chicken.

Agua fresca   Fruit-flavored water, usually watermelon, canteloupe, chia seed with lemon, hibiscus flour, or ground melon seed mixture.

Antojito   A Mexican snack, usually masa-based with a variety of toppings such as sausage, cheese, beans, onions; also refers to tostadas, sopes, and garnachas.

Atole   A thick, lightly sweet, warm drink made with finely ground rice or corn and usually flavored with vanilla.

Birria   Lamb or goat meat cooked in a tomato broth, spiced with garlic, chiles, cumin, ginger, oregano, cloves, cinnamon, and thyme and garnished with onions, cilantro, and fresh lime juice to taste; a specialty of Jalisco state.

Botana   A light snack—an antojito.

Buñuelos   Round, thin, deep-fried crispy fritters dipped in sugar.

Cabrito   Grilled kid; a northern Mexican delicacy.

Carnitas   Pork that's been deep-cooked (not fried) in lard, then steamed and served with corn tortillas for tacos.

Ceviche   Fresh raw seafood marinated in fresh lime juice and garnished with chopped tomatoes, onions, chiles, and sometimes cilantro and served with crispy, fried whole corn tortillas.

Chayote   Vegetable pear or merleton, a type of spiny squash boiled and served as an accompaniment to meat dishes.

Chiles rellenos   Poblano peppers usually stuffed with cheese, rolled in a batter, and baked; other stuffings include ground beef spiced with raisins.

Churro   Tube-shaped, bread-like fritter, dipped in sugar and sometimes filled with cajeta or chocolate.

Cochinita pibil Pig wrapped in banana leaves, flavored with pibil sauce, and pit-baked; common in Yucatán.

Corunda A triangular tamal wrapped in a corn leaf; a Michoacan specialty.

Enchilada Tortilla dipped in a sauce and usually filled with chicken or white cheese and sometimes topped with tomato sauce and sour cream (enchiladas Suizas—Swiss enchiladas), or covered in a green sauce (enchiladas verdes), or topped with onions, sour cream, and guacamole (enchiladas Potosiños).

Epazote Leaf of the wormseed plant, used in black beans and with cheese in quesadillas.

Escabeche A lightly pickled sauce used in Yucatecan chicken stew.

Frijoles charros Beans flavored with beer; a northern Mexican specialty.

Frijoles refritos Pinto beans mashed and cooked with lard.

Garnachas A thickish small circle of fried masa with pinched sides, topped with pork or chicken, onions, and avocado or sometimes chopped potatoes, and tomatoes, typical as a botana in Veracruz and Yucatán.

Gorditas Thickish fried-corn tortillas, slit and stuffed with choice of cheese, beans, beef, chicken, with or without lettuce, tomato, and onion garnish.

Gusanos de maguey Maguey worms, considered a delicacy, and delicious when charbroiled to a crisp and served with corn tortillas for tacos.

Horchata Refreshing drink made of ground rice or melon seeds, ground almonds, and lightly sweetened.

Huevos Mexicanos Eggs with onions, hot peppers, tomatoes.

Huevos Motulenos Eggs atop a tortilla, garnished with beans, peas, ham, sausage, and grated cheese; a Yucatecan specialty.

Huevos rancheros Fried egg on top of a fried corn tortilla covered in a tomato sauce.

Huitlacoche Sometimes spelled "cuitlacoche," mushroom-flavored black fungus that appears on corn in the rainy season; considered a delicacy.

Machaca Shredded dried beef scrambled with eggs or as salad topping; a specialty of Northern Mexico.

Manchamantel Translated means "tablecloth stainer," a stew of chicken or pork with chiles, tomatoes, pineapple, bananas, and jícama.

Masa Ground corn soaked in lime used as basis for tamales, corn tortillas, and soups.

Mixiote Lamb baked in a chile sauce or chicken with carrots and potatoes, used as basis for tamales, corn tortillas, and soups.

Pan de Muerto Sweet or plain bread made around the Days of the Dead (Nov.1–2), in the form of mummies, dolls, or round with bone designs.

Pan dulce Lightly sweetened bread in many configurations, usually served at breakfast or bought at any bakery.

Papadzules Tortillas are stuffed with hard-boiled eggs and seeds (cucumber or sunflower) in a tomato sauce.

Pavo relleno negro Stuffed turkey Yucatán-style, filled with chopped pork and beef, cooked in a rich, dark sauce.

Pibil   Pit-baked pork or chicken in a sauce of tomato, onion, mild red pepper, cilantro, and vinegar.

Pipian   Sauce made with ground pumpkin seeds, nuts, and mild peppers.

Poc chuc   Slices of pork with onion marinated in a tangy sour orange sauce and charcoal broiled; a Yucatecan specialty.

Pollo Calpulalpan   Chicken cooked in pulque; a specialty of Tlaxcala.

Pozole   A soup made with hominy and pork or chicken, in either a tomato-based broth Jalisco-style, or a white broth Nayarit-style, or green chile sauce Guerrero-style, and topped with choice of chopped white onion, lettuce or cabbage, radishes, oregano, red pepper, and cilantro.

Pulque   Drink made of fermented sap of the maguey plant; best in state of Hidalgo and around Mexico City.

Quesadilla   Flour tortillas stuffed with melted white cheese and lightly fried.

Queso relleno   "Stuffed cheese" is a mild yellow cheese stuffed with minced meat and spices; a Yucatecan specialty.

Rompope   Delicious Mexican eggnog, invented in Puebla, made with eggs, vanilla, sugar, and rum.

Salsa verde   A cooked sauce using the green tomatillo and pureed with mildly hot peppers, onions, garlic, and cilantro; on tables countrywide.

Sopa de calabaza   Soup made of chopped squash or pumpkin blossoms.

Sopa de lima   A tangy soup made with chicken broth and accented with fresh lime; popular in Yucatán.

Sopa seca   Not a soup at all, but a seasoned rice which translated means "dry soup."

Sopa Tarascan   A rib-sticking pinto-bean based soup, flavored with onions, garlic, tomatoes, chiles, and chicken broth and garnished with sour cream, white cheese, avocado chunks, and fried tortilla strips; a specialty of Michoacán state.

Sopa Tlalpeña   A hearty soup made with chunks of chicken, chopped carrots, zucchini, corn, onions, garlic, and cilantro.

Sopa Tlaxcalteca   A hearty tomato-based soup filled with cooked nopal cactus, cheese, cream, and avocado with crispy tortilla strips floating on top.

Sopa tortilla   A traditional chicken broth–based soup, seasoned with chiles, tomatoes, onion, and garlic, bobbing with crisp fried strips of corn tortillas.

Sope   Pronounced *soh*-pay, a botana similar to a garnacha, except spread with refried beans and topped with crumbled cheese and onions.

Tacos al pasto   Thin slices of flavored pork roasted on a revolving cylinder dripping with onion slices and juice of fresh pineapple slices.

Tamal   Incorrectly called tamale (tamal singular, tamales plural); meat or sweet filling rolled with fresh masa, then wrapped in a corn husk or banana leaf and steamed; many varieties and sizes throughout the country.

Tepache   Drink made of fermented pineapple peelings and brown sugar.

Tikin xic   Also seen on menus as "tikin chick," char-broiled fish brushed with achiote sauce.

Tinga   A stew made with pork tenderloin, sausage, onions, garlic, tomatoes, chiles, and potatoes; popular on menus in Puebla and Hidalgo states.

Torta   A sandwich, usually on bolillo bread, usually with sliced avocado, onions, tomatoes, with a choice of meat and often cheese.

Torta Ahogado   A specialty of Lake Chapala is made with a scooped out roll, filled with beans and beef strips and seasoned with a tomato or chile sauce.

Tostadas   Crispy fried corn tortillas topped with meat, onions, lettuce, tomatoes, cheese, avocados, and sometimes sour cream.

Venado   Venison (deer) served perhaps as pipian de venado, steamed in banana leaves and served with a sauce of ground squash seeds.

Xtabentun (pronounced shtah-ben-*toon*)   A Yucatán liquor made of fermented honey and flavored with anise. It comes *seco* (dry) or *crema* (sweet).

Zacahuil   Pork leg tamal, packed in thick masa, wrapped in banana leaves, and pit baked, sometimes pot-made with tomato and masa; specialty of mid- to upper Veracruz.

General Index

ACCOMMODATIONS INDEX

RESTAURANT INDEX

FROMMER'S COMPLETE TRAVEL GUIDES

*(Comprehensive guides to destinations around the world, with
selections in all price ranges—from deluxe to budget)*

Acapulco, Ixtapa &
   Zihuatenejo
Alaska
Amsterdam
Arizona
Atlanta
Australia
Austria
Bahamas
Barcelona, Madrid &
   Seville
Belgium, Holland &
   Luxembourg
Bermuda
Boston
Budapest & the Best of
   Hungary
California
Canada
Cancún, Cozumel & the
   Yucatán
Cape Cod, Nantucket &
   Martha's Vineyard
Caribbean
Caribbean Cruises &
   Ports of Call
Caribbean Ports of Call
Carolinas & Georgia
Chicago
Colorado
Costa Rica
Denver, Boulder &
   Colorado Springs
England

Europe
Florida
France
Germany
Greece
Hawaii
Hong Kong
Honolulu, Waikiki & Oahu
Ireland
Israel
Italy
Jamaica & Barbados
Japan
Las Vegas
London
Los Angeles
Maryland & Delaware
Maui
Mexico
Miami & the Keys
Montana & Wyoming
Montréal & Québec City
Munich & the Bavarian Alps
Nashville & Memphis
Nepal
New England
New Mexico
New Orleans
New York City
Northern New England
Nova Scotia, New
   Brunswick &
    Prince Edward Island
Paris

Philadelphia & the Amish
   Country
Portugal
Prague & the Best of the
   Czech Republic
Provence & the Riviera
Puerto Rico
Rome
San Antonio & Austin
San Diego
San Francisco
Santa Fe, Taos &
   Albuquerque
Scandinavia
Scotland
Seattle & Portland
South Pacific
Spain
Switzerland
Thailand
Tokyo
Toronto
Tuscany & Umbria
U.S.A.
Utah
Vancouver & Victoria
Vienna & the Danube
   Valley
Virgin Islands
Virginia
Walt Disney World &
   Orlando
Washington, D.C.
Washington & Oregon

FROMMER'S DOLLAR-A-DAY BUDGET GUIDES

(The ultimate guides to low-cost travel)

Australia from $50 a Day
Berlin from $50 a Day
California from $60 a Day
Caribbean from $60 a Day
Costa Rica & Belize
   from $35 a Day
England from $60 a Day
Europe from $50 a Day
Florida from $50 a Day
Greece from $50 a Day
Hawaii from $60 a Day

India from $40 a Day
Ireland from $45 a Day
Israel from $45 a Day
Italy from $50 a Day
London from $60 a Day
Mexico from $35 a Day
New York from $75 a Day
New Zealand from $50 a Day
Paris from $70 a Day
San Francisco from $60 a Day
Washington, D.C., from $50 a Day

FROMMER'S PORTABLE GUIDES

(Pocket-size guides for travelers who want everything in a nutshell)

Charleston & Savannah	New Orleans	San Francisco
Dublin	Puerto Vallarta,	Venice
Las Vegas	Manzanillo &	Washington, D.C.
Maine Coast	Guadalajara	

FROMMER'S FAMILY GUIDES

(The complete guides for successful family vacations)

California with Kids	New York City with Kids	Washington, D.C.,
Los Angeles with Kids	San Francisco with Kids	with Kids

FROMMER'S AMERICA ON WHEELS

*(Everything you need for a successful road trip, including full-color
road maps and ratings for every hotel)*

California & Nevada	Mid-Atlantic	South-Central States
Florida	New England & New York	& Texas
Great Lake States &	Northwest & Great Plains	Southeast
Midwest		Southwest

FROMMER'S WALKING TOURS

(Memorable neighborhood strolls through the world's great cities)

London	San Francisco	Venice
New York	Spain's Favorite Cities	Washington, D.C.
Paris	Tokyo	

SPECIAL-INTEREST TITLES

Arthur Frommer's Branson!	New York Times Weekends
Arthur Frommer's New World of Travel	Outside Magazine's Adventure Guide
The Civil War Trust's Official Guide to	to New England
the Civil War Discovery Trail	Outside Magazine's Adventure Guide
Frommer's America's 100 Best-Loved	to Northern California
State Parks	Outside Magazine's Adventure Guide
Frommer's Caribbean Hideaways	to the Pacific Northwest
Frommer's Complete Hostel Vacation Guide	Outside Magazine's Guide
to England, Scotland & Wales	to Family Vacations
Frommer's Europe's Greatest	Places Rated Almanac
Driving Tours	Retirement Places Rated
Frommer's Food Lover's Companion	Wonderful Weekends from NYC
to France	Wonderful Weekends from San Francisco
Frommer's Food Lover's Companion to Italy	

FROMMER'S IRREVERENT GUIDES

(Wickedly honest guides for sophisticated travelers)

Amsterdam	Manhattan	Paris	U.S. Virgin Islands
Chicago	Miami	San Francisco	Walt Disney World
London	New Orleans	Santa Fe	Washington, D.C.

UNOFFICIAL GUIDES

(Get the unbiased truth from these candid, value-conscious guides)

Atlanta	The Great Smoky	Miami & the Keys	Walt Disney World
Branson, Missouri	& Blue Ridge	Mini-Mickey	Walt Disney World
Chicago	Mountains	New Orleans	Companion
Cruises	Las Vegas	Skiing in the West	Washington, D.C.
Disneyland			

BAEDEKER
(With four-color photographs and a free pull-out map)

Amsterdam	Crete	Lisbon	Scandinavia
Athens	Florence	London	Scotland
Austria	Florida	Mexico	Singapore
Bali	Germany	New York	South Africa
Belgium	Great Britain	New Zealand	Spain
Berlin	Greece	Paris	Switzerland
Brazil	Greek Islands	Portugal	Thailand
Budapest	Hawaii	Prague	Tokyo
California	Hong Kong	Provence	Turkish Coast
Canada	Ireland	Rome	Tuscany
Caribbean	Israel	San Francisco	Venice
China	Italy	St. Petersburg	Vienna
Copenhagen			

FROMMER'S BY NIGHT GUIDES
(The series for those who know that life begins after dark)

Amsterdam	Los Angeles	Manhattan	Paris
Chicago	Madrid	Miami	Prague
Las Vegas	& Barcelona	New Orleans	San Francisco
London			Washington, D.C.

FROMMER'S BEST BEACH VACATIONS
(The top places to sun, stroll, shop, stay, play, party, and swim, with ratings for each beach)

California	Florida	Mid-Atlantic
Carolinas & Georgia	Hawaii	New England

FROMMER'S BED & BREAKFAST GUIDES
(Selective guides with four-color photos and full descriptions of the best inns in each region)

California	Mid-Atlantic	The Rockies
Caribbean	New England	Southeast
Great American Cities	Pacific Northwest	Southwest
Hawaii		

FROMMER'S DRIVING TOURS
(Four-color photos and detailed maps outlining spectacular scenic driving routes)

America	California	Ireland	Scotland
Australia	Florida	Italy	Spain
Austria	France	New England	Switzerland
Britain	Germany	Scandinavia	Western Europe

FROMMER'S BORN TO SHOP
(The ultimate guides for travelers who love to shop)

Caribbean Ports	Great Britain	London	New York
of Call	Hong Kong	Mexico	Paris
France	Italy	New Egnland	

TRAVEL & LEISURE GUIDES
(Sophisticated pocket-size guides for discriminating travelers)

Amsterdam	Hong Kong	New York	San Francisco
Boston	London	Paris	Washington, D.C.